WILLIAM FAULKNER

Books by Stephen B. Oates

William Faulkner: The Man and the Artist

Biography as High Adventure: Life-Writers Speak on Their Art

Abraham Lincoln: The Man Behind the Myths

THE CIVIL WAR QUARTET:

    Let the Trumpet Sound: The Life of Martin Luther King, Jr.

    With Malice Toward None: The Life of Abraham Lincoln

    The Fires of Jubilee: Nat Turner's Fierce Rebellion

    To Purge This Land with Blood: A Biography of John Brown

Our Fiery Trial

Portrait of America (2 volumes)

Visions of Glory

Rip Ford's Texas

Confederate Cavalry West of the River

Stephen B. Oates

WILLIAM FAULKNER
The Man and the Artist

A BIOGRAPHY

Harper & Row, Publishers, New York
Cambridge, Philadelphia, San Francisco, Washington
London, Mexico City, São Paulo, Singapore, Sydney

A hardcover edition of this book is published by Harper & Row, Publishers, Inc.

First PERENNIAL LIBRARY edition published 1988.

Designer: Sidney Feinberg
Copyeditor: Marjorie Horvitz
Indexer: Brian Hotchkiss

Library of Congress Cataloging-in-Publication Data

Oates, Stephen B.
    William Faulkner, the man and the artist.

    "Perennial Library."
    Bibliography: p.
    Includes index.
    1. Faulkner, William, 1897–1962—Biography. 2. Novelists, American—
20th century—Biography. I. Title.
PS3511.A86Z928   1988   813'.52 [B]   86-46266
ISBN 0-06-091501-3 (pbk.)

88 89 90 91 92 MPC 10 9 8 7 6 5 4 3 2 1

To the memory of

My maternal grandparents
Chris and Freida Baer

And my maternal aunt
Isabel Baer Elder

The primary job that any writer faces is to tell you a story out of human experience—I mean by that, universal mutual experience, the anguishes and troubles and griefs of the human heart, which is universal, without regard to race or time or condition. He wants to tell you something which has seemed to him so true, so moving, either comic or tragic, that it's worth preserving.

WILLIAM FAULKNER, 1962

CONTENTS

ILLUSTRATIONS

PREFACE

He is widely regarded as America's foremost writer of fiction in this century. The novels and stories in his Yoknapatawpha saga constitute a sustained work of the imagination unsurpassed in modern American literature, and they are more extensively read than ever. The world-wide popularity of his art, the impressive body of critical literature, the attention given him in classrooms everywhere—all testify to his continuing hold on our minds, our imaginations, and our hearts.

In many ways, the story of William Faulkner—the lonely, small-town Mississippian who won a Nobel Prize for literature, who struggled all his life with his particular demons and discovered in himself and his world a window to the universe—is as compelling as anything he ever created. In these pages, I have attempted to relate that story in a different manner from that of my predecessors. Joseph Blotner has given us a scholarly chronicle that is invaluable as reference, a massive compendium of information about almost everything Faulkner ever said, did, and wrote. It is still that in its huge one-volume edition. Michael Millgate, Cleanth Brooks, Judith Bryant Wittenberg, David Minter, and many others have produced excellent critical studies that probe the life and the literature, speaking in analytical voices aimed largely at fellow specialists. I have tried to do something else, something directed at a broad reading audience: a "pure" biography, as Paul Murray Kendall described it, whose mission is to elicit from the coldness of fact the warmth of a life being lived.

The pure biographer, as Desmond McCarthy said, "is an artist upon oath." He cannot invent facts, but he can give them narrative form to tell a story. To tell Faulkner's story, I have used novelistic techniques but not fiction itself, for nothing here is made up. Functioning as "the hidden author," I've given Faulkner the stage, seeking to bring him

alive through character development, through his interpersonal relationships, through graphic scenes, revealing quotations, apt details, and
dramatic narrative sweep. I have tried to offer a consistent and coherent interpretation of character, one that uses psychological insights but
eschews psychological jargon in favor of the language of literature. My
narrative voice is empathetic, for empathy is what calls a human being
from the darkness; it is the pure biographer's essential quality, his
"spark of creation." Applying Robert Louis Stevenson's art of omission,
I've endeavored to fashion a portrait of manageable length, to sift the
trivial from the significant, to shape the whole of Faulkner's life so as
to suggest its essence.

In sum, this book is written in the old and honorable tradition of
biography as a narrative art. In Faulkner's case, it seems especially
appropriate to employ the methods of the storyteller to evoke a storyteller's life, to help readers perceive him in all his travail and his glory,
to engage the heart as well as the mind. Faulkner did the latter himself,
powerfully and unforgettably. Moreover, as Faulkner sought to illuminate the universal in a single Mississippi county, narrative biography,
pure biography, seeks to suggest the universal in a single human life.

In the twenty-five years that I have been writing biography, I found
out, as Faulkner said, that "not only each book had to have a design but
the whole output or sum of an artist's work had to have a design." My
biography of Faulkner seems a logical outgrowth of my Civil War quartet, which consists of the intersecting lives of Nat Turner, John Brown,
Abraham Lincoln, and Martin Luther King, Jr., and which spans the
sweep of southern and national history from 1800 to 1968. For years I
wanted to write the life of a major literary figure, particularly a southern figure who was caught up in the thunderous legacies of the Civil
War in Dixie, who captured the great and eternal truths of the human
experience there. I wanted someone who also grappled with the central
tensions of the modern age, with racism and war, with the sense of
alienation, rootlessness, and despair that increasingly plagued humankind in the twentieth century. It wasn't long after my life of King
appeared that I felt the familiar "tapping on the shoulder" that biographers often experience when looking for a subject. I was certain that
Faulkner was in the room with me, standing with my four other figures,
drawing on his pipe and staring at me with those dark, hypnotic
eyes. . . .

PART ONE

FUMBLING IN WINDY DARKNESS

As THE TRAIN ROARED through the Mississippi countryside, the boy and his two little brothers sat transfixed at the open window of the passenger coach, watching the shadowy forests, the hazy fields of corn and cotton, the occasional farmhouses and barns, all slide backward toward Holly Springs. It was an arduous trip for their mother, a small, prim woman with auburn hair and stern eyes. The coach was oppressively hot, and cinder flakes from the locomotive swirled through the open window, sullying the boys' faces and clothes. But Billy, the oldest, had seldom been so excited. Already he had a love for the steam locomotive that rivaled his father's. The sharp burst of its whistle, the hum of its wheels, the throb of the exhaust exploding from its stacks—all thrilled the boy to incandescence.

It was after dark, September 24, 1902, when the train pulled into the depot in Oxford, their new home. They had been on the train for two days, coming from Ripley by way of New Albany and Holly Springs, and they were tired, sweaty, and covered with soot and cinder. Grandfather and Grandmother, with some of their servants, helped them into Grandfather's coach, and they drove homeward through the town square, round an imposing white-columned courthouse, whose cupola housed a four-sided clock and a bell that rang at every stroke of the hour. The courthouse sat imperiously in the center of the square, surrounded by dirt streets, fine board sidewalks, and rows of stores with second-story balconies and balustrades, all lit up by arc lights. The boy had never seen such lights, had never seen so many horses and carriages and so many people. It was said that a thousand people lived here. *A thousand people?* That was incomprehensibly larger than New Albany, where the boy had entered the world almost exactly five years before, on September 25, 1897. Ripley itself, where the family had been living until yesterday, counted only 497 souls, including the boy and his two brothers. By contrast, the size of Oxford boggled his imagination.

Sometime later, the boy's father arrived in a wagon loaded with their household possessions. A tall, gruff, inarticulate man, Murry Falkner was unhappy about the move to Oxford. That was his father's idea: old J. W. T. Falkner, a commanding, self-assured man known as "the Young Colonel," had sold out the family railroad business, which had employed Murry and which he had loved with single-minded devotion. Along with cigars and whiskey, railroads had been Murry's passion since the 1880s, when he had dropped out of the University of Mississippi and gone to work as a coal-shoveling fireman on the family line. He rose through the ranks to engineer, then conductor, then auditor and treasurer in charge of the Traffic and Freight Claims Department, with his base in Ripley.

Then the Young Colonel, from his law office in Oxford, announced that he was selling the railroad and that Murry should move to Oxford, where the Young Colonel would establish him in business. Murry and his family could live in "the old place," which the Young Colonel and his wife, Sallie Murry, were vacating for a fine new home to be called "the Big Place."

Murry was devastated, for the railroad was his life. In desperation, he marched into a bank in Corinth and asked for a $100,000 loan with which to buy the Falkner line himself. But the banker laughed at the idea—who in his right mind would sell a profitable enterprise like that? Offended, Murry stalked out, thus losing his one chance to secure the Falkner line. Back in Ripley, he talked wildly about moving his family out west and buying a cattle ranch, an idea that derived from the western novels he read for pleasure. But his wife, Maud, would have none of it. A brusque, stubborn woman who could not abide weakness in men, she refused to leave Mississippi with the children. Billy, Jack, and Johncy were not going to grow up on some crude cattle ranch on the frontier.

With that, something went out of Murry. His wife and his father had both betrayed him, he felt, yet he lacked the spirit to force a showdown with them. Miserable, lost without his cherished railroad, he surrendered to his father's wishes and in September 1902 moved his family to "the old place" in Oxford.

Shortly after that, Maud's mother, whom the boys called Damuddy, moved into the household with her paintbrushes and easel. She detested liquor and profanity, disliked Murry for indulging in both; yet in she came with her art supplies and rigid ways. A tiny old servant named Caroline Barr—the family called her Mammy Callie—took up residence in a backyard cabin and helped Maud supervise Billy and his brothers. An unhappy Murry bought and managed a livery stable, where his company consisted of several Negroes who tended the horses, two white men who drove the hacks, and numerous cronies who sat around his office stove, sharing his whiskey and swapping tales about hunting and fishing. The father came home promptly at noon for his dinner and imposed total silence at the family table as he consumed his food with heavy breath. Already the boy could feel the tension between his father and mother, could sense his mother's silent disapproval of Murry's drinking, her resentment that this frowning, inarticulate owner of a livery stable had somehow failed her.

Away from his parents, though, Billy frolicked and fraternized with neighborhood chums and got into his share of mischief, often at the expense of his younger brothers. He persuaded sprightly, dark-haired Jack to stick his tongue against an iron hitching post in icy weather. He baffled little Johncy with the question: "How can I be older than you when your birthday is the day before mine?" One day he stood on the gallery of an uncle's second-story office and shot pedestrians with "stink water" from a water pistol.

It was Mammy Callie who tried to discipline him, scolding the boy when he got into trouble, sighing, *Miss Maud, what we goin' do with them boys?* She gave him a nickname, Memmie, which was what Johncy said when he tried to pronounce Billy. *Memmie, Memmie,* she would say with an affectionate scowl, *yo Mammy says to git home.* He loved his Mammy Callie; to him, she seemed "older than God," with her wrinkled face and small, frail body. Born a slave in Mississippi about 1845, she had refused the liberties of emancipation and had elected to stay with "mah white folks." She was proud, she said, to be a Negro, prouder still of her brood of children and grandchildren scattered across northern Mississippi. She didn't share the Falkners' table or sleep in the house, but she did enjoy certain privileges as servant and mammy to the children. She had her own rocking chair by the fireplace, where she sat of an evening with a pinch of snuff under her lower lip, clad as always in a starched dress, smooth white apron, immaculate headcloth, and tiny high-button shoes. It was no wonder that Billy loved her. She rocked him in her lap, gently stroked his head, told him spellbinding stories about little animals struggling to survive, told him about slave times, and the Civil War, and the Ku Kluxers of Reconstruction who rode through Negro communities in their headless sheets, claiming to be dead rebels from hell. Billy could listen to her for hours, transported by his own imagination into the worlds she described.

In the evenings, when the father would come home with whiskey on his breath, Maud would give him a quick, piercing look. The boy felt their tension again at the silent supper table. Later he would see the father sitting alone, absorbed in bitter thoughts of the railroad he had lost and the ranch he had never owned. He would go off for a drink, come back even more irritated, until something would set him off: he would storm and shout at everyone, especially the boy's mother. In Murry's flustered eyes, *she* had played a role in the collapse of his dreams, *she* was to blame for his unhappiness. The boy's mother would endure such outbursts with a fierce reticence, her eyes alone betraying her contempt. Finally the father would stalk away, or lapse into silence himself, his liquored-up rage burnt out.

Murry's drunken tirades frightened Billy. In the boy's view, he could be a maddened giant, violent and unpredictable. Yet there was another side to Murry, a gentler masculine side. Sometimes he would take the boys with him to a family hunting camp called "The Club House," situated north of Oxford at the confluence of the Tippah and Tallahatchie rivers. He taught each in turn how to shoot a gun, how to hunt, fish, track, and ride a horse. When away from Maud, he was not nearly so aloof, so threatening. He told his sons hunting stories, even sang them "The Glow Worm," one of his favorite songs.

Billy felt torn between his parents in vague and painful ways. Yet one thing was clear to him: his mother was around him the most, gave him the most attention. She wasn't loving and warm like Mammy Callie, but she did care for him in her reserved way, did try to shield him from hurt. Moreover, she set an example of stoic resolve, summed up by the sign on the cupboard above her stove: DON'T COMPLAIN—DON'T EXPLAIN.

In addition, she became the boy's devoted teacher, asking his devotion in return. During her own girlhood, her father had deserted her and Damuddy; yet she had found the means to get a college education, had developed her own skills with brush and easel, and had discovered a passion for literature. Now she passed her skill and passion on to her oldest son. She showed him how to paint and draw, and she taught him to read, guiding him confidently through the early primers and Grimms' fairy tales, then introducing him to the magic world of Charles Dickens—all before he started school, at the age of eight. Though his mother usually kept her emotions in check, literature could move her deeply, often to the verge of tears.

For Billy, books and stories opened up a rainbow world of boundless imaginings. In the cavernous library of his grandfather's place, he nourished his imagination on volumes of Scott and Dumas, whose flyleaves bore the name of his grandmother and the date of purchase. He was becoming his mother's boy: precocious, literate, and artistic. Small for his age, with dark, quick eyes and a delicate mouth, the boy clearly resembled his mother. He could even give the father her sharp, piercing glance. She talked about how he would grow up to be an artist. She called him "the light of my life."

SEPTEMBER 1905 began a season of upheaval for the boy and his family. At his mother's insistence, they moved to a little white house almost directly across the street from the Big Place. Now the boy's mother shared a bedroom with Damuddy, he and his little brothers occupied another, and his father took the third. His father was now sleeping alone.

That same September the boy entered the public school, a two-story brick building that housed all ten grades and later an eleventh. On his own for the first time, Billy was quiet and studious and made the honor roll. He was so precocious that the school let him skip the second grade and go to the third. His mother was delighted. On school mornings, he would bolt down a breakfast of eggs, ham, biscuits, and hot chocolate topped with whipped cream, then set off to school carrying a satchel full of books, ruled tablets, and sharpened yellow pencils, with their sweet woody smell.

On late-winter mornings, the boy and his brothers would slip out of the house before daybreak and race to the "dee-po" to watch the fruit trains from Louisiana roar through Oxford. The boys would station themselves on a high bank south of the depot and strain their ears until they heard the first train laboring up Thacker's Mountain south of

Oxford. As it cleared the mountain and descended, there would come the soul-lifting wail of its whistle: "whoo-oo, whoo-ah, whoo-oo, whoo-oo, whoo-ah-ah-ah." Billy knew the locomotive and the engineer of each train by the distinctive sound of its whistle. "That's number 1102," he would say, "with Mr. McLeod." Then they could hear the train enter the level straightaway track that led into town, and the locomotive's exhaust became increasingly sharp and precise. Now it was going full speed: its wheels hummed on the rails, its exhaust exploded in rapid-fire beats, and again that magnificent whistle spread its song across the countryside. And then the locomotive would pound into view, the open firebox door giving off a red glare, the underside of the exhaust smoke swirling low above the cab and tender, and Billy would say it was number 1102 all right—he was always right—and they would turn to await the next train, due to sound its whistle in twenty minutes or so.

Such trains acted powerfully on the boy's imagination and feelings: aggressive iron horses, masculine and irresistible in their furious onward rush. No wonder his father loved them so. The boy even thought about them in school, when he was supposed to be reading and writing as his mother had taught him to do. In the first grade, he had sketched in the back of his reader a detailed picture of a locomotive, complete with wheels and connecting rods, cowcatcher, headlight, smokestack, and bellpull. He had inscribed the book as his grandmother had inscribed the volumes in Grandfather's library: "William Falkner, Oxford, Miss 1905."

I T WAS IN THE THIRD GRADE, in 1906, that the troubled times began. For one thing, his paternal grandmother, Miss Sallie Murry, took ill and stopped coming down to greet the boy and his brothers when they visited the Big Place. Then in the cold of December she "passed away," her soul gone from "the land of life." There was a big funeral in the rain, a burial at St. Peter's Cemetery, a lot of people crying, Grandfather in his panama hat too bereaved to speak. At the same time, Damuddy was dying—of stomach cancer, his mother said. The boy heard that she was taking a potent painkiller called morphine. In June 1907, she, too, was dead. Another funeral, another family grave in the cemetery. His mother was grief-stricken, an ally in the little white house gone forever.

Then came a family announcement: his mother was going to have a baby. Perhaps only Mammy Callie understood the mystery of this, given the hostility between the expecting parents. In mid-August, two days before Murry's birthday, a new baby boy lay wailing in his mother's bedroom. Billy heard his father say, "He's my birthday present." Maud insisted that they name him Dean Swift Falkner after her mother, whose maiden name was Swift. She and Mammy Callie made a fuss over him, tending to his needs, tugging little silk bonnets on his head to cure a bad case of cradle cap. Because the two women devoted so much time to Deanie, the oldest son felt forsaken and lonely.

He found a measure of adult companionship with his grandfather, who felt forsaken, too. Billy could sense how much Grandmother Sallie's death had hurt him. He seemed dazed, lost, without her. At his office, he would drag a chair out to the plank sidewalk and sit there oblivious to his surroundings and his neighbors. Once, Johncy saw him there, all alone; he was writing Sallie's name in the air with his walking stick. Hard of hearing, too, he lived increasingly in a lonesome inner world, drifting with the days, counting over memories of past happiness.

Yet he welcomed Billy's visits to the Big Place, for he and the boy felt a special bond between them. In truth, Billy idolized his grandfather, who stood six feet tall, with thinning white hair and an imposing walrus mustache. He still cut a dapper figure in his panama hat and white suits, a heavy gold watch chain adorning his vest. Billy loved that watch chain, so much so that Grandfather bought him a chain and a vest like his own. The next Sunday, they went to church together, wearing their matching vests and fobs. "I was the proudest boy that ever breathed," Billy said.

At other times, they would sit together on the gallery of the Big Place with their feet propped up on the balustrade, and Grandfather would sip a toddy and enthrall the boy with tales about his great-grandfather, William Clark Falkner. Around 1840, Grandfather said, William Clark, an orphaned boy of fourteen, walked all the way from Tennessee to northern Mississippi, where he moved in with an uncle and grew into a violent, ambitious, arrogant man. After serving in the Mexican War, he killed a rival in a street altercation in Ripley, only to be acquitted of a murder charge. When the Civil War broke out, he organized and commanded a regiment of Confederate infantry and rode to glory at First Manassas, where he fought at the front of his outfit and had two mounts shot from under him. When he galloped back to the battlefront on his second mount, General P. G. T. Beauregard cried out, "Go ahead, you hero with the black plume; *history shall never forget you.*" But his men resented his reckless and ruthless ways, and in the next election they voted him out as regimental commander. Undaunted, he returned to Mississippi, raised a partisan regiment, and fought the Yankees in the Memphis area. After the war, known now as the "Kunnel," he became a powerful figure in Ripley: he practiced law, built a railroad (the same railroad Murry was to cherish so), ran cotton, saw, and grist mills, operated a twelve-hundred-acre plantation, managed one hundred tenants, and lived in an ornate mansion. The Old Colonel had literary ambitions too: he wrote a popular novel called *The White Rose of Memphis,* which among other things romanticized his epic journey on foot from Tennessee to Mississippi and which sold 160,000 copies in thirty-five editions. He also wrote a Civil War play, another novel, and a book of his travels entitled *Rapid Ramblings in Europe.*

Sometimes Grandfather would get out mementos of the Old Colonel: his cane, books, silver watch, even the pipe he was smoking the day he was shot in Ripley. That was on November 5, 1889, Grandfather said, after it became clear that the Colonel had defeated Richard J. Thurmond, a former business partner and a personal enemy, in a bitter election for the state legislature. Late in the afternoon, the Colonel walked to Ripley's public square with an old friend, only to encounter a maddened Thurmond, who brandished a .44 revolver. "What do you mean, Dick?" the Colonel said. "Don't shoot!" Whereupon Thurmond shot him in the mouth, at such close range that Falkner's friend suffered powder burns on his face. The Colonel died that night. And Thurmond himself was tried and acquitted in the most sensational murder case northern Mississippi had ever known. As it happened, Grandfather said, "Kunnel" Falkner had already ordered an eight-foot statue of himself; the family had it placed on a fourteen-foot pediment at his grave in the Ripley cemetery.

Billy could remember the Old Colonel's statue: it loomed against the Mississippi sky, an imposing stone figure that seemed to be addressing a regiment of gravestones laid out in precise formations. Thanks to his statue in the cemetery and his railroad that ran nearby, the Old Colonel remained a living force in Ripley. Billy remembered how people there spoke of the Old Colonel as though he were still alive in the hills somewhere and might come to town at any time.

For Billy, the Old Colonel was a living presence right here in Oxford. Other family members told tales about him, too. And so did a Falkner family servant, Uncle Ned, who still referred to him as "Old Master." Billy strongly identified with his powerful ancestor. He took pride in the fact that they were both firstborn sons and that he, William Cuthbert, shared the Old Colonel's first name. The boy loved to hear stories about him, loved to hold the artifacts of his life—particularly his books—when Grandfather took them out. When asked in school what he wanted to be when he grew up, Billy said, "I want to be a writer like my great grand-daddy."

When he wasn't with his grandfather, Billy was often in the company of a neighborhood girl named Estelle Oldham. She lived in a large house down the street, and her father, known as Major Oldham, was a U.S. Circuit Court clerk and a Republican. Seven months older than Billy, Estelle was petite and feminine, like a fairy. "Even at my age I could tell she was a girl," Johncy said. When she had first seen Billy, she had told her Negro nurse, "Nolia, see that little boy? I'm going to marry him when I grow up." One summer eve, the boy lay beside Estelle, watching Daniel's Comet as it arced through the heavens with its tail of fire. They decided to marry one day and own a chicken farm, but fell to quarreling about what kind of chickens they would raise.

As the months passed, his parents quarreled more than ever. Worse still, Billy himself, who was small and smart like his mother, seemed to be a target for his father's resentments. Even neighborhood boys noticed how much harder he was on Billy than on his other sons. He would call the boy "Snake-Lips," a slur against the boy's mother, too. And his mother would retaliate in her fashion. When Murry would go on a binge, drinking himself into oblivion, she would see to it that he got to a hospital near Memphis for "the cure." She would follow on the train with Billy and his brothers, and together they would wait for the father to emerge, debilitated but sober and chastened. Then, with an air of righteous superiority, Maud, with Billy and his brothers, would take her husband home on the train.

Maud appeared to be demanding a choice from her oldest son. *It's me or your father, Billy,* her actions seemed to say. *You have to decide.* But he could not decide. However profane and disparaging his father might be, the boy still felt something for him, for his world of horses and hunting and trains. Confused, miserable, the boy withdrew from both parents. A friend recalled how moody he seemed, "given to solitary walks, and a disinclination to mingle with his fellows which set him strangely apart from the romping, frolicsome youth of the town." In the fifth and sixth grades, he lost all interest in his studies, and sat staring absently out the window or drawing in his tablet. His grades fell disastrously. During recess, he stood alone on the playground, watching the others at their games. He said he didn't like school and started playing hooky. "He would do anything to get out of school," Estelle observed. His mother was extremely upset: how could Billy do this to her? To himself? Had he forgotten all she had taught him about the value of education? She threatened dire punishment if he didn't behave. But it was no use. "If he couldn't turn her off with a laugh," Johncy noticed, "he simply stood there and listened."

Murry put the troublesome boy to work at the livery stable. Here, he wrote later, he became keenly aware of the rank ammonia-like odor of the horses and learned to harness and curse them "in his shrill cricket voice." He learned about women from the Negro hostlers and the white night man, by listening to their talk. But he became slothful in his chores, rebelling against the livery stable, too, and the whole masculine, fatherly world it represented.

Unable to handle the boy, his parents sent him to live for a time with relatives in Ripley. Later he claimed he ran away to them. Given a few months apart from his feuding parents and the confusion and pain they caused in him, he started on his way toward a resolution.

Back in Oxford, he remained an indifferent, lackluster pupil at school. But at home he sided with his mother, giving himself increasingly to her world of books and art, finding the strength from her to be different in a small town. Under her guidance, he plunged into Shakespeare, into Balzac, Conrad, and Melville, whose *Moby Dick* captivated him. Here was Captain Ahab, bent on self-destruction, drawing others along with a blind and despotic disregard for them as individuals, dragging them toward certain doom in his obsessive quest for the white whale, all set against the earth's most grave and tragic rhythm: the sea. Billy urged Jack to read *Moby Dick,* said "it's one of the best books ever written."

He took a keen interest in people and their habits and stories. When a political uncle went campaigning in outlying hamlets, Billy would go along to watch the farming people, white and black alike, noting how they talked and what they talked about, their gestures and mannerisms.

Back in Oxford, the townsfolk often saw him standing on the south side of the square, entranced, it seemed, as he stared at the white granite statue of a Confederate soldier, erected a few years before by the local chapter of the United Daughters of the Confederacy. The soldier faced forever southward with his musket, an eternal reminder of southern sacrifice and honor in a civil war that Oxonians still talked about. That war, and the part his great-grandfather played in it, captured the youth's imagination. He sat among the old men in the shade of the "cotehouse," listening to their stories about Oxford during the Civil War and the harsh years that followed. He witnessed the Confederate reunions, when the old veterans, men who had screamed the rebel yell and charged Yankees, got out their tattered battle flags and shabby gray uniforms, and marched in memorial parades and wept at speeches of remembered valor. More than anything, he listened to family stories and legends told by his unvanquished aunts, who employed "Damn Yankee" as a single curse word and who had never surrendered. He had heard their tales since he was a child, but now they had a special meaning for him; now he remembered every nuance, scene, event, and character his aunts recounted.

Soon he was telling stories himself, some derived from what he read and heard, others from a mix of fact and fancy. "It got so," a cousin said, "that when Billy told you something, you never knew if it was the truth or just something he'd made up."

Meanwhile he had begun reading poetry and writing his own, which he proudly shared with his friend Estelle. Most twelve- and thirteen-year-old boys regarded girls as their natural enemies, but not Billy. He spent a great deal of time at Estelle's commodious house, talking with her about his verse and drawings. He discovered that he had amazing creative energies and an insatiable need to capture his self and his world at the end of a pencil. In 1911, at age thirteen or fourteen, he evidently submitted a drawing for publication in a national magazine.

He paid a price, though, for being different in Oxford, for embracing his mother's sphere of art and literature. A youth whose best friend was a girl, who shirked his chores, read obsessively, drew pictures, and wrote poetry—no wonder some schoolboys and menfolk thought him "quair." No wonder his own father regarded him as beyond the pale, as completely his mother's boy now. Which was true. Henceforth he was devoted only to her. The father, in Billy's eyes, now loomed dull and contemptible. The youth addressed him with a sarcastic "sir" and went out of his way to provoke him. One day Murry sat down beside his son, said he thought he understood him a little now, and offered him a cigar. "Thank you, *sir,*" Billy said, then crumbled the cigar up in a pipe and smoked it. "He never gave me another cigar," the son remembered with a chuckle.

Yet his rebellion made him even more withdrawn, more unhappy. He did not feel right with himself. He retreated behind a wall of silence, surrendering monosyllabic responses ("Yes'm," "No'm," "It don't matter") in a soft, quick, high-pitched voice, which was still that way after it changed. Even his laughter was soundless. Acutely conscious of his small stature, he longed all his life to be tall like his father, his grandfather, and especially his great-grandfather. Fully grown at five feet, five and a half inches in height, he had his mother's small, shapely feet, thin mouth and delicate chin, her dark, piercing eyes. Billy's eyes could be unsettling. A friend recalled that they seemed to burn right through your flesh and bone, until he could see inside you.

To make matters worse, he had developed something of an inferiority complex about his father's livery business. He had gone through grammar school with boys and girls whose fathers were doctors and lawyers and merchants, men of genteel professions who wore starched collars. He had been unselfconscious then about the difference between their professions and his father's. But not now. All that was changed by his awakening body. "Now," he wrote later in an autobiographical sketch, "he looked after the same girls he had once taken to school in his father's hack, watching their forming legs, imagining their blossoming thighs, with a feeling of defiant inferiority. There was a giant in him, but the giant was muscle-bound." His sexual feelings were so confused, so tangled up with his loyalty to his mother and his anger and bitterness toward his father, that he could not bear to hear a smutty joke. In fact, he would acquire a reputation as a bit of a prude. When someone would start an off-color story, Billy would turn and walk off.

He was more and more confused about Estelle, too. Oh, he continued to share his verse and drawings with her, to cherish their youthful intimacy. But Estelle was developing into an attractive young "belle," with reddish-brown hair that curled over her forehead, blue eyes, round cheeks, and an alluring smile. She spoke in a gushing chatter, her dainty hands conducting the flow of words like music. Already an accomplished pianist, she filled the Oldham home with the swirling sounds of Bach and Beethoven. Billy sat in silent awe as her fingers raced and tumbled over the keyboard.

But he was unsure of her. Apart from their small size, they were opposites: she was coquettish, outgoing, full of laughter; he was morbid, often silent as stone, full of doubts about himself. She loved to dance; he wouldn't even go out on the floor. At parties in the Oldham place, he stood by himself as she glided about on the arms of other fellows. One day, Billy learned that she had caught the eye of a student at the University of Mississippi, which was located in Oxford. His name was Cornell Franklin, and he was captain of the Ole Miss track team and president of the class of 1913. Yet Estelle apparently reassured Billy of her special affection for him, for this shy and brooding young poet who was unlike anyone she knew.

Then came anguishing news: she was going away to school that fall. It was her parents' idea, she said. They were sending her to Mary Baldwin College, a private Presbyterian school in Virginia's Blue Ridge Mountains. When she left by train, Billy was inconsolable. Who his age would share his poems and give him encouragement now? He found school almost unendurable without her.

There were disruptions at home, too. The livery business had fallen off sharply, and Murry had been forced to sell their house in order to make ends meet. He lodged the family in a temporary residence, and with proceeds from the house and a loan from Grandfather he purchased a hardware store on the square. Now three times removed from his beloved railroad, Murry was unhappier than ever. Nevertheless, in December 1913 he was able to buy a new house for the family, a large place at the end of North Lamar, with a fireplace in every room and a pasture in back that stretched out for miles.

Unimpressed with his father's new status as a merchant, Billy continued to be provocative. When he came to the hardware store, he would behave exactly like his grandfather: he would stand an old kitchen chair on its back legs against the storefront and sit there for hours, gazing out over the square. "He was generally almost inert," said a schoolmate, "the laziest boy I ever saw."

ONE SUNDAY THAT SUMMER OF 1914, a thin young man with large ears drove up to the Falkner residence in an impressive seven-passenger Studebaker. He was Phil Stone, the youngest son of "General"

James Stone, a prominent lawyer in town and a Falkner family friend. Phil had heard that Billy was writing poetry; "Miss Maud," in fact, had told Phil's mother that Billy didn't know what to do with his verse. Well, perhaps Phil could help. He asked Billy if he could read some of his work.

The young poet was flattered. Stone, after all, was twenty-one years old—four and a half years older than Billy—and a real intellectual. He had taken one B.A. at Ole Miss and had just earned a second from Yale, where he had concentrated in English and Greek literature. He had hoped to attend Yale Law School, but his father wanted him to enter the law school at Ole Miss instead, which he planned to do that fall. In his room, Billy handed Stone his poetry, then waited as he read it. While Stone didn't think it particularly good, he was surprised and excited all the same. "Anybody could have seen that he had real talent," Stone said later. "It was perfectly obvious."

What this young man needed was a teacher, Stone thought, someone to tutor and guide him. What he needed was Phil Stone, who knew the great works of poetry and believed he understood the art even if he couldn't write verse himself. With training and a lot of hard work, perhaps "Bill" would develop into a real poet and bring prestige to the South, Stone's cherished but maligned homeland.

As the summer progressed, Stone became Billy's self-appointed instructor and friend. And Billy, lonely as he was for male companionship, responded to the proselytizing of the garrulous, more accomplished older male. They went for country rides in Stone's chugging Studebaker and took protracted walks through the forests; Billy listened, taciturn and melancholy, as Stone rhapsodized about how the hills turned blue and lavender and lilac in the sun. Stone brought him to the family's hilltop mansion, an antebellum dwelling with white columns and a wrought-iron balcony in front, and showed him the expansive library on the second floor. Here Stone had spent much of his own lonely and sickly boyhood, finding escape in leather-bound histories of the South and the Civil War. Stone had been reading about that war since he was five years old, and he could discourse at length on the exploits of Lee and Jackson, on Chancellorsville, Gettysburg, and the battles of the Wilderness. They sat in Stone's room, with books and magazines piled everywhere, and Stone lectured about anything that came to mind: about Thackeray and Dickens, Swinburne and Keats, about his sojourn at Yale, where he had heard the great Irish poet William Butler Yeats, about postwar Mississippi politics and the rise of the rednecks—that new breed of acquisitive, unscrupulous farmers who had appeared after the Civil War. He laughed derisively about their crude and persistent ways and taught his morbid protégé to laugh at them, too. In time, they shared a bitter derision that was all their own, with Falkner making a sort of snort and falling into soundless chuckles when Stone recounted another redneck story.

But most of all Stone taught him poetry, putting him through a veritable seminar on Romantic and modernist verse. Stone would send young Falkner off with a stack of books and the Studebaker, and Falkner would drive to a quiet, shady spot in the country and spend the day engrossed in Stone's assignments. He did read the contemporary Imagists, but his sentiments were anti-modern; he went for the Romantics, for Shelley and Keats and Swinburne, especially Swinburne. His musical, sensuous verse, his passionate love for beauty and his melancholy disgust with its human manifestations—all stirred the youth to his depths. It seemed that Swinburne was in the car with him, "springing from some tortured undergrowth of my adolescence, like a highwayman, making me his slave."

Alas, he loved Swinburne so much that he felt as though he had been born out of his time and place. He should have lived in Victorian England, should have gone to Italy with Swinburne. As he gazed at the Mississippi landscape, he saw Swinburne's visions, felt his poignant ecstasies.

With his mind in Swinburne's time, Billy grew more bored with school than ever, finally dropping out for good in his second attempt at the eleventh grade. Phil Stone was all the schooling he needed, Stone and the great poets of those halcyon Romantic years.

In the fall of 1915, Estelle came home and enrolled at Ole Miss as a special student, and Billy saw her a good deal, telling her about his studies and especially about Swinburne, who so satisfied him and filled his inner life. He cared deeply for Estelle. She was tender to him and tried to understand his suffering. In her company, he could be relaxed and open, talk as Stone talked, feel right with himself. Soon he gave her a gold ring with "F" carved on it in gothic, and they reached a private understanding that somehow, in some special way, they belonged to one another.

By now, Estelle's parents had mixed feelings about Billy. He and Estelle were both eighteen, an age when young people traditionally were married or making matrimonial plans. The Oldhams liked Billy well enough, realized how much their daughter cared for him. But they did not want him as a son-in-law. His grandfather may have been a successful man—in addition to his law practice, he had established the First National Bank of Oxford—but Billy's father was something of a failure by comparison. And Billy seemed even worse: a ne'er-do-well and a high school dropout who still lived at home. Miss Lida, Estelle's mother, made it plain that she preferred a handsome, promising young bachelor like Cornell Franklin. To her immense regret, Cornell was gone now, off practicing law in Honolulu.

Because of her parents, Estelle and Billy worked out what others considered a strange relationship. A skilled dancer, petite, fashionable, and flirtatious, she was enormously popular at Ole Miss, as infatuated college boys vied for her attention. She went out with many of them, even casually accepted their fraternity pins. Her mother always accompanied her on dates—no respectable belle could step out without a chaperone. Even with her mother along, Estelle was having the time of her life; she loved the campus dances, which often featured W. C. Handy, the great black trumpet player and "father of the blues," who brought his band down from Memphis. With his hair combed in a pompadour, Billy was often at the dances, but not as Estelle's escort. He might ask her to dance or cut in on her partner. But he was awkward and unsure of himself as he tried to lead her in the fox-trot or the one-step. Most of the time he stood by himself, watching the couples cavort to Handy's golden trumpet. From time to time, Estelle would excuse herself and sit out a dance with him. Afterward, he might go along when Estelle and her mother took a group home for an early morning breakfast. Yet in their moments alone, away from Miss Lida, Billy and Estelle could enjoy their special companionship.

And so he passed his eighteenth and nineteenth years, studying with Stone and sharing his ideas and his heart with Estelle. Sometimes he went hunting with Stone and Stone's tall, hard-drinking father in the Tallahatchie River basin. Every November General Stone and his friends camped there, hunted deer and bear, and drank copiously around a smoking campfire while swapping tales about prey that got away. Billy enjoyed these wilderness outings and drank copiously, too, as he listened to the menfolk. One of their stories especially intrigued him: it was about Old Reel Foot, a huge, crafty bear who had once decimated a pack of baying dogs with his powerful claws.

Back at home, Murry Falkner was growing increasingly alarmed about Billy's weird behavior. What was one to do with a son who pretended to be some kind of intellectual and yet refused to graduate from high school and get a job? Hell, Phil Stone was an intellectual, yet he had two degrees and was in Ole Miss Law School. Murry was even more distressed when he heard that his son stood back silently while other boys danced with his girlfriend. What kind of manliness was that?

Billy's grandfather worried about him, too. Determined to set him straight, the Young Colonel made him a bookkeeper in his bank. Billy told Estelle he hated it. He thought working for money contemptible. Trapped in a situation he detested yet could not escape, he took to drinking brand whiskey from his grandfather's private stock. "Learned the medicinal value of his liquor," Billy said later. "Grandfather thought it was the janitor. Hard on the janitor."

Now it was Maud Falkner's turn to be concerned. Her gifted son, the light of her life, had taken to drink like his father. There was gossip that he even consorted with town drunks, gambling with cards and dice. Uncle John Falkner was so "outdone" with her eldest that he thundered, "Hell, he ain't ever going to amount to a damn—not a damn."

Surrounded by critical family members, Billy cultivated being bizarre. He wore expensive clothes—$17 suits and $12 Johnston & Murphy shoes charged to a Memphis store—and walked down the street like his grandfather, ramrod straight, jaw elevated, eyes staring straight ahead. But such posturing did not ease his boredom or his pain. He spent less time at the bank and more in extracurricular activities at Ole Miss, where two of his drawings—his first published work—appeared in the campus yearbook, *Ole Miss.* One drawing depicted what Billy no doubt wished to be: a tall, debonair man with a mustache, dancing with a fashionably boyish-looking young woman.

Meanwhile, Stone, his mentor and comrade, had graduated with a law degree from Ole Miss and in the fall of 1916 set out for Yale to earn another. With Stone gone, young Falkner appeared even more erratic. "He sure is a nut," one Old Miss student told another. "Hangs around the courthouse, and you can see him sometimes on the square in Oxford, or just sitting by himself on a bench there, doing nothing but looking."

By 1917, his only close friend in Oxford was Estelle. Then came foreboding news. From Honolulu, Cornell Franklin wrote Estelle explicit letters about his regard for her. Worse still, her mother and his mother started talking about how "wonderful" it would be if they got married. That winter Cornell's mother sent Estelle a double diamond ring. *This is your engagement ring,* Cornell wrote her from Hawaii. *I'm coming home in April. We can get married then.*

Estelle came to Billy in tears. Her parents expected her to accept the ring and marry Cornell. "I suppose I *am* engaged to Cornell now," she said, "but I'm ready to elope with you."

What should he do? He was sure he loved Estelle; he did not want to lose her. But he did not want them to run away like cowards. He was the grandson of Colonel William Clark Falkner. They must do this the correct way. "No," he told her, "we'll have to get your father's consent."

He told his father about his intentions and went to Major Oldham for his daughter's hand. If Murry was embarrassed and angry, Major Oldham flew into a tirade. Estelle marry Billy Falkner! Why, he couldn't support himself, let alone a wife. There were impassioned family councils in both households. Nobody was impressed when Billy vowed to support Estelle by working in his grandfather's bank. With both sets of parents opposing them, their own resolve weakened. Christmas came on. Stone, home on vacation, found his protégé sick of his bank job and depressed about Estelle. Frankly, Stone did not like Estelle, thought her "not worth a damn to anybody." If Billy married her, Stone feared it would ruin his chances of becoming a poet.

But a friend of Estelle's believed she was going to marry Cornell Franklin, even though she loved Billy. And Billy, too, felt her slipping away. No wonder he could write later, *"It's terrible to be young. It's terrible. Terrible."* Finally, under increasing family pressure, she announced her engagement to Cornell Franklin, their wedding to take place on April 18, 1918. When Billy realized that she was really going to marry Cornell, "his world went to pieces," his brother Johncy said. He scolded her for not standing up to her parents. He felt rejected, betrayed. In his bitterness, he printed two of his love poems on a sheet of paper, folded it, and gave it to her with the lyrics of a song for voice and piano copied on the front. The composer had taken the lyrics from

a poem, "Obstination," by a French poet and dramatist named François
Coppée.

> *It is all in vain to implore me*
> *To let not her image beguile,*
> *For her face is ever before me—*
> *And her smile.*
>
> *Even though she choose to ignore me,*
> *And all love of me to deny,*
> *There is nought then behind or before me—*
> *I can die.*

I F HE WAS TO DIE, he wanted to go in a blaze of glory, in the great
war in Europe between the Allies and the German-led Central Powers.
From the outset, Billy had closely followed the campaigns, especially
those on the western front. In their bedroom at night, he and his brothers, John and Jack, would spread out a map of Europe and trace the
battle lines from reports in the morning newspaper. By 1916, the opposing armies had committed themselves to deadly trench warfare in
northern France, which produced military stalemate and horrendous
casualties. When ordered to attack, soldiers poured forth from trenches
fronted by barbed wire, dashed across a shell-torn lunarscape called
"no-man's-land," and charged the rival trenches. Enemy machine guns
mowed them down; chlorine gas poisoned them. In parts of France, the
gas was to cling to the tops of caves for twenty years. And yet almost
nothing was gained. In the battle of the Somme in 1916, the British and
French lost 600,000 men, killing and wounding 500,000 Germans, to
win a maximum of eight miles along a twelve-mile front. At Verdun that
same year, French and German forces suffered almost a million combined casualties as they battered one another back and forth for ten
hellish months, leaving a miasmic wasteland of smashed weapons, shattered helmets, shreds of clothings, rotting corpses, and twisted skele-
tons. "Humanity . . . must be mad to do what it is doing," a French
lieutenant wrote at Verdun. "Hell cannot be so terrible."

It wasn't the ghastly ground war that appealed to Billy, for there was little glory in that. What fascinated him was the air war high above the battle lines, a daring, romantic war to him, in which flying knights engaged in spectacular dogfights against a backdrop of sun and clouds. He dreamed of goggled aviators in their frail flying machines, of be-ribboned aces like Immelmann and Boelcke, and Ball and Bishop; he dreamed of going to France and becoming heroic and beribboned, too. He had his chance in the spring of 1917, when America entered the war in a furor of militant idealism and hatred for Germany; Woodrow Wilson pronounced it "a war to end all wars," and American doughboys embarked for Europe, singing "Over There." Billy's parents, however, refused to let him enlist, and so he had decided to bide his time until he turned twenty-one and was eligible for the draft. But a year later, with Estelle gone from him, he vowed to join the American army and become an aviator despite his parents; he stuffed himself with all the bananas and water he could hold and went to the recruiting station, only to be rejected because he was still underweight and under regulation height to boot.

In April 1918, Billy traveled up to New Haven, where he and Phil Stone refined a plan for him to enter the British Royal Air Force. Estelle, meanwhile, cried most of the night before her wedding, but refused to call it off because her father would be furious. "It's too late," she wept. The next day, resigned to her fate, she took her vows as Mrs. Cornell Franklin, then left with her husband for Honolulu.

In June, Billy walked into a Canadian recruiting center in New York City and enlisted in the Royal Air Force, which was organizing squadrons in Canada. He did so by impersonating an Englishman and remaking his unhappy life. He told the recruiting officer that his name was William *Faulkner,* that he was born in Finchley, England, and that his mother, Maud Faulkner, now living in Oxford, Mississippi, was the person to contact in case he died in battle. He made no mention of his father, implying that he was either dead or gone. And so, in a single blow, Billy repudiated his alcoholic father, claimed his mother for himself, and created a new last name for them both. Now as William Faulkner he could start life over again with her; he could be a rootless war hero, a romantic outcast from the world that had hurt him.

For nearly five months he attended RAF training classes in or near Toronto and continued his impersonations. He gave other cadets the impression that he was a Yale student and claimed in his letters to his mother—he never wrote Murry—that he had finished ground school and accomplished a four-hour solo flight. None of this was factually correct. But in his perfervid imaginings he was already another Immelmann, another Ball, flying over the smoking trenches of France in a British Spad.

But then came terrible news. Germany had surrendered to the Allies. The war was over. An armistice had been signed on November 11, 1918. Cadet Faulkner, without so much as a training flight, was discharged. Gone were his fleeting dreams of legitimate heroism and glory. He cursed those who had ended the war and smoldered in "disgusted sorrow" that circumstance could cheat him so.

Well, he was not going back to Oxford as little Billy Falkner, or as a discharged cadet either. He had created one persona to enter the war; he would create another to leave it, one that would put "little Billy Falkner" behind him once and for all. Dressed in a new British officer's uniform he had ordered, he headed for home on a southbound train.

ALMOST THE ENTIRE FAMILY awaited him at the Oxford depot: Maud and Mammy Callie, eleven-year-old Dean and seventeen-year-old Johncy, and his frowning father. Jack was not in Oxford: he had enlisted in the U.S. Marines and had seen action in some of the bitterest fighting in France; he had been badly gassed in one battle, wounded by shrapnel in another. The family hadn't heard anything from him in months. Murry, who favored Jack and Dean, was inconsolable about Jack's fate. "Hush, Buddy," Maud told him. "He'll be back." Fretful about Jack, Murry turned out this day to welcome home his other, insolent son.

Johncy would never forget his brother's appearance when he stepped off the train that early December day. Walking with a limp and sporting a neatly trimmed mustache, he wore an overseas cap, military slacks, and a snappy blue tunic with a Sam Browne belt and a lieutenant's pips on his shoulders, and he carried a swagger stick and a trench coat. On his tunic glittered the wings of the legendary Royal Flying Corps, predecessor of the Royal Air Force. In the car on the way home, he said he had hurt his leg in an airplane crash. He had gone up in a

Camel to celebrate earning his wings, he said, only to crash into the hangar.

It was all an elaborate charade, for Billy Falkner, now William Faulkner, had not earned the wings or the rank of the uniform he wore, or hurt his leg in a plane crash. But never mind truth to facts. He would never have much regard for that. He was recreating himself, this twenty-one-year-old Faulkner, with his British uniform and British ways. He might not have admitted it, but deep down he was seeking acceptance and love; he wanted his father to respect him, young women to find him attractive, people to think him brave and admirable.

In the ensuing days, he wore his uniform and carried his swagger stick about the square, the golf course, and the campus of Ole Miss; he even affected British mannerisms, greeting people with a half salute and calling them by their last names, his dark, shining eyes giving no hint of his masquerade. He embellished the crash story, too, telling his wide-eyed brothers and acquaintances that he had gotten drunk on Armistice Day and had flown up in a rotary-motored Spad with a crock of bourbon, executed an Immelmann turn or two, and gone into a near-perfect loop when a hangar loomed in the way. He crashed through the roof so far, he said, that he ended up suspended from the rafters and had to climb down one of the hangar support poles. And that, he said again, was how he injured his leg.

Then, as if to memorialize his impersonation, he posed for official "war" photographs in various combinations of his military uniform, with a handkerchief tucked in his sleeve, gloves and cane in hand, and a cigarette in his mouth under a small, neatly trimmed mustache. The photographs made him appear cocky, authoritative, and tall.

This was the impression he gave his little brothers, too. Dean, effervescent and carefree, admired his military brother so much that he wore his Boy Scout uniform to school and imitated his big brother's military bearing. Johncy, as loquacious and affable as Faulkner was taciturn, liked to walk around the square with him because of all the salutes he received. Returning doughboys who noticed his overseas cap all saluted him with great respect: they thought he had served in Europe. At times, he claimed that he had fought there, that he had even been wounded in aerial combat and had a metal plate in his head as a consequence.

Meanwhile he resumed his relationship with Stone, who had earned his law degree from Yale and settled in Charleston, Mississippi, where he and his brother managed a branch of the family law firm. Faulkner visited him frequently on the weekends, and Stone gave him more books to read and exhorted him to get on with his own work. More determined than ever to make him a successful poet, Stone cajoled his protégé, browbeat and swore at him, threatened and pleaded. He reminded Faulkner that "the world owed no man anything; that true greatness was in creating great things and not in pretending them; that the only road to literary success was by sure, patient, hard, intelligent work." Later Stone said he doubted that it was Faulkner's ambition to become a poet as much as it was Stone's desire to make him one.

Under Phil Stone's stern tutelage, Faulkner plunged into the works of contemporary poets: he read Robert Frost and Edwin Arlington Robinson with pleasure, and Richard Aldington and Conrad Aiken. But like Stone he still preferred Swinburne and another late Romantic named A. E. Housman. When he read Housman's *A Shropshire Lad*, Faulkner discovered there the secret modern poets were howling after "like curs on a cold trail in a dark wood, giving off, it is true, an occasional note clear with beauty, but curs just the same." Here in *A Shropshire Lad*, he thought, was the "reason for being born into a fantastic world: discovering the splendor of fortitude, the beauty of being of the soil like a tree about which fools might howl and which winds of disillusion and death and despair might strip, leaving it bleak, without bitterness; beautiful in sadness."

By the winter of 1918–1919, he was attempting to create something beautiful and sad of his own, something that derived from his studies but that also drew from his private suffering. He wrote in a romantic haze, with Estelle much on his mind. And other young women troubled him too—ones he saw on the drugstore corner, with "ripening thighs" and "mouths that keep you awake at night with unnameable things— shame of lost integrity, manhood's pride, desire like a drug." Out of his own bittersweet passion and his readings in the English Romantics and Nathaniel Hawthorne's *The Marble Faun* came a set of pastoral poems linked by the yearly seasons, poems about a melancholy marble faun who, imprisoned in a rural English world of leas, wolds, and downs, lamented his "enthralled impotence" and longed in his dreams not only to break his bonds and satisfy his desires but to surpass them, to find a divine fullness in which the ache of longing would be gone forever. . . .

In the spring, Jack Falkner, six feet tall and handsome, returned to

Oxford a genuine war hero. His shorter, older brother, writing poetry in his room, now assumed another posture. "He gave the impression," an acquaintance said, "that he did not have a care or worry in the world, or give a damn about anything or anybody."

In June, Estelle came home for the funeral of her younger sister, Victoria; her dear "Tochie," so much the pretty tomboy in their youths, had died of the dreaded Spanish influenza. Estelle had a four-month-old daughter with her; she was named Victoria, too, but her Chinese nurse called her "Cho-Cho"—butterfly—and so did her family. Faulkner's heart sank. That Estelle was the mother of Cornell's child created an even greater distance between them. Yet the very sight of little Estelle, even more desirable in her fashionable clothes, rekindled Faulkner's longing for her. Before she returned to Cornell in Honolulu, Faulkner gave her a copy of Swinburne's poems with an inscription so passionate that she had to tear the page out.

He worked on another poem that betrayed his stormy feelings. His studies with Stone had led him to the French Symbolist Stéphane Mallarmé, who in 1876 had published a poem called "L'Après-midi d'un Faune," also about a faun and a nymph. Now Faulkner reworked the poem; in his version, the faun followed his nymph through a clouded landscape of desire, mesmerized by her "lascivious dreaming knees" and the "hot quick spark" of her glances. He watched as she whirled and danced, just as Estelle used to do, until at last they walked hand in hand with a breeze caressing her "short and circled breast." But then he had "a nameless wish" to go to "some far silent midnight noon," and he dreamed of another world where ghostly "blond limbed dancers" whirled beneath the moon.

Faulkner took his poem to Stone, who had his secretary type it and mail it off to *The New Republic* for publication. Stone had sent off other Faulkner poems, but they had all come back, rejected. But not "L'Après midi d'un Faune," which *The New Republic* bought for $15 and carried in its issue of August 6, 1919, under the name "William Faulkner." It was his first published literary work. Said Stone later: "Bill and I felt like the lucky country boy at his first crap game: How long has this been going on?" They sent more poems to *The New Republic*, and more, but it declined them all. Still, Faulkner was undaunted. He wrote a female friend: "I am sending you a drawing which, when I have become famous, will doubtless be quite valuable."

While faulkner wrote verse in his room, Murry Falkner had taken a new position as secretary and business manager of the University of Mississippi. He was happy with his work there; his superiors thought him a competent manager of the school, and the students liked him, too. Because he was happy, he and Maud got along better than perhaps they ever had. He bought a new car, a red Buick roadster, and took her on slow afternoon rides through the countryside. With her help, he eventually gave up liquor: she would meet him after work and walk home with him, thus helping him resist temptation when cronies invited him out for drinks.

His relationship with his oldest boy, though, remained painfully strained. He had never understood and never accepted Billy. It was only because Maud considered him a darling of destiny that Murry tolerated the boy at all and let him go on living at home even after he had turned twenty-one. That Billy didn't work, that all he did was write and read poetry up in his room, galled Murry beyond words.

He pressured Billy, now twenty-two, to get a job or at least attend the university. Faulkner didn't want to do either one. But he finally gave in to his father and entered Ole Miss that fall as a non-degree student. Without enthusiasm, he told people that he wanted only to study languages and English.

When he bothered to attend classes, which was not often, he masqueraded as poet and British dandy. He spoke in a British accent, sported a cane or his swagger stick, and wore baggy flannel trousers and a tweed coat with a white handkerchief tucked in the sleeve, British style. To protect his wounded feelings and extreme sensitivity, he retreated behind a facade of arrogant aloofness, staying to himself, seldom speaking to anyone even when spoken to. Fellow students mocked him as the "beau-u-tiful man with [the] cane," or simply dismissed him as "queer." A wag came up with a derisive nickname that stuck. They called him Count No 'Count.

He did have one close friend—a law student named Ben Wasson, who shared his interest in poetry and all but idolized him for his literary talent. A native of Greenville, Mississippi, Wasson was a small man— even shorter than Faulkner—with a boyish face and a shock of hair over his forehead. When they had first met a few years before, Wasson had been so excessively courteous that Faulkner mocked him afterward, saying he looked like "a young Galahad who's just gotten off a rocking horse." But Faulkner liked his sensitivity and his passion for poetry and music—here, clearly, was a comrade in arms. In Wasson's company, Faulkner let himself relax. They shared moonshine liquor, played poker, sat on the square together, and lounged on the campus lawn at Ole Miss, near one of the Confederate monuments. As Stone had done with him, Faulkner read poetry to Wasson and enthralled him with his extensive knowledge of Romantic and modern verse. Faulkner even took him to the Stones' mansion when they were gone—they allowed him the privilege as Phil's friend—and played Beethoven symphonies for Wasson on an old Victrola. "Listen to those horns of triumph and joy," Faulkner once sighed, "crying their golden sounds in a great twilight of sorrow."

A tireless, driven writer, Faulkner turned out an impressive body of poetry and even some criticism that year. He also wrote a short story called "Landing in Luck," an amusing piece about a cadet's initial solo flight in Canada, which drew on the mythic version of his war experience. It appeared in the student newspaper, *The Mississippian*, as did some of his verse and criticism.

By now, he felt a captive to poetry and Phil Stone; he struggled desperately to master the form, to go beyond mere imitation and forge his own poetic vision. As if to show his mentor and master how hard he was trying, Faulkner gave Stone a special present for New Year's: a handmade book of nine of his poems, all hand lettered and bound in a red velvet cover, and entitled *The Lilacs*. Its frontispiece was a watercolor of a sparsely draped female, which set the mood for Faulkner's principal theme and personal fear: that young women, desirable and lovely though they might be, were inaccessible, inevitably unfaithful, and potentially destructive.

In the fall of 1920, Faulkner and Wasson helped form a campus dramatic club, the Marionettes, for which Faulkner served as stage manager and property man. He enjoyed being outrageous. To the shock of other members, he once defended a passage about incest in a Greek tragedy. "You'll have to admit it's lots better to have sex with a sister or a brother, a mother or a father, than with a complete stranger," Faulkner said.

In November, he dropped out of Ole Miss and devoted his creative energies to an experimental play called *The Marionettes,* whose explicitly sensual dialogue would have created an uproar had it ever been staged at the University of Mississippi. Clearly trying to free himself from conventional poetry, he recast the major sexual theme of *The Lilacs* in a drama with poetic dialogue. Gone were the fauns and nymphs of his earlier poetry. In *The Marionettes,* his male character, the white-faced Pierrot of French pantomime, dreamed of seducing a lovely young blonde named Marietta to the music of a guitar. "You are a trembling pool,/Love!" he told her in his dream, "A breathless shivering pool,/And I am a flame that only you can quench." But alas! Pierrot feared that sexual union would kill him and make her a flame instead.

In drawings that accompanied his hand-lettered text, Faulkner portrayed the sensual Marietta, not as a blonde, but as a thin, bosomy, dark-haired flapper who bore a remarkable resemblance to the young woman who had forsaken him. He even bound a special copy for Estelle, inscribing it to her daughter, Cho-Cho, "a tiny flower of the flame," but clearly intended for "the flame" herself.

Hungry for recognition, Faulkner produced four or five additional hand-bound copies of his play and persuaded Wasson to sell them for $5 apiece. Faulkner even printed "First edition" on the title page.

S TILL, HE WAS NOT SATISFIED with *The Marionettes.* He thought it "a shadowy fumbling in windy darkness." During the winter or spring of 1921, he undertook a more ambitious project, a musical poem sequence that reflected the influence of two modern poets he was studying now —T. S. Eliot and Conrad Aiken. He was particularly impressed with Aiken, an American who experimented with subtle musical rhythms and themes of personal identity. Faulkner cared little for the other contemporary American poets, whom he called "a yelping pack" of adolescent bards, "mired in swamps of mediocrity" as they wrote inferior Yeats or sobbed over the Middle West. Aiken, however, was another matter. In the "fog" engulfing modern American poetry, Faulkner thought him the "one rift of heaven sent blue," with his sensational use of musical and narrative lyrics and contradictory points of view.

With Aiken's voice speaking to him, Faulkner composed a verse symphony called *Vision in Spring,* which was really an anguished love song about Estelle, who had married in the month of April. In the title poem, Pierrot, the masked mime, looked back "old and weary and lonely" to a vanished love and wondered "Was my heart, my ancient heart that broke?" He dreamed of unrequited love and unfulfilled ambition, and imagined childlike dancing girls he loved. But this lonely dreamer was "a passive watcher," a "prisoner of echoes and false music."

As the poem unfolded, Faulkner struggled with the form, for within it was a novelistic vision trying to emerge, one that narrative suited best. In "Love Song," a parody of Eliot's poem about J. Alfred Prufrock, Faulkner asked through Pierrot:

> *Shall I walk, then, through a corridor of profundities*
> *Carefully erect (I am taller than I look)*
> *To a certain door—and shall I dare*
> *To open it? . . .*

In a subsequent poem, entitled "Marriage" in one version, Faulkner opened the door to explicit verse about real human beings, using language that was more fictional than poetic. In the opening, a man sat by firelight watching a beautiful woman play the piano, just as Faulkner had done with Estelle. The narrative voice spoke from the man's view, describing the frenzied turmoil in his mind as he dreamed of ravishing the woman, then saw his brain disintegrate "spark by spark." He shut his eyes to banish this terrible vision of sex's destructive power. In the next movement, Faulkner switched to the woman's view as she played the piano: she wanted to dream back to "a certain spring" that "blossomed in shattering slow fixations, cruel in beauty of nights and days." Then suddenly the music stopped. The man watched her climb the stairs with her "subtle suppleness," the swirl of her dress like "a ripple of naked muscles before his eyes." Then a bursting moon: wheels spun in his brain, "shrieking against sharp walls of sanity." At the turn, she shivered and hated him as he mounted the stairs after her.

Faulkner worked on *Vision in Spring* in another room in another house, which the university had provided for his father on the Ole Miss campus. It was the old Delta Psi house, a three-story, red-brick place that resembled a medieval castle, with a tower, stained-glass windows, and a circular stairway inside. The family had moved there in 1920, and

Faulkner occupied a small room in the tower, where he put in a supply of corn liquor and toiled on his verse in solitude.

When he finished *Vision in Spring* that summer of 1921, Estelle was home again, visiting her family with Cho-Cho. Faulkner presented her with a copy of *Vision in Spring,* perhaps lamenting (as he had before) how "I have given my treasures of art, even though she choose to ignore me and my heart." Gone, though, was the hand lettering and watercolors of his previous handbound volumes. *Vision in Spring* was typed like a professional manuscript.

H E OFTEN IMPERSONATED the Bohemian poet now, and went about town barefoot. His father and uncle were dismayed. "That damn Billy is not worth a Mississippi goddamn," Uncle John complained. "Won't hold a job; won't try; won't do anything! He's a Falkner and I hate to say it about my own nephew, but, hell, there's a black sheep in everybody's family and Bill's ours."

Those were Murry's sentiments exactly. He was not impressed when Stone told him, "Mr. Murry, I'm not a writer, I never will be a writer, but I know one when I see one." Bill, he said, "had the stuff." The truth was that Murry thought Stone a bad influence on his improvident son.

To forestall criticism and earn spending money, Faulkner did work at various odd jobs his father secured for him. He painted houses and once helped paint the law building, which had a steeple. Since no one else would paint the steeple, Faulkner tied himself to it with ropes and did the job alone. His mother was horrified. She told Murry not to get him any more jobs without talking to her first.

Much of the time, though, Faulkner gallivanted about the countryside with Stone, who was bored with life in bucolic Charleston and preferred the pleasures of women and cards to the tedium of law. They sallied forth in Stone's car "Drusilla," a Ford coupe with white wire wheels, and headed north for the big city of Memphis, Tennessee, and its flourishing bordellos and casinos along the Mississippi River. Stone went there to test his skill at poker, Faulkner to nourish his taste for beer and bourbon.

It was the early twenties, and national prohibition was in effect—the "noble experiment," Herbert Hoover called it, which the prohibition-ists prophesied would destroy "Demon Rum" forever and bring on the millennium. What it brought on was wide-scale lawbreaking, as drink-ing Americans turned to bootleggers and moonshiners to satisfy their thirsts, or frequented bordellos and speakeasies, which sold liquor in easy defiance of the law. In Memphis, Stone and Faulkner made the rounds of private "clubs" and brothels, Faulkner observing everything —the pungent and smoky rooms, the underworld figures, the pimps and the madams, the businessmen and city officials amusing themselves after hours, and the gentlemen up from Mississippi. He and Stone even befriended a fat, flamboyant madam named Mary, whose two-story brownstone offered clients the diversions of poker and liquor as well as the pleasures of the flesh.

Balding prematurely, Stone wore a hat all the time now, even inside Mary's place. Expansive with the "girls," a *bon vivant* in gentleman's dress, Faulkner's mentor would go upstairs for a poker game while Faulkner lounged about in the downstairs parlor. He would drink and banter with Mary—"I'll put you in a novel someday"—and carry on with her girls, who posed no threat to him. When one of them playfully propositioned him, Faulkner boasted, "No, thank you, ma'am; I'm on vacation."

In his jocular moods, he often contended that a bordello was "the perfect milieu for an artist to work in." It was quiet in the morning, so you could get your work done; it afforded you a social life in the eve-ning, if you wanted one; it gave you a certain social standing, and the girls and the madam and the bootleggers all called you "sir," and all you really needed for writing was a cigarette, some bourbon, and a pencil and paper.

He seems never to have gone upstairs with a prostitute. "I know whores," he said later. "I don't bed down with whores." He was too fastidious and unsure of himself to do so, and anyway, he said he had to love a woman before he would ever sleep with her. In fact, he was in love again—with Stone's Charleston stenographer, Gertrude Steg-bauer. She was "a very pretty little girl," Stone said, and she inevitably reminded Faulkner of his lost love, the object of so much of his anguish and his poetry. He idealized Gertrude Stegbauer. He brought her pre-sents. He and Stone even took her to dances—Faulkner refused to do so by himself. But his blandishments were to no avail. When she did not respond, he took it as another rejection, and it shattered his self-esteem; it broke his heart.

Eventually he found a way out of his suffering. He told Stone he conjured up mental pictures of pretty young Gertrude engaging in the most unromantic act of the human species.

H E WANTED TO LEAVE Mississippi, go up to New York City and live in Greenwich Village like other poets and writers. Maybe he could sell his verse to the big magazines if he were nearer them. Stone feared that he would get up there and *talk* out his writing and not write. But a mutual friend and fellow Mississippian named Stark Young, who lived in New York and wrote and published poetry, urged Faulkner to come there and sleep on his sofa until he could find a room and a job. Determined to get out on his own, be free of his memories, free of Oxford and his disapproving father, Faulkner took a train to New York City in the autumn of 1921. Thanks to Young, who introduced him to the manager, Faulkner got a job as a salesman in a Manhattan bookstore, then moved into a little room in Greenwich Village, where he wrote during his off-hours. But he failed to place any of his work. And so he drank—Stark Young was astonished at how much liquor he could consume for such a short and slender man.

Lonely and confused, Faulkner returned to Oxford when Stone told him to, and with great reluctance took a job as postmaster of the Ole Miss post office. It was a fiasco. Bored beyond endurance, he read and wrote poetry on the job, sold stamps and sorted mail only when he felt like it. He misplaced letters, returned parcels before anybody could claim them, closed mailboxes clients had paid for, and generally went about with a cheerful disregard for his duties and his customers. Soon he refused even to open the general delivery window, ignoring students and teachers who clamored angrily for service.

Still, he was not devoid of responsibility. He did serve as assistant scoutmaster and took gregarious Dean and other scouts on overnight hikes, regaling them with campfire stories about real and make-believe adventures. One Oxonian remembered how kind and patient Faulkner was in his dealings with young people; he showed them how to shoot and repair a gun and to observe the mysteries of the woods, with their cawing birds and fleeing deer.

And he worried about his aging grandfather, who had been so much like a father to him. Now seventy-three, Grandfather still had a law practice, but he sat most of the day in the courthouse yard, a brooding old man too deaf to share in conversation, even with an ear trumpet. Sometimes, in a vain effort to understand someone, he would hold the ear trumpet in his teeth in order to feel the sound vibrations. Then on a quiet afternoon in March 1922, after a hearty midday meal, he lay down for his daily nap—and never awoke, dead of a heart attack. Young Faulkner, in his turn, sat with his grandfather during the vigil in the front parlor of the Big Place, the house where the old man had recounted those glorious tales about the Old Colonel and given his grandson a powerful sense of family heritage that fueled his dreams. The next day, in an old tree-shaded section of the cemetery, Faulkner took his turn in tossing a spade of earth on his grandfather's coffin and telling him goodbye.

B Y NOW, Stone had moved back to Oxford to help his aging father at the family law office. In addition to cheering up Faulkner when he complained about the post office, Stone encouraged him to study prose fiction and to write stories as well as poetry. Faulkner scarcely needed any urging. Under Stone's tutelege, he had continued to read Balzac, Conrad, and Dickens and had studied Flaubert and Joyce, whose *Ulysses* had been excerpted in *The Little Review.* Faulkner was impressed with the stream-of-consciousness technique employed in *Ulysses;* he thought Stone right, that "anyone who wrote fiction hereafter must go to school to Joyce." He admired Flaubert and Conrad, and Melville and "old Walt Whitman too," for breaking out of "the chains of convention" and following their visions, as he'd told Ben Wasson. But for Faulkner and Stone, the greatest writer of fiction was Balzac, whose interconnected novels, "The Human Comedy," captured the rich and vast tapestry of nineteenth-century French society. Stone owned an entire set of Balzac, which he annotated himself, and he and Faulkner now plunged into a comprehensive nightly reading of his work, analyzing character and motivation as they went.

At Stone's urging, Faulkner also took up Willard Huntington Wright's *The Creative Will: Studies in the Philosophy and the Syntax of Aesthetics* (1915), which was Stone's literary bible. Faulkner, too, fell under Wright's spell, pondering and storing one Wright gem after another. Indeed, it must have seemed that Wright was in the room with him, answering his questions and giving him reassurance. Was there a connection between the writing of prose and of poetry? "The ability to write great poetry is an excellent preparation for the writing of great prose," Wright asserted. "Indeed, fundamentally, they should be synonymous." Should a writer belong to a literary "school" or "group"? No, Wright insisted. "His nature is necessarily solitary." What should the writer of fiction strive for? For "progressive innovations" and "emotional intensity." What were the qualities of great literature? Wright stressed "character analysis, the portrayal of realistic segments of life, cosmopolitanism of outlook, spiritual exaltation, dissection of manners and customs, the solution of social and sexual problems, moral and ethical determinism, psychological research, and fanciful creativeness."

Wright cited Balzac as an example, and Faulkner noted what he said. "Balzac creates first a terrain with an environmental climate; and the creatures which spring from this soil, and which are part of it, create certain inescapable conditions, social, economic, and intellectual. Furthermore, the generations of characters that follow are, in turn, the inevitable offsprings of this later soil, fashioned by all that preceded them."

And so, Wright said, "in all great and profound aesthetic creation the artist is an omnipotent god who moulds and fashions the destiny of a new world, and leads it to an inevitable completion where it can stand alone, self-moving, independent. . . . In the fabrication of this cosmos the creator finds his exaltation."

Exalted and excited as never before, Faulkner took to his own work —both prose and poetry—with renewed zeal. He discovered, he said later, that he had a demon which drove him, doomed him, to write, and he struggled to be worthy of it. He made a pencil sketch of himself, the writer, in a herringbone-tweed suit with wide-bottom trousers; his face was thin, with curling hair, dark and narrow eyes, long, pointed nose, and small lips with a thin mustache. Wanting to share his creations, he brought a golfing partner to his tower room and read his verse, glass in hand, "in his shy, almost singing voice."

He kept his work in the mails, striving relentlessly to get it into the national magazines. Alas, everything came back from New York. Stone, giving encouragement, kept a record of submissions and rejections on a suit-box lid.

The writer did have one breakthrough: he had submitted part of *Vision in Spring* to *The Double Dealer,* a new literary magazine put out in New Orleans, and the poem had appeared in June 1922. Now, a year later, he decided to try publishing the entire manuscript. With high expectations, he sent it to Four Seas, a Boston house that had published such prominent poets as Conrad Aiken, William Carlos Williams, and young Stephen Vincent Benét.

Four Seas' response was not what Faulkner expected. The company said it might publish his manuscript if he would pay the costs. Faulkner didn't want this; it was vanity publishing. Besides, he didn't have any money. This was nothing but another rejection. He was crushed about his manuscript, then livid. "It's beautiful," he told an Ole Miss student, "but it's not what they're reading. If they want a book to remember, by God I'll write it."

But Stone dissuaded him from doing that. Counting up the years Faulkner had been writing verse, Stone thought it imperative that he "get some recognition" now, even if they had to pay for it. In Stone's opinion, Faulkner's most publishable manuscript was his earlier cycle of pastoral eclogues about the marble faun. Why not rework that and send it to Four Seas? Faulkner guessed Stone was right—he did need something to show for all his hard work. And so he set about revising his marble faun manuscript, which he finished evidently in the spring of 1924.

Then he went through a mysterious emotional crisis that immobilized him. Whether this involved another idealized young woman, or some lingering attachment to Stone's Charleston stenographer, is not known. But Faulkner could not write anything for months, could not sit down with pencil and paper before getting up again. In his misery, he let Stone handle the business of submitting his reworked poems.

Stone was so anxious to get his protégé before the public that he took care of everything: he negotiated a contract with Four Seas that called for the company to print a first edition of a thousand copies and Stone to defray the $400 publishing costs himself. Stone even gave the manuscript its title, *The Marble Faun,* despite Nathaniel Hawthorne's 1860 novel of the same name, and provided a preface in which he stressed Faulkner's "promise" and hailed his work as signaling a renaissance in southern artistic expression.

Stone even paid for publicity photographs. "We wanted him to look like a romantic poet," Stone said, "you know, like Byron with his thrown-back head and flowing tie. Except we couldn't put on him a tie like that." Faulkner posed with an open collar, tousled hair, and a look of gentle intensity on his face. Stone then launched a promotional campaign, writing his friends and the Yale alumni weekly that "this poet is my personal property and I urge all my friends and class-mates to buy his book." Stone was, he said, trying "to help advertise Mississippi and put it on the map artistically."

Although he left business matters to Stone, Faulkner seemed pleased about his forthcoming book. He told Ben Wasson that Four Seas had been "imperceptive" enough to "accept" it and joked that his photograph would soon be in the Sunday papers. But in a more serious mood: "I believe my book will be an escape for poetry lovers from the scribblings that some authors are presumptuous enough to call poetry."

He dedicated his book about an impotent faun to his mother, apparently indifferent to whatever that suggested to his readers. Yet he ignored his mother and father both in a short autobiographical sketch for Four Seas. In it, he introduced himself as the "Great-grandson of Col. W. C. Faulkner, C.S.A., author of 'The White Rose of Memphis,' 'Rapid Ramblings in Europe,' etc." About to publish his own book, Faulkner added the *u* to his great-grandfather's name and so claimed the Old Colonel for himself. Now it was the two of them against Murry Falkner and the hostile masculine world of Oxford, which Faulkner gave as only his "present temporary address."

Enduring the long wait at the post office, first for galleys, then for published books, Faulkner still felt depressed. Two of his younger brothers—Johncy and Jack—were married now and working. Jack, with a law degree from Ole Miss, took a job that year with the U.S. Treasury Department and soon would be employed as a special agent for what later became the FBI. Faulkner, turning twenty-seven, remained single and without prospects for even a girlfriend.

He suffered on another score, too. The year before, he had become Oxford's scoutmaster, something he cared deeply about. But a local preacher thought this rakish eccentric unfit to work with boys and in the fall of 1924 mounted a crusade to oust him as scout leader. When the preacher retailed stories about his drinking and carousing around, Faulkner quit in disgust.

At the end of October 1924, he resigned as Ole Miss postmaster, too, after the postal inspector in Corinth had sent him a three-page letter charging him with flagrant misconduct and mismanagement. Faulkner felt emancipated. "Thank God," he said, "I won't ever again have to be at the beck and call of every son of a bitch who's got two cents to buy a stamp."

He wrote Ben Wasson, now working in his father's Greenville law office, how heavenly it was to be free of that awful job, "to be able to walk in the sunlight and drink the air and fill the eyes with amazing unbelievable color and then sit down before a sheet of paper and make a pipe and dream." He said he was just now recovering from the emotional ordeal of the past spring: he had a gallon of whiskey, and could at last take up pencil and paper again. In fact, he enclosed "a thing" he had done that morning. As for regular work, he did not think he would ever do that again. In truth, he said he would rather die than measure his brief days by "the moth-eaten fallacies of established society."

But he was still depressed. He worked on a new poem that betrayed his desolate heart; it dealt with his own death and burial in "these blue hills," where the earth that held him fast would find him breath again. He called it "Mississippi Hills: My Epitaph." He visited Wasson in Greenville, a Delta city on the banks of the Mississippi, and the two friends walked down to the levee and sat on the embankment. As the muddy waters of the Mississippi swirled by, Faulkner spoke of his poetry, of the sad brevity of life and the imminence of death. He confessed that for about a year now he had had a premonition that he would die before he reached thirty.

IN EARLY NOVEMBER or so, Faulkner took the train to New Orleans, where Sherwood Anderson lived. Faulkner had read his recent book of stories, *Horses and Men,* and told Ben Wasson that Anderson's "I'm a Fool" and Conrad's *Heart of Darkness* were the best stories he had ever seen. "By God, that's a man," Faulkner had said of Anderson. "I'd sho like to meet him and know him." Wasson said he should go to New Orleans and look him up. His new wife, Elizabeth Prall, had managed the Manhattan bookstore in which Faulkner had worked and could introduce him to her husband.

When Faulkner stepped off the train in New Orleans, he was glad to be back in the old city; he and Stone had visited here before, and he liked the excitement of the French Quarter, with its secondhand stores, art shops, and brassy jazz spots. He walked to Jackson Square, in the very heart of the Quarter, where the St. Louis Cathedral, spired and magnificent, overlooked Jackson Park and the Mississippi River beyond. The Andersons lived in an apartment on the second floor of the Pontalba Building, a historic row house with iron-lace balconies, situated southwest of the square. As Faulkner wrote later, the cathedral and the Pontalba Building looked as though they had been "cut from black paper and pasted flat on a green sky; above them taller palms were fixed in black and soundless explosions."

Faulkner remembered Elizabeth Anderson well enough. A tiny woman from a gentle, academic New York family, she had thought him a good bookstore clerk; she had asked him to wait particularly on elderly women, who loved his southern charm. When Faulkner knocked on the door, he expected to see her, but not Anderson. "I didn't think that I would see him at all, that he would probably be in his study working, but it happened that he was in the room at the time, and we talked and we liked one another from the start."

Faulkner was certainly impressed with the famous Midwesterner. At forty-eight, he was a dramatic, compulsive storyteller, so commanding that Faulkner thought him a big man until he stood. He was actually short and bulky, with auburn hair, prominent brows, and merry, deep-set eyes. The son of an Ohio harnessmaker, he had grown up in a small town as Faulkner had—in a place called Clyde in north central Ohio. Determined to be rich someday, he worked for a Chicago advertising agency, married the daughter of a wealthy Toledo manufacturer, and became a successful businessman himself, first as president of a Cleveland mail-order house, then as president of his own mail-order paint company in Elyria. Meanwhile he cultivated a "hidden vice," as he called it: he wrote fiction at night, working hard to overcome his deficiencies in syntax and spelling. Torn between his desire to be a writer and his commitment to business and money, Anderson suffered a dramatic mental breakdown: he walked out on his company and wandered aimlessly for days, until a pharmacist found him in Cleveland; he was dazed and suffering from amnesia. When he recovered, he found that the breakdown helped him clarify his values and eventually resolve the terrible conflict inside him. He moved to Chicago, befriended writers and artists associated with the Chicago renaissance, divorced his wife, and flung himself into fiction with harried fury and unlimited energy. Enjoying a new, bohemian wife, working on a broad table with candles lit to the inspiration of the gods, he turned out *Marching Men* in 1917 and *Winesburg, Ohio* two years later, both of which, with the subsequent *Horses and Men,* showed his intuitive understanding of ordinary Americans, whose buried psychological lives he uncovered. Faulkner admired *Winesburg, Ohio* for its sympathetic insight into small-town characters, who were similar to real-life people Faulkner knew in and around Oxford. Anderson referred to his characters as "grotesques"—people baffled and stunted by the modern machine age, people whose inarticulateness, misogyny, frigidity, homosexuality, drunkenness, or religious zeal were symptoms of their estrangement, of their inability to love and to give in the middle America of their time. Divorced from his bohemian wife and remarried, this time to aristocratic Elizabeth, Anderson was trying to settle down in the French Quarter after a period of wandering from city to city across the land. With a fanciful autobiography just published, he was now hard at work on another novel, to be called *Dark Laughter.*

Anderson found his little southern visitor fascinating. He invited him back for a dinner party, where Faulkner impressed one guest with his impeccable manners, controlled intensity, and amazing capacity for alcohol. Anderson, a proficient tippler himself, subsequently took him out for drinks at a bordello in the red-light district. Faulkner limped as they walked—he was the wounded war hero again. They sat on a rear patio near a banana tree and drank with abandon, Anderson listening intently as Faulkner talked of home in his Mississippi drawl. Anderson didn't realize what Stone and Estelle knew about Faulkner: that "after a few drinks, he would tell people anything." Wanting to impress the accomplished older writer, Faulkner lied about his RAF service and painful "war injury." Anderson was so affected that he used Faulkner as the model for a character in a short story: the character was "a little Southern man" who lived in "the black house of pain" from injuries sustained in the Great War, and who now wanted to write poetry. "If I could write like Shelley," said the little southerner, "I would be happy. I wouldn't care what happened to me."

Faulkner returned to Oxford and his verse, and impatiently awaited his copies of *The Marble Faun*. They finally arrived a few days before Christmas 1924, and Stone held a little autograph party for him at the family law firm. Then Stone left to peddle copies around the square, and Faulkner took a signed copy to his Uncle John, who had so bitterly criticized him ("He just won't work"), and then dropped copies off at the Oldhams', where Estelle was home for her annual visit. She had Cho-Cho with her and a one-year-old son named Malcolm. She and Cornell now lived in Shanghai, where Cornell was prosperous and distinguished. They had a mansion with a full staff of servants and enjoyed all the social amenities of life in the upper class. Yet their marriage was in trouble: she and Cornell both liked to drink and gamble, and Cornell spent much of his time away from home, tending to business interests, gambling, and pursuing other women. In effect, he had taken up a life separate from Estelle's. She was confused about her marriage, and lonely, and she still loved Billy, her childhood sweetheart.

Faulkner still felt love for her, too, but it was all mixed up with remorse and a nagging sense of betrayal. She still loved him? Well, fine, except that she was married, with two children now, and living in Shanghai. And he was penniless—had just lost the only job he had held for any length of time—and was trying to be a writer. Wary of her, he said he was leaving Oxford, perhaps for good. He and Stone had talked it over and decided that he should go to Europe to establish his literary reputation. Robert Frost had done that, as had others; Ernest Hemingway, a young writer from the Midwest, was doing his work there. Faulkner and Stone thought it was in Europe that he could best gain his fame, now that his volume of poetry was out; he could support himself by writing articles for newspapers.

Estelle understood how much he wanted to go. She accepted her autographed copy of *The Marble Faun*, and they parted. Shortly after New Year's 1925, he was on his way back to New Orleans to catch a ship, heading for Europe and Paris and certain literary fame.

PART TWO

A COSMOS
OF MY OWN

FAULKNER HAD PLANNED to leave for Europe as soon as he could get a boat out of New Orleans. But he liked the French Quarter so much that he ended up postponing his trip. In truth, he had never felt so liberated from the narrow world of Oxford and the confines of his family. Here he found a number of people like himself—not only Sherwood Anderson but other young artists and writers, who stimulated him with their provocative discussions of Freud, of Joyce, Eliot, and Conrad. Here he discovered a whole literary community of Phil Stones.

The literati often gathered at the offices of *The Double Dealer,* whose editors were disgusted with the "colonial mansions and antebellum nostalgia" that infested southern writing and anxious to publish serious literature that would disprove H. L. Mencken's contention that Dixie was a cultural wasteland, a "Sahara of the Bozart." Faulkner's work had appeared in *The Double Dealer,* as had Anderson's, and Faulkner drank quietly with its editors and friends.

He made little impression on them. One artist recalled him as "a skinny little guy" who "was not taken very seriously except by a few of us." Insecure at literary gatherings, he fell into old habits. He made suggestive remarks about all the illegitimate children he had sired in and around Oxford. He claimed that he had been shot down in the Great War, and had a silver plate in his head, and suffered from shell shock. "And he drank enough whisky to support the impression," one observer said. Because he spoke in a high-pitched voice with a clipped British accent, few in the Quarter suspected him of being a southerner, let alone a Mississippian.

He needed inexpensive lodgings, and Elizabeth Anderson helped him out. Anderson was away on a lecture tour—he hated such things, but needed the money in order to write. Until he returned, Elizabeth let Faulkner stay in a spare room in the Anderson apartment. Here he worked in those initial months of 1925, and what he wrote showed Anderson's powerful influence on him. In Faulkner's mind, Anderson had now replaced Stone as his literary hero and mentor. Free of Stone and his overweening efforts to make him a poet, Faulkner produced a series of novelistic sketches about New Orleans life and sold them to the New Orleans *Times-Picayune* and *The Double Dealer* for modest sums. The people in Faulkner's sketches—a young tough, a one-legged drunk, a crippled beggar, a violently jealous husband—were his versions of Anderson's "grotesques" and a light-year's distance from the fauns and nymphs of his early poetry. He continued to write verse, to be sure, but it no longer appealed to him as it once had. The skill and ease with which he composed his sketches suggested that narrative fiction might be more his medium.

In truth, he was ready to try something a good deal more ambitious, something in Anderson's league. In early March, after Anderson returned home, Faulkner borrowed a cot and some bedding from him and Elizabeth and moved into a nearby apartment building in Orleans Alley, a narrow little street that ran beside an immaculate garden in the rear of St. Louis Cathedral. Here, in a small room on the ground floor, looking out over the cathedral garden with its statue of Christ, Faulkner began a novel. It was about soldiers disillusioned by the Great War, and about the pain and uncertainty of love. It began with the soldiers returning home on a southbound train, as he had done in 1918.

His neighbors heard the tapping of his typewriter early in the morning, in the afternoon, and often late into the night. As he worked, he experienced a joy he had never felt before. When Stone, anxiously awaiting news in Oxford, sent him a wire: "WHAT'S THE MATTER. DO YOU HAVE A MISTRESS," Faulkner wired back, "YES, AND SHES 30,000 WORDS LONG."

One neighbor became Faulkner's friend and companion in off-hour amusement. This was William Spratling, a popular raconteur and a gifted artist, whose hand was "shaped to a brush," Faulkner said, as his own was shaped to a pen. Twenty-four then, three years younger than Faulkner, Spratling had dark skin, dark eyes, a large hooked nose, and a neatly trimmed brown mustache. A modest teaching position at Tulane University and assignments for architectural magazines provided him with enough money for an apartment on the floor above Faulkner's room, plus "abundant liquor for all comers, in spite of prohibition," as Spratling said.

His parties were legendary, and Faulkner attended them from time to time. But he preferred Spratling's company alone. During breaks from his composition, Faulkner often sat with him on a bench in Jackson Square park, which featured a statue of Andrew Jackson astride a rearing steed. As sparrows played deliriously in the mimosa trees, Spratling and Faulkner both sketched people, one with his brush, the other with his pen.

Faulkner also saw a good deal of Sherwood Anderson, who was back at work on his own novel, *Dark Laughter.* They took leisurely afternoon walks, strolling past the picturesque two-story homes of the French Quarter, with their ironwork balconies and shaded courtyards. They were a conspicuous pair, the little, limping Mississippian dressed in bohemian poet's garb, the short-bodied, middle-aged Ohioan in attire that was half racetrack and half bohemian, usually a rough tweed suit, a loud tie, perhaps a bright blue shirt and red socks with yellow bands, and a felt hat with a feather stuck in it. In the evenings, they would meet again and drink together until well past midnight.

Faulkner didn't tell Anderson about his own novel in progress. As with Stone, he was content to listen quietly as Anderson expatiated on people, literature, and writing. He urged his young friend to write about America because it gave "ignorant, unschooled fellows like you and me" an opportunity in literature. He even encouraged Faulkner to focus on "that little patch up there in Mississippi where you started from."

Faulkner found him "warm, generous, merry and fond of laughing," but something of a sentimentalist who expected the worst of people, expected them to disappoint and hurt him. It seemed to Faulkner that his mentor could trust only his fictional characters, "the figures and symbols of his own fumbling dream."

Still, he cherished Anderson's friendship, respected his integrity as a writer, looked up to him as the father of modern American fiction. And Anderson, going on forty-nine that year, needed the admiration of the younger man. For all his fame and experience, Anderson was deeply insecure about himself and required constant reassurances that he *was* talented, *was* successful, *was* all right. In truth, Anderson was going through a painful time in New Orleans. He and Elizabeth were not getting along—his third marriage in trouble. She tried to refine his unpolished genius, tone down his outlandish clothes, and he resented it, and finally rebelled against her as he had all the other women in his life. Moreover, he was increasingly unsure of his career, even though he had a new publisher in the firm of Boni & Liveright, who had several other prominent writers on their list and offered Anderson a lucrative financial arrangement for his current and future books. In the first stage of a slow personal and creative disintegration, Anderson was full of dark suspicions, and easily provoked if he thought he had been slighted.

As long as Anderson was the loquacious master and Faulkner the reticent disciple, they got along wonderfully. In addition to their mutual love for literature, they shared an outrageous sense of humor. They even collaborated in making up yarns about an improbable character named Al Jackson, the progeny of Andrew Jackson, whose statue commanded the square. As they embellished his story, Al Jackson went through hilarious metamorphoses, from half horse and half alligator, to half man and half sheep, and finally to a sharklike beast that preyed on obese blond women who swam along the coast. They derived such pleasure from their Al Jackson stories that they started exchanging letters about him. When he read Faulkner's compositions, however, Anderson felt threatened. "You've got too much talent," he told his little protégé. "You can do it too easy, in too many different ways. If you're not careful, you'll never write anything."

THERE WAS A TENSION between them that spring, the inevitable tension in a master-disciple relationship when the master is on the decline and the disciple on the rise, and both know it. One evening that tension flared into an altercation. They were sitting in front of St. Louis Cathedral, after considerable drinking, and Faulkner maintained that the child of a white man and a Negro woman would always be sterile, just like the mule that came from crossing a mare with a jackass. Faulkner was surely sporting with Anderson, enjoying a little boozy fun at his mentor's expense, for Faulkner was aware of the long history of miscegenation on these shores. But Anderson thought he was being serious and took offense. In his view, this was typical of southern white thinking about race. He had watched and talked with black people, and he believed they had the same feelings and impulses that he did. He sympathized with their plight in Dixie, deplored the system of segregation here that oppressed them so, rigidly separating blacks from whites and shackling them to the gutters of the southern social order. Young Faulkner also disliked the mistreatment of Negroes, but he instinctively defended his native land when someone assailed it. And Anderson assailed it. In fact, he believed there was a kind of madness in "those decayed families, making claim to aristocracy, often living very isolated lives in lonely run-down Southern towns, surrounded by Negroes." And Faulkner, who descended from one of those families, had in him "a lot of the same old bunk."

They saw less of one another after that. When Faulkner one day encountered "Miss Elizabeth" and said he was busy writing a novel, she reported that to Anderson. "Good God!" he exclaimed. Did Faulkner want him to read the thing? Tell him, Anderson instructed Elizabeth, that if he didn't have to read Faulkner's "damn manuscript," he would ask Liveright to publish it.

Anderson's response hurt Faulkner. It was Anderson, after all, who had inspired him to write fiction, Anderson whose opinion he valued the most. He would never forget Anderson's remark. A "damn manuscript" indeed! Well, he would get along without Anderson, then. In the little room on Orleans Alley, he forged ahead, composing feverishly in longhand and then transcribing on his portable typewriter. He wrote by hand because words didn't feel right to him when composed on a typewriter. Besides Anderson, his accumulating pages showed the particular influences of Willard Huntington Wright and Conrad Aiken, as Faulkner strove for sharp, realistic characterization, emotional intensity, and multiple points of view. His characters, male and female alike, sprang from fertile ground—from real people he knew and the many sides of himself, and his empathy and imagination.

His central character was a young aviator named Donald Mahon, who had been shot down in France and wounded so severely in the head that his mind was virtually destroyed. Now this quietly suffering youth was going home to die, home to a small Georgia town not unlike Oxford. Faulkner recognized many of his own traits in Mahon, who had carried a copy of Housman's *A Shropshire Lad,* wore a British officer's uniform, and had small hands, a thin face, and a pointed chin. Indeed, Mahon was the injured war hero Faulkner claimed to be around the Quarter.

Home at last, with the help of an unhappy widow named Margaret Powers and another soldier, who had met him on the train, Mahon lay dying in the house of his rector father, who was big-boned and bulky like Murry Falkner. To Mahon came a young woman named Emmy, who had once been his lover and now nursed him tenderly. With great compassion, Faulkner described her memories of their lovemaking.

Another young woman visited Mahon: his onetime fiancée, Cecily Saunders, who had thought him dead. His moribund state shocked her. Her mother pressured her to marry him anyway, but how could she possibly do so now? Cecily, of course, resembled Estelle: she had the boyish looks that were the rage of the twenties; she was flirtatious, with green eyes and desirable knees; she gushed when she talked, walked in a "quick, nervous stride," could be as "graceful and insincere as a French sonnet," and was as confused about men and parental pressure as Faulkner thought Estelle had been. Cecily had to choose between Mahon and young George Farr, who, born of another side of Faulkner, loved and desired her desperately. When he thought he had lost her, Farr seemed to go crazy. He stayed drunk for a week. "In the intervals of belligerent or rollicking or maudlin inebriation he knew periods of devastating despair like a monstrous bliss, like that of a caged animal, of a man being slowly tortured to death." But Farr's story came out differently from that of his creator. He finally persuaded Cecily to sleep with him, then to become his wife, despite the opposition of her parents. And poor Mahon? Before he died, Margaret Powers, the unhappy war widow, married him because he had given her something to live for.

As his novel took shape before him, Faulkner had never been so excited, so confident of success. On May 21, he finished his first draft in a creative burst, writing ten thousand words that day. A part of him didn't want the story to end: he feared he might never again experience such creative ecstasy.

D URING ONE OF SPRATLING'S PARTIES that spring, Faulkner noticed a young woman sitting on the balcony. She was dressed in white and wore what Spratling called her "don't-give-a-damn look." Her legs were sunburned; she had yellow-brown eyes, a pug nose, and a wide, uninhibited mouth. She made Faulkner's heart pound. She couldn't have been more than five feet tall, with a flat-breasted, boyish figure he found incredibly desirable. He was certain she was not thinking of him at all that afternoon, but he spoke to her anyway. Frankly, she said, she couldn't stand people for more than an hour. So Faulkner was a writer, was he? A published poet? She was Helen Baird, twenty-one, from Nashville. She had attended dances at the University of the South in Sewanee. Her mother kept a vacation house at Pascagoula on the Mississippi Gulf Coast. Her father was dead, killed in a freak accident at the Nashville train depot. She was just visiting New Orleans, consorting with the odd and interesting artists there, and planned to join her mother in Pascagoula for the summer.

Faulkner was utterly captivated. Behind her blunt and caustic manner, he sensed a passionate, vulnerable creature, childlike in her innocence as in her size. Already he felt for her what George Farr felt for Cecily in his novel. Later he turned to poetry again to express what was in his heart, "this single stubborn leaf, that will not die, though root and branch be slain."

He thought about her constantly. When summer came on, he left for Pascagoula to be with her, bringing little beyond his typewriter. Stone had arranged for him to stay in the Stone family bungalow there, a ramshackle place not a hundred feet from the ocean.

He and Helen spent much of June together, swimming and walking at the beach and enjoying the ocean smells and gentle breezes. She had now replaced Estelle as the great love of his life. He wrote love sonnets to her and played the role of bohemian poet and beachcomber: he puffed on a pipe, his face often unshaved and his dark-brown hair uncombed, and wore a white shirt and white duck trousers with a rope around the waist. Helen, a sculptress who made figures and dolls, often dressed in a paint-stained smock. When she donned a bathing suit, he saw her terrible scars. "I was burned," she said, and shrugged it off. He loved her unselfconscious gestures, so like a child's. On summer nights, they would lie on the pier and he would woo her by telling her fairy tales. Or they would sit on swings at one of the bungalows and gaze at the spindrift heavens.

"Look," she said one night, "the moon looks like a fingernail in the sky."

Faulkner was delighted. "May I use that?" he asked.

One of his poems, called "Bill," related how "starlight held a face for him to see,/Found wind once more in grass and leaf, and she/Like silver ceaseless wings that breathe and stir/More grave and true than music, or a flame/Of starlight, and he's quiet, being with her." He wrote sonnets about his "fevered loud distress" when he saw Helen's "thin sweet shoulders" and "small grave breasts," and "the brown and simple music of her knees," and "the scarce-dreamed curving of her thighs." He longed, with a terrible ache, to resolve his "dilemma of desire" by touching her soft boy's breasts and gently breaking her "hushed virginity."

When they were together in her house, Helen's mother was certain that he smelled. She glared at him, at his stubby face and shaggy clothes, as though he were something out of Borneo. "How," she demanded of her daughter, "can you stand going around with someone who looks like that wild man?" In truth, Helen herself considered him something of a screwball. She once said of his size and disheveled hair that he reminded her of "a fuzzy little animal." As the summer wore on, she grew tired of him. Once, failing to keep a date, she left him waiting four hours at her doorstep. "That's all right," he said quietly. "I've been working."

He was afraid of showing his feelings, of telling her how much he cared. But his ardor was too much to restrain. One day, in a burst of love for her, he blurted out a marriage proposal. She told him no. He was stunned, hurt to the core. She wouldn't sleep with him, then? Another female rejection? Good night and goodbye? His heart refused to register the finality of her reply.

Somehow he revised and retyped his novel. Then suddenly it was the last week of June and time to leave Pascagoula. He learned that Helen was planning a trip to Europe with her mother, perhaps next winter. Since he still intended to go there, maybe he would see her in Europe. It was not goodbye.

> Let there be no farewell shaped between
> Two mouths that have been one mouth for a day,
> Words can break no bonds, while life is green—
> Time enough for goodbyes when it's gray.

TANNED AND A LITTLE HEAVIER NOW, Faulkner rode the train back to Oxford, where Stone's secretary typed a publisher's draft of his novel. Stone thought it "a damn fine book," but to another friend, "Bill didn't

seem to care a bit about that novel." Faulkner sent it off to Boni &
Liveright, as Anderson had suggested, but didn't wait for a response—
he knew it was good. On July 7, with some $70 to his name, he took his
long-delayed leave for Europe, departing on a freighter with William
Spratling.

Faulkner carried letters of introduction Stone had shamelessly written in his behalf. They were addressed to Ezra Pound, James Joyce, and
T. S. Eliot. But Faulkner wasn't thinking much about them. As the
freighter pushed one empty horizon ahead of it and drew another
behind, he dreamed of Helen, of being with her again. But what if she
still said no? What if she said yes and wasn't even a virgin? While
crossing the Atlantic, while heading across northern Italy for Paris, he
lay many a lonely night with the idea of her. Before they parted company, he told Spratling he was certain that love and death were "the
only two basic compulsions on earth."

In Milan, he stood spellbound before the cathedral on the Piazza del
Duomo. It reminded him of "frozen music," he wrote home. It was "all
covered with gargoyles like dogs, and mitred cardinals and mailed
knights and saints pierced with arrows and beautiful naked Greek
figures." But Stresa repelled him: "Full of Americans—terrible." He
climbed into the Italian Alps above Lake Maggiore and found a charming village, "all stones and cobbles and streets that go either up or
down," which afforded a view of the lake, and boats like toys, and trains,
and three or four towns. "The people eat and sleep and sit on the sides
of the mountains, watching the world pass," he noted. With his pack,
he crossed the mountains above Lake Maggiore, then rode whistling
trains across Switzerland and northern France to Paris.

So he was in Paris at last, the city of the Arc de Triomphe and the
Eiffel Tower, the greatest cultural center in all Europe, where so many
expatriate American writers had made their homes. He was in the Paris
of Scott and Zelda Fitzgerald, of Gertrude Stein and Ezra Pound, of
John Dos Passos and Ernest Hemingway, whose first book—*In Our
Time*—would appear that year from Boni & Liveright, thanks to the
recommendation of none other than Sherwood Anderson. When Spratling rejoined Faulkner in Paris, they visited Sylvia Beach's famous
bookstore, Shakespeare & Company, and saw James Joyce himself in a
café near Place de l'Odéon.

Eager to get to work, Faulkner found an inexpensive room on the
top floor of a narrow-fronted building with a tile roof and chimney pots,

situated around the corner from the Luxembourg Gardens. He wrote a couple of more stories for the New Orleans *Times-Picayune,* which augmented his meager funds a little; turned out still more sonnets to Helen; and began and abandoned at least three novels, one an autobiographical account of their relationship that was more therapy than art. In September, just before his twenty-eighth birthday, he produced a piece of poetry in prose form that excited him beyond measure. "I have just written such a beautiful thing that I am about to bust," he informed his mother. It was about a young woman, the Luxembourg Gardens, and death. "I havent slept hardly for two nights, thinking about it, comparing words, accepting and rejecting them, then changing again. But now it is perfect—a jewel." He said that tomorrow he would probably wake up feeling rotten. "But its worth it, to have done a thing like this."

When he wasn't writing, he enjoyed sitting in the nearby Luxembourg Gardens, watching old men race toy boats as bystanders cheered. In a letter to an aunt, he described one aging sailor with a decrepit derby on his head. "When I am old enough to no longer have to make excuses for not working," Faulkner said, "I shall have a weathered derby hat like his and spend my days sailing a toy boat in the Luxembourg Gardens."

By September, he had added something that made him appear even more the artist: he had grown a beard. "Makes me look sort of distinguished, like someone you'd care to know," he wrote Maud, although a female relative he met in Paris "could see right through it to the little boy I used to be."

In late September, he toured Amiens and Cantigny, where American troops had first entered the Great War, and walked over a vast and terrible battlefield that had claimed a quarter of a million German lives and almost as many British and French. "It looked as if a cyclone had passed over the whole world at about 6 feet from the ground," Faulkner noted. "Stubs of trees, and along the main roads are piles of shell cases and unexploded shells and wire and bones that the farmers dig up."

In early October, he was in London, making his pilgrimage to the homes and haunts of the great English writers. In a fog "greasy" and "full of coal smoke," he visited all the old coffeehouses where Ben Jonson, Joseph Addison, and Christopher Marlowe had sat and talked; he toured Dickens' Bloomsbury, then set out in search of Joseph Conrad, in the verdant countryside around Kent. "I am tramping again," he wrote home—"en promenade, as us french fellers say." He found the sheep-filled meadows around Kent the "most restful country under the sun." No wonder, he thought, that Conrad "could write such fine books here."

En route back to Paris, he had a sensation that something extraordinary had happened to him. He was right: awaiting him in Paris was a letter from Boni & Liveright, telling him that they were going to publish his novel under the title *Soldiers' Pay*, which someone in the office had suggested. Enclosed, too, was a $200 advance. Faulkner probably didn't know it yet, but Sherwood Anderson had written Boni & Liveright about the novel; one editor there said he voted for it "on the strength of Anderson's recommendation."

Faulkner celebrated by posing for the camera. One photograph showed a bewhiskered, pipe-smoking artist, dressed in a hat, a trench coat, and baggy clothes, standing by what appeared to be a Paris church. He sent one of the photographs to Estelle in Shanghai. He celebrated, too, by sending Phil Stone a poem and a pseudonymous letter addressed to H. L. Mencken, the celebrated Baltimore iconoclast and editor of *The American Mercury*. "Enclosed at your usual rate," the letter went, "are poem by Wm Faulkner. He wants to get a start at poetry. And I advise him to try your magazine after I made the corrections. . . . I only made corrections in the above poem without changing its sentiments because the poet himself quit schools before learning to write." An oblique but devastating satire of the kind of letters Stone had often written for him, it indicated that Faulkner, with a novel about to be published, was no longer Stone's poet protégé.

On the verge of a new and independent literary career, Faulkner decided not to remain in Europe. He didn't know where Helen Baird was anyway. Near the end of what had been an extraordinary year, he boarded a steamer for New York City and home.

IN NEW YORK, he dropped by the offices of Boni & Liveright, where he spoke to the editor who had voted for his novel because of Sherwood Anderson; Faulkner told him that he had once fallen out of an airplane and cracked his head. To his surprise, he also ran into Helen, who was in New York trying to sell her figures and dolls. He still loved her desperately. But he wasn't blind. He could sense how little she cared for him that way. Repelled by his shaggy beard, she found him even less appealing than she had the summer before.

With heavy heart, he rode the trains south to Oxford, where his mother, tiny Mammy Callie, and his brothers welcomed him home. His mother, whom he had written devotedly from Europe, took one look at his appearance and ordered him to take a bath.

Home again, with Helen on his mind, he composed a fable about a young knight's quest for perfect love. Like Faulkner, the knight loved three princesses in turn, but with each he felt restless and unfulfilled. In the end, he discovered the woman of all his passion, all his dreams. She was Death. As he had done with his early verse for Estelle, he hand lettered and hand bound his fable, which he called *Mayday,* the anglicized form of the French term for distress. He inscribed it to Helen, the flame of his heart: "to thee/O wise and lovely/this:/a fumbling in darkness." He gave her the only known copy, perhaps in February 1926, just before she and her mother left to visit Europe.

That month found him back in New Orleans, sharing Spratling's new attic apartment on St. Peter Street. The place was littered with painting paraphernalia and lit only by shafts of sunlight coming through its dusty windows. To ward off boredom, the two artists amused themselves with a BB gun. They would lean out the window and shoot at the buttocks of people walking along the street below. They even kept score, with a hit on the rear of a rare type—a Negro nun, for example—earning a special mark.

By now, *Soldiers' Pay* had appeared to generally good reviews, which Faulkner was eager to see. The New Orleans *Times-Picayune,* which had published his sketches, called it the "most noteworthy first novel of the year." But its explicit sex shocked his mother, who wrote him that the book was a disgrace and that he should leave the country. His father, hearing *Soldiers' Pay* wasn't fit to read, continued with his Zane Grey westerns. Stone, who called it "their" first novel, his and Faulkner's, tried to give Ole Miss a copy, but the school refused it. Friends claimed that Faulkner delighted in all the outrage.

He saw Sherwood and Elizabeth Anderson again, and they had an amicable chat, despite the strain in the men's relationship. Grateful for Anderson's help, Faulkner gave him an inscribed copy of *Soldiers' Pay.* Boni & Liveright had recently published Anderson's own novel *Dark*

Laughter, which contrasted the unrepressed song and laughter of the Negro with the spiritual sterility of white people. It was Anderson's first financially successful novel. Yet he was not in a good mood, was sick of people. And in late winter or early spring, he took umbrage at something Faulkner did or said. Faulkner never did know what happened; all he knew was that Anderson got so mad that he wouldn't speak to him.

Elizabeth herself probably expressed what was troubling her insecure husband. She complained that Faulkner had a superiority complex. Perhaps, in addition to Faulkner's threatening talent, this referred to something he had written the previous spring, a critical discussion of Anderson's work that had appeared in the Dallas *Morning News.* In it, the gifted and ambitious protégé had mixed some disapproval with his praise. That he found any fault with Anderson's books (some showed "a fundamental lack of humor," another "a bad ear") could only have infuriated a man so plagued with suspicion and self-doubt as Anderson.

He and Elizabeth were leaving New Orleans—they had bought a farm in Virginia, where he hoped to get on with his writing. In mid-April 1926, he wrote Horace Liveright that Faulkner was a potentially successful commercial novelist and should be encouraged, but added: "I do not like the man personally very much. He was so nasty to me personally that I don't want to write him myself."

WITH HIS HEART STILL LONGING for Helen, Faulkner worked on another novel that spring in New Orleans. He intended it as a satire about the intelligentsia there, about Anderson, the *Double Dealer* set, even Helen and himself. He thought it all rather clever and hoped to impress Helen with it, to woo her back somehow. As one of his main characters said, "I believe that every word a writing man writes is put down with the ultimate intention of impressing some woman that probably don't care anything at all for literature, as is the nature of women."

The novel focused on the escapades of a group of people who rented a yacht and spent the day on Lake Pontchartrain, just north of New Orleans. Faulkner had gone on just such an outing with Anderson and a group of friends, and he drew from that experience to tell his story and shape his characters. Dawson Fairchild, a relaxed, folksy writer who bored everyone with Al Jackson stories, clearly derived from Sherwood Anderson. Young Patricia Robyn, by turns selfish, ingenuous, overconfident, and inconsiderate, came just as clearly from Helen Baird. Another character, a male sculptor, thought her the embodiment of the ideal girl-woman: virginal, young, and epicene. When first meeting her in his New Orleans apartment, the sculptor was aroused by her "flat breast and belly, her boy's body which the poise of it and the thinness of her arms belied. Sexless, yet somehow vaguely troubling."

Another character, born of Faulkner's feelings for Helen, found Patricia more than a little troubling. David West, a young steward on the yacht, worshiped her with a doglike devotion; he would go anywhere with her, do anything she asked. As the story progressed, Faulkner actually introduced himself in a scene that reflected his special sense of humor. A female character told Patricia about meeting Faulkner on a previous outing. He was "a funny man. A little kind of black man." "A nigger?" Patricia asked. "No. He was a white man, except he was awful sunburned and kind of shabby dressed—no necktie and hat." She remembered the funny things he said. "He said if the straps of my dress was to break I'd devastate the country. He said he was a liar by profession, and he made good money at it." She said, "I think he was crazy. Not dangerous; just crazy." His name? "Faulkner, that was it." "Faulkner?" Patricia said. "Never heard of him."

When summer came on, Faulkner headed for Pascagoula in hopes of seeing Helen there. He brought a gift for her: a hand-bound volume of his sonnets, fifteen in all, called *Helen: A Courtship*. Perhaps to please her, he had shaved off his beard. But he still wore a mustache, smoked a pipe, and went about in white duck trousers, often without a shirt or shoes.

As it turned out, Helen was not there, and Faulkner was crestfallen. He sought out her aunt, who lived in a small cottage in Pascagoula and liked him despite his long hair and thin, ragged appearance. With great intensity and passion, he told her how much he loved Helen and wanted to marry her. He said he thought of her "as an amber flame."

He tried to work on his novel. But Helen, as "bitter and new as fire" to him, loomed in his thoughts and his writing. He wanted her to come back, wanted to share the warmth of the summer with her, the star-flung nights, the whisper of the wind in the wild palms. He kept thinking of Cyrano de Bergerac, the unsuccessful, large-nosed lover in Edmond Rostand's play. In August, resorting to drink to assuage his pain, he wrote Helen an almost illegible letter on the back of a manuscript page. "Helen," he said, paraphrasing a line from Cyrano, "your name is like a little golden bell hung in my heart." He told her about his visiting her aunt and writing chapters of a novel in her front yard. "Your book is pretty near done," he said of the novel, and added, "I have made you another book. It's sonnets I have made you, all bound. . . . you must come back."

Later, in a more sober mood, he crossed out each line of that letter and never sent it. And Helen never came back, at least not to him. The next he heard, she was planning to marry someone named Guy Lyman. And so went the pain of love. Was he doomed to heartbreak, then? Was it always to be this way for him? He did not know what to tell young women anymore, did not know what they wanted. He had made poetry and fiction for them—his beautiful words and images, all to no avail. Well, he would not do that again. What he wrote from now on would be strictly for the sake of art, not for some young woman. He intended to be a "proud and self-sufficient beast," as he described himself later, who "walked by himself, needing nothing from anyone."

He turned back to his book, taking a measure of solace from his novelist character, Dawson Fairchild. "You don't commit suicide when you are disappointed in love," Fairchild counseled. "You write a book." Which Faulkner did, transforming his anguish into art. At the climax of his story, Patricia and David, the lovesick steward, left the yacht and had an unromantic adventure together in the sweltering countryside around Lake Pontchartrain: exhausted, plagued by mosquitoes—which was what Faulkner called his story—they returned to the boat and the sterile, often profane chatter of its literary guests.

A bold and explicit tale for 1926 America, *Mosquitoes* contained references to constipation, masturbation, incest, lesbianism, perversion, and syphilis, and words in dialogue like "bastard" and "whore." Despite its flaws as a work of art, Faulkner did think of himself as a novelist now. "So I can't write poetry any more," said novelist Fairchild, speaking for his creator. "It takes me too long to say things, now."

Faulkner dedicated his novel "To Helen, Beautiful and Wise," and mailed it off to New York. Later, on second thought, he deleted "Beautiful and Wise." In New York, Horace Liveright did not like the new novel so well as *Soldiers' Pay.* In his opinion, it showed little development in Faulkner's spiritual and artistic growth. Yet he agreed to publish, thanks to a rave editorial report from a young woman at the firm named Lillian Hellman. By the time he heard from Boni & Liveright, Faulkner was back in New Orleans, certain that he could never enjoy it as he once had.

H E FOUND SOME PLEASURE in a bit of satirical mischief with William Spratling. In December, they collected Spratling's New Orleans sketches into a book, and Faulkner contributed a foreword that gently parodied Anderson's views and simple, "primer-like style," as Faulkner described it. An example: "We have one priceless universal trait, we Americans. That trait is our humor. What a pity it is that it is not more prevalent in our art. . . . Our trouble with us American artists is that we take our art and ourselves too seriously. And perhaps seeing ourselves in the eyes of our fellow artists, will enable those who have strayed to establish anew a sound contact with the fountain-head of our American life."

The frontispiece was a sketch of a small-bodied, big-headed man in garish dress, with a double chin, large eyes, and bushy hair hanging over his right forehead. This, the caption said, was "Mister Sherwood Anderson." The last sketch depicted the two collaborators sitting at a desk: there was a black-mustached, big-nosed Spratling, and an impish Faulkner wearing a scruffy sweater, with whiskey bottles under his chair. On the wall hung a Daisy BB gun and a sign proclaiming, "VIVA ART." With barely restrained chuckles, the collaborators dedicated the book "To all the artful and crafty ones of the French Quarter" and paid a local press to print it under the title *Sherwood Anderson & Other Famous Creoles.*

Faulkner intended his introduction to be "warm and delicate" satire, as Spratling styled it. But Anderson, now living in Virginia, was not amused. That same year, Hemingway had served up a savage, condescending parody of Anderson's style in *The Torrents of Spring,* and it had wounded Anderson to the core. He had helped "Hemy" publish his first book with Liveright, and this was the thanks he got. Anderson had received what he considered a "raw," "pretentious," "patronizing" letter from "Hemy," which convinced him that Hemingway was trying to knock him out as a writer, and he had replied in kind. And now here was Faulkner, another ingrate, ridiculing him, too. Anderson could not understand Faulkner's "hatred" for him. "What is the matter with Bill?" he wondered. "Why is he so against me?" Anderson never doubted Faulkner's talent—"he was, from the first, a real writer"—and conceded that he had in him "something finer and certainly more generous" than Hemingway did. Nevertheless, Faulkner's parody annoyed Anderson so much that he resolved not to speak to him again.

Faulkner came to regret "the unhappy caricature affair," as he called it. Yet it epitomized his own ambivalent attitudes toward another mentor he had outgrown, toward "a fine, kind, sweet man who talked much better than he wrote." He would always regard Anderson as "a giant," the "father of all my generation," and yet would insist that he had made only "two or perhaps three gestures commensurate with gianthood." Worse, he had made "almost a fetish of simplicity" when it came to his style, until Faulkner thought that style was all he had left.

W HEN FAULKNER TOOK UP his pen again that winter, he worked without much purpose, speculating idly about time and death. Certain that at twenty-nine he was "on the verge of decrepitude" and about to lose the world he knew, he heeded some advice Anderson had once given him. He began a couple of interrelated stories about "that little patch up there in Mississippi" where he had started from. As it happened, he was so poor that he had to leave New Orleans and go home again, to the very town and county he had started writing about. By January 1927, he was once again a penniless ward of his parents, toiling on his Mississippi stories in the little tower room of their home at Ole Miss.

His two stories were different from anything he had tried before. One was about a redneck clan called the Snopeses, a rapacious, fecund bunch swarming like vermin out of the Mississippi backwoods and infiltrating a hamlet near the fictional town of Jefferson. The story grew out of Stone's farcical tales about the redneck tenant farmers who appeared after the Civil War and challenged the rule of the old patrician families. The other tale was about the decay and decline of one of those families, the Sartorises of Jefferson, who in real life were the Falkners of Ripley and Oxford. As he worked simultaneously on his stories, Faulkner thought of an entire saga about the Snopeses, as "a bolt of lightning lights up a landscape and you see everything." He realized that it would take a whole book, maybe more than one, to chronicle the Snopeses' greedy climb to power. Right now, the Sartoris story was even more compelling, drawing as it did from his own family history. With rising excitement, he put the Snopeses aside and concentrated his creative energies on the Sartoris story.

In it, Faulkner saw the most powerful male figures in his life reemerging in two of his principal characters. His grandfather came back as old Bayard Sartoris, who found himself in the attic, pondering forgotten family relics—a cavalry saber, a Bible—and recalling the history of the Sartoris clan. As he did so, Faulkner's great-grandfather, the legendary Old Colonel, reappeared in the form of Colonel John Sartoris, who had commanded Confederate troops in the Civil War and afterward had restored the land and built a railroad in northern Mississippi, only to die in the metallic blaze of a rival's gun. As a younger generation of Sartorises sprang to life before him, Faulkner worked with great intensity, knowing that he was onto something profound. He had discovered in his own "little postage stamp of native soil," as he described it later, a wealth of people and events to write about. He remembered what Willard Huntington Wright said: in creation the artist was an omnipotent god who fashioned a new cosmos that could stand alone, self-moving and independent. If Faulkner could sublimate the actual to the apocryphal, he could create a cosmos of his own, moving his people around like God, not only in space but in time. In truth, they seemed to be moving about on their own, independent of any artistic process. They were so real to him he could hear them talking. He strove to get them down on paper, to capture their entangled and doomed lives, their entire cursed and glorious past. . . .

If his inner world excited him as never before, the exterior world was as troubling as ever. That January, Estelle was back in town with her children. Her marriage had failed, and she had filed for divorce. Cornell, off with his gambling friends and lovers, was never home anymore. And she had been unfaithful, too. "While Cornell had his lovers," she said, "you don't think I was sitting at home, do you?" Yet she had been so miserable; last year she had come home with bandages on both her wrists. Not that filing for divorce had made her feel any

better. She dreaded the thought of returning to Oxford as a divorcee
with two children. She was sure to be gossiped about, even ostracized.
Yet she had nowhere else to go. Faulkner, still her friend, did what he
could to help her through this ordeal. He was sensitive to her suffering;
it showed in her grave, unhappy eyes.

When Ben Wasson came for a visit, Faulkner was reading the galleys
of *Mosquitoes* and complaining that Liveright had "toned down" certain passages—one had a lesbian element, another suggested an incestuous relationship between a brother and a sister. He and Wasson took a
long walk, and Faulkner confessed that he was in love. "Her name is
Helen Baird," he said. Wasson knew her: he had met her at Sewanee;
her family was from Nashville.

"Yes," Faulkner said. "It's hell being in love, ain't it?"

April, Eliot's cruelest month, brought murderous thunderstorms
and rumors of tornadoes. The violent weather matched the turmoil in
Faulkner's heart. It rained so hard and so often that the Mississippi rose
to the danger level, then broke through the levee near Greenville and
rampaged across much of the Delta. It was the worst flood in recorded
Mississippi history. Faulkner would not forget the swirling roar of the
flood, or the travail of its victims, as "the Old Man" transformed "the
whole face of the adjacent earth." In all directions, swollen carcasses of
horses, mules, cows, sheep, and deer floated in the currents, and the Old
Man's human flotsam, white and black, clung precariously to the tops
of trees, the roofs of sheds, cotton gins, and floating cabins, and the
second-story windows of flooded houses and office buildings. From the
Gulf came a hodgepodge convoy of shrimp trawlers, pleasure cruisers,
and coast guard cutters to rescue whomever and whatever they could
find in the flat sheet of brown water that stretched across the vanished
roads and fields. Below the surface, as if from another stratum, men
could hear a deep and faint rumble, like the muffled roar of a speeding
subway train, which was the furious rush of the flood itself.

At the end of April, with some 27 million acres of Mississippi under
water, Faulkner's *Mosquitoes,* the book he had written for Helen and
dedicated to her, appeared in a modest printing in New York. A few
days later, on May 4, Helen married Guy Lyman in New Orleans.
"—Be still, my heart, be still: you break in vain," Faulkner wrote. "Why
did I wake? When shall I sleep again?"

Hurt though he was, Faulkner kept in touch with Helen. He was not
one who let rejection turn him to bitterness. When he visited New

Orleans, he called on her and Guy sometimes. And he occasionally phoned and sent her letters. In one undated letter, he told her he was writing well now, as he had done in Pascagoula when he would go to her aunt and ask about marrying her. But the memory of that summer, and the previous one when they had been together, reminded him anew how much he still loved and wanted her. "Helen," he wrote in closing. "Helen Helen Helen." There was no signature.

H E WROTE A FEMALE FRIEND in New Orleans that he didn't have "heights or depths any more" and that he was fearfully withdrawn. More than ever now, he sought refuge in his imagination, in a cherished inner sanctum in which he could escape the vicissitudes of the outside world and record what his voices said to him. By the summer of 1927, when the flood had begun to recede, his tale of the Sartoris family, which was really the story of his own family, had developed into a full-fledged novel. As he worked on in his little tower room, an entire fictional kingdom stood revealed to him, a kingdom born of all he had assimilated in a near lifetime of observation in the "little, lost town" that was his home. There was Jefferson, the seat of Yacona County, patterned after Oxford, the seat of Lafayette County. There was the court-house in the center of the town square, and the Confederate soldier who stood there like a white candle, and Negroes who flowed along the sidewalks, murmuring, with something grave and sad in their laughter, and old Civil War veterans who lounged on the benches beneath the porticoes of the courthouse, and trains that roared into the station with steam hissing from their locomotives. And there were the outlying hamlets and rivers, and the pine hills, and around all, the unemphatic land. From a distance, at twilight, the lights of the courthouse clock shone like yellow beads suspended on the horizon, and a column of smoke sometimes stood like a balanced plume against the green after-glow of the west.

Above all there were the characters of his story, characters so fully alive to him that they existed beyond the confines of any book. There was Colonel John Sartoris, who was long dead when the story opened, but whose spirit was a potent presence in the Sartoris bank and household in Jefferson. He seemed to stand above and all around his descendants, "with his bearded, hawklike face and the bold glamor of his dream." There was his son, old Bayard, a Jefferson banker "cemented by deafness to a dead time," who left the running of his large house to his aunt, Miss Jenny Du Pre. A blustering man, he rode to his bank in a carriage and walked stiffly erect, greeting people with his hand raised in a half-military salute. Behind his "wall of deafness," he brooded about the reckless driving of his grandson, his namesake and bearer of the arrogant Sartoris heritage. This was young Bayard Sartoris, the central figure of the story, who took on facets of his creator as he struggled with his violent family legacy and the whole issue of "doomed immortality and immortal doom." Returning from the Great War in Europe, blaming himself for his brother's death in aerial combat, young Bayard turned a cruel, derisive face to the world of Jefferson: he drove his car at breakneck speed, his teeth showing in a lipless sneer as he shot forward "on a roar of sound like blurred thunderous wings," whipped past Negroes in a carriage, zoomed by the very cemetery where his great-grandfather, "in pompous effigy," gazed across the valley and the railroad he had built.

Young Bayard was incapable of affection, yet there was one who loved him despite his cold, destructive ways. This was young Narcissa Benbow, a sweet and slender belle like the idealized young women of her creator's poetry and dreams. When she looked on young Bayard, "her own patient and hopeless sorrow" overflowed in pity for him. Caught in his headlong violence, she was "like a lily in a gale which rocked it to its roots." Unable to help herself, she married young Bayard and then carried his child. Meanwhile, on a reckless ride with his grandfather, who tried to slow him down, young Bayard lost control of the car, and it hurtled off the road, crashing down a ravine and back up the shallow bank and onto the road again, where Bayard brought it to a stop; but his grandfather, old Bayard, was dead. How death stalked the Sartorises, endowing them with whatever significance they could claim. Embittered, beset with guilt, young Bayard finally fled Jefferson and his family heritage, only to meet his own violent doom in a plane crash in Ohio.

On that same day, Narcissa bore his son, whom she named Benbow Sartoris, as if that would somehow save him from the Sartoris legacy of codes, quixotic schemes, and violent oblivion. But Miss Jenny Du Pre knew better. "Do you think," she told Narcissa, "that because his name is Benbow, he'll be any less a Sartoris and a scoundrel and a fool?" A slender, erect, indomitable old woman, with shining eyes and dried cheeks, she shared with Narcissa "that fine and passive courage of women throughout the world's history." She was the embodiment of Faulkner's own unvanquished aunts, who had inspired him with their family and Civil War tales and their implacable loyalty to the doomed and defeated South.

Miss Jenny visited the cemetery where young Bayard lay with his grandfather and great-grandfather, but she didn't cry. As John Sartoris' sister, she had lived with "these bullheaded Sartorises" for eighty years, and had vowed never to give "a single ghost of 'em the satisfaction of shedding a tear over him." Well, she thought, the last one was buried now. The dust of all of them lay moldering beneath their gravestones, the "pagan symbols of their vainglory."

Beyond the Sartoris clan, there were other memorable characters, such as twisted Byron Snopes, a member of the rapacious clan from outlying Frenchman's Bend, who worked in old Bayard's bank as a bookkeeper. Tormented with sexual fantasies about Narcissa, he sent her obscene anonymous letters; one climactic night he even broke into the deserted Benbow home, lay on Narcissa's bed, and pilfered one of her undergarments as he retrieved his letters. Then he fled Jefferson after robbing the Sartoris bank, a harbinger of what the town could expect from the infiltrating Snopeses.

By contrast, there was idealistic and sensitive Horace Benbow, Narcissa's brother, for whom she had possessive, even incestuous feelings. She sharply disapproved when he had an affair with a married woman and then wedded her himself after she was divorced. Like Phil Stone, who recognized himself when he read the story, Horace was a lawyer in the family tradition who "spent so much time being educated that he . . . never learned anything."

Faulkner loved his creations. He believed he had learned to control "the stuff" now and to "fix on something like rational truth." Unhappily for him, creation didn't pay his expenses, resupply his moonshine. As the summer wore on, he was so desperate for money that he had to borrow several hundred dollars from Phil Stone in order to keep on writing. Evidently Stone assumed that their relationship hadn't changed, that Faulkner was still his protégé, and undertook to tell him what to write.

Faulkner rebelled. "Phil Stone lent me that money," he told a friend, "but I'm not gonna be obligated to him. I'm gonna pay that money back. Nobody dictates to me what I can write and what I can't write." He even considered severing their relationship. While he stopped short of that, Faulkner did eschew the services of Stone's secretary; this time he typed his own publisher's draft, working with soaring confidence, even exaltation. In September, four days after his thirtieth birthday, he finished his novel in a burst of excitement. "I have written THE book," he informed Liveright, "of which those other things were but foals. I believe it is the damndest best book you'll look at this year." He called it *Flags in the Dust,* which caught the significance of the buried Sartoris clan. The title was so good, he told Liveright, that not even "the bird" who named *Soldiers' Pay* could improve on it. He even asked for an advance—and for "a good reason." He was "going on an expedition with a lady friend, for purposes of biological research."

With the manuscript off to New York, he took odd jobs, perhaps to help finance his expedition, and waited impatiently for Liveright's response. It came late in November. "It is with sorrow in my heart that I write to tell you that three of us have read Flags in the Dust and don't believe that Boni and Liveright should publish it."

Faulkner was shocked. His eyes scarcely registered the rest of Liveright's report: "We don't believe that you should offer it for publication. . . . we're frankly very much disappointed in it. . . . We think it lacks plot, dimension and projection. The story really doesn't get anywhere and has a thousand loose ends."

His first reaction was blind protest. He had found his fictional voice in this novel; how could Boni & Liveright fail to see its originality, its genius? He plunged into depression, unable to turn to anyone in Oxford —certainly not to Stone. Then he tried to be objective. Perhaps some revisions would make *Flags in the Dust* more acceptable to another house. But when he reread it, he didn't think he could revise his story, and he hid his eyes in "the fury of denial." He worked spasmodically on other fiction, but nothing seemed right. He wrote bitterly to Liveright: "I have a belly full of writing, now, since you folks in the publishing business claim that a book like the last one I sent you is blah. I think now that I'll sell my typewriter and go to work—though God knows, it's sacriledge to waste that talent for idleness which I possess."

But he did take up *Flags in the Dust* again and made extensive revisions. "Every day or so I burn some of it up and rewrite it," he told an aunt, "and at present it is almost incoherent." Finally, in February

1928, he sent the fifth draft to Ben Wasson, who was in New York now, working for a major literary agency called the American Play Company. "Will you please try to sell this for me?" Faulkner said, and added that he couldn't afford the postage to send it around. Although Ben was working on a novel himself during his off-hours, he thought *Flags* a splendid book and agreed to function as Faulkner's agent.

Well, thank God for Ben at least. While he painted signs and houses for money, Faulkner felt terrible. It was the blackest period of his life so far. Then came the news from New York: Ben had shown *Flags in the Dust* to several publishers, but none wanted it. As the rejections piled up, Faulkner alternated between bafflement, hurt, and rage. He believed he would never be published again. In odd moments, he found himself singing morbid lyrics. He thought about how he would die and where he would be buried.

To make matters worse, Estelle was home for good now, and she needed him more than ever in this, her own bleakest hour. Her divorce had been granted and would be final next year, yet she was far from happy about it. She was very confused about her feelings for Cornell and what was happening to her. She felt rejected, felt like such a failure. She feared that all this was her fault—that there was something wrong with her. What was to become of her now? And her children, Cho-Cho and Malcolm? In desperation, she looked to Faulkner, her childhood friend and onetime sweetheart, for salvation. Surely Billy would marry her. Surely he would save her from the humiliation of being a divorced woman with two small children, a failure and an outcast in a small Mississippi town.

Faulkner, in his own misery, no longer knew how he felt about Estelle, beyond sympathy and compassion for her suffering. As was his penchant, he made light of his difficulties. He wrote an aunt that he wanted to show her someone, a woman of course, whose "utter charm" and shallowness were intriguing. She was "like a lovely vase" who helped the days pass for him. He thanked God that he had no money or he would marry her. "You see," he said, "even Poverty looks after its own."

Here was a hint of his pain, of the hurt he felt from his failures in art and in love. Under "severe strain" caused by "difficulties of an intimate kind," as he said later, he took refuge in a new work, begun as a short story in the late winter or early spring of 1928, but rapidly growing into something larger. Here, in his inner kingdom, he found a "lovely vase" that would never torment him, never cause him pain. Like Anderson, he no longer trusted people in the outer world; he trusted only his fictional characters, the figures and symbols of his own fumbling dream. Shut off from Estelle and the publishing world that had rejected him, Faulkner wrote in such secrecy in his tower bedroom that no one in Oxford knew what he was about.

PART THREE

VOICES
IN THE
SANCTUARY

IN THE SANCTUARY of his imagination, he heard children's voices in a pasture, and he realized that the children had been sent away from their house during the funeral of their grandmother Damuddy, the nickname of his own maternal grandmother, who had died when he was a boy. One of the children was a girl named Candace, or Caddy, the others her brothers and some young Negroes. As Faulkner wrote, an image loomed in his mind: Caddy, bolder and more adventurous than her brothers, was climbing a pear tree to see what was happening inside the house, and the other children were looking up at the muddy seat of her drawers. Faulkner was entranced. Then another image flashed before him—of Caddy and her smallest brother splashing in a brook, Caddy falling, the smallest brother sobbing until she comforted him. As Faulkner wrote this down, the entire story seemed to explode on the paper, a short story about the blind self-centeredness of innocence, typified by children.

One of Caddy's brothers was truly innocent—an idiot named Benjy, similar to an idiot Faulkner knew in Oxford, who only understood what happened, not why. The other brothers were Quentin and Jason. Now Faulkner realized the meaning of Caddy's climbing the pear tree and the brothers and the young Negroes peering at her muddy drawers. Hers was a wonderful courage, demonstrated here, that in later years would enable her to confront honorably the shame she engendered, a shame neither Quentin nor Jason could ever face. One would take refuge in suicide, the other in a vindictive fury he would turn on Caddy's illegitimate daughter

Now the story came powerfully alive. The fused image—of the funeral, the innocence of the children, Caddy in the pear tree—was so striking that it filled Faulkner with love. For him, Caddy was "the beautiful one." She was his "heart's darling." He loved her so much that he couldn't give her life only for a story; she deserved more than that —a novella at least.

But it would be strictly for himself, since he thought his publishing career was finished. In fact, a door seemed to close between him and all publishers and book lists, and he said to himself, "Now I can write." Now he could make for himself a lovely vase in darling Caddy, a vase that couldn't hurt or trouble him like Estelle and Helen. Like the old Roman, he could keep his vase at his bedside and kiss it so much its rim would wear away. So he who had never had a little sister, and had failed so often at love, set out to make for himself "a beautiful and tragic little girl," his own idealized female, "a maid that life had not had time to create."

I N APRIL 1928, in the privacy of his tower bedroom, he began again, tentatively calling his novella *Twilight.* The Compsons, like the Sartoris family, lived in Jefferson, the town the Snopeses were invading from the backwoods. But Faulkner didn't tell the story of Caddy and the Compsons through her eyes. No, she was too beautiful to reduce to narrator. He thought it would be more passionate to see her through the eyes of her idiot brother, who loved her with such trust and innocence that she was his whole world. So he told Caddy's story from Benjy's view, in a first-person narrative that was set in April 1928—the story's "present" —and that weaved back into past events in various time levels, including Damuddy's funeral in 1898. So it was that the scene of Caddy in the pear tree grew into a story of the entire Compson family over the first three decades of the twentieth century.

When Faulkner finished the Benjy section, he wasn't satisfied. Somehow Benjy's view of events needed to be clarified. On inspiration, Faulkner let Quentin, the firstborn son, tell his version in a stream-of-consciousness style. But Faulkner still didn't think the story was right. He tried again, this time switching to the voice and view of Jason. But the story, growing into a fair-sized novel, still wasn't clear. Perplexed, Faulkner tried for a month to clarify matters. Finally, in the last section, he told the story himself, trying as omniscient narrator to fill in the gaps and gather the pieces into a coherent whole.

But he still wasn't satisfied. No matter how hard he tried, he couldn't capture the story as it lived in his dreams, in the other world of his imagination. He had never anguished so much, never worked so hard, to bring a story off. He wrote his "guts" into that novel, he said later; he almost died in the pain of its creation.

Yet it was pure ecstasy, too. Each morning when he sat down to write, he felt an "eager and joyous faith and anticipation." He could hardly wait to discover what surprises the unmarred sheets of paper held for him. In his pages, he found what he had anticipated in *Mosquitoes:* a work "in which the hackneyed accidents which make up this world—love and life and death and sex and sorrow—brought together by chance in perfect proportions, take on a kind of splendid and timeless beauty." No wonder he felt more tenderness and love for this novel than for any of the others. Here was a pure work of art, uncontaminated by a publisher's contract and expectations of profit. When he finished the novel in September 1928, with no plans to submit it for publication, he realized that "there is actually something to which the shabby term Art not only can, but must, be applied."

Only now did he take Stone, his onetime mentor, into his confidence. He invited Stone up to his tower room in the Delta Psi house and exultantly showed him the work. Then Faulkner read him the entire manuscript, night after night, in his high, soft voice, as if to say, *See what I have created on my own, out of my own vision and experience, without writing by your dictates or trying to impress anyone else?* The novel was now remarkably complex, with each of its four narratives having its own fullness and integrity and its own "present." For three of them, the present fell around Easter, the time of the Crucifixion and the Resurrection. As Faulkner read through Benjy's section, dated April 7 (Holy Saturday), 1928, Stone immediately recognized the local Chandler idiot in Benjy, but could not make "head nor tail" of what was going on. "Wait," Faulkner kept telling him, "just wait." As soon as Faulkner reached Quentin's section, an interior monologue set eighteen years earlier, "the whole thing began to unfold like a flower," Stone said, and he was spellbound. Here in the Compsons was a dark and compelling tale about the moral impotence of the old established southern families in the modern South, about their aimlessness and sense of doom. The father was an alcoholic like Murry Falkner, the mother an egocentric and a hypochondriac like Stone's own mother. The Compson children were doomed like their parents to empty lives and hopeless dreams, although only Caddy knew and accepted that. She was kind and gentle to slobbering Benjy, and she loved Quentin, too, though she realized he was incapable of love, thanks to their tortured, neurotic parents. Doomed, she had a bastard child, then left the girl in her mother's care and fled Jefferson, to the despair of poor Benjy, who whimpered and bellowed in his grief for her departed love.

As Faulkner read on, taking Stone through Quentin's version of events, Stone was impressed with the stream-of-consciousness technique employed here, which showed how much Faulkner had learned from "his apprenticeship with Joyce." Quentin himself was a fascinating creation, an exaggerated reflection of Faulkner's own psyche and experience. Like Faulkner, Quentin was a firstborn son who suffered irreversible damage from the impact of his parents. Like Faulkner, he personified the feminine sphere of art in contrast to the masculine world of action. Insecure about his masculinity, unable to find the love he needed because he was incapable of giving love, Quentin mourned the idealized Caddy of his childhood, as Faulkner had mourned Estelle. He went on to Harvard with the help of his parents, who sold part of the family land to the Golf Club in order to raise the necessary funds. At Harvard, Quentin drifted into madness, tormented by incestuous fantasies about Caddy and a jealous and impotent rage at her seducer, all the while his drunken, nihilistic father lurked in the background of his mind, behind and beyond him "in the rasping darkness of summer." Unable to bear Caddy's dishonor (do you love him . . . I'll kill you . . . there is a curse on us), Quentin finally drowned himself in the Charles River, finding in suicide the "clean flame" that expunged all guilt and all consciousness.

Jason, too, was doomed—to repressed violence and hatred. A hybrid of Faulkner and his father, Jason talked like Murry and was the "worst member of the family," like his creator. "Cold and shrewd, with close-thatched brown hair curled into two stubborn hooks" and "hazel eyes with black-ringed irises like marbles," he hated his father and was devoted only to his black-eyed mother. In his section, which shifted the story to Good Friday 1928, Jason was now the head of the family, a bitter cynic who treated Benjy cruelly and hated both Caddy and the "whore" of a daughter she had left behind, so much so that he stole the monthly money Caddy sent home for her. Above all, he hated Dilsey,

the Negro cook and the only honorable member of the Compson household, yet was too afraid of her to throw her out. When, in the last section
of the book, Caddy's daughter ran away with his savings, plus the
money he had purloined from her mother, Jason lashed himself into a
distempered rage. Robbed! By that bitch! With aching head, he went
after her, only to return empty-handed, more embittered than ever.

The book's final section, set during Easter Sunday 1928, told the
Compson story from the view of Dilsey Gibson, with Faulkner functioning as omniscient narrator. Dilsey habitually wore a black straw hat atop
her turban, her face "myriad and sunken," her once-large frame now
an indomitable skeleton. Nominally the Negro cook for the Compsons,
Dilsey was the moral center of the household. Her deep religious faith,
honesty, and powerful sense of honor contrasted sharply with the moral
decay of the Compsons, as they degenerated into alcoholism, hypochon-
dria, idiocy, promiscuity, hatred, madness, and suicide. Through her
patient, Christ-like strength, she alone kept the Compson family together—hence the telling of her story on Easter, which for Faulkner
suggested the possibility of redemption, the continuation of the human
story, for it was the Dilseys who endured. Dilsey treated whimpering
Benjy with care and tenderness, tended Mrs. Compson after her husband drank himself to death, and tried to protect Caddy's daughter
from hateful Jason. Temperamentally like Mammy Callie, whom
Faulkner had loved since his childhood, Dilsey was one of his favorite
creations. For him, she was a living person, as much as anyone in the
exterior world. She was "a fine woman," he said later, "a good human
being." And he was "proud of her."

He was proud of all his people, even malignant Jason. In their
doomed lives, he had found an antidote to the pain and despair of his
own. Yes, he loved his novel. He thought it his "most gallant, most
magnificent failure," for in it he had tried to do the impossible—to
produce a perfect work of art that matched the dream.

Stone was impressed, too. Always possessive about Faulkner's art, he
even claimed that he contributed the book's final title. Since it was "a
tale told by an idiot," he suggested that they borrow from the famous
passage in *Macbeth* and call it *The Sound and the Fury*. But Faulkner
remembered differently. The phrase from Shakespeare, he said, had
struck him one day out of his unconscious, and he had adopted it at once
as an apt title for his "dark story of madness and hatred."

Faulkner could scarcely believe the news from New York. After some ten publishers had rejected *Flags in the Dust,* Wasson had shown it to Harrison Smith at Harcourt, Brace and Company, and Smith wanted the book. He did think it too long, however, and suggested that Wasson edit it himself, trimming it down by about 25 percent. If Faulkner agreed, Harcourt would advance him $500 and pay Wasson $50 to do the editing.

Faulkner was delighted about the acceptance, if not about the terms. He feared that *Flags in the Dust* would die if cut. Nevertheless, he signed and returned the contracts. He had stopped thinking of himself in publishing terms, yet here was a reputable New York house offering to publish him again. Harcourt was the publisher of Sinclair Lewis, so Faulkner would be in excellent company there. This remarkable turn of events changed his mind about *The Sound and the Fury,* too. If Harcourt was willing to gamble on *Flags in the Dust,* maybe it would also take a chance on *The Sound and the Fury,* which Faulkner was now revising. But that raised a problem with Liveright, to whom he owed money and the option on his next book. He certainly didn't want to submit his new novel to Liveright, not after the treatment he had given *Flags in the Dust.* According to one friend, Faulkner thought that Liveright ought to be a stockbroker, not a publisher of creative literature.

In October, he went to New York with his manuscript, to settle matters himself. Wasson, the diminutive southern gentleman, still looked up to Faulkner as his literary hero, and squired him around the world of New York publishing. It was Wasson who introduced Faulkner to his new editor, Hal Smith, a slight, absentminded man who viewed the follies of the world with ironic amusement. His nose twitched nervously when he had to make a decision; perhaps it twitched when he learned about *The Sound and the Fury,* about its sensational themes and potential technical problems. Nevertheless, he apparently gave Faulkner assurances about publishing it.

"Well, I'm going to be published by white folks now," Faulkner wrote an aunt in Mississippi. "Harcourt Brace & Co bought me from Liveright. Much, much nicer there. Book will be out in Feb. Also another one, the damndest book I ever read. I dont believe anyone will

publish it for 10 years. Harcourt swear they will, but I dont believe it."
He added, "Having a rotten time, as usual. I hate this place."

Faulkner rented a small flat in Greenwich Village and there revised
and typed the final draft of *The Sound and the Fury*. But almost every
day he dropped by Wasson's room, to check on his progress with what
was now called *Sartoris*. The manuscript had come to Harcourt without
the original title page, "Flags in the Dust," and someone there had
devised the new title.

"The trouble is that you had about six books in here," Wasson said.
"You were trying to write them all at once."

Faulkner retorted that this demonstrated his breadth of vision.
When Wasson showed him what he meant and what he was deleting,
Faulkner realized, for the first time, that he had done better than he
knew. As he pondered "those shady but ingenious shapes" in his book,
he speculated again on time and death and wondered whether he had
invented this fictional world, or whether it had invented him, giving
him "an illusion of greatness."

At first Faulkner adamantly refused to help reshape his book, leaving the cutting and smoothing of transitions up to Wasson. Painful
though it was, Faulkner did lend a hand in the end. He told Wasson,
with a hint of sarcasm: "You've done a good job, and it ought to suit
them." But stripped of a quarter of its rich detail and correlated scenes,
Sartoris was a considerably reduced thing, so much so that Faulkner
preserved a composite typescript of the original story, almost six hundred pages' worth, probably with the hope that someday *Flags in the
Dust* would be published in its entirety.

Nevertheless, Faulkner hoped that *Sartoris* would be a popular and
critical success. In his dedication, he expressed his gratitude to his
second former mentor, the man who had urged him to write about that
"little patch" in Mississippi where he came from. "To Sherwood Anderson," the dedication read, "through whose kindness I was first published, with the belief that this book will give him no reason to regret
that fact."

The day after Wasson completed his work on *Sartoris*, Faulkner
came to his room and dropped a large envelope on his bed. "Read this
one, Bud," he said. "It's a real son of a bitch." It was *The Sound and the
Fury*. He couldn't revise and polish it any more. Wasson could show it
to Hal Smith now.

Wasson truly admired Bill's work and thought his own inferior by contrast. But the sheer originality and technical outrageousness of *The Sound and the Fury,* especially in the Benjy section, made it difficult for Wasson to follow. Faulkner admitted that it was a demanding book, but indicated that he would use italics to identify different time levels.

He wanted a quick decision from Smith, Faulkner told Wasson. Because deep down he didn't think Harcourt or anyone else would ever publish *The Sound and the Fury.* He expected another rejection. Well, he hadn't written the book for editors and publishers anyway. And now he was finished, done with his cherished Compson story, the hardest and yet most exhilarating novel he ever hoped to write, and he felt empty and depressed. Writing a book was always like that: you got swept up in the protracted demands and ecstasy of creation, and when you were done, it left you drained, disoriented, and lonely. He felt that way now, more than ever. In his room, in a huge, cacophonous city far away from Oxford and its fictional counterpart, Faulkner locked his door and reached for a bottle of bootleg gin, drank that, then reached for another, and another, until he passed out on the floor and into blessed oblivion.

H E LINGERED IN NEW YORK, trying to sell some short stories he had written, one of them entitled "As I Lay Dying." But the New York magazines still closed their doors to his work, and in December he went home again to an uncertain future.

He needed money as always—to pay off his debt to Stone and meet basic expenses. And there was Estelle—a looming question mark. If he did decide to marry her, he would need money to support her. He hadn't decided anything yet, but his financial situation had become a chronic problem in any case, and he was tired of it. He wanted to write a book that would sell and free him from his nagging money woes. No potboiler, though. He was a serious artist and always had been. Surely he could produce something that was both artful and commercially appealing.

He remembered a story he had once heard from a young hooker in a Memphis nightclub. She had taken up with a strange, twisted gangster nicknamed Popeye, who had raped her with a corncob and kept her in a brothel. Faulkner thought this a real possibility for a commercially successful novel and also a work of art: a mystery-gangster story that mirrored the corruption and violence of America in the roaring twenties. Faulkner had certainly seen plenty of that himself in the underworlds of Memphis and New Orleans. Given its appetite for sensationalism, the reading public ought to relish the story of Popeye and the prostitute, especially if narrated by a skilled storyteller. In January 1929, Faulkner set to work on the most horrific tale he could imagine. It was going to be a "shocker."

That same month, *Sartoris* appeared in an edition of 1,998 copies, and Faulkner started feeling "again as a printed object." But the reviews, calling it loose and uneven, with inconsistent themes and characters, were scarcely reassuring for Faulkner or his publisher. February 1929 brought a letter from Alfred Harcourt himself, who rejected *The Sound and the Fury* on the grounds that it was not likely to find "a profitable market." "That is all right," Faulkner replied. "I did not believe that anyone would publish it."

As it turned out, though, Harrison Smith had formed his own publishing firm with Jonathan Cape, and Smith wanted the novel himself. "You're the only damn fool in New York who would publish it," Harcourt told him. Smith was willing to gamble on Faulkner's strange but brilliant tale, because he wanted a serious novelist on his new list.

Counting Four Seas, it was Faulkner's fourth publisher in five years. But he gladly signed the contracts, which gave him a $200 advance and a standard royalty rate of 10 percent for the first five thousand copies and 15 percent thereafter. He noted with pleasure that Ben Wasson had joined the new firm and would be his editor.

But Faulkner was far from being solvent and happy. His short stories still weren't selling; *Sartoris* was limping along; *The Sound and the Fury* was not likely to break any sales records. He wondered if he was capable of writing something many Americans would read. One evening in his tower room, he showed Stone some of his work in progress, but Stone was skeptical. "Bill," he said, "this won't sell. The day of the shocker is past." Faulkner admitted that he was discouraged. He had hoped that *Sartoris,* the novel in which he had found his fictional voice, would be a popular book. But Harcourt hadn't cared much for it, and obviously the reading public didn't either. Faulkner told Stone he didn't know why he kept writing—maybe just to stay out of regular work. He was sure he would never make any money from what he wrote, or enjoy any literary recognition.

"Bill," his friend said, "forget about trying to please them. Just go on and write what you damn please."

Nobody in Oxford, of course, cared about his books save Stone and Maud Falkner, who was again defending her son against the local critics. Druggist Mac Reed did stock *Sartoris* for the rare soul who might want a copy, "but anything without pictures, selling for more than 50 cents is indeed a drug here," Faulkner said. Away from his writing desk, he often visited the drugstore on the square, to greet Reed and browse in the magazines. The townsfolk would see Faulkner carrying a crooked stick and wearing a floppy hat, an English tweed coat, work khakis, and dusty shoes when he wasn't barefoot. He seemed remote, in a daze. Sometimes he walked right by lifelong acquaintances without speaking or even seeing them.

The townsfolk also saw him with Estelle, the divorcee, and her children. They saw him giving candy to Malcolm and Cho-Cho during school recesses and heard that he even sat with them at the Oldham place when Estelle was out. They saw him there so much that wags dubbed him "Major Oldham's yard boy," which they considered a damn sight more respectable than what he did do, which was nothing except write dirty books that didn't sell. When they didn't see him, they knew he was in that tower in the Delta Psi house, up to no good, still bumming off his parents at age thirty-one, more than ever Count No 'Count, with his British accent and lazy ways.

In May, Faulkner came down from his tower with a completed manuscript and sent it off to New York with hopes that here at last was a best-seller. Called *Sanctuary,* it was "about a girl who gets raped with a corn cob," as he described it to Wasson. The girl, Temple Drake, was an Ole Miss coed with a doll face, blond legs, and a bad reputation. Beyond Popeye's raping her, Faulkner's artistic interest was in "how all this evil flowed off her like water off a duck's back," which demonstrated to him that "women are completely impervious to evil." But his real focus was on Horace Benbow, who had come to *Sanctuary* from *Flags in the Dust* and had taken over the story. The incestuous element between him and his sister Narcissa, which had been trimmed away in *Sartoris,* was back emphatically in *Sanctuary.* "You're in love with your sister," his wife taunted him. "What do the books call it? What sort of complex?" Narcissa herself had changed from the sweet innocent of

Sartoris into a cruel, destructive, manipulating female who sought to dominate her brother, a transformation perhaps influenced by what was now going on between her creator and Estelle Franklin.

A story about seven violent murders in addition to rape and incest, *Sanctuary* was a shocker all right. "It's horrible," Estelle said when she read a carbon copy. "It's meant to be," Faulkner said, and added, "It will sell."

It wasn't long before he heard from Hal Smith in New York. "Good God," he told Faulkner, "I can't publish this. We'll both be in jail."

Faulkner was stunned. This was an even flatter rejection than *Flags in the Dust* had gotten from Liveright. "You're damned," Faulkner told himself. "You'll have to work now and then for the rest of your life."

W HILE FAULKNER WORKED ON *Sanctuary* that spring, Estelle's divorce became final, and everybody involved was bickering and taking sides about him and Estelle. The Oldhams were concerned about his hanging around the house so often—what were the neighbors thinking? After a fiery family argument in late spring, a sister of Estelle's phoned Faulkner and told him to stop stalling; it was time he married her. But Major Oldham still objected to Faulkner as a son-in-law, still called him a wastrel. And Stone still opposed the idea of Faulkner's marrying Estelle. Stone liked her even less now and feared that the burden of supporting her would ruin his friend's art. And Maud Falkner didn't want her Billy marrying anybody, let alone a divorced woman who drank. She couldn't bear the thought of sharing her brilliant and gifted son with another woman. She liked things exactly as they were, with thirty-one-year-old Billy living and working at home under her care.

Faulkner continued to vacillate. He had wanted to marry Estelle eleven years before, but now he was not at all sure, not with the wounds he carried in his heart. He wasn't certain he had ever forgiven her for marrying Cornell, or ever gotten over Helen, who had rejected and hurt him even worse than Estelle had. The bitchy young females in *Sanctuary*—Narcissa and Temple—suggested how angry he felt toward young women when he stopped idealizing them.

His stalling and uncertainty threw Estelle into a panic. Unless he married her, how could she go on living—she, a thirty-two-year-old divorcee with two children? A failure in the eyes of her family and friends, worse than that to the town at large? Billy was her childhood friend and sweetheart. Without him, she felt she had nothing, was nothing. For the sake of her sanity, of her life, he must marry her. She had no one else to turn to. Her nerves were gone, her mind, too. He was her last hope.

Estelle's frantic helplessness appealed to Faulkner's sense of honor. And it touched a deep need in him, a need to be wanted and depended on. What was more, she appeared to be his last hope, too. He couldn't go on living at home under the care of his mother—no, he recognized the danger in that. And there were no other prospective mates in his life. Here was his chance to assert his independence and get out on his own. Here was his chance to prove to his father and Major Oldham and all his other detractors that he was a *man,* not a wastrel, who could support a wife and have a family.

While his dreams for *Sanctuary* had collapsed, he resolved to act. He wrote his publisher. "Hal, I want $500.00. I am going to be married. Both want to and have to. THIS PART IS CONFIDENTIAL UTTERLY. For my honor and the sanity—I believe life—of a woman. This is not bunk; neither am I being sucked in. We grew up together and I don't think she could fool me in this way; that is, make me believe that her mental condition, her nerves, are this far gone. And no question of pregnan[c]y: that would hardly move me: no one can face his own bastard with more equanimity than I, having had some practice. Neither is it a matter of a promise on my part; we have known one another long enough to pay no attention to our promises. It's a situation which I engendered and permitted to ripen which has become unbearable, and I am tired of running from the devilment I bring about. This sounds a little insane, but I'm not in any shape to write letters now." He added that he would never again bother Hal for money, because from now on he would have to work at a regular job. "And I work well under pressure—and a wife will be pressure enough for me."

Evidently Smith couldn't come through. One of Faulkner's cousins claimed that her husband loaned him the money for his honeymoon.

Faulkner's parents and Phil Stone were not happy about his decision. Major Oldham didn't know about it because Estelle was afraid to tell him. On June 20, their wedding day, Faulkner picked up Estelle in his mother's Chevrolet and drove to the courthouse for the license.

Then, to her surprise, he went straight to her father's law office on the square. His honor required that he tell Lem Oldham in person.

"Mr. Lem," Faulkner said, his back ramrod straight, "'Stelle and I are going to be married."

"Billy," said old Major Oldham, "I've always been fond of you as a friend but I don't want you marrying my daughter." He stared at the fierce-eyed little man in front of him. "But if you're determined, I won't stand in your way."

Faulkner marched out to the car and drove Estelle, dainty and happy in her wedding dress, to College Hill Presbyterian Church, where he took her as his wife, with no hope that his art would ever support them.

A FEW DAYS LATER, they were sitting in a ramshackle beach house in Pascagoula, sipping drinks and watching the boats slide across the Gulf horizon. She was dressed in an imported satin gown and a large hat, and was smoking cigarettes and chattering away over her drink, as high-strung and outgoing as ever. Her husband, whom neighbors thought "a regular Chesterfield" with his gallant manner and sartorial tweeds, drank and watched the boats in silence.

They were on their honeymoon, in the little Gulf town where he had loved Helen Baird and written poetry about his desire for her as she swam in the moving sea. Now he was married to his loquacious little companion, who had also rejected him for another man, not so long ago. And they were not alone: her children, Cho-Cho and Malcolm, were with them, as was the silver-haired female servant of her former mother-in-law.

The newlyweds were a sensation at Pascagoula: the reticent, dapper little man with the trimmed mustache, his talkative, birdlike bride in her gorgeous gowns. It seemed to their neighbors that they dressed up in banquet finery for every dinner, even for walks on the beach against the sundown sea.

Yet behind their glamorous facade, all was not well between them. To her dismay, he sometimes went about unshaven and barefoot, wearing soiled old clothes. And he shut her out a good deal, too, unable to tolerate her garrulous ways. Even when they sat together in the June twilight, he could be withdrawn and unresponsive. When he was like that, she began to realize that she would never have as much of him as she needed. To occupy herself, she tried to read Joyce's *Ulysses,* but put it down, complaining that it was too difficult. "Read it again" was all he said.

In July, galleys of *The Sound and the Fury* arrived, and he left her for long periods then, off in his inner sanctum with Benjy, Quentin and Jason, Dilsey, and above all Caddy, his real "heart's darling." Even more preoccupied now, he resented family intrusions. When provoked, "he could say things that would cut you to the heart," Cho-Cho found out. He was on edge for another reason: Ben Wasson had made editorial changes in Faulkner's cherished book, substituting spaces in place of the italics Faulkner had used to distinguish different time levels. Faulkner angrily eliminated the spaces, restored the italics, and wrote Wasson a warning: "Don't make any more additions to the script, bud. I know you mean well, but so do I." Later he apologized for his tone, but still insisted he was right.

The galleys were an unbearable ordeal for his bride. Only a visit by her sister helped Estelle get through it. She was overjoyed when he mailed them off and took her to New Orleans for a welcome interlude. Now this was more to her liking: a room in an elegant old hotel, fashionable breakfasts and lavish dinners in restaurants more suitable for her hats and gowns than a Pascagoula beach house. They strolled through the narrow streets of the French Quarter, where Faulkner had once walked with Sherwood Anderson, had written his first novel in a state of joy, and had met Helen Baird, who had broken his heart. It was not the same city to him now.

Back at Pascagoula, Estelle couldn't bear the contrast: the run-down beach house, her husband laconic and remote again. She started missing Cornell, missing their mansion in Shanghai and her staff of servants, missing the whole extravagant life she had enjoyed there. Inevitably, she turned to alcohol as an escape. One evening, after she had drunk steadily for several hours, something happened between her and her husband. Dressed in a silk gown, she walked down to the beach and waded out into the water, searching for the place where the shelf ended and the channel began. Unable to stop her, Faulkner ran to a male neighbor, shouting, "She's going to drown herself!" The neighbor raced into the water and waded and stumbled after the receding figure, finally overtaking her just short of the point where the channel began.

The tiny figure broke loose and lunged for the deep water that would carry her away, out of her doomed life. But the man pulled her back from the edge, subdued her somehow, and dragged her back to the hated beach house, where a doctor gave her a sedative.

She remained in bed for several days, then, sober and perhaps repentant, returned to Oxford with her children and brooding husband. They rented the downstairs of a large white house on University Avenue, equipped the rooms with her furniture, and began their life together.

It was not a happy life. Estelle had counted on him to save her from the pain of her broken marriage and shattered self-esteem, to make her secure and happy. And he had hoped to oblige her. But there was a wall of irreconcilable differences between Faulkner and Estelle which made real intimacy impossible. A vivacious extrovert, she loved to dress up and go out for the evening, to dine at a nice restaurant, talk, and dance. He did take her out occasionally, but preferred to eat at home—she was a good cook, after all, particularly adept at Oriental dishes—and to spend a quiet evening with a book. Worse than that, he was unable and unwilling to open up to Estelle and trust again. He had experienced too many personal hurts, too much torment in his parents' home, too many rejections, to do that. As with everyone else, he kept an impregnable carapace around his inner self, refusing to share his deep personal feelings and thoughts with her.

Almost entirely dependent on him for her own happiness, Estelle could never adjust to the creative artist in him, to his moods, his shut-mouthed ways, his long absences when he was off in his fictional kingdom. Without open communication between them, they both drank too much: Faulkner when he wasn't writing, Estelle when he was.

And there was the accursed money problem. Estelle was accustomed to a large checking account, to an expensive wardrobe, a mansion, servants, and other luxuries, but enjoyed none of that with her impecunious husband. While she did receive child support payments from Cornell, Faulkner still needed a job to support them all. Bitterly, he went to work on the night shift at the university power station. He left the house at 6 P.M., returned at six the next morning, took his breakfast, slept for two hours, then wrote in the parlor, on a spindle-legged table his mother had given him, with breaks for catnaps in the afternoon. While he wrote, he expected no intrusions or unnecessary noise from Estelle and the children.

It was an arduous schedule for all of them. To make matters worse,

Faulkner each day performed the filial duty of calling on his mother in the Delta Psi house and sharing coffee with her in the parlor. Still slight and stern-eyed, she had aged gracefully, with strands of gray in her hair. Sometimes Estelle came along, but Maud Falkner made it clear that she wasn't welcome. Maud thought Estelle "flighty—a sort of butterfly," violently disapproved of her drinking, and was not reconciled to her as Billy's wife. She was cold, distant, and rude to her other daughters-in-law, too, turning them all away at the front door. When Johncy came to pay his respects, his wife, Lucille, had to wait in the car. Estelle, for her part, could never adjust to such treatment, or accept Billy's loyalty to his mother. It seemed that he loved her more than his own wife, and it grated on Estelle; she couldn't stand it.

Not long after the honeymoon in Pascagoula, Malcolm told a friend an astonishing story. His father, Cornell, and his new wife, Dallas, paid a visit to his mother and Mr. Bill, Malcolm said. Mr. Bill was in the garden with Dallas while his mother and father were together in the parlor. Mr. Bill was polite to everyone, but after a while he walked out, went away to Memphis, and stayed there until Cornell and Dallas left. Cho-Cho, watching her mother carry on, was sure she regretted marrying Mr. Bill and hoped Cornell would come back to her.

But he wasn't coming back. She had to resign herself to that finally. Well, she had sought her life with Billy; she must make the best of it somehow. And he did have many fine qualities. He was trying to take care of them. He was good to her children, treating them as though they were his own. And he was kind to her when she was ill and needed his care. Yes, he was especially tender then. But lonely and insecure, needing more than he could ever give her, she still drank.

O N OCTOBER 7, 1929, *The Sound and the Fury* appeared to considerable critical attention but an indifferent reading public. Not that Faulkner was surprised. He knew his book wouldn't sell. Still, he could take heart from one thing. Atop the season's best-seller lists were Erich Maria Remarque's *All Quiet on the Western Front* and Ernest Hemingway's *A Farewell to Arms.* Here was proof that serious works of fiction could also be commercial successes.

Meanwhile Faulkner went about his nightly chores at the Ole Miss powerhouse. From six to eleven, he would pile coal into a wheelbarrow, push it over, and dump the coal where the fireman could shovel it into the boiler. Between eleven at night and four in the morning, most people were asleep and the homes and buildings didn't require as much steam. Faulkner and the fireman could rest then; the fireman would doze in a chair and Faulkner would make a table out of an overturned wheelbarrow in the coal bunker and write on legal-size onionskin paper, while a dynamo whirred nearby.

On his wheelbarrow desk, he set down what his voices were telling him now—a story about another family in Faulkner's mythic Mississippi kingdom, which he renamed Yoknapatawpha County. Yoknapatawpha was a Chickasaw Indian word that meant "water flowing slow through the flatland." As he wrote, minor characters came in from earlier novels, and he began to see the larger picture of his fiction. "I found out," he said later, "that not only each book had to have a design but the whole output or sum of an artist's work had to have a design." As *Sartoris* and *The Sound and the Fury* had dealt with the decay and decline of two of the old patrician families in Jefferson, his new work was about a poor family of "misfortunates" who toiled on a hardscrabble farm beyond the town. As with the Sartoris and Compson families, the story of the Bundrens had a familiar autobiographical theme. It was about wounded, inadequate parents and their doomed children.

The voices of the seven Bundrens spoke clearly in Faulkner's imagination, yet he wrote with none of the ecstasy and anticipation of surprise that *The Sound and the Fury* had given him. This was a "deliberate" book, he said. He intended it to be a tour de force. In a letter to Smith, he reported that he was composing in a coal bunker next to the dynamo room, whose steady hum was "the finest sound to work by I ever heard." Faulkner said the new novel was "a son bitch sho enough." Borrowing the title of an earlier short story, he was calling it *As I Lay Dying*. "How's that for a high?"

Eschewing omniscient narration, Faulkner let his characters tell the Bundren story from various perspectives—by now a Faulkner trademark. When the story began, the one who lay dying was Addie, the wife and mother, a bitter, willful woman who had simply given up living. A former schoolteacher, she had once been capable of love, only to become poisoned against it. She had married Anse in bitterness and remained bitter when she bore their first two children, Cash and Darl, who only violated her sense of aloneness. Feeling betrayed by Anse's word "love," which she considered "just a shape to fill a lack," she slept with a local preacher in the woods and had his boy, Jewel. She favored Jewel and hated herself for it, but favored him all the same. To compensate for Jewel, she gave Anse two more children, Dewey Dell and Vardaman. Then Anse had four children that were his and not hers, and she could get ready to die. After all, her father had told her, the reason for living was getting ready to stay dead.

When she finally willed her death, the children, grown but unmarried, were still living at home. With Anse, they placed her in a coffin fashioned by Cash, loaded it in a wagon, and set out for Jefferson to bury her in the family cemetery, as she had requested. Only Darl, the second oldest, realized what a sight they were: five of them riding in the wagon with their mother's decomposing corpse, while Jewel rode alongside on his spotted horse. The only surviving Bundren capable of love, Darl in many respects was a reflection of his creator: he had hypnotic eyes, a poetic imagination, and a tendency to muse about who or what he was, all of which prompted folks to call him "queer." A neighbor summed him up: "He don't say nothing: just looks at me with them queer eyes of hisn that makes folks talk. I always say it aint never been what he done so much or said or anything so much as how he looks at you. It's like he had got into the inside of you, someway."

Darl alone knew about Jewel, knew that he was the preacher's son, not Anse's. "Jewel's eyes look like pale wood in his high-blooded face," Darl thought. "He is a head taller than any of the rest of us." Jewel went about in a permanent rage, furious even in his approach to the spotted horse—the only thing he came close to loving. And his sister, Dewey Dell, was almost as angry. She hated Darl because he had figured out her secret—she was carrying the child of a local farmer. Like Temple Drake and Narcissa Benbow Sartoris in *Sanctuary,* Dewey Dell was a surly young woman, "pretty in a kind of sullen, awkward way," as another character said. She was so obsessed with her pregnancy that she could not fully comprehend her mother's death. All she could think about, save hating Darl, was buying pills from a Jefferson druggist that would abort the unwanted child.

Anse, the father, had his own selfish reason for pressing on. Humped and toothless, with a hangdog look and feet twisted from wearing homemade shoes in his youth, he intended to get himself some store-bought teeth in Jefferson. Throughout the whole dramatic journey, he kept thinking that now he could get them teeth. That would be a comfort. But it vexed him when Darl started acting queer again. Sitting back there on the plank seat, with his dead ma lying in her coffin at his feet, Darl started laughing. Anse thought, "How many times I told him it's doing such things as that that makes folks talk about him, I don't know." Anse thought Darl ought to show his ma more respect, thought, "The Lord will pardon me and excuse the conduct of them He sent me."

Meanwhile they survived a terrible mishap in the flooded river south of Jefferson and pressed on, determined to get there come what may, Anse to buy his teeth, Dewey Dell to get those pills, with Jewel furious astride his horse and Darl laughing at the bizarre spectacle they made. When the corpse began to stink and buzzards to circle overhead, Darl tried to end the obscene pageant: he set fire to a barn where the coffin rested for the night. But Jewel rescued it from the flames in a frenzied, single-handed effort; later he learned from Dewey Dell—who had found out from Vardaman, the youngest—that Darl had started the blaze. Finally the Bundrens reached Jefferson, where they buried Addie in her family graveyard as Anse had promised. But afterward authorities from an insane asylum were waiting in the lane for Darl. It was a trap, laid with vicious cunning by Dewey Dell and Jewel, who had convinced Anse to incarcerate their "crazy" brother. To Cash's astonishment, Dewey Dell leaped on Darl "like a wild cat," scratching and clawing at him. Then Jewel, screaming "kill the son-of-a-bitch," helped throw Darl down and hold him. When he finally surrendered, Darl sat there and laughed and laughed. And Cash, the oldest and least wounded of the children, gained compassion for his doomed brother, thinking that "this world is not his world; this life his life."

In the end, Dewey Dell gave herself to a young druggist in exchange for some worthless pills, and Anse got his teeth and something else. He approached his four remaining children with a woman in tow—a duck-shaped woman, all dressed up and carrying a grip, with hard-looking pop eyes that seemed to dare them to say something. "Meet Mrs. Bundren," Anse said.

Faulkner finished the manuscript draft in six weeks, typed it up with some revisions, and sent it off in January 1930, with high hopes that this would make his fame. He told Hal Smith, to whom the book was dedicated, that by it he would stand or fall.

FAULKNER CREATED *As I Lay Dying* in the midst of the stock market crash of October and November 1929, which shook American business to its foundations and imperiled the nation's entire financial structure. By the time Faulkner completed his novel and turned to writing short stories for immediate income, panic had set in across the land; rumors flew of suicides on Wall Street; thousands of investors and speculators had lost their fortunes, and banks were calling in their loans. The country seemed on the verge of a violent economic smashup, of a calamity on the scale of the Civil War.

Despite the grim economic picture, Faulkner wanted to buy a house. Apparently done with working at the university generating station, he sent off a flurry of short stories to the high-paying national magazines, which had systematically rejected his earlier work. But with four novels published, Faulkner had a growing reputation. The long drouth ended when *Forum* took "A Rose for Emily," a chilling tale about a Jefferson spinster who kept something grotesque in her bed. "A Rose for Emily," which appeared in the April issue, was Faulkner's first publication in a national magazine. Meanwhile the *Saturday Evening Post* bought another story, for $750—more money than he had earned from any of his novels. *The American Mercury* took another story, *Scribner's* still another. Faulkner was elated about the money he earned, if not about writing commercial short stories. When forced to turn them out for income, he felt he was "whoring."

With money coming in, Faulkner had his eye on the old Shegog place in a secluded, wooded area of Oxford. It consisted of a two-story, colonial-style main house, a smokehouse in back, a barn on the northwest side, and a surrounding tract of land. The main house loomed majestically in the trees, with a balcony and a four-columned portico in front, a cedar-lined walkway that led to a formal garden beyond, and a curving, cedar-lined drive. True, the place lacked electricity and plumbing and was so run down that the beams were rotting and starting to sag. But it had an aura of history to it that inflamed Faulkner's imagination. "Colonel" Robert R. Shegog, a wealthy Irishman, had built the house with slave labor back in 1844, on a tract of land originally granted to a Chickasaw Indian named E-Ah-Nah-Yea. The house had witnessed the golden age of the South's *ancien régime* and its obliteration in the Civil War, in the Yankee occupation and the end of slavery. There was a legend about it and the war which Faulkner and Estelle had heard since childhood. When the Yankees had captured Oxford, Judith Shegog, the colonel's beautiful young daughter, had fallen in love with a Yankee lieutenant. But when she tried to elope with him, she fell from the balcony and plunged to her death at the very feet of her horrified lieutenant. A short time later, the story went, the Yankees burned a home across the Old Taylor Road, but left the Shegog place unscathed out of deference to the doomed lovers. On some nights, when the moon was out, and dogs bayed in the far-off woods, and the wind moaned at the windows, a subsequent owner thought she could hear the steps and sense the ghostly presence of the dead girl.

That kind of tale appealed to a creative artist with a taste for the macabre and a tragic sense of history. What if the old place was run down and haunted-looking? It could be restored with a little imagination. Besides, it reminded Faulkner of his great-grandfather's mansion in Ripley. He had always wanted to be like the Old Colonel, to write books and own a mansion like him. With his own antebellum home, a wife, and children, Faulkner could walk proudly in the Old Colonel's footsteps and thumb his nose at everybody in Oxford who called him Count No 'Count. That would give him exquisite satisfaction indeed.

Because the Depression had made money scarce, the current owner worked out an arrangement with Faulkner, which they legalized in April 1930. Faulkner could have the house, satellite buildings, and four acres of land for $6,000 at 6 percent interest, without a down payment; he would pay off the mortgage at $75 a month. When he added taxes, insurance payments, and expenses for renovation and repairs, Faulkner knew he would be sorely pressed, with his erratic income. But he was happy nevertheless. Daring to be different in a small Mississippi town, he had become a landowner on his own terms, in his own way. Like the planters of old, he gave his home a name. He called it Rowan Oak, after the rowan tree of his ancestral Scotland, a tree symbolic of security and peace.

If Faulkner was happy about Rowan Oak, his wife was miserable. She wanted a home all right, but not this ramshackle dump. When they moved there in June, she sat on the front porch and wept. Look at this place! It had no lights, no plumbing, no running water. It looked as though it would collapse in the next rainstorm. God, nobody would visit them here. They would be social outcasts.

Ignoring her complaints, Faulkner put them all to work: they cleared dust and debris from the rooms, raked shedded snakeskins from one of the closets, pulled down cobwebs, raised windows to release the musty, closed-up odor, and arranged Estelle's furniture throughout. At least they had enough room for all of it now, even her piano, which went into the parlor to the right of the front door; the other parlor, across the hall, would be Faulkner's library and workroom. Adjacent to the parlor with the piano was a formal dining room, with a kitchen in back. A stairway in the hall led to three upstairs bedrooms.

To Estelle's horror, they had to bathe outside that summer, in the courtyard by the cistern, first she and Cho-Cho, then Faulkner and Malcolm. But Faulkner was handy with tools and a paintbrush, and he worked hard to make the old house livable. With a helper, he put in new beams, installed plumbing in the kitchen and bathroom, scrubbed and painted the outside, and wired the place for electricity, watching all the while for hibernating snakes in the attic.

At the same time, he gathered a staff in the manner of his great-grandfather and grandfather. He hired a Negro cook to tend the kitchen and relieve Estelle of that responsibility. Old Mammy Callie, small and frail, dressed as always in a starched dress, smooth white apron, immaculate headcloth, and tiny high-button shoes, came to help Estelle supervise the two children. Soon Mammy Callie was regaling Malcolm with her tales, the two of them sitting outside under a big oak between the barn and the smokehouse, Malcolm in a swing, Mammy in her rocking chair. Sometimes Faulkner would break from his renovations, sit on a woodpile nearby, and listen again to the stories that had enthralled him as a boy.

Another old Negro functioned as an all-purpose servant, as yard man, stock tender, and butler. This was Uncle Ned, a tall, portly man of erect and gentle dignity, with a round, pleasant face and a ring of white hair about his balding head. He was so fastidious about his appearance that he wore a tie even while chopping wood or milking the cow. He had served three generations of Falkner men, and he brought a chest full of clothes they had given him during his long tenure with the family: a blue brass-buttoned frock coat and plug hat he had worn as coachman for both the Old Colonel and his son, high-crowned hats, broadcloth suits, and broadcloth frock coats which the Old Colonel himself had worn and then bequeathed to Ned, pigeon-tailed coats of the Young Colonel's time, and even a short coat from Faulkner's own father. On Saturday afternoons, he would dress in sartorial splendor and go to town to collect debts. He liked to loan money to fellow blacks, and referred to those who repaid him as "colored gentlemen," those who didn't as "niggers." On Sunday mornings, preparing for church, he would don yet another costume and douse himself with toilet water. Sometimes Estelle would drive him to church in the family car, but would keep the windows down because of the pungent aroma of Ned's toilet water. Sitting in the back seat, as black men had to do when riding with white women in Dixie, he would pray aloud that her driving wouldn't kill him.

At thirty-two, Faulkner was more sensitive to black folk than in his earlier years. He watched Mammy Callie and Uncle Ned as they went about their tasks, listened to them talk with whites and with one another, and he began to comprehend the roles they assumed around whites, to sense their special pain and suffering in a land of rigid white supremacy, to realize how little whites understood about black people. He felt real love for Uncle Ned, just as he did for Mammy Callie, and would never forget the sight of Ned going to town on Saturdays. Referring to himself in the third person, Faulkner recalled that he might glance idly out the library window and see "that back, that stride, that coat and hat going down the drive toward the road, and his heart would stop and even turn over."

For Faulkner, it was a good summer, a productive summer. As he hammered and painted at Rowan Oak, the *Post* bought two more of his stories for $750 apiece, which helped defray the mounting cost of renovations. Better still, Hal Smith liked *As I Lay Dying* and put it on his fall list. And Faulkner's books were starting to appear in Britain, too. Chatto & Windus brought out *Soldiers' Pay* that summer, with plans to publish *Mosquitoes* and *The Sound and the Fury* as well. One British critic announced that Faulkner wrote "generally like an angel," while another ranked him ahead of Hemingway and D. H. Lawrence.

Perhaps even more profound news came from Estelle: she was pregnant. Because she was so thin and frail, doctors had warned her against any more pregnancies. But it had happened anyway, and Faulkner was delighted. He loved Cho-Cho and Malcolm, but he really did want a child of his own. That would sho-nuff give the town something to wonder about: Count No 'Count a father as well as the squire of Rowan Oak.

With expenses sure to mount now, Faulkner turned out a procession of short stories, working feverishly on his fragile table in the library, where he soon installed bookcases for the volumes piled on the floor. When *As I Lay Dying* appeared in October, Faulkner was disappointed perhaps that Smith had printed only 2,522 copies. Obviously Smith didn't think it would become a best-seller.

When his copies arrived, Faulkner put them in a special glassed-in bookcase and paid no further attention to them. He was increasingly indifferent about his books once they appeared. For him, his characters lived on beyond the volumes about them, growing older and changing just like ordinary people. He knew that his characters, many of them, would be back again for his next book, and his next, all part of a larger story, which he knew now was the story of himself and the world.

By now, his life at Rowan Oak had settled more or less into a routine. An insomniac, he slept fitfully, seldom more than five hours a night. He rose around 4 A.M., even before the blue jays began their quarrelsome song. He was a ritualist about breakfast, treating himself each morning to a tremendous meal of fruit, eggs, grits, bacon or broiled steak, toast with Dundee marmalade, and hot black Louisiana coffee. Then he retired to the library for much of the morning. The library door had no lock, so he would remove the doorknob and take it inside with him. "No one can get in," Estelle told a visitor, "and he is quite secure." She added, wistfully, that "he is difficult to get along with when he is working hard on something." He complained, of course, that nobody understood the demands of creative writing, that interruptions and undue noise broke his concentration. When that happened, it was hard to get back into his story and characters.

So Faulkner insisted on a quiet house when he was working: radio, doorbell, telephone—all were "forbidden items," Malcolm said. Faulkner did permit a telephone in the house, but he abhorred the thing and for good reason: people thought they could ring him anytime, oblivious to the fact that creative writing was different from compiling a grocery list. An artist who cherished his solitude, Faulkner had "a natural and sustained aversion to the telephone anywhere, anytime, and under any conceivable circumstances," said his brother Jack.

In his library sanctuary, he followed no set routine about writing. "Ah write when the spirit moves me," he told a visitor, "and the spirit moves me every day." He would put off actual composition as long as possible, trying to get a passage right in his head before committing it to paper. He liked to write when he was "hot," which was usually in the morning; then he might break for a rest and return to his desk in the afternoon. When he was really inspired, he could work for twelve or thirteen hours in a single day. Sometimes he referred to his inspirations in sexual terms. "When I have a case of the hots," he said, "I can write like a streak."

He still composed in longhand—"I've got to feel the pencil and see the words at the end of the pencil," he said. He wrote in a cramped, almost illegible script, going so rapidly, often in a demon-driven fury, that he had to type up a day's work lest he not be able to read it the next morning. Though critics and readers alike complained that his sentences were tortuous, his plots convoluted and inaccessible, he revised his material with painstaking devotion to craftsmanship, once turning out a dozen versions of a single story. And he prided himself on the sharpness of his imagery, the extraordinary originality of his characters, and the multiple perspectives in his narratives, which sought to convey his understanding of the nature of truth. No individual, Faulkner maintained, could fully comprehend an event, since he saw only one phase of it. Someone else who observed the same event saw it from a different perspective. And so it went with other witnesses. When taken all together, the truth emerged from what they all saw, though none saw the truth intact. The truth, or as close to it as mortals could get, came when the reader went over all the different viewpoints and put them together into a kind of synthesis. That was what Faulkner aimed at in *As I Lay Dying*, which gave readers the Bundren story from the perspectives of fifteen different narrators.

When a story or a novel mired down, Faulkner would vent his frustrations on the bitterweeds that grew in the pasture beyond the barn. Malcolm would see him out there with a hoe, hacking furiously at the bitterweeds until he resolved the problem. Then he might settle into ordinary hoeing to uproot the hated plants. At other times, he would go for a long walk down the Old Taylor Road to Thacker's Mountain, or head into town for his mail. As always, the denizens of Oxford stared at this strange little man in their midst, who continued to wear outlandish clothes—a tweed jacket with an old pair of greasy khaki farm pants—even though his work now appeared in the *Post*. A lot of people still sneered and laughed at him. Some even concluded that Phil Stone wrote his stories, because Faulkner didn't have sense enough to do it himself.

At noon, in the southern tradition, Faulkner joined Estelle and the children for dinner in the formal dining room at Rowan Oak. He was

hardly more demonstrative at the head of the table than he was anywhere else, and meals often took place in silence. In the afternoon, if
he wasn't writing, he might curl up for a nap and then tend to chores
about the place. Toward sunset, often dressed in coat and tie, he would
relax in a large rocking chair on the front porch, smoking his pipe and
nursing a glass of bourbon while birds chortled in the tall cedars and
dogs barked in the distance. Estelle often joined him with her glass—
it was their time together. Later, to ensure privacy, they added a veranda to the east side of the house, with a wall that closed off the east
lawn from the front lawn and the cedar-lined drive beyond. Here, on
the east veranda, they could enjoy their cocktail time shielded from the
view of meddlesome neighbors and strangers. After supper, he liked
nothing better than to make his pipe and open a favorite book, turning
again and again to Balzac, to Conrad and Dickens, to Shakespeare,
Melville, and the Bible. By the time Estelle and the children were in
bed, he might be back at his writing table, working in the silence and
shadows of the night.

Busy and preoccupied as he was, he did find time for Malcolm and
Cho-Cho. After dinner he might entertain them with Civil War stories
or read to them from the books he loved. Or he might tell them ghost
stories, as he did ritually at Halloween, when the children would invite
their friends and Faulkner would frighten the wits out of them with
animated tales about Judith Shegog's ghost. He would sit on the steps,
shoulders squared, legs crossed, smelling of pipe tobacco and bourbon,
as he told about Judith and her Yankee officer in a soft voice, the
costumed children wide-eyed in the flickering candlelight. But he
added something to the legend, saying that after Miss Judith plum-
meted to her death near the very steps where they were sitting, she had
been buried at Rowan Oak, and so eventually had her lover. Recently,
he said, she had made a pilgrimage on each anniversary of his death:
she would descend from the top of the stairs and glide out the front door
and out across the lawn to the spot where her officer lay in his grave.
As he spoke, Faulkner would reenact her pilgrimage with both hands
raised, the children all seeing her absolutely instead of him. Then he
would urge them to visit Judith's grave under the big magnolia beyond
the house. As he watched from the steps, they would step through the
gloom by candlelight, only to come running back, screaming in an
ecstasy of fear.

Malcolm and Cho-Cho relished Mr. Bill's stories and believed that

Judith's ghost really did inhabit Rowan Oak, just as he said. Sometimes they could hear piano music coming from the empty parlor, and Mr. Bill would say, "That has to be Judith playing." One night Cho-Cho thought she *saw* Judith: she awoke with a start and there, standing by her bed in a filmy, swirling gown, was a young woman with exquisite features, just as Mr. Bill had described her. Suddenly she turned and fled into the hall; and Cho-Cho caught a glimpse of her drifting off the balcony, and then saw her receding down the walkway between the towering cedars, only to disappear in the formal garden beyond.

Through stories and shared experiences, Faulkner, who had never really known a father, tried to be a father to his stepchildren. He could be difficult to live with, but he could also be kind and sensitive, especially to Malcolm, who came to idolize him. He took "Buddy" squirrel hunting in the woods nearby, even invited the boy to share his eccentricities. On Armistice Day in November, Mr. Bill might put on his RAF uniform, take Malcolm out of school, and walk with him around the square in honor of the day.

ONE DAY THAT NOVEMBER, 1930, Faulkner sat at his desk in the library, staring morosely at a set of unexpected galleys. They were the galleys of *Sanctuary*, the story about Horace Benbow and the rape of Temple Drake, which Faulkner had all but forgotten. Hal Smith, who had rejected the book lest he and Faulkner both end up in jail, had changed his mind about publishing it. In financial trouble in these uncertain times, Smith was now willing to gamble on a shocker like *Sanctuary*. If it sold, it would justify the risk.

Faulkner read the galleys in despair. The book seemed so badly written to him now, so cheaply approached, so obviously conceived to make money, that he could not let it go. His pride as an artist was at stake. He wrote Smith not to publish, but Smith replied that the firm had already invested too much to stop now. "You can't print it like this," Faulkner retorted, "it's just a bad book."

He had to think this through. It irked him that the reading public had ignored *The Sound and the Fury* and *As I Lay Dying* in favor of the kind of ephemera that usually made the best-seller lists. He felt a tremendous obligation to his two deeply cherished novels, could not put his name on one that didn't measure up to them. He had no choice but to rewrite *Sanctuary,* trying to make it into something that wouldn't shame *The Sound and the Fury* and *As I Lay Dying.* Given its sensational themes, *Sanctuary* still might have popular appeal. "It might sell," he thought with contempt. "Maybe 10,000 of them will buy it."

Smith's reply was blunt: if Faulkner wanted to redo the book in galleys, he would have to assume half the cost. Faulkner agreed to "pay for the privilege," tore down the galleys, and rewrote the book. In the first version, Horace Benbow, the sensitive, idealistic lawyer with incestuous feelings for his sister, had dominated the story. Now, in calling back his characters, Faulkner reduced the incestuous element between Horace and Narcissa Benbow and made Temple Drake's the central story. Indeed, Temple emerged full-blown now, an unforgettable character in her own right, a "little doll-faced slut," as another character described her, who appeared impervious to the maelstrom of evil swirling around her. She seemed a malignant offspring of the nymphs of Faulkner's early poetry, of the virginal, childlike young women he had once idealized and still fantasized about.

Seventeen when she entered the story, Temple was the daughter of a prominent judge and a student at Ole Miss in Oxford. Thin-armed, with small, high buttocks and curled reddish hair, Temple was "a small childish figure no longer quite a child, not yet quite a woman." She went about in scant, narrow dresses, which showed off her long legs. On campus, she could be seen with "a snatched coat under her arm and her long legs blonde with running, in speeding silhouette against the lighted windows of the Coop, as the women's dormitory was known." At dances, she whirled about "with her high delicate head and her bold painted mouth and soft chin, her eyes blankly right and left looking, cool, predatory and discreet."

On her way to a baseball game in Starkville, she joined an inebriated young collegian who took her on a drunken auto ride to fetch a bottle from a bootlegger southeast of Jefferson. After plowing into a fallen tree, they ended up at the old Frenchman's plantation house on the Yoknapatawpha River; it was now "a gutted ruin rising gaunt and stark out of a grove of unpruned cedar trees." Here they fell captive to a gang of bootleggers and spent the night. At one point, Temple actually fled, ran clear to the road and down it a ways, only to turn and come back to the house, drawn to the danger there. In a room with a bed, she removed her scant dress, hurled it away, and covered herself in her coat, with a raincoat over that. One of the men, a halfwit, watched her closely. So did another, a vicious-looking man in tight clothes, with eyes "like rubber knobs," a face of "queer, bloodless color," and an ever-present cigarette dangling from his lips. This was Popeye, who sensed something in Temple, a perverse affinity between them. When she tried to hide in a corncrib, Popeye followed her there, found and murdered the halfwit, and raped Temple with a corncob, in what for her was "a half-desired nightmare."

Afterward, the raped girl accompanied Popeye into the Memphis underworld, which Faulkner had visited with Phil Stone and now described in scenes rich with detail. Popeye installed Temple in a private room in a brothel and stood over her again, savage and impotent, whinnying like a horse, "saliva drooling between his fingers," as his hand advanced on her and her body thrashed furiously from side to side. As his kept woman, Temple became "wild as a young mare," the madam said. When Popeye presented Temple with a virile young man named Red, she became his lover, copulating in orgasmic abandon as Popeye looked on with hissing, emasculated desire. Temple wallowed in all her squalor. "You're not even a man!" she taunted Popeye, "hanging over the bed, moaning and slobbering like a—" "Dont you wish you were Red? Dont you? Dont you wish you could do what he can do? Dont you wish he was the one watching us instead of you?" Lusting after Red, Temple tried to run away with him, but Popeye aborted that by shooting Red to death; then he took off for Florida.

Meanwhile Horace Benbow, the idealistic lawyer, came to the aid of one of the other bootleggers, a violent, stubble-faced man named Lee Goodwin, who was falsely charged with the murder of the halfwit. Still the Yoknapatawpha counterpart of Phil Stone, Benbow was a tall, thin man with "a quick, faintly outlandish voice, the voice of a man given to much talk and not much else." His sister Narcissa, a widow of ten years now who lived with Miss Jenny at the Sartoris place, ruthlessly opposed Horace's efforts to defend the bootlegger. What would respectable people think of her if he got mixed up with "moonshiners and streetwalkers"? But Benbow kept the case—and thought he had it won when Temple agreed to testify that it was Popeye who had killed the halfwit. Instead, to Benbow's horror, she gave perjured testimony against his client, insisting that Goodwin had murdered the halfwit and raped her with a corncob. In the courtroom in Jefferson, Temple was the picture of female duplicity, sitting there in her black hat, her hair escaping in tight red curls "like clots of resin," her blond legs slanted, her eyes fixed on something at the back of the room, "her mouth painted into a savage and perfect bow." After the court convicted the doomed bootlegger, men on the square said of Temple, "She was some baby. Jeez. I wouldn't have used no cob."

Elsewhere in Dixie, Popeye was arrested and convicted of another murder, which he did not commit. Only now did his background come out, the cruel formative years—a syphilitic father, a demented grandmother who almost killed him when she set the house afire—that twisted him into a violent, impotent man. On the scaffold, he made a final gesture. "Pssst!" he whispered to the sheriff. "Fix my hair, Jack!"

In the closing scene, Temple was visiting Paris with her father; they strolled through the Luxembourg Gardens, where an old man "in a shabby brown overcoat" sailed toy boats on a pool. It was the old man Faulkner had watched during his own stay in Paris. While a band in the pavilion played Berlioz and Massenet, Temple sat on a bench beside her father, yawning behind her hand, seemingly unaffected by the appalling events she had left behind.

Faulkner looked on Temple and Popeye with morbid fascination. To him, all that evil sliding off Temple proved again that women were impermeable to it. And Popeye was a monster, a "protagonist of evil," as Faulkner described him. Still, as he said later, it was coincidental that Popeye appeared to symbolize the wickedness endemic to modern society, for Faulkner maintained that he was writing about people, not about symbols and ideas. Once he even felt compassion for Popeye, characterizing him as simply "another lost human being."

And so *Sanctuary* was done. He had made it as honest and moving and significant as he could. Now perhaps it wouldn't embarrass *The Sound and the Fury* and *As I Lay Dying* too much. He returned the galleys to New York; his share of the cost of resetting them came to $270 —"at a time when I didn't have $270." He claimed he had to take a job "passing coal" to pay for it.

A t christmastime, the Faulkners made it a custom to invite relatives and friends to Rowan Oak, to sip eggnog from a silver bowl in the parlor. By then, Estelle was almost seven months pregnant, but still terribly thin and frail. One bitter cold night in January 1931, she woke Faulkner and complained of pains. She thought it was the baby, but he was skeptical: the baby wasn't due until March. But when the pains kept coming, he called her doctor and rushed her to the hospital.

The next day, he gazed on a tiny baby girl, born two months prematurely, whom they christened Alabama after Faulkner's favorite aunt. The baby stirred his heart; she was such "a puny, little thing," almost too fragile to survive. Anxious about what to do with her, he conferred with Estelle's doctor, John C. Culley, a brusque, opinionated, handsome man Faulkner disliked. There was no incubator in the hospital, and bills were mounting, so Faulkner elected to take Alabama and her frail mother back to Rowan Oak. He was certain that he and Mammy Callie could look after them best.

The tiny child lay in a bassinet in the middle upstairs bedroom, where Malcolm and Cho-Cho, standing on tiptoes, looked down at her in wonder. Although Dr. Culley came every day and Faulkner and Mammy Callie tended to their every need, mother and child both took a turn for the worse. At dawn on January 20, an alarmed Mammy Callie shook Faulkner, asleep in an adjacent bedroom, and said it was the baby. They hurried to the bassinet, where Alabama was struggling to breathe. Frantically, he phoned Dr. Culley, but the doctor, curt as ever, said there was nothing he or anybody else could do for the child. Back at the bassinet, Faulkner and Mammy Callie looked on helplessly as Alabama, only ten days old, passed from this world.

Faulkner was devastated. He had loved Alabama more than anything, and now she was already gone from him, and he did not think he could bear the pain he felt. But even in his despair he took precautions not to awaken Estelle, who needed desperately to rest. Quietly, the family gathered for the funeral, with the dead child lying in a tiny casket before them. Then came the procession of automobiles out to the cemetery. On the way, Faulkner held the little casket in his lap, so numb from grief that he scarcely knew where they were. At the cemetery, he gave his daughter back to the earth, so that in some distant time it might give her breath again. Then Murry Falkner, tall and old and visibly moved, uttered a tender prayer to a departed grandchild he thought had resembled his son.

Back at Rowan Oak, Estelle lay in her bedroom, unaware of what had happened. Faulkner waited until she took a sedative, then entered and sat down beside her bed. Overwhelmed with grief and bitterness, he could not at first find the words to tell her. But finally it came out —"Alabama's dead, Estelle"—and then he cried. She had never seen him cry before.

"Bill," she said, "get you a drink."

"No," he said in his misery, "this is one time I'm not going to do it."

The rage came afterward, an almost paralyzing fury that fixed on Dr. Culley as the author of their misfortune. Faulkner fantasized about seeking violent retribution, as the Old Colonel would likely have done. Soon fantasy became reality in his mind, and he spread an apocryphal story that he had punished the doctor for refusing to come to Rowan Oak when Faulkner had called. He claimed that right after Alabama died, he had grabbed a gun, plunged into the dawn, summoned Dr. Culley from his home, and shot him with full intention to kill. But the bullet only wounded him, Faulkner said, and he recovered and didn't press charges. Faulkner added, "The bastard deserved to die."

He told the story many times, with various embellishments, until it passed into local lore. While it wasn't true, it revealed the depth of his grief and anger—and his guilt. Deep down, he feared that he was really to blame. If only he hadn't brought Alabama home from the hospital, if only he hadn't been asleep. . . . To assuage his guilt, he later contributed an incubator to the hospital. But nothing seemed to ease the hurt inside—not his work, not even furious hacking at the bitterweeds out in the pasture.

Sanctuary, the story of doomed people who had no home or sanctuary anywhere, appeared in February 1931 and created a sensation. Reviewers were shocked. The book was "putrid," an "inhuman monstrosity," even if it did have artistic power. But Faulkner had correctly gauged popular tastes: *Sanctuary* sold more copies in three weeks than the combined totals of *The Sound and the Fury* and *As I Lay Dying* since their publication. By April 1931, six to seven thousand Americans had bought the story of Temple Drake, Popeye, and Horace Benbow; by July, the book had gone into six printings, and one Maurice Edgar Coindreau, a professor of French literature at Princeton, had written Faulkner that he wanted to translate it into French. Yet, spectacular though its sales were for a Faulkner novel, *Sanctuary* was only a modest seller compared to the truly popular books of the season: Vicki Baum's *Grand Hotel,* Warwick Deeping's *The Bridge of Desire,* and Anne Green's *Reader, I Married Him.*

In Oxford, as elsewhere in Dixie, people reacted in horror—even when they hadn't read the book. What they wanted were tales about gallant gentlemen and pretty belles in crinoline, living romantically in columned mansions under the magnolias. What Faulkner gave them, they cried, was obscene and blasphemous. His in-laws were stunned. A cousin asked him face-to-face if he was drunk when he wrote such things. "Not always," Faulkner replied. One woman vowed never to speak to him again; another declared that she would rather have her right arm torn off than sign her name to such "filth." An Ole Miss professor could not fathom why anybody should write "a book like *that.*" Mac Reed, the druggist, did stock copies for local readers, but those bold enough to buy copies usually wanted theirs wrapped.

Murry, of course, was scandalized. Hell no, he hadn't read the book —and wasn't going to. "It's trash," he said. If his boy had to write, Murry stormed, why didn't he write westerns like Zane Grey? Johncy claimed that Murry was so mad about *Sanctuary* that he tried to suppress it. Even Dean, Faulkner's youngest brother and one of his most ardent admirers, admitted to a female friend that "the book isn't fit for a nice girl." Maud, however, stood resolutely behind her son, more than ever the darling of her life. When a woman asked how Billy could write such an outrageous book, Maud drew up straight, announced that "My Billy writes what he has to write," and never spoke to the lady again.

Stone defended Faulkner, too, though by now they had drifted even farther apart. Faulkner still regarded Stone as a close friend and frequently dropped by his law office for a visit or for legal counsel. But after *Sanctuary* appeared, Stone told Faulkner, "You don't need me any more," and added that he was through "reading manuscripts and fooling with writers." "I have to see about making a living for my old folks," Stone said.

In truth, Stone was in dire financial straits. The Depression had hit Mississippi, the poorest state in the Union, with crushing force. A searing drought had set in, burning up corn and cotton fields across Mississippi, and the combination of drought and plummeting cotton prices imperiled the state's entire fragile economy, based as it was on agriculture. In all directions, banks foreclosed on farmers who failed to pay their mortgages; croppers and tenant farmers faced eviction, even starvation; unemployment soared; and banks and businesses toppled. In 1930, fifty-nine banks had closed their doors in Mississippi; fifty-six more would fail in 1931. Conditions were desperate all over America, but nowhere worse than in this impoverished state, where annual per capita income began a disastrous plunge—to an incredible $177 by 1933.

In Oxford, people found themselves out of work, their savings lost, their hopes shattered. General Stone, Phil's father, had lost his bank and faced $50,000 worth of debts, bankruptcy, and dishonor. A proud man and a loyal son, Phil Stone assumed his father's debts and vowed to pay them off—an act of great personal sacrifice, since his only income derived from a small-town law practice in the midst of the Depression. Stone struggled under the staggering burden of his father's debts, fending off creditors, battling lawsuits, in a desperate attempt to uphold the family honor.

By the time *Sanctuary* appeared, Stone really did have little time for Faulkner's writing, really did have to care for his "old folks." But there was more to their estrangement than that. Because Stone had lost his proprietary status with his onetime protégé, he felt injured, deeply ambivalent about "Bill," even hostile. He could say that Faulkner had "made a great reputation," that "no one in the world knows him and his progress in writing as well as I do," and that he was "the sanest and most wholesome person I have ever known." On the other hand, he could assert that Faulkner was "the most aggravating damned human being the Lord ever put on this earth," and that he lacked the humility, maybe even the talent, "to ever become truly great."

SUMMER 1931 came with scorching heat and deepening depression. At Rowan Oak, Faulkner and Estelle were both going through a bad time. Estelle was down with an intractable anemia, the result of her difficult pregnancy and the loss of her child. Faulkner worried about Estelle's health and commiserated with her sorrow, for Alabama's death still tortured him, too. To make matters worse, he had little money— royalties from *Sanctuary* weren't due until September. Hal Smith agreed to publish a collection of his stories, including the popular "A Rose for Emily," under the title *These Thirteen*. But that scarcely relieved Faulkner's immediate financial needs. With so many troubles, he found it difficult to work. He wrote Ben Wasson in New York, "I may be up there in the fall. I hope so. I need a change. I'm stale. Written out."

But in August he heard the voices again, Civil War voices this time, and with them the pounding hooves of cavalry horses. A vision flashed before him of Earl Van Dorn's 1862 raid on Grant's supplies at Holly Springs. Then a character appeared named Gail Hightower, a tall, gaunt-shouldered man, with skin the color of a flour sack. He was a doctor of divinity, and his grandfather had died in that raid. But in Faulkner's imagination, the scene of action shifted from Holly Springs to occupied Jefferson, in Yoknapatawpha County. In the story taking shape in his mind, it was in Jefferson that the rebel cavalry came thundering down the streets to sack the Yankee stores, here that Hightower's grandfather fell from a Yankee bullet. Two generations later, Gail Hightower returned to Jefferson in hopes that he, too, could be heroic and do something bold and tragic like his ancestor. He would sit alone in the shadows of his house, preoccupied with that moment of glory when his grandfather's cavalry had swept into Jefferson, fearing that nothing remained for him, that all the heroism and honor belonged to his grandfather's time. In his youth, Faulkner himself had known that fear.

A novel was struggling for birth, but Faulkner couldn't get it in focus. Tentatively he called it *Dark House*, which captured Hightower's reveries on several levels. But Faulkner wasn't pleased with the initial jottings on the desk before him. What were the voices saying to him? What was trying to come out about the dark house?

One late afternoon that August, he and Estelle were sipping drinks on the east gallery and gazing across the grass at the sunken garden. At this time of year in Mississippi, there was often a luminous quality to the twilight that made it seem centuries old, Faulkner thought, a twilight for classical times, for fauns, satyrs, and gods. Presently, Estelle said, "Bill, does it ever seem to you that the light in August is different from any other time of the year?"

Faulkner stood up. "That's it." And he walked inside to his worktable, crossed out "Dark House," and wrote "Light in August" as the title of his new novel. For it was at twilight, "in the lambent suspension of August," that Hightower brooded over the vision of the cavalry charge, as coming night surrounded itself "with a faint glow like a halo."

And so Faulkner began *Light in August,* conceived like *The Sound and the Fury* at a time of acute personal suffering. As he toiled at his writing table, other characters emerged as counterpoints to Hightower —a serene, strapping country girl on the road in search of her runaway lover, a strange, hostile, death-bearing man who did not know who or what he was. Yet Faulkner struggled with his composition, experiencing none of the ecstasy he had felt in writing *The Sound and the Fury,* the novel he still loved best. Each morning, he sat down without the anticipation and joy that alone made writing a pleasure for him; he moved his characters around and shifted scenes, searching for the right narrative stratagems to make the story cohere. As he said later, "I was deliberately choosing among possibilities and probabilities of behavior and weighing and measuring each choice by the scale of the Jameses and Conrads and Balzacs. I knew that I had read too much, that I had reached that stage which all young writers must pass through, in which he believes that he had learned too much about his trade."

In October, he left Rowan Oak to attend a southern writers' conference at the University of Virginia, with plans to travel on to New York. He detested literary conferences, but it was a chance to get away, see Charlottesville, and talk to Hal Smith in New York about his financial needs. Estelle also thought the trip would be good for him, and Hal offered to pay his train fare and some of his expenses; and so he went, taking his manuscript with him.

The farther he got from Rowan Oak, the more he missed his sickly wife. Their marriage, in deep trouble before Alabama's death, had rebounded in the terrible ordeal they had shared. Faulkner had even dedicated *These Thirteen* to her and Alabama. When he reached Charlottesville, he wrote Estelle a tender letter about how grand the autumn was here and how much he cared for her. "I dont think that I will need to tell you to give my love to the children, any more than to tell you that you already have about 1,000,000 tons of it yourself. But I do, nevertheless. Get well fast, darling, darling, darling."

Anxious and insecure, he turned up at the writers' conference wearing an aviation cap—he had served in the Canadian air force, he explained. The conference was a disaster for him. He detested the endless rounds of talks, addresses, receptions, detested all the attention he received. His Mississippi novels, especially *The Sound and the Fury* and

Sanctuary, had made his reputation in southern literary circles, and he was far and away the most popular writer there, even more popular than Sherwood Anderson, who studiously avoided him. "The focal point of every gaze," as one reporter observed, Faulkner felt exposed and vulnerable. While conversation and argument raged around him, he would only murmur, "I dare say." Unable to escape or endure an intolerable situation, he yielded to "the chemistry of craving," as he described it, and got drunk and stayed that way for the rest of the conference. When people approached him at one reception, he vomited.

Fortunately for him, Hal Smith had come down for the conference and managed to get him away to New York. But when other publishers tried to court the author of *Sanctuary,* Smith had him smuggled out of town and sent him to Florida and then South Carolina until the pursuit stopped. By early November, Faulkner was sober and back in the city, asserting that he didn't like literary people, never associated with other writers, and was here only to see Hal Smith, "my one friend in the North."

At once the clamor started up again, as magazine editors swept him off to luncheons and publishers hounded him with contract offers. Viking, Alfred A. Knopf, and Random House all tried to woo him. Faulkner was utterly bewildered. Four years ago nobody in New York wanted to publish him. Now, thanks to *Sanctuary,* editors and publishers were battling for his favors. "It's just like I was some strange and valuable beast," he wrote Estelle.

Smith, with his nose twitching nervously, did his best to keep Faulkner sober and close by. The house of Cape and Smith was in serious financial trouble and couldn't afford to lose an author of Faulkner's stature. As it turned out, Cape and Smith dissolved their firm while Faulkner was in New York, and Smith formed a new one under his own name—a brave move in the midst of the Depression—and wanted to take Faulkner with him. Faulkner might have secured better terms with another publisher, but he was loyal to Smith, the "one man I like." He turned down Viking, Knopf, and Random House. He was sticking with Hal.

In all, Faulkner spent seven weeks in New York, caught up in a whirlwind of receptions and parties. He kept asserting his dislike of such things, but after years of scorn and rejection, toiling virtually alone in the literary backwoods, he couldn't resist all the attention and flattery. "I have created a sensation," he wrote Estelle in mid-November.

"I have learned with astonishment that I am now the most important figure in American letters. . . . I'm glad I'm level-headed, not very vain. But I dont think it has gone to my head." He added that he was going to write a movie script for Tallulah Bankhead. "How's that for a high?"

Oh, he was high all right, as the stars of the New York salons lined up to pay him court. There was Bennett Cerf, the young cofounder of Random House, a tall, dark, bespectacled bachelor with a winning smile and a fund of anecdotes. Cerf made it clear how much he wanted to be Faulkner's publisher: he bought *Sanctuary* for his Modern Library series, took Faulkner to lunch, and invited him to soirees at his posh apartment overlooking Central Park South.

There was Dorothy Parker, poet, playwright, short story writer, and celebrated conversationalist, who introduced Faulkner to the Round Table, the literary group that met at the Algonquin Hotel. Though Faulkner thought they were "showing off," he enjoyed "Miss Dorothy." She was a small woman with plaintive, hands-to-bosom gestures and a savage wit. For a time, everything malicious or brilliant said in New York was attributed to her. Observing her in action against a flirtatious southern blonde, Faulkner told Ben Wasson: "Miss Dorothy is a mighty tough lady, ain't she?" Even so, she was sensitive to Faulkner's vulnerabilities. "You just wanted to protect him," she recalled.

He did meet other writers he liked, among them Dashiell Hammett and Lillian Hellman Kober. Twenty-six and New Orleans born, Hellman had a special rapport with Faulkner, a fellow southerner: she had been the reader at Boni & Liveright who gave *Mosquitoes* the rave report back in 1926. She was a prominent screenwriter now, not to mention an aspiring playwright, and "Dash" Hammett's lover and companion. Red-haired and Jewish, she was a stylish dresser, ambitious, idealistic, and fiercely independent; she delighted in salty language, but refused to tolerate Hammett's promiscuous ways, refused to accept his contention that this was "the way men are." Eleven years older than she, Hammett was a tall, thin, white-haired man, a popular mystery writer, and a legendary boozer and womanizer. When Faulkner met him, he was in bad shape, plagued with headaches and a suicidal gloom; he may have actually tried to kill himself that autumn. He had read *Sanctuary* and thought Faulkner had "a nice taste in the morbid and gruesome," but was "overrated." It drove Dash crazy that Faulkner could knock out books the way he did, and yet was as big a drunk as Hammett. Still, Faulkner was "a hell of a nice guy and good drinking buddy," and the three of them spent long intemperate evenings together, boozing and fraternizing at obscure watering holes.

By then, Faulkner was off on another binge and unable to stop. One day he and Hammett, both wearing tweeds, turned up drunk at a formal dinner party given by Blanche Knopf, the publisher's wife. Horrified, Bennett Cerf lectured them to behave themselves, and they tried to be quiet as they swiped glasses from trays that went by and gazed at couples in tuxedos and evening gowns. Soon Hammett slid off the couch onto the floor and passed out. Faulkner, however, seemed perfectly sober. He stood, announced his departure—and collapsed. As someone helped Hammett away, Faulkner rose again, repeated that he was leaving, and once more sank to the carpet. Luckily for him, Wasson was there and helped get his inebriated friend back to his hotel.

Not long after that Faulkner disappeared. Nobody knew where he was. Several days later Hal Smith and a woman from his office found him at the Algonquin; he was agitated and didn't want to be alone. They drank with him until midnight, then tried to get him to bed. But he protested: he couldn't sleep without a bottle. How would they like to wake up at three in the morning without a bottle? They procured one for him, and afterward Smith talked to Wasson, who wired Estelle to come up as soon as possible. Anemic though she was, Estelle caught the train in Memphis, eager to see New York as well as to help Billy. In Memphis, she boasted that her husband was going to Hollywood.

When she reached New York, Faulkner was glad to see her, but fretted about her health. She appeared exhausted, her eyes enormous in her thin face. One look at her husband told her that he was in trouble. He said he had taken about all the parties and pressures he could stand. She tried to shield him, to ward off invitations, but how could she resist New York? She adored the glamour and excitement. Soon both of them were swept up in the social whirl, lunching with celebrities and attending parties at the Algonquin. But each worried about the other's drinking too much.

Already in precarious health, Estelle couldn't handle the strain. Worn down from all the excitement and drinking, she showed signs of deep emotional stress. At one of the Algonquin parties, with Faulkner sitting on the floor beside a glass of bourbon, Estelle got into an unpleasant argument with Hal Smith's wife. After a shopping expedition with Dorothy Parker, she became hysterical, ripped her dress, and threatened to kill herself. Parker was astonished at her behavior. So was playwright Marc Connelly, who often came to the Algonquin. To Connelly, Estelle appeared "a very nervous girl" who occasionally had strange mental lapses, or slips in her thinking. When this occurred one night, Connelly remembered, Faulkner looked at Estelle "quite objectively, without a bit of reproachment," then reached out and slapped her face, hard. According to Connelly, "she went right back to completely normal conduct, and Bill, without any apologies or anything else, continued whatever he had been talking about."

Cerf remembered another night, at a party in his Manhattan apartment. Estelle stood at a window, gazing at the glittering skyline. She shivered. "When I see all this beauty," she told Cerf, "I feel just like throwing myself out the window."

Alarmed, Cerf pulled her back. "Oh now, Estelle, you don't mean that."

Her eyes widened. "What do you mean?" she said passionately. *"Of course I do."*

Sober now and concerned about Estelle, Faulkner was ready to go home. Cerf gave them a farewell party, but Estelle grew bored with all the literary talk and retired to another room to read. Cerf followed her, put on a record, and asked her to dance. Around a man she found attractive, Estelle could be "kittenish" and "altogether seductive," as Wasson put it. While unhappily married to Cornell Franklin, she had kissed Wasson in a moment of passion. Now, unhappily married to Faulkner and deeply troubled, she danced for a long time with Cerf, flattered that this wealthy New York bachelor could find her charming. Before she left New York, he gave her a photograph of himself.

When the Faulkners reached Rowan Oak, Estelle put the photograph next to one of her husband on the mantel. Malcolm was certain she did it to irritate Mr. Bill. As for Mr. Bill, he said he'd never been "so tired of literary people in his life." He even went on the wagon, allowing himself only one dispensation: a bowl of eggnog with a pipe and a book at Christmastime.

FORTIFIED BY BLACK COFFEE, Faulkner devoted three profitable months to *Light in August,* his most complicated novel thus far. In the midst of his composition, he did something rare for him: he granted an interview to Henry Nash Smith, an English professor from Southern Methodist University, who found him standing in front of a coal fire in the library, wearing a blue shirt and carpet slippers. Faulkner's comments revealed something of his thinking about the new novel. He insisted that he had no theory of fiction, but believed he had passed through three stages in his attitude toward people and thus toward his characters. "There is the first stage when you believe everything and everybody is good. Then there is the second, cynical stage when you believe that no one is good. Then at last you come to realize that everyone is capable of almost anything—heroism or cowardice, tenderness or cruelty."

Which was a major theme of *Light in August,* whose characters were among the most complex and contradictory Faulkner had ever conceived. By the time he finished the book, in February 1932, and started revisions, his people were more vivid to him than his stepchildren and unhappy wife in another part of the house. The story now began with Lena Grove, one of two central figures, the serene, strapping young country girl who had left Alabama in search of the feckless man who had seduced her and fathered her child. Six months pregnant now, she faced her task with an "inwardlighted" serenity, her face pleasant and friendly under her faded blue sunbonnet. Her travels brought her to the small town of Jefferson, Mississippi, the home of the Compsons, Sartorises, and Benbows. It was also the home of four isolated people whose lives and fates were to become dramatically linked with her own.

One was Byron Bunch, who worked at the Jefferson planing mill and led a country church choir. Like Faulkner, he was a small, nondescript, compassionate man living on the fringe of the community. When he first met Lena, Byron fell in love with her and became her devoted companion. As it turned out, Byron's only friend in Jefferson was Gail Hightower, the eccentric recluse and sometime amateur physician, whose preoccupations with the Civil War had given Faulkner his initial inspiration for *Light in August.* Hightower had once been the minister of the Presbyterian church in Jefferson. But he had lost everything now —his church, his wife, and his spirit—and lived "outside life" in his lonely house, obsessed with the heroic deeds of his Civil War grandfather, much as Faulkner had been with the Old Colonel's. As the story progressed, Byron Bunch drew Hightower back to the present, back into life, by involving him in Lena's difficulties and those of the other central figure and Lena's counterpoint, Joe Christmas.

Christmas was one of Faulkner's most memorable creations. Indeed, he was "the tragic, central idea of the story," as Faulkner said later, for Christmas had no idea who or what he was—"didn't know whether he was part Negro or not," and would never know. Yet he feared he was, and it poisoned him. At a Memphis orphanage, where he grew up, a female dietician called him a "little nigger bastard" and tried to have him transferred to a Negro orphanage, and there began the destructive confusion about his identity that was to ruin his life. It was also the first of several damaging experiences with women that twisted him, too. Faulkner could sympathize with Christmas, for he carried permanent scars himself from the women in his life. As a young adult, Christmas had an affair with a small, blond, childlike waitress named Bobbie. Despite the fact that she was a part-time prostitute, Christmas wanted to marry her; he even confided to her that he thought he had some Negro blood. One terrible night, Bobbie blew up at Christmas; two of her friends beat and robbed him. "He told me himself he was a nigger!" Bobbie screamed. "The son of a bitch! Me f---ing for nothing a nigger son of a bitch."

Tormented by what had happened, Christmas wandered aimlessly for fifteen furious years, running through a thousand savage and lonely streets in search of peace, perversely telling people he was part Negro, provoking fights, and copulating with women of both races, until at age thirty-three he turned up in Jefferson, a hostile, death-bearing man whose gaunt face had the color of dead parchment. As Faulkner perceived him, Christmas was a southern version of the completely alienated man. Determined to establish a lonely identity beyond black or white, he took up bootlegging, wore a white straw hat, lodged at the Burden place, and made violent love to its proprietress, Joanna.

Joanna Burden was a plump spinster in her forties, with a long, prominent, almost manlike face. Her inheritance, like Hightower's, haunted and imprisoned her, cutting her off from the rest of the community. Her abolitionist parents and grandfather had come to Jefferson after the Civil War to educate and help the former slaves. Her grandfather and brother had both been murdered by Colonel Sartoris for attempting to register Negro voters, and her father had warned her that the Negro race was "doomed and cursed to be forever and ever a part of the white race's doom and curse for its sins." She felt as Faulkner felt: "I had seen and known Negroes since I could remember. I just looked at them as I did at rain, or furniture, or food or sleep. But after that I seemed to see them for the first time not as people, but as a thing, a shadow in which I lived, we lived, all white people, all other people. I thought of all the children coming forever and ever into the world, white, with the black shadow already falling upon them before they drew breath. And I seemed to see the black shadow in the shape of a cross." And now, with her father dead and buried, too, she lived alone in a dark house on the edge of town, cursed by the thing her ancestors had abominated, atoning for that curse as an ardent benefactor for Negroes and Negro institutions, somehow enduring her "burden" with a brave and quiet dignity.

When Joe Christmas entered her life, she surrendered to him without tears or self-pity, and they became desperate lovers, the prim spinster and this twisted man who thought himself "part nigger." And it released forbidden lusts in Joanna, who gasped "Negro, Negro, Negro" as she thrust at him in bed, thus denying him the peace he yearned for. Christmas watched her pass through every avatar of a woman in love: she was seized with fits of jealousy, she trapped him in lies, then wept and cried at him. But then she abandoned her perverse ways, embraced religion, and tried to convert Christmas himself into a missionary to Negroes and manager of her affairs. Christmas couldn't stand her female possessiveness. When she started praying over him, he bristled with hatred. He felt the violence gathering in him *(I am going to do something)* and then slashed her throat with a razor, set the house afire, and fled into the woods. But a week later he emerged, the picture of defiance now, determined to face his doom like a man. Feeling a measure of peace in that, he strode boldly into Mottstown, bought a new shirt, a tie, and a straw hat with money stolen from the dead Joanna, and walked the streets "like he owned the town." When asked, he admitted straight out that he was Christmas and offered no resistance when the sheriff took him off to jail in Jefferson. And that was what caused the angry crowd to form: "He never denied it," the townfolk said. "He never acted like either a nigger or a white man. That was it. That was what made the folks so mad."

Meanwhile Byron Bunch had told Hightower about Christmas and the ghastly events at the Burden place. By degrees, Byron had been drawing him out of his lonely reveries, and Hightower felt compassion now. "Is it certain, proved, that he has Negro blood?" he asked about Christmas. "Think, Byron; what it will mean when the people—if they catch . . . Poor man. Poor mankind." When Christmas was arrested and jailed, Byron implored Hightower to save the doomed man, by saying that he was with Hightower on the night Joanna was murdered. Hightower refused to do that; he couldn't tell a lie to save a murderer. But at Byron's urging he did deliver Lena's child—in a cabin she was now occupying at the Burden place. Hightower was elated. "I showed them!" he thought. And he walked home like a man with a purpose. Life had come to him, after all. Lena had given that to him; she had given both life and love to Byron. The simple country girl had saved them both.

But there was no hope for Christmas. On the very day Lena's baby was born, Christmas unaccountably broke away from a clutch of lawmen and ran handcuffed through the town, with a special deputy in close pursuit, a fanatical young racist and chauvinist named Percy Grimm. Christmas raced first to a Negro cabin, then sprinted to Hightower's place, entered by the back steps, struck the minister with a pistol, and barricaded himself behind a kitchen table—but refused to shoot when Grimm burst into the room. In a sadistic rage, Grimm shot Christmas five times and then castrated him. When other lawmen reached the kitchen and saw what was happening, one of them gave a choked cry and vomited. Grimm sprung back, flung the bloody butcher knife away. "Now you'll let white women alone, even in hell." Christmas lay there with his eyes open and something, a shadow, about his mouth, until his face, body, all appeared to collapse in on itself, and from the slashed garments about his loins "the pent up black blood seemed to rush like a released breath."

Some weeks later, Lena Grove, as innocent of evil as Christmas was its victim, left Jefferson with Byron and her baby. A repairman and furniture dealer who gave them a ride could not fathom what a good-looking gal like her was doing with a nondescript like Byron. Once he saw Byron crawl into the truck where mother and baby were sleeping, and nothing happened to the count of fifteen or so, "and then I heard one kind of astonished sound she made when she woke up, like she was just surprised and then a little put out without being scared at all, and she says, not loud neither, 'Why, Mr. Bunch. Aint you ashamed. You might have woke the baby, too.' " And so the curtain closed on Lena, as it had opened. Reaching Tennessee, she sighed and said, "My, my. A body does get around. Here we ain't been coming from Alabama but two months, and now it's already Tennessee."

Faulkner felt great compassion for Lena and Byron, for Christmas,

Hightower, and Joanna Burden: his own complexity as a man allowed him to embrace their attitudes with equal insight and sensitivity. Yet he admired gentle Lena most of all, for she was "the captain of her soul," as he put it later. Like Caddy Compson, he said, Lena knew her destiny, which was to have a husband and children, and she attended to that without asking for help, without confusion, fright, or alarm. Hers was the strength of the earth, Faulkner believed, which was different from Dilsey's strength, which came from oppression. But like Dilsey, Lena radiated passive courage and endurance, traits Faulkner greatly valued. And her speech to Byron about waking the baby warmed Faulkner's heart. It was, he recalled, "one of the calmest, sanest speeches I ever heard."

When he finished his typescript in March 1932, he was exhausted and broke. Cape and Smith owed him $4,000 from the sales of *Sanctuary,* but when his former publisher had liquidated, all its assets, including Faulkner's royalties, had been frozen. He would never receive a dime of that money. To make matters worse, Estelle had run up charge accounts in Memphis and Oxford, which had to be settled. And he needed money for household expenses and repairs, not to mention taxes and insurance. His financial worries only exacerbated the inevitable depression that followed the completion of a novel. And he and Estelle quarreled, about her spending, about his writing all the time on his novel. At one point she got so angry at him that she flung *Light in August* out of their car, and he had to chase down the scattering pages.

With his finances a shambles, Faulkner tried to serialize *Light in August* in the magazines, but nothing came of that; he had to settle for whatever it would earn in book form. Desperate for money right away, he jumped at an offer from Metro-Goldwyn-Mayer to come out to Hollywood and write screenplays for six weeks at $500 a week, beginning May 7. But he was so destitute that he had to borrow $5 to wire his acceptance. At his request, the studio sent money to cover an overdraft at the bank and buy his train ticket.

He said goodbye to his mother, who was living with Murry in a little house on South Lamar which she had designed; Murry had retired from the university and was sickly now, bothered by a bad back, irritated by doctors who ordered him to give up fried foods. The family saw him pacing back and forth on the front gallery, "almost like a demented person." To Faulkner, he seemed bored with living.

In early May, Faulkner boarded a train for Los Angeles. He was afraid of what awaited him out there in that strange city. What if he couldn't write movie scripts? He had no experience at it, no training. How he hated to leave the security of Rowan Oak and his writing desk, even if he and Estelle were not getting along. It was terrible that a man of thirty-four, with six novels published and another in press, had to leave his work in order to make enough money to do the work.

The train roared westward across deserts and mountains he had never seen before.

Billy Falkner (center) with his brothers, circa 1910–1911: Jack (left), Johncy (right), and Dean (front).

Estelle Oldham

Childhood sweethearts: Estelle Oldham and Billy Falkner. Billy gave her a gold ring with "F" carved on it in gothic, and they reached a private understanding that somehow, in some special way, they belonged to one another. But in 1918, to Billy's bitter despair, Estelle married Cornell Franklin.

Phil Stone, Billy Falkner's garrulous and well-educated first mentor, put him through a veritable seminar in literature and urged and browbeat him to become the poet Stone thought he could be. In the early 1920s, the two friends often sallied forth in Stone's wire-wheeled Ford coupe and headed for Memphis and its flourishing bordellos and casinos.

Ben Wasson was so excessively courteous that Falkner initially thought him "a young Galahad who's just gotten off a rocking horse." Wasson became Billy Falkner's close friend at Ole Miss and later served as his agent and editor.

Back from Canada, December 1918, Billy Falkner was now William Faulkner. His few months service as an RAF cadet in Canada inspired him to play out a charade for gullible folk in Oxford. With suitable props—a cane and an RAF lieutenant's uniform—Faulkner artfully impersonated a wounded aviator and war hero.

The poet, 1924, posing for a publicity photograph for *The Marble Faun,* his first published book. Stone said, "We wanted him to look like a romantic poet —you know, like Byron with his thrown-back head and flowing tie. Except we couldn't put on him a tie like that."

Sherwood Anderson, Faulkner's second mentor, helped turn him to narrative fiction. During their talks in New Orleans, Anderson urged his young friend to write about "that little patch up there in Mississippi where you started from."

Faulkner in Paris, 1925, with a newly grown beard. Faulkner thought the beard made him look "sort of distinguished," but admitted that a female relative he met in Paris "could see right through it to the little boy I used to be."

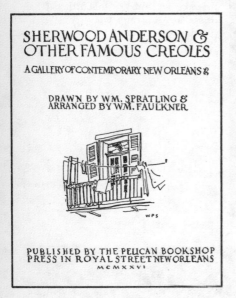

SHERWOOD ANDERSON &
OTHER FAMOUS CREOLES

A GALLERY OF CONTEMPORARY NEW ORLEANS &

DRAWN BY WM. SPRATLING &
ARRANGED BY WM. FAULKNER

WPS

PUBLISHED BY THE PELICAN BOOKSHOP
PRESS IN ROYAL STREET NEW ORLEANS
MCMXXVI

THE LOCALE, WHICH INCLUDES MRS. FLO FIELD

In 1926, Faulkner and artist William Spratling collaborated on *Sherwood Anderson & Other Famous Creoles,* which was privately printed in New Orleans. The sketch on the right shows the neighborhood in which French Quarter artists congregated.

Spratling's caricature of Anderson, which appeared as the frontispiece of *Creoles*, and Faulkner's satirical foreword, left the older writer unamused.

The last sketch in *Creoles* was a self-caricature of the two collaborators, complete with Faulkner's whiskey jugs and inevitable glass. Faulkner's capacity for drink was already phenomenal.

Helen Baird, Faulkner's second great love, was a blunt and caustic young woman with a fashionably boyish figure. She did not return his affections and desire, however, and ultimately broke his heart by marrying Guy Lyman.

Faulkner in 1931, posing for publicity shots for a UPI write-up on *Sanctuary*. Put off by the whole procedure, he wore an old tweed coat and white seersucker pants smeared with paint.

Estelle Faulkner with Jill, 1933. Faulkner had married his childhood sweetheart after her divorce from Cornell Franklin. She had expensive tastes in clothes, especially exotic gowns and hats. Although this was a relatively peaceful time for the Faulkners, their marriage became increasingly unstable, fraught with drunken arguments and mutual lack of understanding, and made even more difficult by Faulkner's extra-marital affairs.

Meta Carpenter, Faulkner's Hollywood mistress, loved him deeply and wanted to marry him. He was grateful for her devotion. "You save my damned life out here, Meta," he told her. "You keep me alive and sane."

Faulkner circa 1936, in one of the most difficult periods of his life, when he was grieving over Dean's death, drinking heavily, fighting with Estelle, carrying on a love affair with Meta, and working on film scripts in hated Hollywood. Yet it was in this period that he completed perhaps his greatest novel, *Absalom, Absalom!,* which appeared in October 1936.

Howard Hawks, the noted film director, engaged Faulkner again and again to write or revise screenplays for his movies. Faulkner detested Hollywood, but he liked working for Hawks. "Writing for pictures is not exactly my racket," Faulkner said, "but I get along with him." In fact, the two men enjoyed one another's company and became close friends.

The writer in his library sanctuary at Rowan Oak, posing with his cherished old portable. He actually composed in longhand—"I've got to feel the pencil and see the words at the end of the pencil," he said. But he wrote so rapidly, often in a demon-driven fury, that he had to type up a day's work lest he not be able to read it the next morning.

Winner of the 1949 Nobel Prize for Literature. "I believe that man will not merely endure: he will prevail."

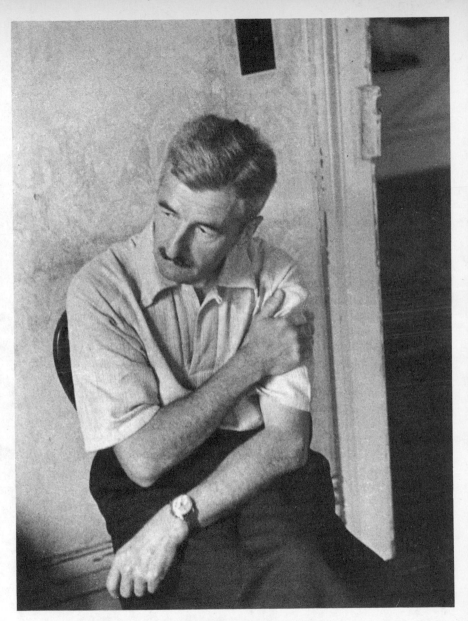

Even at Rowan Oak, Faulkner had to contend with that mortal enemy of prize-winning artists: an incessant public clamor for photographs, interviews, and details of his private life. Yet, as he told Malcolm Cowley, "It is my ambition to be, as a private individual, abolished and voided from history, leaving it markless, no refuse save the printed books."

When Faulkner was with Joan Williams, thirty-one years his junior, it was like walking in April again. "I do need you," he once wrote her. "So I can believe again that work is worthwhile and do it. . . . Damn it, I want somebody to give to," somebody "to say yes, yes to me and I want to say yes, yes, yes to the dear face in return."

With Saxe and Dorothy Commins, Princeton, Thanksgiving, 1952. Saxe was not only Faulkner's editor, but his close personal friend and confidant. Commins booked Faulkner's plane flights and hotel rooms, accepted awards for him, listened to his marital troubles, saw him through his binges, and looked after him in countless other ways.

Faulkner and Estelle at Rowan Oak, May 1955. The previous year, Estelle had almost filed for divorce, complaining to Saxe Commins about Faulkner's drunkenness and infidelity. In 1957, Estelle did offer him a divorce, but Faulkner refused; in the end, they reconciled and stayed together.

Jill Faulkner Summers, 1959, on the University of Virginia campus in Charlottesville. After their marriage in 1954, Jill and her husband Paul had settled in Charlottesville and started a family. Two and a half years later, Faulkner became writer-in-residence at the University, and he and Estelle began dividing their time between Oxford and Charlottesville. For Jill, growing up with a hard-drinking, creative father had not been easy, but by 1959 she was amazed at how much he had changed. "He had in a sense finished the creative side of his life and wanted to have something else," she said. "He became so much easier for everyone to live with—not just family, but everybody."

The aging man of letters, cultural emissary, and public spokesman had come a long way from the often barefoot Bohemian of early Oxford days.

PART FOUR

SOJOURNS
DOWN
RIVER

Hᴇ sᴛᴏᴏᴅ ᴏɴ ᴛʜᴇ ᴅᴜsᴛʏ ᴏᴜᴛsᴋɪʀᴛs of Los Angeles, a lonely little man from Mississippi, staring at MGM's Culver City studio. MGM was the biggest motion picture company in Hollywood, grossing $100 million a year even in the Depression, and the sheer size of its operation overwhelmed him. He had scarcely met his superior when he bolted the studio. A week later he returned. He had been wandering in Death Valley, he said, a hundred and fifty miles away. He was contrite and ready to work now, determined to get through his enslavement here.

His first assignment was to prepare a "treatment"—a synopsis of a story line and its characters that prepared the ground for an actual script. This was far different from the rolling narrative sequences, uninterrupted monologues, and flashbacks that he liked to use in his fiction. "I have not got used to this work," he wrote home. "But I am as well as anyone can be in this bedlam."

Faulkner was soon "homesick as the devil." He was too mad and too busy to write Wasson, who had helped get him this infernal job. He liked nothing about Hollywood: the thankless work, the mayhem, the loud extroverts who gave him orders, the pretentious people. Once a gushing woman said, "Mr. Faulkner, I understand that an author always puts himself in his books. Which character are you in *Sanctuary?*" "Madam," Faulkner retorted, "I was the corncob."

When his contract ended in late July, he would have gone home had it not been for Howard Hawks, the noted movie director. Hawks had read Faulkner's work, ranked him among "the most talented writers of this generation," and wanted to make a movie based on Faulkner's "Turn About," a story about aviators of the Great War that had appeared in the *Saturday Evening Post.* A slim six-footer with blue eyes and silver-blond hair parted in the middle, Hawks exuded confidence and a potent charm. He persuaded MGM to renew Faulkner's contract, convinced him to write the treatment, and then offered him a drink. As it developed, Hawks matched Faulkner shot for shot. The next morning, he woke up in a motel room in Culver City and saw Faulkner groping for cigarette stubs in a mint julep glass.

It was the beginning of a close collaboration and friendship. A year older than Faulkner, Hawks had a droll sense of humor and a lifelong passion for stories and machines. He had driven racing cars, flown planes in the army, and still thundered about on a motorcycle. He was fascinated with "rugged individualism" and daredevil pilots, and it showed in films like *The Dawn Patrol,* his ninth as director. And now, with Faulkner's help, this deliberate, hard-drinking man set to work adapting "Turn About" into another film about aerial combat, to star Gary Cooper, Franchot Tone, and Robert Young.

In the ensuing weeks, Hawks put Faulkner through a crash course in how to write screenplays, pointing out that the complex techniques of flashbacks and montages employed in his fiction would not work for motion pictures. Hawks left tricks and fancy experimentation to the Europeans. "The first thing I want is a story," Hawks said; "the next thing I want is character." Hawks showed Faulkner what he meant, helping him develop a treatment into a full script with dialogue. As it turned out, though, MGM wanted Joan Crawford to be one of the stars, and they had to revise the script to accommodate a female role. That, Hawks said, was the film business.

Hawks appreciated Faulkner's work, praising him for his inventiveness, his ability to solve problems and "to characterize the visual imagination." Faulkner returned the compliment. "I like working for Hawks," he said. "Writing for pictures is not exactly my racket, but I get along with him."

The galleys of *Light in August* arrived, but Faulkner was too busy with *Turn About* to read them. Then on August 7 came news from home. His father had died of a heart attack early that morning, just short of his sixty-second birthday. With the galleys and the movie script, Faulkner returned to Oxford for the funeral. He felt little sense of loss, for the man being lowered into his grave at St. Peter's Cemetery had never been a father to him—had never understood or approved of him, or given him enough love. Still, as the oldest son, Faulkner was the head of the clan now; he must look after the welfare of the family, as his grandfather and the Old Colonel had done. "It was a natural role for him," Jack said, "and he assumed it at once, without fanfare but with dignity and purpose." Murry had left Maud solvent for about a year. "Then it is me," Faulkner wrote Wasson. He would have to look after Dean, too, who still lived at home. And Jack and John, if they ever needed him.

In his library, sitting at the little table his mother had given him, he finished the film script and mailed it off to Hawks, then turned to the neglected galleys of *Light in August*, long since due back in New York. What he found there irked him to the core. The copyeditor had little understanding of his style and almost no sympathy for his inventiveness, which included a number of compound words *(womansmelling, manvoice, backglaring)* in the manner of Joyce and John Dos Passos. Worse still, the editorial interrogations had an impatient, condescending tone. Faulkner's replies fairly bristled: "O.K. damn it." "O.K. as set, goddam it." "O.K. as set/and written/Jesus Christ." He returned the galleys with orders to let the book "stand as it is."

He wrote Hal Smith in September: "Things are going pretty well here. My father died last month, and what with getting his affairs straightened out and getting Hollywood out of my system by means of a judicious course of alcohol in mild though sufficient quantities before and after eating and lying down and getting up, I am not working now. But I seem to have a novel working in me; when the cool weather comes, I will probably start it."

But Hawks called him back to California for final revisions on the film script, now called *Today We Live,* and he left, swearing his hatred for Hollywood. Once back in Culver City, he received astounding news: Paramount had taken up the option on *Sanctuary;* the story of Temple Drake and Popeye was to be made into a movie. Faulkner's share of the sale came to more than $6,000—a small fortune for him. Back home in October—"thank God"—he appeared "justifiably pleased at this turn of events," a townsman said, "and in as good spirits as I had ever seen him."

He had other reasons for cheerful spirits. Despite Estelle's fragile health and the troubles between them, she was pregnant again. She was thirty-five now, but with proper care and a little luck, everything would go all right and he would be a father yet. For a Democrat like Faulkner, things were hopeful on the national front, too. In the presidential election that November, Franklin D. Roosevelt buried Republican incumbent Herbert Hoover by a margin of more than seven million popular votes; Roosevelt swept the "solid South," capturing 96 percent of the vote in beleaguered Mississippi. He had promised, in his warm and ringing voice, to end the Depression and launch a new deal for America, and Democrats everywhere were singing "Happy days are here again."

By then, *Light in August* had appeared under the imprint of a new house, Smith & Haas, which Hal Smith and Robert Haas had formed. But Faulkner was indifferent to the finished book. He said he "didn't even want to see what kind of jacket Smith had put on it." He had a vision of himself looking at a row of his books "with flagging attention which was almost distaste," until a voice seemed to say, "Thank God I shall never need to open any one of them again." He had even less interest in the reviews; in fact, he had stopped reading reviews altogether. Who knew the faults of his work better than he did? he liked to say. But his brother John thought he ignored reviews for another reason: he couldn't bear the pain of adverse criticism. "He was simply protecting himself from hurt," John said.

I<small>T WAS A DISPIRITING DECEMBER</small> at Rowan Oak. The weather turned rotten, and Faulkner was busy much of the time caring for a sick household. Estelle and the children were ill in rotation, and the day after Christmas, pregnant Estelle took a bad fall down the stairs and had to stay in bed for a couple of weeks. Well, at least Faulkner had a store of English tobacco and a keg of moonshine to help him cope.

At his writing table, he toiled on another accursed movie script—thanks to Hawks, MGM let him work in Oxford at regular wages, an unorthodox arrangement that raised hackles at Culver City. Meanwhile Faulkner had put together a collection of his verse called *A Green Bough*, which included mostly old poems, still derivative even with revisions; Smith agreed to publish the book, but Faulkner ignored his pleas for an introduction.

When it came to serious fiction, he felt uninspired, producing little of consequence that winter and spring of 1933. The spirit used to move him every day; had it deserted him now? Had he forgotten how to write during his "sojourn down river," in the servitude of Hollywood? For years he had written novels and stories with the voices singing to him. But they sang fleetingly now, if at all.

He took up flying as a diversion. Each week he made the seventy-mile trip to Memphis for lessons with Captain Vernon Omlie, who ran a flying school there. Aloft in Omlie's bright red Waco, a powerful biplane with a four-passenger cabin and brown leather bucket seats, Faulkner loved the drone of the 210-horsepower motor, the rush of the wind at his goggles. He had always wanted to do this, had told imaginative lies about getting shot down in France during the Great War, had written stories and helped produce a movie script about wartime aviators. Now he was making fantasy real. In April, he attended the premiere of *Today We Live* in Memphis, saw his name on the credits, and no doubt strongly identified with the aviators who flew and fought on the screen. Eight days later, he was ready to solo: he strode out to the Waco alone, wearing goggles and an aviator's cap, took it up in the steep, throbbing Waco climb, and circled against the skies for three quarters of an hour.

In May, MGM removed Faulkner from its payroll because studio people had complained about his unorthodox working arrangement. But thanks to months of regular pay and the movie sale of *Sanctuary,* released that May in a sanitized version called *The Story of Temple Drake,* Faulkner had more money in the bank than ever in his life. He splurged and bought Omlie's bright red Waco for himself. That summer a Memphis paper reported that the author of *Sanctuary* had found "peace in the sky."

O N A CLEAR NIGHT IN JUNE, the Faulkners went for a ride together, enjoying the soft moonlight that illuminated the countryside. On the way home, Estelle complained of pains. Faulkner didn't question her this time; he drove straight to the hospital, and at daybreak, June 25, 1933, she presented him with a healthy baby girl, whom they named Jill. At thirty-five, his hair beginning to gray, Faulkner was a father at last. Brought to see his new sister, Malcolm thought his mother was happy and noticed a rare smile on Mr. Bill's face. When they took the child home, Faulkner gathered the servants upstairs, handed out shot glasses, and proposed a toast to "little Miss Jill."

He adored little "Missy." She was his "heart's darling." He hovered over her bassinet with an aura of radiance about him. He was so proud of her, so thankful that she was healthy, that he vowed not to drink anything for a year. He lasted about four months before "the chemistry of craving" destroyed his resolve.

After Missy came, he worked "spasmodically" on a novel and wrote a few stories, but it was a dry season for his creative side. He flew a good deal in the Waco—he would have his pilot's license before the year was out—and often took his brother Dean up with him and Omlie. The fact was, he worried about his youngest brother, who was suffering from a broken love affair and seemed to lack purpose and direction in his life. Although he was twenty-six, Dean worked only when he felt like it, and still lived at home with Maud, who needed him for emotional security now that Murry was gone. Faulkner, seeing how much she depended on Dean, feared that he would never be able to leave. Faulkner knew about that danger—he had lived at home, on and off, until he had married Estelle.

To get Dean out of the house, Faulkner paid Omlie to give him flying lessons. As it turned out, Dean had a passion and a talent for flying that surpassed his big brother's. Soon he could pilot the Waco like a professional, putting her through loops, wingovers, and stalls. Jack, who had taken up flying too, said that Dean had the "surest, most delicate touch of any pilot I ever saw." Thanks to Faulkner, he had found something he excelled at, something he loved.

In truth, Dean idolized his oldest brother, so much so that he grew a mustache, too, and adopted Faulkner's spelling of his last name. And Faulkner loved Dean in return, enjoyed and needed his companionship. He was such a compassionate and gregarious kid, and a first-rate hunter, often bringing quail to Rowan Oak for Estelle's table. Moreover, when Faulkner went on a binge, it was Dean who came out to Rowan Oak and stayed with him, often in a room by themselves, until it was over.

By October, Faulkner was broke again, what with the costs of flying and mounting family expenses. He tried to work on his novel about the Snopes clan, but put it aside and started one about "a nigger woman" called *Requiem for a Nun.* But he was dissatisfied and unhappy, complaining that it had been sixteen months since he had written anything original. On top of that, he had to worry and fret about money. The sale of a few stories didn't help. By wintertime, he was indigent and living on credit while trying to make headway on his novel. In despair, he outlined his needs to Smith: in addition to his own family and servants, he had Maud and Dean to support, plus whatever demands his other brothers might make on him. In March, he would owe $1,500 in taxes and $700 in insurance. He seemed to be running back and forth from pillar to post. Unless he could grind out salable short stories, he would have to sell himself back into slavery and return to Hollywood.

Once again, desperation stimulated his imagination, and in midwinter 1934 the voices were singing again, clear and irresistible. He had heard them before in short stories, the voices of Colonel Thomas Sutpen and his children and an old poor white named Wash Jones. Now their brooding chorus suggested something far more ambitious than a short story, and he set aside *Requiem for a Nun* to pursue the Sutpens in a novel. He wrote Smith that it was about "the more or less violent breakup of a household or family from 1860 to about 1910. . . . Roughly, the theme is a man who outraged the land, and the land then turned and destroyed the man's family. Quentin Compson, of the Sound & Fury, tells it, or ties it together; he is the protagonist so that it is not complete apocrypha. I use him because it is just before he is to commit suicide because of his sister, and I use his bitterness which he has projected on the South in the form of hatred of it and its people to get more out of the story itself than a historical novel would be. To keep the hoop skirts and plug hats out, you might say. I believe I can promise it for fall." He needed $1,500, he told Smith, reassuring him that he was sober and had been since November.

But he had a terrible time with the beginning and the narrative line; the novel seemed to defy being written. In mid-February 1934, he left his desk to attend an air show in New Orleans with Captain Omlie. He met some aviators and drank, flew, and caroused with them. At the meet, he watched, spellbound, as the frantic little planes turned and twisted overhead and raced around the pylons. The atmosphere was charged with violence: the day before, a pilot had crashed while attempting a full-throttled loop. On this day, in full view of spectators, a plane plunged into Lake Pontchartrain in a geyser of spray. To Faulkner, there was "something frenetic and in a way almost immoral" about nomadic daredevils like these, courting death and living hand-to-mouth as they dashed around the country from race to race. They seemed beyond respectability and love, even beyond the range of God.

Back at Rowan Oak, he was so bereft of money that he shelved the Sutpen novel and resorted to writing potboilers for the big-circulation magazines. By now, Ben Wasson had relocated in Hollywood, and Faulkner was using Morton Goldman's New York agency to peddle his stories, firing them off with frantic pleas. In April, Smith & Haas brought out another Faulkner collection, called *Dr. Martino and Other Stories,* but Faulkner was desperate for immediate cash to pay his taxes and insurance. Finally he surrendered himself to a series of Civil War stories for the *Saturday Evening Post.* Hal Smith thought this the low point of Faulkner's writing career and despaired of ever seeing his novel that year.

The stories were "trash," Faulkner admitted, but what choice did he have? He was backed against the wall. Even when "boiling the pot," though, he tried to be an artist; he did the best he knew how. But he bogged down in the stories, too. Finally he threw up his hands and headed for Hollywood, this time to hack out scripts for Universal Studios at $1,000 a week. He did get to see Ben Wasson, but otherwise suffered dreadfully. He brooded about the Sutpens, about his problems with the plot and his inability to work on the book in accursed Hollywood. He hated like hell to be here. He was so "jumpy" to get home that he was at "the fingernail chewing stage," he wrote Estelle. "I wasted a whole week doing nothing at all; that's what frets me about this business." But he had one consolation at least: he earned enough money to meet some of his debts.

In August, he was back at Rowan Oak. How could he write creatively on this roller-coaster life? His desk was crowded with half-completed projects—with movie scripts, the *Post* stories, bits and parts of three novels. To make matters worse, it was "hot as hell here," he wrote Morty Goldman, his agent. "I have to work in front of a fan; I write with one hand and hold the paper down with the other." He tried to push ahead with the Sutpens: he could hear and see them and the other characters, he understood the dimensions of their tragedy, but making sense of all that on paper was like imposing order on a whirlwind. He wrote Smith in despair: "I still do not know when it will be ready. I believe the book is not quite ripe yet; that I have not gone my nine months, you might say." But at least he had a title, taken from 2 Samuel. It was *Absalom, Absalom!,* the story of "a man who wanted a son through pride, and got too many of them and they destroyed him."

LEAVE IT TO DEAN to do something impulsive like this. Faulkner was beaming. Back in the spring, his gregarious little brother had gone into the aviation business in Memphis with Captain Omlie; they had formed Midsouth Airways, and Faulkner had given Dean free use of the Waco to haul passengers at air shows. Happy-go-lucky as always, Dean roomed with Omlie in his Memphis apartment and commuted back and forth to Oxford to visit Maud and Bill. In June, he met a pretty young blonde named Louise Hale, took her with him on barnstorming weekends, and won her heart with his good-natured charm. At an air show in September, they married on impulse, and drove to Oxford to tell Maud and Bill. Louise understood and accepted Dean's intense loyalty to them. "Mother and Bill will always come first," he said. As it turned out, Louise fared better with Maud than Estelle and the other daughters-in-law. Maud actually accepted her.

The newlyweds now stood in Rowan Oak, telling Bill and Estelle the news. Faulkner could not have been happier for them both. He summoned the families to Rowan Oak for a wedding celebration, and offered a toast: "To the best wife of the best flier I have ever known." After that, Dean and Louise were "happy transients," sharing Omlie's apartment in Memphis and flying the Waco from one air show to the next. They were never in one place long enough to unpack their suitcases.

By the autumn of 1934, Faulkner was off liquor again, which was all the more remarkable given his frustrations with *Absalom, Absalom!* The novel simply refused to cohere. It was a complicated work, in some ways even more complex than *Light in August,* with Quentin Compson trying to sort out the Sutpen tale from various witnesses in different times. Of the inchoate pile of pages on his desk, Faulkner found only one chapter acceptable. Unable to make headway, he turned to something else, something easier. Maybe that would help him break through with *Absalom, Absalom!* In October, he began a novel about peripatetic aviators, based on the air meet he'd attended in New Orleans the previous February. Driven by all his pent-up frustrations with the Sutpens, the new book exploded out of him. He wrote so rapidly that he abandoned his routine and mailed chapters off to New York as he completed them. By mid-December, he was done. By mid-January 1935, he was reading galleys. Born of his anguish with a major work,

Pylon was a strange, often unintelligible book about human "ephemera and phenomena on the face of a contemporary scene," as Faulkner described it. The characters, an air-circus pilot, a parachutist, the woman they both shared, and a drunken, cadaverous reporter, had no place and no past. "They were as ephemeral," Faulkner said, "as the butterfly that's born this morning with no stomach and will be gone tomorrow."

To his mother's delight, Faulkner remained sober, even in the aftermath of completing a novel. Despite his myriad woes, he had had a productive year, not only writing a novel but publishing a second book of stories and nine other stories in national magazines like *Harper's, Scribner's,* and *The American Mercury,* not to mention *The Saturday Evening Post.* And that wasn't all. "Lo!," his humorous tale about the Indians of Yoknapatawpha, was to appear in *The Best Short Stories 1935.*

Yet his relationship with Estelle had steadily deteriorated. Perhaps that was why she drank too much at Christmastime. He could have written a grisly tale about their troubled marriage, about how it had rebounded after Alabama's death, then worsened, then rebounded again with Jill's birth, only to curdle with mutual resentment and hostility. After Jill came, Estelle moved into the back bedroom upstairs, and she and Faulkner stopped sleeping together. Not that he wanted her anymore. He bristled at her unladylike bouts of drunkenness, her flighty and flirtatious ways, her spending sprees in Memphis. Bird-thin, nervous woman, she seemed to live in the illusion that he was rich, like Cornell Franklin. Look at the expensive junk she brought home. It was all frivolous. She didn't care that her extravagance impinged on his work, forced him to write trash for the popular prints to pay her goddamn bills. What did she care? She didn't understand his art, the demands of his fiction. He remembered her fit when she hurled *Light in August* out of the car. It was a good thing he had hired a Negro nurse for Jill. Estelle couldn't take care of her. All she could do was spend money, smoke cigarettes, and drink.

In her view, he was just as bad. He never talked to her, never asked about her feelings, what she wanted; he never talked to her the way he did to Maud. God, how she resented him for that. She felt so inferior, so unwanted. Was all this her fault? Was she to blame? Was there something wrong with her? She realized she wasn't passionate anymore. Given her fragile health and four difficult pregnancies, she might be forgiven that. But she wasn't the only one who was cold. She could write a book about his withdrawals, hiding out in that library of his with the doorknob off and expecting everyone to be quiet, no piano playing, no radio, all of them shut out completely. And Hollywood was another thing, his going out there. He had all the glamour in their lives; she had all the isolation, stuck at Rowan Oak with the children, except when she could manage a trip to Memphis. Why wouldn't he take her to Hollywood with him? Oh, she knew; she had heard his reasoning: "You're only looking for a good time. I don't want to go. I want to stay here. This is the only place I can write about." But nobody could tell her he wasn't having a good time in Hollywood, with all those movie stars and great places to dine and dance. God, she could be so angry with him sometimes. But she didn't like the fighting: the constant carping about money, then the silences, then the fighting again. She wanted everything to be all right, all of them to be happy. But Bill seemed incapable of loving her, of giving her what she needed. He seldom took her dancing or anywhere else; all he wanted to do at night was sit alone, whiling away joyless hours with a book or a play nobody else could understand. Was this a husband? she once wrote. Was there a man who breathed "with soul so dead?" She was so tired of all this. Sometimes she didn't care whether she lived or died.

Shut up in her bedroom, she smoked her cigarettes and tried to sew or to paint at her easel. Then she would get depressed again and drink and drift through the days, caught in a lonely battle against alcohol, drugs, and suicide.

B Y THE NEW YEAR, 1935, Faulkner needed money "to beat hell." Hal Smith came down, read over what he had of *Absalom, Absalom!,* and advanced him $2,000. It wasn't enough. He needed $10,000. Then he could pay his debts and really write. He told Goldman he was disappointed in his advance and thought he could get more money from another publisher. One thing he knew for certain: "I cannot and will not go on like this. I believe I have got enough fair literature in me yet to deserve reasonable freedom from bourgeoise material petty impediments and compulsion, without having to quit writing and go to the moving pictures every two years. The trouble about the movies is not so much the time I waste there but the time it takes me to recover and settle down again; I am 37 now and of course not as supple and impervious as I once was."

With creditors pressing him from all sides, he turned to his old anodyne and started drinking again. Alarmed, Miss Maud came to Rowan Oak and poured his whiskey down the drain, but he only found more and stayed in his room. Finally an old flying companion went up there and somehow got him out of bed and sobered him up. He was all right now. The binge had been aborted.

On March 30, with *Pylon* out and collecting mixed reviews, Faulkner went back to *Absalom, Absalom!*, back to the "inchoate fragments" on his desk. But this time the book felt ripe for him, and he worked through the spring with unbroken intensity. It was developing into a first-rate suspense story. What did Quentin know about Sutpen from the vantage point of 1910, when Quentin was a student at Harvard? What did he pull together from other characters in the past, from his father, from the spinster Rosa Coldfield? *What had gone wrong in Sutpen's design? What had turned one son against the other?* Faulkner was hot; the voices were singing again. By June, he had sent the first two chapters to Smith. The third went off in July, the fourth in August.

By September, he faced bankruptcy. Damn these money troubles! Whoever said that the "pinch of necessity" was good for the artist was a damned fool. He owed $500 in Memphis and $1,200 in Oxford, more than half that to the grocer; he was trying to give Miss Maud $100 a month; and taxes and insurance premiums were coming due again. If he didn't get money soon, he would lose his house and insurance, everything. Then God knew what would become of his novel.

In desperation, he went to New York, prepared to leave Smith & Haas if he couldn't secure better terms for his book. To everyone's surprise, he drank little this time. He talked to Cerf at Random House, and Cerf assured him that they were eager to publish his books and meet his terms. It was tempting, but Faulkner wanted to see Smith first. He felt "good and ready and 'hard-boiled' now," he said, "enough to cope with Shylock himself." At Smith's office, he made his case and listed all his expenses, and Smith agreed to loan him enough money to get through the winter. It was either that or lose Faulkner to another publisher.

"I have settled the business," he wrote Estelle in jubilation. "There are strings to it, of course, and I have agreed to go to California for 8 weeks in March if Hal can get me a contract and so pay back the money which they loaned me." It wasn't a huge sum, but it would pay their outstanding bills, taxes, and insurance premiums, provide winter clothes for her and the children, and buy him five precious months of freedom to devote to *Absalom, Absalom!*

Home again in October, he plunged back into Yoknapatawpha County and the mystery of Thomas Sutpen. Old Rosa Coldfield was telling the story now, as she and Quentin rode out to Sutpen's Hundred after the violent breakup of all Sutpen's dreams; they were certain that Sutpen's mulatto daughter was hiding something out there, and they intended to find out what. On the way, Rosa related how Sutpen had pursued his evil design, how the "demon" had destroyed his own sons during the war, had then made her a shocking offer that had left her indignant, blazing with hatred, and finally had brought about his own violent death. . . .

On Sunday, November 10, Faulkner was called to the telephone. He hung it up and stood there in a state of shock. Dean was dead, killed in a plane crash that day ten miles west of Pontotoc. The news refused to register. Faulkner had recently seen Dean, had visited him and Louise in Memphis. Everything seemed to be going right for them: Louise was pregnant, Dean happy and busy as a professional pilot, thanks to his big brother, who by then had sold him the Waco. This weekend, Dean had flown down to Pontotoc, southwest of Oxford, for an air show to take place on Monday, Armistice Day. He had taken three other men aloft and something had happened, nobody knew what, and the Waco had crashed, killing all four.

Faulkner drove to get his mother, and they rode up to fetch Louise and bring her back to Maud's house in Oxford. They were all in shock. Maud wanted to know if she had ever done anything to make Dean unhappy. She wanted to see him. Billy would bring him home, so she could see him one last time. She lay motionless in her bedroom, her tiny hands locked across her chest.

Relatives came to stay with her and Louise, and Faulkner set out for Pontotoc to bring his brother home. It was the longest thirty miles he had ever driven. He knew few details about the crash, only that rescue workers had removed the bodies with hacksaws and blowtorches and had taken them to a funeral home in Pontotoc. Faulkner shuddered at what awaited him there. He had a photograph of Dean in his pocket, in case the undertaker should need it to reconstruct him.

What he found in the funeral home was ghastly. Dean "was so badly disfigured," Faulkner said, "that I spent the whole night with the mortician at the side of a bathtub trying to put his face back in some shape." Faulkner didn't think he could ever get into a bathtub again. The next morning, numb from shock, whiskey, and lack of sleep, he accompanied his brother back to Oxford. But a cousin dissuaded him from letting Maud look into the coffin. Faulkner went into Louise's bedroom and spoke gently to her. It was best to leave the coffin closed, he said, and remember Dean the way he had been.

It was Monday, Armistice Day. Jack and John were there now, and the three brothers gathered round their mother for a brief service in her living room, then for the burial at St. Peter's Cemetery—the same cemetery that held little Alabama. The full realization of what had happened smote Faulkner like a physical blow: his kid brother, the happy-go-lucky guy who had liked everybody, who had stayed by Faulkner's side when he was under the weather, who had admired and emulated him, was really gone. He was really dead.

Afterward, Faulkner was overcome with guilt. *He* was to blame for this. *He* had set the example for Dean, *he* had encouraged him to fly, *he* had sold him the Waco. "Don't reproach yourself," Jack said. "What happened wasn't your fault. You weren't responsible for it."

"No," Faulkner said. "But I bought him the plane, I paid for his lessons."

In his guilt and grief, he reached out, trying to find comfort by giving it. For several weeks he lived at Maud's house, doing what he could for her and especially for pregnant Louise, who had come there to stay. Each evening he drew a bath for her, despite the terrible memories the bathtub evoked. Before she went to bed, he brought her a glass of warm milk and a sleeping pill. But nothing seemed to ease his own suffering. He told Louise that he dreamed about the accident every night: the Waco smashing into the ground in a burst of flames, the disfigured body lying in the bathtub. . . . Once he broke down in front of visitors; he became so hysterical that Louise had to lead him from the room. Inevitably, he turned to whiskey to numb his pain. But even that failed him. One afternoon, as he and Louise sat talking about Dean, she could see that he had been drinking. Suddenly he started to cry. "I have ruined your life," he sobbed. "It is my fault." He was so miserable, so hopeless, that she burst into tears.

Finally he pulled himself together. He put the whiskey away and took out *Absalom, Absalom!* At night, after Louise and Maud were asleep, he wrote by candlelight at the dining room table, pushing into the last half of his novel. As so often before when grief-stricken, he found a measure of comfort in creative work, in his compassion for the sufferings of others, even Thomas Sutpen. By December 4, he could write Goldman: "I am working like hell now. The novel is pretty good and I think another month will see it done."

B︎UT A FEW DAYS LATER, terrible news came from New York. Smith and Haas were in financial trouble and had to call in their loan to Faulkner. It was the same old story. To pay off Smith, he had to interrupt his novel yet again and return to Hollywood for another "tour of duty." This time, Howard Hawks got him a contract with Twentieth Century–Fox—Darryl Zanuck's studio—to work on a French film about trench warfare during the Great War, which Hawks was adapting for the American screen. Faulkner was to be coauthor of the film script at a salary of $1,000 a week. When he reported for duty in mid-December, Faulkner warned Hawks he was not likely to do his best work with his mind on *Absalom, Absalom!* and his brother's death. Hawks asked only one favor: don't get drunk until after we finish the picture.

In Hawks' outer office, a young woman sat working at a typewriter. Faulkner could not take his eyes off her. She was lovely: tall and boyishly thin, with fine blonde hair that fell to her shoulders in a straight sweep. When she walked, she was lithe as a ballerina, with a waist that was only a handspan around. She looked about nineteen. She turned out to be twenty-eight, and her name was Meta Carpenter; she was Howard Hawks' personal secretary and "script girl." She was from Mississippi, too, from the Delta. He was *"the* William Faulkner"? She was impressed, despite his ill-fitting tweed suit. Still, she was sure she had read that he was married.

At the studio, then at his hotel room in Beverly Hills, he could not stop thinking about her. It had been more than two years since he had slept with Estelle, and he was lonely for a woman, a young woman, someone sweet and slender like Miss Carpenter. He started drinking. At the studio, with glassy eyes and unsteady legs, he asked her out to dinner. Flustered, she ran into Hawks' office, and Hawks came out with her answer. No, she wouldn't have dinner with him.

Later he asked her again. She said with obvious irritation: "I don't want to go out with you, Mr. Faulkner, and you know why. Please don't keep asking."

"I'm sorry, ma'am."

He tried to get his mind off her. Each morning, he rose early and worked "furiously" on *Absalom, Absalom!* for three or four hours, then put in a full day at the studio, sometimes grinding out thirty-five pages of script in a single day. On his desk was a photograph of his baby daughter, his "angel," his "cherub." But Miss Carpenter was around him much of the time, taking dictation from him and typing his script. He couldn't help but stare at her. It was as if she had materialized out of his youthful fantasies about whirling young nymphs with lascivious knees and hot, quick glances. . . . In fact, she was stealing glances at him, thinking, *He has a small, sensitive mouth behind his mustache, a hawk-like, austerely handsome face.* She could smell the talcum he used after he shaved.

He asked her out again, and this time she accepted. Unlike other men in Hollywood, he was not a womanizer, she decided, but "a gentleman of incontestable probity." That evening they drank cocktails and dined at Musso & Frank's Grill on Hollywood Boulevard. Initially lighthearted and "boyishly engaging," Faulkner became solemn, then silent. He was thinking about Dean again. But the mood passed. He asked about her life in Hollywood, her Mississippi past, her dreams. He found out she was recently divorced—her marriage had been "a youthful mistake." He called her "pretty thing" and "Miss Meta" and referred to himself as "a book-writin' man." After dinner, they found a bookstore and searched in vain for a copy of his book of verse, *A Green Bough.* She settled for a copy of *Sanctuary* instead.

The next night he treated her to an expensive dinner at LaRue's on Sunset Strip. Afterward, they strolled along the Strip, she almost an inch taller than he. He said he had flown combat missions in France during the Great War, had crashed, and had a silver plate in his skull; he tapped it with his hand. He was enjoying himself immensely. "I have to see you every night," he said.

"Every night?" she asked.

"You save my damned life out here, Meta. I swear you do. You keep me alive and sane." He admitted that he was a married man, and "piss poor," and couldn't give her anything, but he had to see her every night. And she felt the same way now. She wanted him "to be the only man who opened doors for me."

In the mornings, she would pick him up and drive him to the studio in her car. In the evenings, they would drop by the Hofbrau to drink beer and listen to German music, or play miniature golf, or eat out when he could afford it. She was falling in love with him, with his "lightning-like brain," his kind and courteous ways, his gentleness. He would chuckle softly and call her "m'honey." He sang her songs and told her stories; he quoted Housman and Swinburne and wrote her poems—he always felt poetic around a desirable young female. He even confided in her about Dean's death and the excruciating guilt he felt.

Then one night he showed her photographs of Jill. "I worry, even with Mammy around, that something will happen to Jill when Estelle goes on one of her drinking binges. I worry that she will set the house on fire with her cigarettes and matches." He said, "Listen to me. You have to know this. When Jill was born, from that time on, Estelle and I have not had anything to do with each other as man and woman." His eyes burned brightly. "Estelle goes to her bed at night, I go to mine. You hear me, Ma'am?" Meta was shocked; she said nothing. Faulkner closed his eyes. "It is hard on a man like me to be without a woman that way. A woman should be able to understand that as well as another man." She nodded. "Yes." He said he never went with prostitutes, not here, not in Oxford, not anywhere; he went to bed with a woman only when he loved her.

A week later he still hadn't kissed her. But she could sense his desire. One night, as they walked after dinner, he held her hand tightly, kneading it in his own, and she returned the pressure. He led her back to the hotel and up to his room. He trembled at the sight of her, fought for his breath. "Oh, my God," he whispered. He tried not to hurt her, and afterward kissed her eyelids, her face and throat, and she noticed what a massive chest and muscled shoulders he had for so small a man. When they parted, he said, "You've brought me out of a deep and bottomless pit, Meta. You and no one else."

B Y THE END OF THE YEAR, Faulkner and his co-writer had completed the screenplay for *The Road to Glory*, though the associate producer had contributed much of the dialogue. In fact, before Hawks would be ready to shoot, the script would go through several additional drafts and revisions, with which Faulkner was uninvolved. Most Hollywood scripts were like that: the result of combined efforts, with writers, directors, and producers all taking part. The final screenplay was apt to be impersonal, without the stamp of any individual. No wonder screenwriting was inimical to a creative artist like Faulkner, who needed to work in solitude, to follow his singular vision and inspiration, and to produce something uniquely his own.

Which, of course, was what he did in his hotel room, as he pushed on with *Absalom, Absalom!* He finished the manuscript early in January 1936, almost two years exactly from the time he had begun it. He was euphoric. At the studio, he showed the manuscript to an associate. "I think it's the best novel yet written by an American," he said.

Then came the emptiness and the drinking, which not even Meta could ease. He was drunk and depressed. He wanted to go home, home to Rowan Oak and to Jill. Hawks wouldn't need him for a while; he would return when he felt better. He had no choice but to come back —he needed the money. On January 7, the studio released him "temporarily due to illness." When he could travel, Meta drove him to the train station. He left her a gift—a puppy she could pick up at the kennel.

H E FOUND LITTLE PEACE at Rowan Oak. He was glad to see his daughter again, but the tensions in his marriage were as bad as ever. He missed Meta, missed their lovemaking. He shut himself off in the world of *Absalom, Absalom!*, reading over his manuscript and making marginal corrections, losing himself in the lives of his characters. He still had to type a final draft and would make additional revisions, but it was already a powerful novel, maybe his best. What he had created, in a sense, was a novel of voices, in which people sat and talked in monologues and soliloquies, approaching and interpreting the Sutpen saga from different perspectives at different times. The circular plot was taut with suspense, with gradual revelations and repetitive climaxes that raised additional questions, all building to an astonishing curtain. On one level, Faulkner was making an eloquent statement about the South's racial and historical obsessions, which he'd pondered much of his life. But on a higher level, he was suggesting a profound and disturbing truth: that human beings could never fully know their past, that the highest level of understanding—in this case that of Quentin Compson and his Harvard roommate, who functioned as observers and commentators—remained fleeting and speculative. As Faulkner said through Quentin's father, "We have a few old mouth-to-mouth tales; we exhume from old trunks and boxes and drawers letters without salutation or signature, in which men and women who once lived and breathed are now merely initials or nicknames . . . we see dimly people . . . performing their acts of simple passion and simple violence, impervious to time and inexplicable— Yes, Judith, Bon, Henry, Sutpen; all of them. They are there; yet something is missing; they are like a chemical formula exhumed along with the letters from that forgotten chest. . . . the words, the symbols, the shapes themselves, shadowy inscrutable and serene, against that turgid background of a horrible and bloody mischancing of human affairs."

Yet four of Faulkner's characters, doomed never to know the full truth, struggled heroically to comprehend the "horrible and bloody mischancing" of Colonel Sutpen's affairs, in the process exposing the tragedy of pride and the curse of race in Dixie. Indeed, the rise and fall of Thomas Sutpen paralleled that of the Old South itself. Quentin, the central narrator and protagonist, was still an exaggerated reflection of Faulkner: a brooding, firstborn son who hated the ugly sides of a region that both shaped and haunted him. At Harvard (it was some five months before his suicide), he tried to sort out the mystery of Colonel Sutpen on the basis of what Rosa Coldfield had told him, what his grandfather General Compson, Sutpen's "first Yoknapatawpha County friend," had told his father, and what his father in turn had retailed to him. Quentin became so obsessed with the mystery that he drew his Canadian roommate, Shreve McCannon, into it as well. They sat in their Harvard dormitory, "the morose and delicate" southerner trying to reconstruct remembered events, while the cherubic-faced Canadian, with his twin-moon spectacles, brought an objective outsider's perspective to bear in attempting to interpret them. Faulkner thought that Shreve held "the thing to something of reality. If Quentin had been let alone to tell it, it would have become completely unreal . . . would have vanished into smoke and fury."

And this in essence was what they and their creator came to know of those faded years: that Thomas Sutpen, the son of a poor western Virginia mountain farmer, once humiliated by the haughty Negro servant of a tidewater planter, set out to become a planter himself, to build a dynasty of material wealth and rich progeny. This was his "design," to which he devoted himself with single-minded zeal. He repaired to the West Indies and there amassed slaves and gained a wife and a son. Alas, Sutpen discovered that his wife had Negro blood, a fact that imperiled his design in that white supremacist time. So he put them aside (or so he thought) and sailed for mainland America with a retinue of wild Haitian Negroes, turning up finally in Jefferson, Mississippi, in 1833. According to Jason Compson, Quentin's father, Sutpen was about twenty-five then, a big man with a gaunt frame, a short, reddish beard, and pale eyes at once visionary, alert, and ruthless. With "secret and furious impatience," he set about building his dynasty anew: he deviously acquired one hundred square miles of virgin wilderness twelve miles from Jefferson and with his wild Negroes and a "grim unflagging fury" cleared the land and built a mansion and landscaped garden known as Sutpen's Hundred. Next he acquired a wife, Ellen Coldfield, the oldest daughter of a Jefferson storekeeper, a small, shallow butterfly swept up "in bewildered and uncomprehending amazement" in Sutpen's gale. Nevertheless, she gave him a son, Henry, and a daughter, Judith. With a big plantation, slaves, a wife, and children to bear him grandchildren, Sutpen was close to achieving his design in the South's paternalistic, slave-based world.

But cracks appeared in Sutpen's edifice. Henry grew into a fiery young man, "given to instinctive and violent action rather than to thinking," as Jason Compson said. He entered Ole Miss in Oxford and returned one Christmas with a fellow student, one Charles Bon of New Orleans, a passive, sardonic, catlike man of exquisite manners and sartorial elegance. He had captivated Henry, who clownishly aped his dress and manner and invited him home to meet his family, especially his beautiful sister. As Henry had hoped, Bon captured young Judith's heart, too, and they became engaged. But Bon harbored a secret now, something he had discovered about himself and Judith's father. Yes, he was Thomas Sutpen's son by the Haitian woman, the discarded off-spring tainted by a strain of Negro blood. All Bon wanted was Sutpen's recognition that he was his son; if Bon got that, he was willing to leave Judith alone. But Sutpen, when he discovered who Bon was, would never grant him that, or allow him to marry Judith, because of the miscegenation issue. Sutpen had no objection to miscegenation on principle, or incest either; he was too obsessed with purpose to care about principle or morality. He opposed miscegenation in this case because it threatened the purity of his design.

At Christmastime 1860, with civil war threatening the nation, Sutpen took a bold step to save his own house. Certain that Henry would never permit an incestuous union, he told Henry that Bon was his brother. But Henry refused to believe it. He loved Bon, as much as Judith did. As the town heard it from Sutpen's Negroes, Henry abjured his father, renounced his birthright, and stormed out, riding away with Bon into the night. Sutpen's dynasty, like the nation itself, was collapsing in domestic discord.

When the Civil War broke out, Sutpen helped John Sartoris raise his Mississippi regiment and rode off to war on a gaunt black stallion, erect in a faded gray uniform, determined to help save the South and what remained of his dynasty. He was almost fifty-five now, without his old swagger, seemingly bemused as he tried to hold his design above the maelstrom of unreasoning and unpredictable mortals. His mutinous sons also joined the rebel army, and Henry gradually accepted the idea of an incestuous union between Bon and Judith, thinking, "But kings have done it! Even dukes!" Through the speculations of Quentin and Shreve, Faulkner suggested what happened next. During the war, when Sutpen realized that Henry would not block Bon, he played his trump card: he sought Henry out and summoned him to his army tent. There, in a climactic scene, Sutpen told his son that Bon was part Negro.

As Quentin and Shreve imagined it, drawing on the information they had, Henry left his father's tent, stumbling in the dark, knowing what he would do, what Bon would force him to do. When he confronted Bon about his father's revelation, Bon retorted, *"So it's the miscegenation, not the incest, which you cant bear."* Henry's heart was torn to shreds. *"You are my brother,"* he said, fighting for his breath. Bon taunted him. *"No I'm not. I'm the nigger that's going to sleep with your sister."* Henry grabbed him by both shoulders, panting. *"You shall not!"* he cried. *"You shall not! Do you hear me?"* Bon said gently, *"You will have to stop me, Henry."*

At war's end, back at Sutpen's Hundred, the two men faced one another again, and this time Henry shot and killed Bon, the brother he loved, in order to save the sister he loved and the family's honor. Afterward, Henry stood there, "hatless, with his shaggy bayonet trimmed hair, his gaunt worn unshaven face, his patched and faded gray tunic," and yelled at Judith that she couldn't marry Bon now, and then vanished.

Colonel Sutpen returned home to find his mansion a "grim decaying presence," his dreams as vanquished as his defeated homeland: his wife Ellen had died, his slaves had run off after the Yankees, his son on whom his dynasty depended had disappeared without a trace. Sutpen's Hundred had dwindled to two women: Judith and Clytie, the latter Sutpen's mulatto daughter by one of his slaves. So it went for a region of men who erected their economic edifice on "the shifting sands of opportunism and moral brigandage." Yet Sutpen was undaunted. He would build another dynasty, hoping (as Quentin said) to restore "by sheer indomitable willing the Sutpen's Hundred which he remembered and had lost." He turned to Rosa Coldfield, his dead wife's sister—a tiny, implacable spinster—and offered her marriage as he might call a dog. And she accepted, she told Quentin many years later, speaking in a poetic, rhetorical voice that often bordered on hysteria. She thought, she said to Quentin, that maybe the war had slain the ogre in Thomas Sutpen, and in any case she feared that this was her last chance to marry. And so she accepted. But with his violent impatience, his sense of wasted years and time fleeing from under him, he offered her a monstrous proposition: let us try it first and if it is a male I'll marry you. Shocked, Rosa left him, retreated in a rage back to Jefferson, where the public mocked her: "Rosie Coldfield, lose him, weep him; caught her man but couldn't keep him."

In the postwar years, Sutpen became a fat, pathetic old man, epitomizing the shame and decay of the former patrician class in defeated Dixie. He lived at Sutpen's Hundred and ran a country store that preyed on whites and blacks alike; his partner and clerk was a gangling, malaria-ridden poor white named Wash Jones, who worshiped him. Wash would look at Sutpen and think: *"A fine proud man. If God himself was to come down and ride the natural earth, that's what He would aim to look like."* In a final effort to gain a son and build his elusive dynasty, Sutpen, now sixty, seduced and impregnated Wash's fifteen-year-old granddaughter, Milly. And Wash gave his approval, thinking that the colonel would make it right, that Milly's child would inherit Sutpen's dynasty—something Wash's blind loyalty, he believed, had earned for him and his descendants. But when Milly gave birth to a daughter, not a son, Sutpen turned his back on her in contempt. At that, Wash went berserk. He dispatched Sutpen with a rusty scythe, then killed Milly and her baby with a butcher knife. When a sheriff's posse came after him, he grabbed the scythe and charged to his own bloody doom.

Now only Judith remained of Sutpen's design, the daughter who had bravely buried Bon and now bravely buried her father. But when she died of yellow fever, this in 1884, all that was left at Sutpen's Hundred were two tainted offspring—or so the town thought. One was Clytie, Sutpen's mulatto daughter, now a dried-up little woman scarcely larger than a monkey. The other was a retarded, slack-mouthed grandson of Charles Bon and an octoroon mistress, whom Clytie had raised. But Rosa Coldfield was convinced that some one else was out there, some one Clytie was hiding. In 1909, as Quentin told it to Shreve, Rosa took him out to the ghostly mansion to find out who was there; she forced her way upstairs, and there, lying in bed, his body wasted now, his eyelids closed, almost transparent, was Henry Sutpen, who had come home four years earlier to die. That was Clytie's secret; that was the secret of Sutpen's Hundred. Clytie was trying to shield the presence of her half-brother, to protect him because of Bon's murder all those years before. When Rosa returned with an ambulance, Clytie panicked, certain that officials were coming to arrest Henry. She set the mansion ablaze, and both of them died, incinerated in the swirling flames and smoke.

So Quentin told Shreve, who recapitulated it, trying to comprehend its meaning. "Now I want you to tell me just one thing more," Shreve said. "Why do you hate the South?"

"I don't hate it," Quentin said, quickly, immediately. "I dont hate it," he said. *"I don't hate it* he thought, panting in the cold air, the iron New England dark; *I dont. I dont! I dont hate it! I dont hate it!"*

Quentin spoke for Faulkner, who also had deep ambivalences about his native land. He scorned its sentimental plantation tradition and hated its violence, its bigotry and injustice, and yet he loved it despite its faults, for he had made his art of it, had risen from its soil and would return to it one day. As he contemplated his lyrical creation, with its biblical themes of pride and vanity, he pitied Thomas Sutpen. As he said later, this ruthless, self-centered man thought he was outside the human family and could take what he wanted; but people like him were destroyed ultimately, "because one has got to belong to the human family." Put another way, the story of Thomas Sutpen was like a Greek tragedy: he set out to establish a dynasty—he didn't care how—"and he violated all the rules of decency and honor and pity and compassion," Faulkner said, "and the fates took revenge on him." In the end, only "the idiot negro" remained of Sutpen's progeny. At night, the town could hear him out there, howling in the ruins.

While reading over and correcting his manuscript, Faulkner had held his drinking in abeyance. But after he dated the last page, the combination of post-manuscript depression and memories of Dean overcame him: he surrendered himself to another binge, stopped eating, and sank into an alcoholic stupor. It got so bad that his family had to take him to a small sanitarium in Byhalia, fifty miles north of Oxford, to dry out under medical supervision. In this particularly he was his father's son.

He was nothing if not resilient. Back at Rowan Oak, sober and chastened, he plunged into the long and arduous process of typing a publisher's draft of *Absalom, Absalom!* On that score, momentous news had come from New York. Random House had bought out Harrison Smith and Robert Haas and would thenceforth publish Faulkner's works, including *Absalom, Absalom!* Smith and Haas would be partners with Bennett Cerf and Donald Klopfer, cofounders of Random House, and Smith would continue to work closely with Faulkner—which, given all their years together, could not have pleased Faulkner more. While nobody at Random House believed that Faulkner would ever be a commercial success, Cerf said, he was "the greatest possible adornment to the Random House list." That was high praise indeed, for Cerf's expanding trade list now included James Joyce and Eugene O'Neill, who would win the 1936 Nobel Prize for literature.

In better spirits now, Faulkner took his manuscript up to Stone's columned hilltop mansion. Faulkner was so enthusiastic about his book that he had to share it with his cantankerous friend, who was still struggling with his father's debts and protesting his lack of time for writers and manuscripts. Much had changed in Stone's life. A confirmed bachelor all these years, he had recently married a schoolteacher named Emily Whitehurst; he was forty-two, bald, and burned out; she was twenty-six, statuesque, and awed by his learning. While Stone's elderly parents occupied the downstairs of the Stone mansion, Phil and his bride made their quarters on the second floor. Emily met Faulkner at the top of the stairs and escorted him along the book-lined hallway, pointing out some changes she had made in the sitting room. Faulkner said he recognized a new hand here.

"You surprise me," she said. "Phil says you never see anything."

"I see everything," Faulkner said.

In the old antebellum mansion, brimming with volumes of southern and Civil War history, Faulkner read rapidly from *Absalom, Absalom!* in a deadpan voice. Stone was not impressed, complaining later that the book was "absolutely ruined" because Faulkner apparently lacked any "comprehensive sense of design," any "consistent and comprehensive theory of aesthetics."

After the reading, when they were alone, Faulkner evidently confided in Phil about his marital troubles and his affair with Meta Carpenter. No matter what Stone thought of Estelle, which wasn't much, he advised Faulkner to stay married. Faulkner's place in American letters, Stone seemed to think, required that his personal life be exemplary.

B Y LATE FEBRUARY 1936, he was back in Hollywood, slaving away on a movie treatment by day and making passionate love with Meta by night. "Seized with a consuming sexual urgency," as Meta put it, he could not get enough of her. He confessed that he had once worried "a whole lot" about himself and women—still did, in fact. Yet with an adoring young woman like her, he felt confident as a lover. Never had he been so uninhibited, so erotic. Like Lady Chatterley's lover, he named their sexual parts—his was "Mr. Bowen," hers "Mrs. Bowen"— and wrote poetry that celebrated Mrs. Bowen's red blossoms and golden brown hair, which gave "one of earth's sons" such warm delight.

One weekend, they drove to Santa Monica, on the Pacific, and registered at the Mirabar Hotel as "Mr. and Mrs. Bowen." That night, in their spacious cabana bungalow, he sprinkled gardenia and jasmine petals across their bed, and they loved one another with the windows open to the ocean breeze and the moonlight. Before, she had always returned to her room after lovemaking in his hotel room; now, for the first time, they slept together all night, like man and wife.

With the warmer weather of spring, they went to the Mirabar as often as possible, to sun on the beach and swim in the rolling Pacific. He got his weight down to 140 pounds and looked better than he had in years. At thirty-eight, he felt young again, in love again. He joked about his tan—"they just might ride me out of Oxford"—and enjoyed sitting by an umbrella, watching Meta splash about in the waves, admiring the curve of her body as he had admired Helen Baird's body on another beach long ago. With his blond young Meta, he had come a long way from that sad, one-sided romance, a long way indeed.

He would watch Meta for a few moments, then motion her back to the umbrella. "I won't have that rare white skin marred by ugly red and blistering," he said, and added, "I have to find a way to describe that white skin. It's not blanched out white but with a suffusion of ivory and alabaster. I've never seen any woman with such a skin." He gave her a variation of Keats' "Ode on a Grecian Urn," which ended, "Forever shall I dream / And she be fair. / Meta, my darling, my love. / My dear love. / My dear, dear love."

He found a kind of sweet, virginal innocence to her that inflamed his desire. She was his Caddy Compson, his beautiful one, his "heart's darling." Meta noticed that he sometimes treated her as though she were much younger than she was; it seemed to her that he needed to turn her into "a sweet, tremulous little girl," even "a girl-child."

After lovemaking, he was voluble and outgoing. He liked to make her blush. He told bawdy stories and kissed the flame in her cheeks. He wrote her erotic notes about how her "long girl's body" was "sweet to fuck." In one missive, he called her "my heart, my jasmine garden, my April and May cunt; my white one, my blonde morning, winged, my sweetly dividing, my honey-cloyed, my sweet-assed gal."

"Meta, my honey," he told her one weekend, "I've never been as happy in my life as with you right here." Had he met her before he'd married Estelle, he said, he would have married her instead. He would have known instantly that she was the one for him.

Meta already thought of herself as his wife; she put Estelle out of her mind and dreamed about really being married to him soon. Ten years older than she, gentle, romantic, and passionate, he was to her "the all encompassing figure—the friend, the lover, the mentor, the guide, the mature father figure—all melded into one." He was her "guiding light," her "Rock of Gibraltar." She wanted to spend the rest of her life with him.

Yet there were things about him that troubled her. For all his passion and tenderness, he kept a certain distance between them, as he did with everyone. "The insularity that he drew over himself like a second, tougher skin put him beyond common query," Meta found out. Like Estelle, she realized that she could never know his private thoughts, his inner self. "The great carapace was impenetrable," she said, "even in our most intimate moments." She did not know why, did not know about the confusion and hurt of his early years, about his loveless father and demanding mother and their marital battles, all of which had caused him to build that impregnable shield in the first place, then to stay behind it after all his subsequent troubles with young women. No, Meta knew none of that, because he wouldn't tell her, couldn't tell her.

Other things bothered her too: his dark moods, his inattentiveness when his mind was on his characters, his refusal to discuss his work, his want of spoken sentiment out of bed, which was part of his insulation. "I knew he loved me by looks, by touch, by the poems and the letters, only seldom by what he said to me."

There was another problem, a major difference between them. She loved music with such passion that it could move her to tears, sweep her off into another world. Had she been talented enough, she said, she would have been a concert pianist. As it was, she did play the piano regularly and attended concerts whenever she could. When she first played her piano for Faulkner, however, she noticed him squirming in his seat.

She said, a little irritated, "You don't like my playing."

"You play very well, m'honey."

"But it didn't do anything for you."

"I don't appreciate music as much as I ought to," he said. "It's one of my flaws I reckon." He added in a moment, "Language is my music. All I'll ever need."

Perhaps Meta's piano had unhappy associations for him, reminding him of Estelle and her piano playing, even Estelle and her dancing. Certainly it annoyed him that music could possess Meta the way it did. It was his turn to feel left out. Once, while listening transfixed to a radio broadcast of *Tristan und Isolde,* she waved him off impatiently. He looked at her in disbelief, his face reddening, and then stalked out.

Later she apologized for her gesture, but he wasn't mollified. He asked her repeatedly how she could be a vassal to music, to something so "white and opaque and distant." According to Meta, he could no more accompany her into her world of recitals and symphonies than she could enter the interior domain of his fiction.

Even so, she thought she could rationalize all their differences. She wanted to marry Faulkner more than anything. And Faulkner did give her hope. He took her to parties in Hollywood, posed for snapshots with her, and introduced her to Dorothy Parker and to his old friend Ben Wasson.

"That is the girl I'm in love with," he confided to Wasson. "Can't get her out of my mind or system. And don't want to. You don't know what a wonderful person she is."

"She's certainly attractive," Ben said. Tall, good-looking, and young, he thought. He hadn't heard Faulkner talk about loving a woman since Helen Baird; Faulkner had never told him that he loved Estelle.

"She's brought me peace of mind," Faulkner said of Meta. "I haven't said anything yet to Estelle, who's already suspicious, I think. I want to marry Meta."

BUT HE FELT A STRANGE COUNTERPULL. When he was at Rowan Oak, he wanted Meta. When he was in Hollywood, he missed Jill and the warm familiarity of Rowan Oak. "I wish I was at home," he wrote Estelle that March, "still in the kitchen with my family around me and my hand full of Old Maid Cards. Bless the fat pink pretty. In haste, but with much love." As the spring passed, he became increasingly confused, his heart torn between Meta and home. Unable to talk openly to her or anyone else, he turned to bourbon for relief. Meta, unsure of what was wrong, observed that he was no longer content with one or two straight shots at dinner; now he belted down four or five. Sometimes he could consume an entire fifth. She worried about the look of futility in his eyes. A studio friend, certain that Faulkner was drinking at work, warned Wasson that his job was in jeopardy. Faulkner became belligerent. "You're spying on me. I can tell. You want to tell Estelle. Go ahead. I don't give a damn what you tell her."

He drank until he was insensible, oblivious to his whereabouts or his pain. One Sunday, Meta returned to her apartment to find him huddled on the corner of her bed with his hands stretched out. He was screaming. "They're going to get me! Oh, Lordy, oh, Jesus!"

"Who," she asked him. "Who's trying to hurt you?"

"The Jerries!" he cried. "They're trying to shoot me out of the sky. . . ."

Horrified, she summoned a musician friend who worked as a male nurse. Faulkner had the "DTs," he said. They helped him to a dry-out center, his eyes turned upward in their sockets.

When he was sober, he decided to go home. He didn't want to leave Meta, but Jill's third birthday was approaching in June; he couldn't miss that. As it turned out, he had a break in movie work until August 1, when he was to resume scriptwriting for Darryl Zanuck at $750 a week. But his contract contained a contingency clause about good behavior. Translated: if he got drunk on the job, he would be fired. In mid-May, he wrote Estelle that he was returning to Rowan Oak. "Damn this being an orphan," he said.

On his last night with Meta, his lovemaking was frantic and furious. Afterward, she asked, "What about us?" But he put a finger to her lips, entreating her to ask no more. She cried when they parted—she had never done that before. The next day, they shared a final meal together. He was silent and remote. But when she blotted her lipstick on a napkin, he put it in his pocket. He told her to write him in care of Phil Stone. "Phil's my closest friend. He will see to it that I get every letter." She cried again. She would wait for him forever. En route to Mississippi, he wrote a letter to his "darling" Meta, his "love, dear love, dear, dear love," saying on paper the tender things he found it difficult to tell her in person.

H E WROTE HER AGAIN from Rowan Oak. He wasn't drinking now —no credit to him; it was "just too damned hot." Yes, he had received her letters, and he missed her. He still had the napkin with the mark of her kiss.

By now, Louise Faulkner had given birth to a girl, named Dean after her dead father, and Mammy Callie was going to Maud's every day to look after the baby. Standing by the wrecked Waco, Faulkner had promised his brother that he would be a father to his child, and he no doubt repeated that now. He wrote Meta that he and Jill, now a chubby, blue-eyed blonde, liked to lie on his bed and watch the horses from his window. He was gentle with Jill; he loved it when she called him "Pappy," her nickname for him. But there was nothing but bitterness between Faulkner and Estelle. She was drinking worse than ever, "getting blind, staggering drunk," as he put it later. Once again, she had run up charge accounts while he was away—"for things like a radio and overstuffed furniture," Faulkner wrote Meta, which he took "a certain amount of sadistic pleasure" in throwing out of the house. He was so furious that he published a personal notice in both the Oxford *Eagle* and the Memphis *Commercial Appeal:* "I will not be responsible for any debt incurred or bills made, or notes or checks signed by Mrs. William Faulkner or Mrs. Estelle Oldham Faulkner."

The notice created an uproar, as reporters for the national press descended on Rowan Oak like locusts. They found "the famed novelist," as *Time* put it, helping his wife stage a birthday party for their daughter. Author Faulkner denied any family ruckus. "It's just a matter of protecting my credit until I can pay up my back debts," he told the reporters. He hated publicity—even if he had brought it on himself. Had his anger at Estelle caused him to take leave of his senses? He was so embarrassed and mad that he canceled all scheduled reprints of the notice.

At least his work went well, despite the sweltering heat. In Hollywood, he had continued to type *Absalom, Absalom!* and had added a chronology of events to clarify the story. Now, sober and unimpeded by movie scripts and demanding producers, he blazed through to the end of the text, mailing the final section off to Smith in New York. By his own standards, he had failed again to match the dream, which was to produce a perfect work of art. But he had done his best—that was what counted in the end.

At some point, he appended a map of Yoknapatawpha County, "William Faulkner, Sole Owner & Proprietor," which gave a graphic picture of his life's work. Crossing the Tallahatchie River from the northwest and heading for Jefferson, the visitor passed the fishing camp on Sutpen's land where Wash Jones killed Colonel Sutpen with the scythe. On down, to the right, was Sutpen's Hundred, where the inscrutable events of Christmas 1860 presaged the downfall of Sutpen's design. Farther down, on the left, was the Sartoris plantation, where Narcissa lived with irrepressible Miss Jenny. Entering Jefferson, the hub and county seat, the visitor saw the Burden place, where Joanna and Joe Christmas did their strange pas de deux before he slit her throat. Across the road and down by the railroad tracks was the sawmill where Byron Bunch first saw serene and bonneted Lena Grove. Across the tracks was Miss Rosa Coldfield's place, where on a "long still hot weary dead September afternoon" she began telling Quentin Compson about the "demon" Thomas Sutpen. Beyond the road, to the east, was the Compsons' house and the pasture they sold to the Golf Club so that Quentin could go to Harvard, there to ponder the enigma of Thomas Sutpen and later to drown himself in the Charles River. At the center of the square stood the courthouse, with its four-sided clock and hourly bell, where Temple Drake committed perjury and condemned Lee Goodwin to death. South of the courthouse stood the Confederate soldier, frozen in white granite, facing forever southward, which Benjy had to pass always on the left. On the northeast side of the square was Old Bayard Sartoris's bank, which Byron Snopes robbed and which Flem Snopes took over as president. Heading north, away from the square, the visitor found the jail, where Goodwin and Joe Christmas were taken, and Reverend Hightower's house, where Christmas met his ghastly fate at the hands of Percy Grimm. Behind the jail was the Benbow residence; north of it, the cemetery where the Bundrens buried Addie at last and where the statue and effigy of John Sartoris gazed on his railroad, which ran nearby. North of town the visitor could locate the spot where Old Bayard died in young Bayard's car. And on around to the southeast of Jefferson, down along the Yoknapatawpha River, lay Frenchman's Bend and the Old Frenchman place, where Popeye murdered the halfwit and raped Temple with the corncob, and south of that the Bundren farm, where Anse and his children set out for Jefferson with Addie's corpse. . . .

This was Faulkner's "keystone in the Universe," as he called it later. In his view, the people here were like people everywhere: all were struggling with the conflicts in their hearts, with their backgrounds and their fellow human beings. He wasn't writing about the South here; he was merely using that as his setting, because he knew its people and its history. But what he was trying to capture was the universal human condition as it found expression in a single Mississippi county. As he said a few years later, he was writing from his heart about the eternal verities—"about honor, truth, pity, consideration, the capacity to endure well grief and misfortune and injustice and then endure again." Yes, that was what he attempted to capture at the end of his pencil, as he listened to the voices that spoke only to him.

He was due back in Hollywood on August 1, but he couldn't bear to leave Jill after so short a visit. He worried that Estelle's drinking might bring harm to his daughter—he saw himself worrying about that all the while he was in Hollywood. His only choice, he decided, was to bring them along, so that he could look after Jill. Estelle wasn't hard to persuade: she had wanted all along to go with him. They would take Jill's nurse, Narcissa, and another servant, named Jack. With mixed emotions, Faulkner warned Meta what to expect and asked for her forbearance.

In mid-July 1936, the Faulkner entourage climbed into a new Ford he had bought and headed for California, with Jill singing "Oh! Susanna!" over and over. On Route 66, they passed dust-covered jalopies bursting with household possessions and towheaded children. Faulkner knew about them—they were "Okie" migrants who had lost their farms in the dust bowl. In the last two years, "black blizzards" had swept across the midwest, laying waste to thousands of square miles. In Oklahoma, the storms had turned farmlands into shifting sand dunes and forced the owners to scrap the tenant system, evict their renters, and bring in the machines. With no place else to go, the Okies set out for California, the legendary land of beginning again. Their overloaded cars and trucks became familiar sights on Route 66—symbols of a calamitous time even the New Deal seemed powerless to end.

In Los Angeles, the Faulkners stayed in a hotel until they could find a home. As soon as he could manage it, Faulkner went to see Meta, who had moved to a bungalow court on Crescent Heights. "My love," Faulkner whispered. "My long-legged, big-mouf gal." They made love with half their clothes still on.

Still, Meta was vexed. Estelle was no longer some vague form off in Mississippi; now she had invaded Meta's domain, intruded on her life with Faulkner. For the first time, she felt threatened. "Bill, how are we going to see each other?" she asked. "You with a wife and child to go home to every night from the studio?" He had spoken vaguely about getting a divorce, had said he wanted Meta always for his own, had held out hope for them. How long did she have to wait for Estelle to let him go? *Would* she let him go? Faulkner stared at her, then turned abruptly and walked out to his car, looked back, then drove away.

The truth was, he felt ambivalent about a divorce, fearful of what it would do to Jill. In Mississippi, he reminded himself, the divorce courts always gave the mother custody of the child. What would happen to Jill if he were not around? If all she had was a drunken, chain-smoking mother to raise her? He shuddered at the idea of leaving his daughter to such a fate. Still . . . he held some hope that he might reach an accommodation with Estelle that would give him his freedom without hurting Jill. It would be a struggle; he had to prepare himself for that. In the meantime, he and Meta would have to see one another whenever they could. Somehow they would work this thing out.

AFTER A WEEK IN THE HOTEL, the Faulkners and their two servants moved to a rambling, two-story brownstone near the ocean; it afforded a good view of the mountains from the dining room windows. On the sun deck, Faulkner read galleys of *Absalom, Absalom!*, wearing tennis shorts and pilot's sunglasses and smoking a long-stemmed briar, his face tanned, his hair short and iron gray. But behind the tranquil facade, he felt as though he were living in purgatory. He would come home from the studio in a tirade, complaining about his lackluster assignments. Here he was, the author of *Absalom, Absalom!*, in his view the best novel written by an American, having to supply dialogue for tripe like *The Last Slaver* and *Splinter Fleet;* the latter was so bad that he couldn't find the damn story line. And Estelle made him madder still. Oh, at first they tried to maintain some semblance of marital respectability: they invited people over for drinks, and Estelle, wearing a long-sleeved gown, entertained them at the piano. But the marital truce soon collapsed, and they drank and fought. Sometimes their altercations turned violent. Once Estelle scratched his face. Later she came at him with a croquet mallet. He showed up for work with a bump on his forehead.

When conditions at home became unbearable, he turned to Meta for comfort. But Meta was having a hard time, too. She wasn't used to being the other woman in his life. And that wasn't all. Earlier that year, while Faulkner was back in Oxford, she had met and gone out with another

man, a young Austrian pianist named Wolfgang Rebner. It wasn't simply his musical talent that attracted her. He was charming, worshipful
—and single. Rebner was on tour now, off in Japan, but he wrote her
every day about his regard for her, about how she had changed his life,
and she felt obligated to reply. She had told Faulkner about this, reassured him that he was the man she loved, but she hadn't put Rebner
entirely out of her mind.

Faulkner gave her all he could, even invited her into his other life.
One morning when Estelle was drunk in her room, he introduced Meta
to Jill, and the three of them went on a ride in her car and then had
lunch in her apartment. When Estelle was indisposed again, Faulkner
would call Meta, and she would pick Jill up and take her to the park to
play with Meta's puppy and lunch on sandwiches and milk. Meta loved
Jill and wanted to be her mother. She imagined what it would be like
for the three of them to live together. She hated Estelle. In her mind,
Estelle was a "commanding, baleful woman," who made everyone
miserable.

Then Faulkner did a strange thing, a cruel thing. He went to Meta
and Ben Wasson with an astonishing request: he wanted Estelle to meet
Meta, but didn't want her to suspect anything, so he asked Ben to bring
Meta to dinner as his date. Faulkner had told Estelle they were seeing
one another. Wasson thought it "a terrible idea" and felt "a sense of
betrayal," and Meta didn't like it either. She thought it a "punitive act"
against Estelle. Yet she and Wasson agreed to go along with the bizarre
charade.

They showed up at the Faulkners' promptly at 9 P.M., after Jill was
in bed. Faulkner, puffing on his pipe, played his role to perfection: he
mixed martinis with a steady hand and looked on serenely as Estelle
made idle conversation, asking Meta what she did and how she had met
"my Billy." Face-to-face with her adversary, who had loomed so menac-
ingly in her imagination, Meta was startled to find her "a small, gray
wren of a woman in a nondescript dress." If she had ever been pretty,
Meta thought, she showed little trace of it now. As she confronted this
"pale, sad, wasted creature," Meta felt her hatred evaporate.

At dinner, Faulkner carved the meat with authority. They made
polite talk, sipped, picked at their food. Meta sat there cringing; she
wanted to crawl under the table and hide. Afterward, in the car, she and
Wasson scarcely said a word.

The next morning, Estelle phoned Wasson in a rage. "You didn't fool me for a second, you and Billy. I know that the person you brought to my house last night is Billy's girl out here and not your girl at all! I know about that movie actress you're so crazy about. I don't appreciate it one bit your flinging his mistress right in my face, and all these years you've been like a member of the family!" She hung up.

Faulkner phoned next. "If Estelle called you up, I'm sorry. Ain't there something you can do to get her off my back?" He paused. "Get her a lover, anything, so she'll leave me alone." Wasson muttered "platitudes" and thought this was "surely the end of their marriage."

Faulkner seemed to be steeling himself for a showdown with Estelle. Perhaps, if he was outrageous enough, she would agree to terms just to get rid of him. One Sunday, despite his dislike for such things, he took Estelle to a musicale, and Meta was there, as he'd asked her to be. He even persuaded Meta to invite him and Estelle to one of her own parties. "Why do I do whatever you ask?" Meta said, annoyed. She found that she did hate Estelle after all; she was "foolish, all pride drowned in whiskey and lovelessness."

Still, Faulkner avoided talking to Estelle about a divorce. He knew it would be an ugly scene, and he dreaded it. One night, Meta told him that Wolfgang Rebner had phoned—he was in Arizona now—and said he thought he was in love with her. He was coming back to Hollywood after his tour ended. Meta didn't intend this as a threat, she said. But Faulkner was worried—she sensed it through all the webbing he kept around his feelings. He told her good night. At the doorway, he pivoted, looked at her wildly. Alarmed, she called his name. But he held up his hand in apology and hurried away.

Shortly after, perhaps that weekend, he braced himself and went to Estelle. It was time for them to talk.

WHEN FAULKNER CALLED ON META a few days later, he had been drinking. He threw himself into a chair and put his head back. "Damn, damn, damn," he muttered. Meta tensed; he had done it, she thought, had asked Estelle for a divorce and for custody of Jill; from his appearance—he was trembling violently—she was sure there had been a terrible argument.

"It's Jill, isn't it?" she guessed. "Estelle won't let you have Jill."

"I expected she'd give me a fight over Jill," he said. "That I was braced for. What I didn't expect is that she would want to take everything. I didn't dream she would go that far."

But Estelle would go that far. She was fighting for her sanity and her life. No, she would not give up her daughter to him and that Miss Carpenter. She would not give up Rowan Oak or his name either. The truth was, she didn't want a divorce; she couldn't bear the pain and humiliation of yet another round in court, another marital failure. Her marriage to Billy was terrible for her, too, but it was all she had. She would fight for it to the bitter end, if it came to that.

What were his alternatives? If he filed for divorce, he would have to make Jill a ward of the court. But he could never do that. Moreover, he was convinced that in a divorce action Estelle really would strip him of everything he owned and leave him a pauper. He had so many people to support—his mother, Louise and baby Dean, the servants. He was already insolvent. The financial penalties of divorce, he feared, would ruin him.

With heavy heart, he told Meta the truth. "I can't get free," he said. "Not for a long, long time." She couldn't believe it. "Are you telling me there's no chance for us?" None, he said, at least not until Jill was old enough to go before a judge and choose between him and Estelle. "Good Lord," Meta said, "that's ten years."

He left her that night in the stubborn expectation that somehow they would have to go on as before. Which for Meta was intolerable. It meant subterfuge, games, deceit, living "in the Back Street . . . of a married man's life." She had dated him, slept with him, fallen in love with him, in the vain hope that he would divorce Estelle and marry her. It was clear now that that had been "a foolish dream."

It was a difficult fall for them both. He could tell by her distance, by the quaver in her voice, how angry and disappointed she was. Then one day at lunch she told him it was over between them. She and Wolfgang had been corresponding, and he had proposed. He came from a wealthy Jewish family, commanded top fees as a concert pianist, and played "like an angel." She was almost thirty years old. When he had pressed her for a decision, she had told him yes. Faulkner was distressed and deeply hurt, but he had figured this would happen. He did try to dissuade her, but she had made up her mind. She realized now that he couldn't live in Hollywood any more than she could live in Oxford.

And so Meta was gone from him, his sweet, long-legged girl, his honey. He missed her fiercely. Once, for old time's sake, he asked her to have a drink with him, and she agreed. How could she refuse? He kissed her hair, called her "dear love," asked her to go to bed with him.

"No," she said, "I'm not going to sleep with you anymore."

"Not even one last time?"

"No," she said.

He felt rejected. It was Helen Baird all over again. How could Meta do this to him? A week later, he went to her and exploded. He wasn't a monk. She and Rebner weren't married yet. Why wouldn't she sleep with him? To keep him at bay, Meta asked an aunt to move in with her until her marriage to Rebner in the spring.

Absalom, Absalom! had appeared in late October, in a special limited edition of three hundred copies and a first printing of six thousand more. But Faulkner's mind was on his departed love. He opened the first copy of the special edition and wrote: "Inscribed for Meta Carpenter, wherever she may be."

He felt trapped in a vortex of unhappiness. He couldn't talk to anybody—who would understand him? He felt isolated and alone, cut off from his characters with no novel to work on, shackled to a bad marriage and to hated Hollywood. "All of a turmoil inside," he became the suffering drinker again. Wasson let him stay at his place while he was away, but returned to find Faulkner passed out on the couch in his undershorts, with a half-filled page in his typewriter and empty bottles everywhere. The air reeked of alcohol fumes and stale cigarette smoke.

The new year 1937 began with another loss: Hal Smith, Faulkner's longtime editor, publisher, and friend, resigned from Random House largely because of a conflict of styles. Robert Haas assured Faulkner that he and his remaining partners, Cerf and Klopfer, were among Faulkner's most enthusiastic admirers, and Smith sent him a tender letter. "I do not have to tell you what publishing your books has meant to me through all these years since the time of 'Sartoris' and Harcourt, Brace, or how important for the future and for literature your work has always seemed to me." Yet Hal's warmth failed to cheer him. Another close relationship was over. He felt terribly alone.

The winter and spring spun by in an alcoholic haze. In early April, just before Meta's marriage to Rebner, he found himself in the car with Estelle. He was driving, she sitting in the next seat. They were quarreling over Meta. He told her Meta was getting married—it was all over between them. But Estelle didn't believe that he'd given Meta up, that he no longer wanted her, and she flung an expensive compact out the window. He lost his temper and railed at her; she raked her fingernails down his face. He thought she wanted to kill him.

Later, after midnight, he made his way to Meta's place. He was still livid, his cheek gashed and bloody. Meta was shocked. "Estelle's signature," he said. "Do you have anything to drink?" She poured him what remained of his own bourbon and listened, incredulous, as he related what had happened. Her aunt called from the bedroom, but Meta assured her it was all right. As it happened, Wolfgang had just left. They were to be married day after tomorrow and would honeymoon in Europe. Faulkner pulled her to the couch.

"I wish you every happiness," he said. "I'll see you in New York—when you come back from Europe."

"Will you really?"

"You don't think I'm going to let you out of my life?"

On her wedding day, he went on a nonstop binge. Bill Spratling, his old friend from New Orleans days, called for a visit and found him and Estelle both miserable; Faulkner passed out after a few drinks, and Estelle showed Spratling bruises on her arms. By now, Faulkner was out of control, spinning in an inner midnight of hallucination and terror. He awoke in the Good Samaritan Hospital, suffering from an acute alcoholic condition. When he left in late April and returned to the studio, people talked about him: he was "skin and bones, and hardly recognizable." A colleague urged him to see a psychiatrist, but Faulkner refused. He distrusted psychiatrists even more than regular doctors. Outside his fiction, he didn't trust anyone.

In MAY 1937, Estelle took Jill home to Rowan Oak. Cho-Cho had married and was expecting a baby in the fall, and Estelle wanted to be with her. And anyway, she had had enough of Hollywood and marital combat. Faulkner fretted about Jill's safety, felt even more isolated without her. "Take care of my little baby for me, Sister," he wrote Cho-Cho. "She is little and helpless and wants little save to be happy and loved and looked after." He repeated, "Take care of my baby."

As summer came on, he was determined to pull something out of himself. He returned to his series of Civil War stories, which had appeared in the *Saturday Evening Post,* and set about revising and expanding them into a book, which Cerf agreed to publish. It wasn't a major work, he knew that, but at least he was back home in Yoknapatawpha County and writing again. The setting was Civil War Mississippi, the central figure a youthful Bayard Sartoris, "Old Bayard" of *Sartoris.* During the war, Bayard idolized his father, Colonel John Sartoris, and tried to emulate his deeds of valor and his creed of violence. Bayard's constant companion was Ringo, a black youth who was like a brother to him and shared his military adventures during the war. Indeed, their close relationship reflected one of Faulkner's observations about race relations in the South—that youngsters there tended to be innocent of bigotry and unaware of racial differences. As Bayard recalled, "Ringo and I had been born in the same month and had both fed at the same breast and had slept together and eaten together for so long that Ringo called Granny 'Granny' just like I did, until maybe he wasn't a nigger anymore or maybe I wasn't a white boy anymore, the two of us neither, nor even people any longer: the two supreme undefeated like two moths, two feathers riding above a hurricane."

After the Civil War, Bayard's father returned home with a young woman named Drusilla Hawk, who was a hardened version of the epicene young females Faulkner had always liked. Drusilla had a sunburned face and savagely cropped hair, with a "boy-hard body," Bayard said, "not slender as women are but as boys are slender." When her first husband had died at Shiloh, Drusilla had discarded her woman's role and fought in Sartoris' irregular regiment as a man. After the war, in a man's shirt and pants, she returned to Jefferson with Colonel Sartoris and worked and slept at his plantation, until the indignant ladies of the town arranged for them to be married.

Colonel Sartoris, the fictional counterpart of Faulkner's great-grand-father, had been a ghostly presence in *Sartoris.* Now he was fully alive, with grizzled hair and the eyes of a man who had killed too much, busily building his postwar empire in Jefferson as Faulkner's great-grand-father had done in Ripley. Colonel Sartoris died like him too—gunned down in the street by his former business partner. By then, twenty-four-year-old Bayard had outgrown his father's life of violence. But he was *the* Sartoris now, and Drusilla and the Colonel's followers, even Ringo, all looked to him to avenge his murder. Ringo, who had found a new identity after the war ("I ain't a nigger any more. I done been abolished"), even tried to help Bayard; he was ready to blast Redmond with a gun. But Bayard would have none of it. Alone and unarmed, he confronted Redmond in his law office, forced him to fire two shots aimlessly and then to flee Jefferson, never to return. Back home at the Sartoris plantation, Bayard found that Drusilla had reconciled herself to his brand of courage—and then had left for good. Aunt Jenny Du Pre, overjoyed that Bayard had broken with his family's violent legacy, still deplored the pride that had led him to risk his life. "Oh, damn you Sartorises!" she cried. "Damn you! Damn you!"

Beyond the current story, of course, her joy wouldn't last. For Bayard's grandson, young Bayard of *Sartoris,* would fall heir to the family tradition of violence. But for now Aunt Jenny could bask in her happiness. By late summer, Faulkner was done, the book off in New York; he would call it *The Unvanquished.* It was a retread of mostly old material —only the last chapter was new—yet it gave him a sense of accomplishment in an otherwise abysmal time for him.

In August, Twentieth Century–Fox declined to take up the option on his contract. He was free to leave Hollywood, having earned nearly $20,000 in 1936 and more than $21,000 in 1937. Sick of movies, "worn out from them," he was ready to go home, even to Estelle. Yet he felt terrible. He missed Meta. In a black gloom, he left Hollywood with Ben Wasson, who was going home to Greenville for a visit. When they crossed the Arizona-California line, Faulkner stopped his Ford and looked at the sun-parched landscape. On the California side, he thought a sign ought to be erected for travelers: "Abandon hope, all ye who enter here." Well, it was behind him for a while, anyway. He took out a pint of bourbon and sipped it as he headed across Arizona.

It was a tense trip for Ben, who watched Faulkner consume one bottle of whiskey after another, his face etched with unhappiness, his eyes sometimes filled with tears. In tourist courts at night, Faulkner would call out Dean's name. Back on the highway, with the arid wastes of the Southwest passing in the car windows, Wasson tried to engage him in conversation. Once, in a burst of courage, he even asked what Faulkner thought about the critics' reception of *Absalom, Absalom!* "I don't know what they said about it," Faulkner replied, "but I'm told they didn't like it. But they don't know everything. Some day they'll grow up to that book. It's too much for them." Faulkner managed a half grin. Then he grew solemn again. "I do know, though, Bud, that *Absalom* is the last big one I'll write. It takes too much out of me."

By September 1, Faulkner was home again after a long year's absence. There was still tension between him and Estelle, but they did reach a kind of truce after all the trouble in Hollywood. With Meta and Helen Baird both on his mind, he wrote a short story about tragic lovers called "The Wild Palms," then celebrated his fortieth birthday. His hair was grayer now; there were wrinkles at the corners of his eyes.

In October, he headed for New York City to see Meta when she and Rebner returned from their honeymoon. Not entirely sober, he met them for coffee and shook hands with Rebner, who was tall, assertive, and altogether charming. Meta was glad to see Faulkner, glad to have him back as her friend. But she could tell that he still wanted her.

He called at Random House and saw Bennett Cerf, who could commiserate with his problems of the heart. Two years ago, Cerf and movie star Sylvia Sidney had eloped from Hollywood in an airplane, but their marriage had ended a few months later when Miss Sidney sued for divorce on the grounds that Cerf objected to her career and "did not understand motion-picture people." Well, Faulkner could sympathize with that: he didn't understand them either.

Faulkner also met his current editor, a onetime dentist named Saxe Commins, who was Eugene O'Neill's editor and close friend. Faulkner liked this tense, slender, sad-eyed man, who had a fondness for hats and chain-smoked cigarettes. Commins made room for him in his cramped third-floor office so that they could go over *The Unvanquished* and Faulkner could work on revisions.

Meanwhile he discussed financial arrangements with Robert Haas, a partner in the firm, who now supervised the publication of his books. A Yale graduate and winner of a Distinguished Service Cross for heroism in the Great War, Haas had helped found the Book-of-the-Month Club before becoming a publisher. Gray-haired and impeccably dressed, he had the reserved manner of a Jewish patriarch, with a wry wit and a vast vocabulary that dazzled his associates. Although he admired Faulkner, he agreed to advance him only $1,000 on his next novel. Faulkner had earned that much in one week in Hollywood.

At a cocktail party later, Faulkner spotted Sherwood Anderson, sixty-one now, with double chin and thinning gray hair, his short, bulky frame still conspicuous in a crowd. Anderson had refused to speak to him since the "unhappy caricature affair" in New Orleans eleven years before. By now, Anderson had divorced Elizabeth and married a fourth time, and Faulkner would wonder if he wouldn't have been happier as a monk. Faulkner remembered how upset Anderson had been when he and Hemingway had both parodied Anderson's style, how much he thought he'd been betrayed. Well, Faulkner hadn't intended to hurt him; his satiric little foreword in Spratling's book of sketches hardly matched what "Hemy" had done in *The Torrents of Spring*. But Faulkner still regretted his part in their estrangement, and he wanted to make amends.

Anderson noticed Faulkner, too, but tried to avoid him. Finally Faulkner came over and pulled Anderson aside. "Sherwood," he said, grinning, "what the hell is the matter with you? Do you think I am also a Hemy?" For a moment, Faulkner thought, Anderson "appeared taller, bigger than anything he ever wrote." Then Faulkner remembered *Winesburg, Ohio* and some of the stories in *Horses and Men,* and he knew that here truly was a giant in a world of pygmies, even if Anderson had made only those two or three gestures equal to giant-hood.

As his stay lengthened into November, Faulkner drank steadily, unable to cope with his tempestuous feelings for Meta. He had made a dinner engagement with her and Rebner, but when he awoke in his room in the Algonquin and thought about seeing her that night with another man, a man she belonged to and slept with, he hit the bottle in a frenzy of jealousy and heartbreak. He was so drunk that he fell against a steam pipe in the bathroom, burning his back severely. He lay there, face down on the floor, clad only in his shorts, oblivious to the icy November wind blowing through an open window, until anxious friends got the management to open his door and found him. They helped him to bed and summoned a doctor, who treated him for a third-degree burn and gave him an evil-tasting potion, paraldehyde, to curb his craving for alcohol.

"Why do you do this?" the doctor asked.

"Because I like to," Faulkner snapped.

Meta and Wolfgang entered the room, having waited for him in the lobby for nearly an hour. They were shocked to find Faulkner lying naked in bed, heavily sedated. The acrid smell of medication permeated the room. "I started drinking," he whispered to Meta. "Last night I was all right. This morning, thinking of seeing you tonight . . . belonging to someone else—" She sponged his face with a wet towel, and he mumbled that he would be better tomorrow.

The next day, convalescing in bed, he asked to see Sherwood Anderson. This time Anderson didn't avoid him. At his bedside, the older man was warm and solicitous to his onetime protégé. He realized that Faulkner suffered from an acute drinking problem, and he tried to soothe him now, as if to forgive him for everything.

Within a week, Faulkner was up and about despite the excruciating pain in his back. He saw Meta and Rebner again, and Meta had the impression that he had completely shut out the fact of their marriage. Before Faulkner left for Oxford, she met him once more, alone. As they sat together on a bench in Central Park, she told him about Rebner's difficulties in trying to be a concert pianist and about their precarious finances. He offered money to help them, but she said no. He told her about the truce with Estelle, then asked, "Carpenter? Are you happy?"

"I love Wolfgang very much," she said. "I can say that to you, can't I?"

"Yes, ma'am."

"I love being in his world. In the center of everything that's exciting to me." She added, "It's fine with us. It really is."

There was so much he could have told her: about his suffering and terrible confusion since their breakup, his wondering if *he* wouldn't have been happier as a monk. Still, he could not regret the love they had shared. "Meta." He took her hand. "Meta, one of my characters has said, 'Between grief and nothing I will take grief.' "

PART FIVE

VANISHED FIELDS OF GLORY

IT WAS A SUNLESS NOVEMBER in Oxford, with cold, gusty winds crying at the window by Faulkner's writing table. Before going to New York, he had written a short story about tragic lovers. Now, despite the pain of his burn and the insomnia this caused him at night, he was developing "The Wild Palms" into a novel. He wrote this, he said later, "in order to stave off what I thought was heart-break." Once again, he turned his pain into art, as his characters sprang to life and spoke to him in their own distinct voices. The setting was not Yoknapatawpha County, but the themes derived from his own suffering over doomed love, first with Helen Baird and now with Meta.

At first the novel was only about the doomed lovers, a onetime New Orleans intern named Harry Wilbourne and a free spirit named Charlotte Rittenmeyer. But suddenly Faulkner realized that "something was missing" in his story: "it needed emphasis, something to lift it like counterpoint in music." At this juncture, a tall, hillbilly convict emerged in his imagination, telling a parallel story to that of Harry and Charlotte; the tall convict—he never gave his name—had been betrayed by one woman yet saved another in the great Mississippi River flood of 1927 and then returned to prison. Faulkner saw that Harry ended up in prison like the tall convict. They were both there largely because of their entanglements with women. Faulkner was delighted with his creation, in more ways than one. He had often thought of retreat as the only alternative to the destructiveness of sexual love. Yet he'd told Meta that he preferred grief to nothing. Now he could put his own ambivalent feelings into his fiction, as counterpoints in the lives of his characters. He called the convict's story "Old Man"—Faulkner's name for the Mississippi—and worked back and forth on the concomitant stories, alternating a chapter of "The Wild Palms" with a counterpoint chapter of "Old Man." Later he would title the book itself *The Wild Palms*.

He wrote in great travail, beset by family and back complications. Cho-Cho's husband had left her and her newborn baby, and Faulkner did all he could to comfort her—"He kept me alive," she said emphatically. On top of that, his nerves were frayed from constant back pain and inability to sleep. In February 1938, he consented to skin grafts on his burn, but they didn't take. Disgusted, he said "to hell with it, let it all rot off and be damned." Then he got the damn thing infected and had to have it scraped and treated constantly for two weeks. In April, he wrote Bob Haas about his difficulties and said he had only now returned to his book, though he still felt pretty bad.

Because of all the turmoil, he couldn't tell whether his novel was all right or pure drivel. It seemed to him that he was sitting on one side of a wall and the paper was on the other side, and he wrote with his pen hand thrust through the wall, scribbling in pitch darkness. Sometimes he didn't even know "if the pen still wrote on paper or not."

By mid-June 1938, he was finished, his characters fully realized despite the ordeal of their birth, his anguished heart especially evident in the story of Harry and Charlotte. Initially, Harry had been a nondescript intern in a New Orleans hospital; still a virgin at twenty-seven, as perhaps his creator had been, Harry found the hospital a sanctuary from love and involvement. Then he met Charlotte at a New Orleans party, as Faulkner had met Helen Baird. In fact, Charlotte resembled Helen. She was a short young woman, not fat as Harry had first thought, just broad, simple, a "profoundly delicate and feminine articulation of Arabian mares," with a face that laid no claim to prettiness, lacking makeup save for her painted broad mouth. Her eyes were brown with a yellow cast, and her cheek had a faint inch-long scar, from a childhood burn.

Charlotte was a strong woman, outspoken, passionate, and uninhibited. She confessed to Harry that she had a husband and two children, then set out to seduce him. Captivated, Harry succumbed to her, letting her overcome his fear of women and end his virginity. Charlotte became the great love of his life. He spoke of her as "an amber flame" (as Faulkner had spoken of Helen). Her eyes had a "fierce affirmation . . . in which he seemed to blunder and fumble like a moth." Feeling trapped in marriage and motherhood, Charlotte ran away with Harry, to pursue the eternal romance of true love, which she thought attainable only in an unmarried, unconventional relationship. She set the rules and held Harry to them with a ruthless, almost unbearable honesty. "Listen," she said, "it's got to be all honeymoon, always. Forever and ever, until one of us dies."

She made love by striking her body against his, hard, as she might pull his hair to awaken him. To her horror and disgust, he began thinking of her as his wife. In Utah, she became pregnant, and they fought bitterly. "Oh, God, Harry, make me stop! Make me hush! Beat the hell out of me!" Finally, she persuaded him to abort her, but his hand shook so badly that he bungled the operation. She started bleeding. They hurried to New Orleans, then to a town like Pascagoula on the Mississippi Gulf, where she died in a rented cottage, and palm trees danced and moaned in the Gulf wind. In the end, Harry went to prison, where he rejected an opportunity to commit suicide and cherished Charlotte's memory with a fierce joy. *"Between grief and nothing,"* he thought, *"I will take grief."*

Meanwhile, the tall convict had also become entangled with a woman, as the chapters of his story alternated with those of "The Wild Palms." His saga began with him in the penitentiary at Parchman, serving fifteen years for armed robbery. About twenty-five, the tall convict was lean and flat-stomached, "with a sun-burned face and Indian black hair and pale, china-colored outraged eyes." He felt secure at Parchman; it was his sanctuary, as the hospital was Harry Wilbourne's. Then came the great 1927 flood, which wrenched the tall convict out of his secure little world. First, prison officials put him on a chain gang to help shore up a levee; then the guards ordered him into a small boat and sent him to rescue a pregnant woman trapped in the flood. When the boat overturned in the swirling waters, the authorities gave him up as dead and so recorded it. But he wasn't dead. A man of towering strength and humanity, he made it back inside the skiff, found the pregnant woman as he had set out to do, and tried desperately to return her and the boat to the guards. Now it was him against the rampaging "Old Man," which bore him and the woman violently southward, through thickets, over cotton fields, past Vicksburg, down past Baton Rouge, and finally to an old Indian mound, where he helped deliver the woman's baby. In the end, he brought his charges to safety and returned eagerly to the penitentiary. The authorities, of course, were astonished, since he'd been listed as dead and could have gone free. Now they added another ten years to his sentence for trying to escape.

And so the tall convict ended up in a prison cell like Harry Wilbourne, except that the tall convict was there of his own volition. Only now did it come out why: as a youth, he had had a young girlfriend, with ripe breasts and dull eyes; in fact, he had attempted armed robbery in large part to impress her. After he'd gone to prison, she had come to see him once and wept; later he received a picture postcard from her, which showed a Birmingham hotel where she had spent her honeymoon. After that, the tall convict wanted only one thing in life: to stay in prison and away from women, who were nothing but grief. The last line repeated what Faulkner himself had often thought. "Women ---t!" the tall convict said.

WHILE HE WORKED ON THE NEW BOOK, *The Unvanquished* had come out and had brought him an unexpected windfall. Random House had sold the motion picture rights to MGM for $25,000. After commissions, Faulkner's share came to $19,000—a veritable fortune in Depression Mississippi. "I am in fair shape now," Faulkner wrote his agent, Morton Goldman; "for a year or so now I can write in leisure, when and what I want to write, as I have always someday fondly dreamed."

Faulkner wanted to protect his money in a wise investment. He had long dreamed of owning a farm as the Old Colonel had done, and his brother John found exactly the one for him: a 320-acre spread situated in the hills seventeen miles northeast of Oxford, which Faulkner bought and named Greenfield Farm. Situated on a slope, the tumbledown farmhouse commanded a sweeping view of the remote countryside, of the bottomland and its winding creek and the wooded hills beyond. Faulkner loved the isolation and solitude—here he could retreat from Oxford and the pressures of money and family; here he could commune with the woods, the land, and the hill people like those he wrote about; here, when he needed an escape, he could work without the noisy intrusion of "civilization." What was more, the farm gave him another role to play: "I'm not a literary man," he would tell interviewers and others who made him feel uncomfortable. "I'm just a farmer who likes to tell stories."

He and brother John walked over the land together, two small figures silhouetted against the hills and sky. As John rolled a cigarette, his resemblance to his older brother was startling—not only the same small stature, but the same delicate movements, thin mustache, and short, graying hair. John agreed to run Greenfield Farm for Faulkner, to hire some Negro hands and raise mules, feed corn, and hay. By now, John had writing aspirations himself, and Faulkner would give him advice as to magazines and publishers. John admired his novelist brother almost beyond measure. "I think Bill is the greatest writer that's ever lived, including Shakespeare." But he was sensitive to Faulkner's volatile moods. "My brother is the most even-tempered man in the world," he once remarked, "mad as a hornet all the time."

In the fall, squire Faulkner engaged a new agent in New York, Harold Ober, a friend and neighbor of Bob Haas. "Mr. Ober," as Faulkner addressed him in their correspondence, cared deeply about his writers and fought to secure the best possible terms for them. Among his clients were Agatha Christie, Faith Baldwin, and F. Scott Fitzgerald. Ober had helped Fitzgerald far beyond their business relationship; Ober and his wife had even taken Fitzgerald's daughter into their home and become her foster parents. Yet this tall, beetle-browed New Englander was so withdrawn that he could sit through an entire lunch with scarcely a word. Faulkner once described him as "horribly shy, and I mean horribly," and swore he would not want to be marooned on an island with him. Nevertheless, Faulkner would rely a great deal on this reticent, indefatigable man in the hard years ahead.

By then, Faulkner felt better. Writing *The Wild Palms* had restored his confidence and his energy. On November 19, 1938, he sent Ober a story called "Barn Burning," intended as chapter one of a new novel, and Ober promptly sold it to *Harper's* for $400. The barn burner in the story was Ab Snopes, the hard-bitten father of the Snopes clan and the central character of "Father Abraham," which Faulkner had begun back in the winter of 1926–1927, then set aside to write *Flags in the Dust.* For years, Faulkner and Phil Stone had swapped humorous tales about the Snopeses, patterned after the proliferating rednecks of the post–Civil War era; and Snopeses had come and gone as supporting characters in Faulkner's Yoknapatawpha saga. Now, in the approaching winter of 1938, the Snopeses crowded Faulkner's imagination in a cacophony of voices, some so funny they made him laugh. In December, Faulkner wrote Haas that he was planning an entire trilogy about the way that comical, lowborn, money-grabbing, blackmailing bunch gradually took over Jefferson from the old inhabitants, the gentry and their ghosts. The central character of the trilogy, Faulkner explained, was Flem Snopes, Ab's son and the clan's chief, who first rose to power in outlying Frenchman's Bend (volume one), then moved to Jefferson, schemed and manipulated his way from a side-street café to the presidency of the Sartoris bank (volume two), then devoured Jefferson itself until there was no more of the old gentry to replace and nothing left to take (volume three). Faulkner told Haas that he was well into the first volume, which included some previously published stories, and that it was "going to be pretty damned sound."

Meanwhile, to the delight of his publisher, Faulkner gave an interview to Robert Cantwell, the literary editor of *Time* magazine, which planned to do a cover story on him and his forthcoming *The Wild Palms.* Cantwell believed that the South was enjoying a literary renaissance, what with the critical success of the literary magazine *The Southern Review,* the astounding sales of *Gone With the Wind* (1,750,000 copies thus far), and Faulkner's growing popularity with the French, who compared him to Poe. A novelist himself, Cantwell considered Faulkner the central figure in southern literary life, and would so argue in his cover story and review of *The Wild Palms.* Faulkner must have liked Cantwell. As a result of their interview, Cantwell could report a few details about Faulkner's background, including an accurate account of his war record. For once, Faulkner had apparently told the truth about that. As for his work, Faulkner said that his current project, a three-volume novel about the Snopes clan, would wind up his saga of Yoknapatawpha County. He saw himself as "a social historian," Cantwell said, who hoped to suggest the changes that were transforming the entire South.

The new year 1939 brought Faulkner unprecedented recognition in the United States. On January 18, he was elected to the National Institute of Arts and Letters, along with novelists Marjorie Kinnan Rawlings and John Steinbeck, whose *Grapes of Wrath,* which immortalized the Okie migrants, would win the Pulitzer Prize that year. *Time*'s cover story about Faulkner appeared in the January 23 issue, and called him "the most talented but least predictable Southern writer." Faulkner's picture on the front cover made him look like the farmer he insisted he was, and an unsmiling one at that, dressed in thick suspenders and a work shirt. *The Wild Palms* came out at about the same time, and by March was selling more than a thousand copies a week, which made it the most popular Faulkner novel thus far, even surpassing *Sanctuary*.

Later in the year, Faulkner's "Barn Burning" won the first O. Henry Memorial Award for the best short story of 1939. And Conrad Aiken, whom Faulkner had emulated in his youthful verse, published in *The Atlantic Monthly* the first sensitive and sensible discussion of Faulkner's style, which critics had almost universally damned as slipshod, whimsical, and incoherent. Aiken, who counted himself among Faulkner admirers, did describe his style as "a jungle of rank creepers and ferocious blooms taking shape before one's eyes,—magnificently and endlessly intervolved," but argued that Faulkner wanted to make readers "go to work" and that those who did were in for rich rewards. Aiken compared Faulkner to Balzac in verisimilitude and alternating viewpoints, and argued that what set him above his contemporaries was his James-like preoccupation with the novel as form.

Meanwhile Faulkner had heard from Meta again, and what she said raised his hopes of getting her back. A telegram from her indicated that her marriage to Wolfgang was finished and that she needed money for train fare from New York City to Arizona, where her parents now lived. Faulkner asked Bob Haas to give her $150 out of his royalties, and wired Meta to route herself through southern Mississippi. In early April, he met her at a rain-swept depot and drove her to New Orleans, where they found a hotel room in the French Quarter. She was exhausted, anemic, and shivering from a slight fever; he gave her raw whiskey to kill the cold. She felt miserable about her marriage. Rebner's hopes for a concert career had faded, and they were badly in debt. Sometimes he verbally abused her. Meta had come to Faulkner because he was her best friend and because he loved her. They made love that night and slept until noon. By then her fever was gone. "Good whiskey." He smiled. "And Mr. Bowen."

He asked her to stay in New Orleans and promised to come to her when he could, but she said no. She felt so worn out and confused—it was best for her to go home, where she could rest and try to get her mind together.

Later he received a letter from Meta with a New York postmark: she had gone to Arizona all right, but then had returned to Rebner, to try and salvage her marriage. She believed they were reconciled now. Faulkner didn't answer right away. When he did, he protested that he didn't see her enough and that it was bad physically to live as he did now. He knew he ought to find a girl—"a physical spittoon," as he put it. But although he'd tried, he hadn't been successful. "I simply won't rise," he wrote Meta. "That's strange isn't it? After what I know and don't ever seem to stop remembering very long, all else is just meat."

By late spring, he was hard-pressed for money again, thanks to a magnanimous gesture on his part. Phil Stone's father had died of a heart attack, and Stone had tried to sort out the old General's chaotic estate and pay off his creditors. By March 1939, one of them was suing on a $7,000 debt, and Stone, with only $1,000 to his name, was in severe financial trouble. Faulkner had not forgotten how much Stone had helped him with money and support in his early years as a writer. By securing an advance from Random House and selling his personal life insurance policy, Faulkner raised $6,000 for his beleaguered friend. "I have known him all my life," Faulkner told Haas, "never any question of mine and thine between us when either had it." But the loan left Faulkner so short of funds that he had to borrow $1,500 from the bank; it was either that or take another "sojourn down river" to Hollywood. But God knew what he would do when the $1,500 was gone. "Maybe what I need is a bankruptcy," he wrote Haas, "like a soldier needs delousing."

Nevertheless, he had more than two hundred pages done on his Snopes book and was soaring with confidence. "I am the best in America, by God." When the bank loan ran out, he did have to "boil the pot" again, cranking out detective and other stories for the big-paying magazines and haunting the post office for checks with which to pay coal and grocery bills. But he pushed on with the Snopes novel too—his capacity for work was astonishing—and by year's end he was done. He called it *The Hamlet* because it dealt with the Snopeses' invasion of Frenchman's Bend, a hamlet situated on the Yoknapatawpha River southeast of Jefferson. The sequels, he wrote Haas, were to be called *The Town* and *The Mansion,* which followed Flem Snopes' rise to power in Jefferson itself.

Faulkner began his story with Will Varner, the aging mogul of Frenchman's Bend, a lazy, mild-mannered man, thin as a fence rail, with reddish-gray hair and mustache and bright innocent blue eyes, who punctuated his speech with "Hell fire." His holdings comprised most of the good land in the area and mortgages on the rest, as well as a store, a cotton gin, and a combined gristmill and blacksmith shop.

It was Varner's little empire that Flem, the head of the Snopes clan, first targeted for infiltration. He came in from the backwoods to clerk in Varner's store, wearing a new white shirt, disreputable baggy pants, and tennis shoes, "a thick squat soft man," as Faulkner described him, "of no establishable age between twenty and thirty, with broad still face containing a tight seam of mouth stained slightly at the corners with tobacco, and eyes the color of stagnant water" and "a tiny predatory nose like the beak of a small hawk." The name Flem described him perfectly. With illimitable cunning, chewing his tobacco and spitting "contemplative bullet-like globules of chocolate saliva," Flem slowly and relentlessly invaded Varner's empire, usurping his son's place in the family business, moving into Varner's village, then into his place, and finally into his family.

He'd been watching Eula Varner, Will's indolent and voluptuous teenage daughter, her hair all honey in the sunlight. Flem had no lust for her like the other men, for he was sexually impotent; what he had was cold, calculating ambition. When Eula turned up pregnant by another man, Flem was there, ready to marry her. Will arranged the wedding with alacrity, glad to avoid a blot on the family honor and to reward the seemingly honest and energetic Flem. Eula, for her part, passively acquiesced in her father's decision, her face "a calm, beautiful mask." For Faulkner, hers "was not a tragic face; it was just damned." Part of Will's arrangement with Flem included the useless Old Frenchman place, with its "jungle-choked lawn" and "fallen baronial splendor." To be sure, Flem would find a way to turn it and his new family connections to profit. The newlyweds took off for Texas, the spitting, froglike Snopes scarcely reaching the shoulder of the blond and blank-eyed Eula, whose lovely legs had long aroused the men of Frenchman's Bend. That Flem had won Will Varner's daughter filled them with envy and wonder.

By now, Flem's relatives were swarming over Frenchman's Bend. Lancelot "Lump" Snopes had succeeded Flem at Varner's store. Weasel-like I. O. Snopes, quoting proverbs in a Niagara flow of chatter, had become the schoolteacher. Isaac Snopes, Flem's idiot cousin, had materialized there, pulling a wooden block with two snuff tins attached, gazing back with dim-witted absorption at the dust it raised in the road. "Another of them," a local man said. The most repugnant Snopes was an incorrigible, vicious little man with a cold flat dead voice and a face "like a mask of intractability carved in wood." This was Mink, another of Flem's cousins, who worked a hardscrabble farm near Frenchman's Bend. While Flem was off in Texas, Mink threw the little community into an uproar. When another farmer won a $3 judgment against him,

Mink went berserk, grabbed his shotgun, and annihilated the man. During his trial, Mink expected cousin Flem to return and save him. But Flem did not return and Mink, convicted and given a life sentence, went to prison cursing "that son of a bitch" and vowing to get even. Clearly Flem, and Yoknapatawpha County, had not seen the last of him.

As the Snopeses multiplied and spread, V. K. Ratliff, an itinerant sewing machine salesman, became their chief opponent and the spokesman for the independent farmers they victimized. Ratliff was one of Faulkner's favorite characters, an affable, tenderhearted countryman who somewhat resembled Sherwood Anderson, with shrewd, intelligent eyes and a pleasant, drawling, anecdotal voice. Based in Jefferson, he rode about the countryside in his buckboard wagon, watching Flem and his kinsmen and talking about the menace they posed in Frenchman's Bend. After Flem returned from Texas, Ratliff tried desperately to check his nefarious operations. But Flem was not to be outdone. He tricked Ratliff and two of his friends into buying the useless Old Frenchman place for cash, a mortgage on a farm, and Ratliff's half of a side-street café in Jefferson. In the end, Flem departed for Jefferson with his wife and her new baby daughter, and the denizens of Frenchman's Bend spoke about him in amazement, certain that nobody but Flem Snopes could have outwitted V. K. Ratliff.

Faulkner sketched Flem with sardonic pleasure, astonished that such a monster could exist, or even be imagined. But exist he did in Faulkner's world, his evil schemes threatening the downfall of people like Faulkner's own ancestors. Yes, Flem was now on his way to greater rewards in Jefferson, but readers would have to await the sequel to find out what happened. Faulkner dedicated *The Hamlet* to Phil Stone, and Random House put it on its spring list for 1940. It would be Faulkner's twelfth novel.

Faulkner read about events in europe with grave concern. By 1939, Adolf Hitler had built Nazi Germany into a dangerous military state, a new Reich, he proclaimed, that would avenge German dishonor in the Great War. On September 1, 1939, Germany invaded hapless Poland with fifty-six infantry divisions and fifteen hundred Luftwaffe planes, which pounded baroque Polish cities and wooden villages. The tank-led German panzer divisions introduced blitzkrieg, or lightning war, as they smashed relentlessly across the Polish countryside. To the Poles, the swarming tanks and planes seemed like visitations of the Apocalypse. Warsaw, besieged with screaming Stuka dive-bombers and artillery barrages, fell in late September, and the Polish state, pummeled by Germans from the west and Russians from the east, ceased to exist. The German invasion plunged Europe into another war, as France and Britain mobilized against Hitler and his thousand-year Reich. While the United States remained neutral, Roosevelt and other national leaders sympathized with the Allies and believed they could defeat Germany if they had enough weapons. By 1940, Hitler was massing his armored forces along France's Maginot Line, and all Europe—and much of America—awaited the inevitable trumpets of battle.

It was a portentous winter at Rowan Oak, too, for tiny Mammy Callie, in her mid-nineties now, was in precarious health. For years, she had lived in a cabin in the backyard, sewing her quilts by the light of kerosene lanterns. She spurned electricity and wouldn't use her spectacles, which she wore across the brow of her white headcloth. Long ago, she had decided that the family was in arrears to her—the figure she'd fixed on was $89—and even now she would send Jill to remind her father of his debt. "Pappy," Jill would say, "Mammy said to tell you not to forget you owe her eighty-nine dollars." The previous spring, when Jack flew in from Seattle in a new plane, the family went up for rides; and Mammy decided to go, too, despite her age and her fear of "them flyin' contraptions." Jack said, "her snuff stick was as rigid in her tightly clenched teeth as her little body was in the seat." But she relaxed once they were aloft; she tried to lift herself high enough to look out the window, glanced at Jack, smiled, and tapped his knee. "Dis here is good, Jackie. Dis here is *good!*"

But her health had steadily declined, until one day she had suffered a stroke while eating watermelon at Rowan Oak. As she lay in her cabin, "the generations of her loins began to arrive," Faulkner wrote later, "from her own seventy and eighty year old children, down through their great-and-twice-great grandchildren," and Mammy, conscious now and sitting up in bed, became "matriarchial and imperial, and more: imperious." At ten or eleven at night, while Faulkner lay alone in his bedroom, reading, he would hear the sound of stocking or naked feet on the back stairs, and a strange black face would appear in the doorway and say, "She want the ice cream." Dutifully, Faulkner would dress and drive up and down the highway until he found an all-night "juke joint" that would sell him a quart of ice cream.

As the fall turned to winter, Mammy seemed to improve; soon she was up and walking. "But," Faulkner remembered, "it was as if she knew herself that the summer's stroke was like the throat-clearing sound inside the grandfather clock preceding the stroke of midnight or noon," because she never again touched her last unfinished quilt. The cold came on and the days shortened, and she spent more and more time in the big house. Around Christmas she told Estelle, "when them niggers lays me out, I want you to make me a fresh clean cap and apron to lay on."

The new year 1940 brought bitter cold to Oxford; by January 25, the temperature stood at zero, and a half foot of snow lay on the ground outside Faulkner's library windows. He was reading the galleys of *The Hamlet* now. There was little news from the western front in Europe; both sides appeared to be waiting for the spring thaw. At Rowan Oak, Faulkner could hear Mammy out in the kitchen, where she took her meals now. On January 27, she suddenly collapsed, seized by another stroke, and then lapsed into a coma. The Faulkners kept vigil at her bedside; her kinfolk gathered again. But there was no hope this time. On January 31, with Estelle at her side, Mammy Callie died.

They dressed her in a fresh cap and apron, as she had wanted. Then her black and white mourners gathered round her casket in the parlor, and Faulkner gave the eulogy, as she had asked him to do, recalling in his quick, high-pitched voice how much Mammy Callie meant to him. Since his childhood, he said, she had stood "as a fount not only of authority over my conduct and of security for my physical welfare, and of active and constant affection and love. She was an active and constant precept for decent behavior. From her I learned to tell the truth, to refrain from waste, to be considerate of the weak and respectful to age. I saw fidelity to a family which was not hers, devotion and love for people she had not borne.

"She was born in bondage and with a dark skin and most of her early maturity was passed in a dark and tragic time for the land of her birth. She went through vicissitudes which she had not caused; she assumed cares and griefs which were not even her cares and griefs. . . . She was born and lived and served, and died and now is mourned; if there is a heaven, she has gone there."

Her death left an emptiness at Rowan Oak, so much so that Faulkner for a time had little heart for work. But in his grief for her, he thought a good deal about white-black relations in Dixie, about the estrangement of the two races and "that impenetrable wall of ready and easy mirth which negroes sustain between themselves and white men," as he once wrote. Out of his reflections came several stories about black folk, which Faulkner referred to as his "negro stories." In them, especially "Pantaloon in Black," Faulkner tried to penetrate the inner lives of black people, to probe behind the masks they wore in white society, so that he might understand their feelings and thoughts as human beings. "Pantaloon in Black," one of the most powerful stories Faulkner had ever written, introduced a big young Negro named Rider, who worked at the sawmill in Jefferson. When his wife of six months suddenly died, Rider was heartbroken and desperate. He got drunk and then joined a dice game at the mill, only to catch a white man cheating. When the man brandished a gun, Rider slit his throat with a razor. The next day, the victim's relatives lynched Rider from the bell rope in a Negro schoolhouse. A white deputy sheriff told his impatient wife about Rider while she was preparing dinner. Oblivious to Rider's feelings and suffering, the deputy was a monument to white insensitivity. "These damn niggers," he said. "I swear to godfrey, it's a wonder we have as little trouble with them as we do. Because why? Because they aint human. They look like a man and they walk on their hind legs like a man, and they can talk and you can understand them and you think they are understanding you, at least now and then. But when it comes to the normal human feelings and sentiments of human beings, they might just as well be a damn herd of wild buffaloes."

The deputy was merely mouthing what whites in the exterior world of Mississippi said every day, and it troubled Faulkner. Yet he admitted that it was hard to fathom black people because they did conceal so much of themselves from whites. He realized why, of course. It was a way of surviving a brutal caste system that threatened their very humanity. Every time he went to town he could see evidence of that, in the WHITES ONLY signs that hung in every white restaurant, bar, lunch counter, barbershop, hair salon, and hotel, over public water fountains and the doors of public rest rooms . . . in the way whites addressed a Negro man as "boy," a Negro woman as "auntie" . . . in the segregated schools and whites-only elections . . . in the ever-present threats of beatings, cross-burnings, and lynchings that "kept niggers in line" . . . in the whole fabric of southern law and custom that elevated one race over the other, dividing them into the blessed and the wretched of their Christian world.

Faulkner sent his "negro stories" off to Ober, but Ober couldn't place them that March, not even "Pantaloon in Black." *Collier's,* in turning it down, admitted that it was an excellent story, but said there was no place for it in their magazine.

B Y April 1940, Faulkner was broke again. To make matters worse, the federal government "put the finger" on him for an additional $450 on his 1937 tax. It was an old story by now: the worries about money distracted him so much he couldn't write. He seethed and raged about his inability to care for his family on the meager returns of his art. Once again, he prevailed on his publisher for help. Could Random House advance him $1,000 immediately and $400 a month, even $300, over the next two years? Haas and the others at Random House wanted to publish everything he wrote, but his books didn't sell enough to warrant that kind of arrangement. *The Hamlet,* published on April 1, had sold almost seven thousand copies by month's end, but Haas warned Faulkner that no book of his would ever earn him more than $3,000. Haas proposed a three-novel arrangement that would pay his harried author $1,000 now, $2,000 the next year, and $250 a month for the following two years.

Faulkner thanked him for his prompt response and generous offer, and asked for the $1,000 at once. He was desperate. Then his anger boiled over. "Every so often," he wrote, "I take these fits of sort of raging and impotent exasperation at this really quite alarming paradox which my life reveals: Beginning at the age of thirty I, an artist, a sincere one and of the first class, who should be free even of his own economic responsibilities and with no moral conscience at all, began to become the sole, principal and partial support—food, shelter, heat, clothes, medicine, kotex, school fees, toilet paper and picture shows—of my mother . . . [a] brother's widow and child; I inherited my father's debts and his dependents, white and black without inheriting yet from anyone one inch of land or one stick of furniture or one cent of money. . . . I am 42 years old and I have already paid for four funerals and will certainly pay for one more and in all likelihood two more beside that, provided none of the people in mine or my wife's family my superior in age outlive me, before I ever come to my own."

He fretted about the war, too, and the malaise that caused in him. By the end of May 1940, Hitler's armies had stormed into the Low Countries, sent the British and French reeling, and cornered last-ditch survivors at Dunkirk. Meanwhile, on the other side of the world, the Japanese were plundering China, bombing her cities and seizing her territory. "What a hell of a time we are facing," Faulkner wrote Haas. He said that he had tried on his old RAF uniform—it still fit him too—and that he might have to wear a uniform again. "Of course I could do no good, would last about two minutes in combat. But my feeling now is better so; that what will be left after this one will certainly not be worth living for."

Maybe "watching all this coming to a head" for the past year explained why he couldn't write, didn't seem to *want* to write. But he could still write, he told Haas. He hadn't said at forty-two all that was in the cards for him to say. Surely it was still possible for him "to scratch the face of the supreme Obliteration and leave a decipherable scar of some sort."

But no new novel would come. And his expenses still outran his advances. Here he was, drawing money from Random House for a novel he couldn't write, and the money wasn't enough anyway. It all gave him insomnia. He conceded that he was spending too much for his value as a writer, but if he didn't raise another $4,000 by next January he would have to liquidate himself and sell some of his property. He couldn't bear the thought. "It's probably vanity as much as anything else which makes me want to hold onto it," he told Haas. "I own a larger parcel of it than anybody else in town and nobody gave me any of it or loaned me a nickel to buy any of it with and all my relations and fellow townsmen, including the borrowers and frank spongers, all prophesied I'd never be more than a bum."

To justify an additional $4,000 advance, he proposed a book of his Negro stories, to include "Pantaloon in Black" and the others he had written the past winter; he promised that it would have "a more or less continuous narrative," like *The Unvanquished.* If Haas couldn't get more deeply involved, then let Faulkner try another publisher. To his regret, Haas replied that Faulkner's sales did not permit the extra advance he needed. So Faulkner contacted Harold Guinzburg at Viking, who had once intimated that Faulkner could write his own ticket there. Guinzburg made him an offer of $6,000, which Faulkner relayed to Random House. The inference, he pointed out, was that Viking would publish him from now on.

"All of us are absolutely sick at heart at the thought of your leaving Random House," Cerf wrote him in June. But Cerf didn't give up without a fight. He threw in a modest counteroffer for the book of stories; at the same time he made it plain to Guinzburg that it would cost him to "buy" Faulkner. For Random House to give up its contractual claims, Viking would have to pay $1,500 for the plates and current stock of *The Hamlet*. At that, Guinzburg backed off. In July, he wrote Faulkner that Random House's demands made the project too expensive for Viking and that he was withdrawing his offer. Faulkner was almost back where he began.

Cerf tried to palliate matters. "I beg you to put aside all thoughts of going to another publisher," he wrote in August. "I promise you that we will do everything in our power to make things as easy for you as we can. In my opinion, you and Eugene O'Neill are the two keystone authors on the whole Random House list and we simply cannot afford to lose you." These were reassuring words, but Cerf didn't offer any more money for the book of Negro stories. Faulkner had no choice but to shelve the project and resume writing commercial short stories.

At last, in late summer, Ober came through for him, placing several of his stories, including "Pantaloon in Black" with *Harper's,* for a total of $2,700. "I am doing no writing save pot-boilers," Faulkner told Haas in October. "Ober sells just enough of them to keep my head above water."

HE CONTINUED to "fret and stew" about Europe. In June, German armies had overrun France, stampeding soldiers and civilians alike; the German swastika now flew over Paris, and German soldiers strolled in Faulkner's cherished Luxembourg Gardens. By the fall of 1940, German planes were bombing London by night and by day, and the survival of Britain was still in doubt. Meanwhile Germany, Italy, and Japan had signed an axis pact, and Japan's ruling war party had adopted a program of conquest and expansion that menaced U.S. interests in the Pacific. Following events from Rowan Oak, Faulkner worried about bringing children into this war-racked world; he feared they might all be liquidated in a Nazi-Japanese takeover.

In November, he escaped into the wilderness with a group of Oxford hunters, some of whom had been members of General Stone's old hunting party. In his youth, Faulkner had gone out with the General and his friends; he remembered the tales they had told about Old Reel Foot, the huge, elusive bear who had once fought off an entire pack of dogs. Since then, timber companies had mowed down the woods where the old Stone camp had stood, and Faulkner brooded about the fate of the wilderness in the modern age, with its rapacious, exploitive technology.

Now the hunters gathered each autumn on the Big Sunflower River down in the Delta, to hunt deer and enjoy boozy masculine camaraderie around nighttime campfires. Faulkner was a regular member of this ritualistic annual retreat; he found it a wonderful way to forget his money troubles, his moribund marriage, and now his anxieties about the war. To be sure, he enjoyed the evenings of drinking and tale telling, the huntsmen laughing silhouettes in the glare of the campfire. He liked to stalk deer, too, to pit himself against the cunning of a wild animal. But beyond that, he felt a sacred kinship with the big woods, which allowed him a temporary refuge from the corruptions of civilization. Out here a man could remember his values—his honor and pride and independence, which alone made him worth saving but which civilization threatened with its dehumanizing technology, its onerous government controls and handouts.

With heavy heart, he returned to civilization and more desperate days. By mid-January 1941, he was too poor to pay his $15 electricity bill; Ober wired him $100 at once to keep his lights burning. Feeling victimized, out of control of his life, he would retire to his "drunk bed," as Malcolm called it, and descend into the hell of Old Crow. He might be gone for a week, two weeks, even longer.

With family help and sheer willpower, he pulled himself through the worst of it. To help the drying out, he took after the bitterweeds with his hoe. Malcolm said he would attack them like a man obsessed. Meanwhile money trickled in from the sale of his commercial stories. In May, sick to death of writing them, he returned to his long-delayed collection of Negro stories, for which Random House at last furnished him a $1,500 advance. He told Haas that his new book, a set of interrelated tales, would explore the "relationship between white and negro races here." To be called *Go Down, Moses,* it would include the powerful "Pantaloon in Black" and his other stories about black folk, which he now set about revising. He intended to make this a coherent book that would read like a novel.

When Jill entered the library, she could see him sitting in his backless chair, with his feet curled around the bottom of the legs, and tapping on his portable typewriter. She was eight in June, "fat and fair" as her father said, with a light, fairy-tale voice. She loved it when he read her stories, or sang "Oh, Dear, What Can the Matter Be?" or told her about the escapades of Virgil Jones, the guitar-playing squirrel. But he couldn't do that when he was writing. She noticed how distracted he was then. Sometimes she would see him lying on his couch, but he would tell her not to bother him because he was still working, "making things up."

With summer came a creative breakthrough. Never mind how terrible things were in the outside world (the Germans launched a massive invasion of Russia, relations between Japan and the United States were increasingly tense). His recent retreat into the big woods, and his memories of Old Reel Foot, inspired a chorus of Yoknapatawpha voices, some of which he had heard before and written down in previous stories. But now they came together in a long and magnificent new tale called "The Bear." Because of his accursed need for money, he wrote a version for the magazines, entreating Ober to sell it anywhere for anything he could get; Ober finally got $1,000 for it from the *Post.* Meanwhile Faulkner wrote a much longer version of "The Bear," which he incorporated into *Go Down, Moses* as its showpiece story and one of the triumphs of his art.

Isaac "Ike" McCaslin was the main character in "The Bear" and one of the central figures in Faulkner's entire Yoknapatawpha saga. In fact, Ike was closer to Faulkner in spirit than were any of his other characters. He was the grandson of Carothers McCaslin, an arrogant planter whose improbities with one of his slave girls—who also happened to be his daughter—led to a line of mulatto descendants. In fact, most of *Go Down, Moses* was about the tangled genealogies of the black and white strains of McCaslin's "cursed" progeny, including his white grandson Ike McCaslin.

In "The Bear," ten-year-old Ike joined the menfolk for their yearly trip to Major de Spain's hunting camp on the Tallahatchie River. There Ike came under the spell of Sam Fathers, one of Faulkner's most remarkable characters, an incorruptible old man of mulatto and Indian ancestry, who wore frayed, faded overalls and a five-cent straw hat, once his badge of slavery and now "the regalia of his freedom." The group's chief woodsman, Sam taught the boy how to hunt and survive in the forest, inculcating in him the notion of man's holy relationship to the wilderness. Under Sam's tutelage, Ike became keenly aware of the contrast between the purity of the woods and the corruptions of civilization beyond.

Ike now joined the hunt, an annual "pageant-rite" in which the menfolk and their baying dogs stalked a great, two-toed bear named Old Ben. None of them really thought they could kill their formidable prey, who was "ruthless with the fierce pride of liberty and freedom," and Faulkner suggested that the pursuit of the totemic bear was a kind of ritual, almost a religious ceremony, which afforded the men an escape from mundane society and a moment of cleansing and renewal. Once Ike actually saw the great bear; but only after he had put aside his gun and compass, the symbols of civilization, and met nature on its own terms. Then Old Ben *let* himself be seen.

Later, when Ike was thirteen, Sam Fathers captured a wild, violent dog and trained it to hunt; it was the kind of dog they needed if they were ever to bring the great bear to bay. Yet neither Sam nor Ike really wanted that, for it would mean the end of their ritual in the wilderness. Yet if that happened, Ike would not grieve. "He would be humble and proud that he had been found worthy to be a part of it." In the next hunt, both the bear and the dog perished, and Sam went down, too, from exhaustion, shock; a doctor said he "just quit," as if his own life depended on what the bear had symbolized. Following his directions, a fellow hunter, also part Indian, killed him and placed his corpse on an Indian funeral platform. After that, the hunters abandoned the campsite, the ritual of cleansing and renewal finished for them. Two years later, on his last journey into the woods, Ike was acutely oppressed by what he saw—a half-completed planing mill, stacks of steel rails, a logging train roaring by—which portended the doom of the wilderness.

Faulkner could have ended "The Bear" with the death of Sam Fathers and the end of the hunt. Instead, as Faulkner would say, Ike McCaslin kept talking, kept casting a shadow. Wanting to trace his family history, Ike, now twenty-one, plunged into the ledgers of his father and uncle, and there discovered not only his grandfather's incest, but the profoundly interrelated relationships of slaves and owners in the McCaslin genealogy. The entire exploitive saga of the white McCaslins shocked and disgusted him. To find peace of spirit, Ike renounced his claim to the family's slave-built plantation, a plantation founded on ruthless exploitation and rapacity and still sustained by savagery to sharecroppers and animals alike. He renounced it, too, because of his deep conviction, learned from Sam Fathers, that no man could own nature, any part of it. Having repudiated his ancestors, Ike embraced Sam as his father, old Sam who had smeared the blood of the buck on the boy's face and taught him his own spiritual view of the wilderness. Exalted, Ike exclaimed, "Sam Fathers set me free." But he paid a price for giving up his legacy, for it led to the breakup of his marriage, thus denying him children and a family of his own.

The next story in *Go Down, Moses* found Ike a bespectacled and childless old man, known in the county as "Uncle Isaac." It was about 1941, and he and his friends talked about the war in Europe. As it developed, Isaac had the unpleasant task of dismissing the mistress of one of his younger white kinsmen, Ross Edmonds, who lacked the heart to do so. The woman had her infant child with her—Edmonds' child. She loved Edmonds and had tried desperately to get him to return to her, but to no avail. As they talked, Isaac found out that she was a McCaslin descendant herself. But that was not what shocked him. He discovered, too, that this intelligent and articulate young woman, with her pale lips and dark, tragic, foreknowing eyes, was part Negro, and he cried, in a voice of pity, astonishment, and outrage, "You're a nigger!" It was still going on, then: the latest white descendant of old Carothers McCaslin had begat a child of McCaslin's latest black descendant. As Isaac cried out, he thought to himself about the chances of a Negro marrying a well-born southern white: *"Maybe in a thousand or two thousand years in America. . . . But not now! Not now!"* When the woman said she was going back north, he gave her money, he touched her hand with his gnarled, bone-dry, old man's fingers. "That's right," he said. "Go back North. Marry: a man in your own race. That's the only salvation for you."

"Old man," she retorted, "have you lived so long and forgotten so much that you dont remember anything you ever knew or felt or even heard about love?"

Later, lying on his cot in a sorrowful rage, the old man associated the destruction of his beloved wilderness with his kinsman's treatment of the young woman, both terrible violations to him—and to Faulkner, who made such violations central themes of the entire book.

By Christmas season 1941, the last section of *Go Down, Moses* was with Saxe Commins at Random House. "I think it's good stuff," Faulkner told his editor. "But then I always do." Faulkner would dedicate the book to Mammy Callie, "Who was born in slavery and who gave to my family a fidelity without stint or calculation of recompense and to my childhood an immeasurable devotion and love."

ON DECEMBER 7, the Japanese bombed Pearl Harbor, crippling the U.S. Pacific Fleet in a holocaust of destruction. America was stunned. Roosevelt pronounced it "a date which will live in infamy," Congress declared war, and Germany and Italy retaliated with war declarations against the United States. In a single surprise attack, the Japanese had swept America into a global conflict whose consequences were beyond calculation for those caught up in its flames.

At Rowan Oak, Faulkner read the news with alternate alarm and patriotic fervor. He was determined not to miss this war as he had the last. He would join the navy; if not that, the Army Air Corps. Was he not a licensed pilot? Could he not do his part? Estelle, however, tried to discourage him. He was forty-four years old; none of the services would take him at his age. But Faulkner was undaunted. Other men he knew were gone or going. His brother Jack had a commission in the counterintelligence and would soon be leaving for England. Faulkner, too, wanted a chance to paw "the earth a little in a plume and sword."

In the spring of 1942, he flew to Washington for a round of talks with military authorities, but the air corps turned him down, and nothing else worked out for him either. It was terribly distressing. Bob Haas was on temporary duty as a major in the national guard, his partner Don Klopfer a captain in the Army Air Corps. Both Malcolm and John's son

Jimmy would soon be in boot camp. Why couldn't Faulkner serve?
What the hell was wrong?

Go Down, Moses came out in May and sold well enough for a
Faulkner book, but he had drawn so many advances from Random
House that his royalties for the entire year would come to a paltry $300.
"Harrassed to hell for money," he sent Ober another batch of commercial stories. He thought them hackneyed. "I know where the trouble lies
in what I write now," he told Ober. "I have been buried here for three
years now for lack of money and I am stale." If he failed to get a military
commission, he thought he would go somewhere for a while, probably
to California. He would try for something in pictures, even for $100 a
week, until he could get back on his "mental feet."

Bitterly frustrated, he unleashed a diatribe against his family, especially the women in it. "I have been trying for about ten years to carry
a load that no artist has any business attempting: oldest son to widowed
mother and inept brother and nephews and wives and other female
connections and their children, most of whom I dont like and with none
of whom I have anything in common, even to make conversation about.
I am either not brave enough or not scoundrel enough to take my hat
and walk out: I dont know which. But if it's really beginning to hurt my
work, I will choose pretty damn quick. I don't think that yet; it is only
my earning capacity which is dulled; possibly because I have too little
fun." He added, "Incidentally, I believe I have discovered the reason
inherent in human nature why warfare will never be abolished: it's the
only condition under which a man who is not a scoundrel can escape
for a while from his female kin."

There was another reason for Faulkner's explosion—and his interest
in returning to Hollywood. Meta was back there now, without Rebner.
Their marriage was really finished this time; she had filed for divorce
in the Los Angeles courts. Faulkner needed Meta in the worst way. His
head swam with erotic thoughts. In late June, when Cerf informed him
of a possibility at Warner Bros., Faulkner wrote Meta at once that he
was going out to Hollywood and that he loved her passionately.

But in July, Faulkner found himself in an absurd crisis. In his harried
state, he had authorized two agents to represent him in Hollywood.
One was Ober's veteran West Coast associate. The other was an independent young agent named William Herndon. Unaware of one another, both agents approached Warners in Faulkner's behalf. After
young Herndon arranged a contract for him at $300 a week, Ober's

man stepped in, certain that he was Faulkner's authorized agent and that he could get him $500 a week. At that, Faulkner wired Herndon that his contract was invalid. Herndon in turn blew up, threatened to "cause trouble," accused Faulkner of having "failed in integrity." Faulkner was furious, resenting both the threat and the accusation. But he thought Herndon sincere, if naive and wrong. In the end, Faulkner's honor compelled him to abide by Herndon's terms. But it was galling all the same. The $300 weekly salary was less than Faulkner had earned as a novice ten years before. Out of that he would have to pay Herndon a 10 percent commission, send money to Maud and to Estelle, pay on his debts, and try to live on whatever he had left.

O N A SATURDAY EVENING IN LATE JULY 1942, he was sitting with Meta at Musso & Frank's Grill, in their favorite booth against the wall. Despite the emotional ordeal she had been through, she was still young-looking and attractive to him, with her flowing blond hair and wide, gentle mouth. As for Faulkner, she thought he had aged perceptibly: his hair was almost completely gray now, his mustache full and bristly, his eyes pouched. Gone were the traces of youth she had seen in his face before. His sharp nose and furrowed brows gave him an "old guarded eagle look," she thought.

He told her about the fiasco with Herndon and his salary with Warners—only $300 a week, compared to the $1,200 he had made when he left Hollywood the last time. Top writers now commanded $2,500 a week. Meta was furious. He was "America's greatest novelist," yet even beginning screenwriters earned more than he did. There were rumors that he had been blackballed—"Hollywood's punitive response to his excessive drinking and go-to-hell arrogance," she contended.

Back at her apartment, she proposed boldly that they live together, but he refused. "It would be a grievous error for us," he said.

"Estelle?" Meta asked.

"She wouldn't say a word this time," Faulkner said.

"Then what, Bill?"

"My southern rectitude," he said. "The mystery of each other, mainly mine for you, if I have any."

She said, "You are not easy to know, Bill Faulkner."

They became lovers again, but on different terms. Before, she had expected that they would marry. Now she asked for nothing, expected nothing, except his love and encouragement. "It was not enough," she said, "but I made it enough."

When he reported to Warner Bros., he got the shock of his life. He had thought his contract called for a thirteen-week stint in Hollywood. Now he found out it was for seven years. *Seven years!* He couldn't believe it. Even after Herndon verified the terms, he still couldn't believe it. At first he refused to sign the contract. But Herndon said he had to. "You authorized me to represent you. I have already committed you to it," Herndon said. Mad at himself "for getting things bitched up like this," Faulkner finally signed. But it was like consigning himself to purgatory.

Every workday morning, he dragged himself to Warners' Burbank studio, girded with walls like a prison. At the writers' building, he found himself in a corner office called "the ward," where he and six other screenwriters turned out production-line scripts for a firm that happily called itself the Ford of the motion picture industry. Faulkner hated everything about his slavelike conditions. But most of all he hated Jack Warner, Hollywood's Simon Legree. A cigar-puffing dandy with a deep tan and a pencil-line mustache, Jack Warner disdained writers—"You're all schmucks with Underwoods," he told them—and bragged that he had America's best writer on his payroll at $300 a week.

Faulkner did befriend a fellow writer named A. I. "Buzz" Bezzerides, a dark, massive man of Turkish birth, who all but worshiped him. As an engineering student at Berkeley, "Buzz" had read all of Faulkner's novels in an "inexplicable, confounding, passionate fascination," and had gone on to write a novel himself about truckers, which Warners had made into a movie. But even with Buzz on the ward with him, Faulkner felt like a man in chains, forced by the whip of debt and family obligation to hack out scripts for *The De Gaulle Story* and other films. He enjoyed a brief reprieve when Howard Hawks, his friend, called him in to resuscitate a couple of moribund scenes in Hawks' *Air Force*. Back on Warners' production line, Faulkner handed over exactly twenty-five pages a week, which he believed was all the studio deserved for his miserly wages.

After work, he saw Meta for drinks, dinner, and perhaps a walk on Hollywood Boulevard, in surging crowds of men and women in uniform. Signs of the war were everywhere in Los Angeles—in the meat and butter shortages, the hooded streetlights and nightly blackouts, the barrage balloons along the coast, and the antiaircraft batteries set up in school playgrounds and out in the canyons. Far across the Pacific, the Japanese had driven westward clear to the borders of India, smashed southward toward Australia, bombed the Aleutians off the coast of Alaska, and pushed across the central Pacific to Midway, where American naval forces at last turned them back in a momentous U.S. victory. Nevertheless, bombing scares plagued Los Angeles into the winter of 1942, and night wardens patrolled the city to enforce the blackout.

Faulkner had rented a room with a terrace on the top floor of the Highland Hotel; it afforded a scenic view of the Hollywood Hills, dotted with Spanish stucco houses. Here, high over Hollywood, he made love to Meta, trying to shut out the war, the studio, his neglected art. Yet things were not the same between them. Thirty-five now and twice divorced, Meta was no longer the dependent, submissive young woman who had so ignited his desire. She was her own woman now, making her own way, solving her own problems. He could still be passionate with her and concerned about her wants, but there was a distance between them. When she realized that he did not need her company as he once had, Meta herself broke their "night-after-night pattern," as she phrased it. She loved him more than ever, she thought, but she wanted to see him on her terms: when she had ardor of her own, when she could no longer stay away from him.

After that, Faulkner often spent whole evenings at bars with other male writers. It pained him to think of his lowly salary compared to theirs. He wished to hell he could get out of here and into the war somehow; it distressed him to see so many men in uniform, some of them no younger than he. Lonely, unproductive, and miserable, he went on another drinking spree. Once, with Meta, he tossed down nine or ten straight double bourbons, and she became alarmed. Yet she had an idea what was troubling him, beyond Hollywood, the indignity of his job, the terrible war. "You miss Jill, don't you?" she said. Yes, he confessed, he sure enough missed Jill. She kept writing and asking when he would come home; she wanted him to sing her songs and tell her stories about Virgil the squirrel. He made a phonograph record about Virgil and sent it to her; he wished her, and Estelle too, plenty of ghosts and goblins on Halloween. He missed his mother, his brother John, and Malcolm and Cho-Cho. He might complain bitterly about them when he was at Rowan Oak and want desperately to get out. Yet when he was out, he became unbearably homesick.

Meta said, "You really are a family man, Faulkner." And she thought to herself: he didn't sleep with Estelle, had no guilt about making love to another woman, but he wasn't made for adultery. She thought it violated his deep feeling for family and southern respectability.

At Christmas, he headed home on "furlough," took pleasure in being the lord of his manor for a month, and returned feeling restored, with his sense of humor intact. In April 1943, he wrote Cho-Cho that he had come down with "the damned worst bloody rotten bad cold in human captivity," and that it was now one of triplets: lumbago and earache, with leprosy, bubonic, and death still to go. But "I've got used to it now. Of course I can't hear on my left side, and when I creep out in the A.M. to go to work, I am a rachitic old man in the last stages of loco-motor ataxia. But I can still see the red lights to cross the street on, and I can still invent a little something now and then that is photogenic, and I can still certainly sign my name to my salary check each Saturday."

Later in the spring, Howard Hawks rescued him again from the ward at Warner Bros. and put him to work on what was to be Hawks' epic war film *Battle Cry*. Hawks installed him in his office on the Warner lot, a little house with kitchen and icebox, messenger boys and stenographers, and the two of them produced a treatment and later a temporary revised screenplay. Faulkner wrote Maud that Hawks was "a cold-blooded man, but he will protect me if I write a script that will make money for him." The new assignment brought him and Meta together almost every workday, since she was back with Hawks as his secretary and script girl. Meta kept an eye on him, begging him to stay sober. He swore he would try.

He kept trying to get out of his seven-year contract and its "pittance of a salary." But Warners and Herndon both kept him shackled to it— Herndon because he needed his steady 10 percent commission. The studio did raise Faulkner's salary to $400 a week, but it was still a pittance. Faulkner wanted so badly to escape Warners and go home that he was "about to bust." But at least he had work to do with Hawks, something he believed in. If it weren't for *Battle Cry*, he reckoned he would blow up.

Yes, he believed deeply in Hawk's film, which celebrated the contributions of all the Allies to the coming victory. And victory did seem a little more possible in the summer of 1943. By then, the Russians had turned back the invading Germans in a series of titanic land battles and were counterattacking at the center of the eastern front. In the Pacific, U.S. and Australian forces had driven the Japanese out of the Solomons and New Guinea, and U.S. strategists were planning an aggressive island-hopping campaign into the heart of Japan's Pacific empire.

For Faulkner, one casualty in the Pacific brought the war close to home: Bob Haas's only son, a torpedo-bomber pilot, was killed in June 1943. Faulkner sent his condolences to Haas and said he feared that his nephew Jimmy, who was training to fly torpedo planes, would also get killed. Then who knew? Faulkner told Haas. *Maybe your son and my nephew will sit together in the mythic hall at Valhalla, where the souls of slain heroes gathered, and will hold two places for us, too, not because we were heroes, but because we loved them.* Faulkner remembered that Haas' daughter was serving in the Women's Ferry Squadron, and that all the Haases were Jews. He hoped he didn't run into some one-hundred-percent American Legionnaire until he felt better.

Meanwhile he kept apprised of developments in North Africa and the Mediterranean, too. American forces had joined the desert war, and an Allied juggernaut had swept the Axis out of North Africa. In May and June 1943, while Faulkner worked on *Battle Cry,* Allied bombers, including a squadron piloted by American Negroes, pounded the Italian-held island of Pantelleria into submission, thus clearing the way for an Allied invasion of Sicily in July.

Faulkner read about the Negro pilots, and he read something else, too. On the very day they distinguished themselves over Pantelleria, the worst American race riot of the era broke out in Detroit, with roving gangs of whites beating Negroes in the streets and torching their cars. The rioting was so terrible that Roosevelt had to send in six thousand federal troops to restore order, but not before twenty-five blacks and nine whites had been killed.

What in hell was going on here? Negro fighting men were risking their lives overseas while Negroes were getting mobbed and murdered in Detroit? Faulkner was fuming. In *Battle Cry,* he had included a sequence suggesting that the wartime solidarity of blacks and whites might lead at last to the fulfillment of Lincoln's promise. Now it seemed even more urgent that the war usher in a new era of racial justice. "A change will come out of this war," he wrote Malcolm. "If it doesn't, if the politicians and the people who run this country are not forced to make good the shibboleth they glibly talk about freedom, liberty, human rights, then you young men who live through it will have wasted your precious time, and those who don't live through it will have died in vain."

The more he brooded about the war, the more convinced he became of something else. Woodrow Wilson had vowed that the first great war would be "a war to end all wars." Instead, it had created the combustible conditions that ignited the current inferno, which threatened the lives, not to mention the freedom and human rights, of countless millions of people the world over. Well, it must not happen again. He wrote Malcolm, "We are fighting, as always, the long battalioned ghosts of old wrongs and shames that each generation of us both inherits and creates. We will win this one, then we must, we must, clean the world's house so that man can live in peace in it. I believe we will. I envy you being young enough to have a part in it."

Still, was there not something he could do? He was too old to fight like Malcolm and Jimmy, too old to answer the trumpet call of battle. The military centers had all made that clear to him. What, then, was left for the older men? His mind raced forward to the postwar years. "When you and Jim and the young men have cleaned the house," he told Malcolm, "maybe there will be a part for me, who cant do anything but use words, in re-arranging of the house so that all mankind can live in peace in it."

He could write something, then: something that would convert people to the idea of peace and racial justice. In the meantime, he could work on an epic film like *Battle Cry*, doing some small part to win the war and bring on the glad tomorrow when older men like him would have their chance.

Later in the summer, Hawks came to him with an exciting proposal. Once they finished *Battle Cry*, Hawks hoped to form his own independent production company and hire Faulkner as his scriptwriter. By now, Warner Bros. had promised to let Faulkner out of his seven-year contract once he wrote a successful film. Surely *Battle Cry* would be that. Then Faulkner could go with Hawks! The tall director exuded confidence. He was certain that he and Faulkner as a team could command two million dollars a picture and divide the profits. The possibilities sent Faulkner soaring. A partnership with Hawks would not only emancipate him from Warners; it would make him financially secure for the rest of his life. He could go home, back to the town, the land, and the people he loved, and there write things that might effect social change.

But his dream collapsed when Warners refused to approve Hawks' multimillion-dollar budget for *Battle Cry*. Faulkner didn't know the details. There were rumors of a confrontation, a report that Hawks had walked off the studio lot. Later, word came that *Battle Cry* had been canceled. Gone, too, was Hawks' plan for an independent partnership —and Faulkner's chance for freedom. Steeped in gloom, Faulkner walked across the street to a bar.

HIS FORTUNES SEEMED TO CHANGE like the desert wind. Before him stood a couple of Hollywood veterans, director Henry Hathaway and producer William Bacher. As Bacher explained it, they wanted to make a movie about the reappearance and second crucifixion of Christ during the First World War. Christ would turn out to be the Unknown Soldier buried under the Arc de Triomphe in Paris. The two men wanted Faulkner to do the film script. Bacher, a spellbinding talker, was forceful on this point. In their judgment, he said, Faulkner was the only writer in Hollywood who could do the script properly. To attract him further, Bacher offered a three-way profit-sharing arrangement, plus a $1,000 advance. Since Warners had a technical claim on all his script-writing, Faulkner could produce a synopsis now and a full screenplay once he had cleared up his contractual status with the Warner studio. He could also write a novel or a play of his own, retaining all rights for himself.

Faulkner leaped at the chance. In August 1943, he secured a leave without pay from Warner Bros.—the $1,000 advance from Bacher would help carry him over—and headed home to work on the synopsis. The project was exactly what he had hoped for: an opportunity to help rearrange the postwar house. He wrote Harold Ober what he was about and said it would be "a fable, an indictment of war perhaps, and for that reason may not be acceptable now."

Free of Hollywood for six months, he worked almost exclusively on the synopsis of his fable, hoping to shape it into a novel. In January 1944, he tried to explain its message to Haas. Christ, representing a movement in mankind to end war forever, reappeared and was crucified again in the First World War. "We are repeating," Faulkner explained, "we are in the midst of war again. Suppose Christ gives us one more chance, will we crucify him again, perhaps for the last time." Faulkner went on: "That's crudely put; I am not trying to preach at all. But this is the argument: We did this in 1918; in 1944 it not only MUST NOT happen again, it SHALL NOT HAPPEN again. i.e. ARE WE GOING TO LET IT HAPPEN AGAIN? now that we are in another war, where the third and final chance might be offered us to save him."

In February his leave ran out. With sinking spirits, he packed his fable and headed back to Hollywood, back to his slave cell on the ward at Warners. But unexpected good news awaited him there. Once again, he was to be a scriptwriter for Hawks, who had patched up things with imperious Jack Warner and was doing another film, *To Have and Have Not,* based on the Hemingway novel. As Hawks told it, the idea for the film came from a bet: during a fishing trip with "Papa" Hemingway, Hawks had wagered that he could make a picture out of Hemingway's worst book. What was that? Papa asked. "That goddamned piece of junk called *To Have and Have Not,"* Hawks said. "You can't make a picture out of that," Papa said. "OK," Hawks retorted, "I'll get Faulkner to do it. He can write better than you can anyway."

Hawks and Warner had high hopes for *To Have and Have Not.* The male lead was Humphrey Bogart, currently the most popular motion picture star in America, commanding a salary of $3,500 a week from Warner Bros. In his forties now, "Bogey" stood five feet ten and weighed about 150 pounds, with short hair, dark eyes, and taut lips, usually drawn around a cigarette. His hard, unhappy face, said a writer for *Life* magazine, looked as if it had "just smelled something unpleasant." As an actor, he had appeared in more than forty movies, mostly as a gangster and tough guy. Then in 1942 came his breakthrough—a starring role in *Casablanca* opposite Ingrid Bergman. It was in *Casablanca,* a critical and popular success, that Warner Bros. realized what a romantic leading man it had in Bogart. In truth, *Casablanca* made him a screen idol, a strong, solitary, no-nonsense actor whom women found irresistible and men widely imitated. Because Bogey was the star, Jack Warner expected *To Have and Have Not* to rack up enormous profits, filling theaters across the land.

The film's female lead was a nineteen-year-old named Lauren Bacall, who had never acted in pictures before. She had appeared on the New York stage and begun a career as a fashion model when Hawks saw her picture on the cover of *Harper's Bazaar.* Since he was looking for a young woman to play opposite Bogart in *To Have and Have Not,*

Hawks summoned her west for a screen test, thought her face sensationally photogenic, and promptly signed her to a seven-year contract. Tall and blond, with catlike eyes and spectacular legs, she impressed studio bigwigs as a potential sex symbol. The young woman also had promise as an actress. Hawks, who hoped to produce a major film, thought she would be excellent as the hard, passionate counterpart of Bogart's character, a tough fisherman who ran revolutionaries and liquor between Havana and Key West.

Another writer had already produced a screenplay, but Hawks thought it too political and too faithful to the novel. He handed it to Faulkner and told him to reshape the entire thing. Through the late winter and into spring, Faulkner struggled with the story line, changing the location to Martinique and sharpening characterizations. The sole author of the "Second Revised Final" script, he worked under tremendous pressure, staying only a day ahead of Hawks, who shot from Faulkner's revisions. But Faulkner still hadn't mastered the motion picture style. At one point, Bacall saw him come on the set with a new scene, including a speech for Bogart that was six pages long, like the soliloquies in his fiction. Bogey read the speech in amazement. "I'm supposed to say all that?" Hawks assured Faulkner it was fine, and later, with Bogart's help, revised the scene himself. In fact, Hawks changed so much of the story to suit his style that the final picture bore little trace of either Faulkner or Hemingway.

Faulkner was used to that by now. And in any case he respected Hawks' movie judgment and liked both of the stars. Beautiful Miss Bacall reminded him of "a young colt." And he and Bogart had taken to one another from the start, so much so that they often lunched together. Like Faulkner, Bogey had an air of cool independence, disdained imbeciles and hypocrites, and cultivated friendships with a few select people, mostly fellow iconoclasts. Faulkner liked him for another reason: he refused to take Hollywood or himself too seriously. He spoke with a slight speech impediment—an old war injury, he said—and had a muscle tic over his left eye. His lunches invariably consisted of two martinis, a bottle or two of beer, two fried eggs, and coffee. A man to him was "junior," a woman "baby." Bacall was a real "baby." Anyone who annoyed him was a "creep." Sometimes he referred to Jack Warner strictly as a creep. Faulkner could agree with that, emphatically. He could relate to something else too: Bogey's third marriage, to a plump blonde he called "Sluggy" (their marital battles were legendary), was doomed when young Miss Bacall entered his life. "Bogie's got a new girl friend," Faulkner said with admiration. In fact, Bogey and Bacall had fallen in love. Reports of an offscreen romance filled gossip columns and added immensely to the appeal of the picture, to be released in October. Bogart would soon divorce "Sluggy" and marry young Bacall, and "Bogey and Baby" would become one of Hollywood's most glamorous couples, on screen and off.

Because of the picture, Faulkner had been unable to write a word on his fable since returning to Hollywood. He wasn't sure he could get back to it. He told Ober that wartime was bad for writing anyway, what with "the sublimation and glorification of all the cave instincts," preempting art and literature. But in truth, he was developing a bad case of self-doubt, worried that at forty-six he was losing his talent. On the weekends, unable to write, driven by his demons, he succumbed to hopeless bouts of drunkenness. But he hadn't lost control entirely. To save his job at the studio, he'd hired a male nurse to see that he got to work on Mondays.

He did have an encouraging exchange of letters with Malcolm Cowley, the prominent critic and literary historian, whose *Exile's Return* chronicled his own ordeal of estrangement and reconciliation as a member of Gertrude Stein's "Lost Generation" of the twenties. Now the literary editor of *The New Republic,* Cowley was concerned about Faulkner's sagging reputation. Faulkner's eleven books about Yoknapatawpha County, Cowley said, constituted "a sustained work of the imagination such as no other American writer had attempted." Yet almost nobody in America knew about it. Of his seventeen total books, all were effectively out of print and likely to remain that way; the New York Public Library had cards for only two of them. In publishing circles, Cowley said, Faulkner's name was "mud." Among critics, it was worse. Academic critics were almost universally contemptuous of his work, as were the daily and weekly reviewers who aped them. Cowley wanted to correct all that, by writing a long critical essay that would reassess Faulkner's achievement and give him the credit he was due.

In these dreary days, Faulkner needed all the reassurances he could get. Yes, he wrote Cowley in May, he would like very much to have the piece done. "I think (at 46) that I have worked too hard at my (elected or doomed, I dont know which) trade, with pride but I believe not vanity, with plenty of ego but with humility too (being a poet, of course I give no fart for glory) to leave no better mark on this our pointless chronicle than I seem to be about to leave."

But Faulkner cautioned Cowley not to include any biographical matter in his essay. "I think that if what one has thought and hoped and endeavored and failed at is not enough, if it must be explained and excused by what he has experienced, done or suffered, while he was not being an artist, then he and the one making the evaluation have both failed."

Later in the year, Cowley published part of his essay in *The New York Times Book Review*. Faulkner saw and liked it, and wrote Cowley that in his books he was trying mainly to tell a story, in the most effective and moving way he could, and that story was himself and the world. And this accounted for the so-called obscurity of his style and the long sentences. He was trying to say it all in one sentence, put it all on one pinhead. His current project wasn't Yoknapatawpha, but in it he was still attempting to "put all mankind's history in one sentence."

HE AND JILL HAD EXCHANGED letters, too, with mutual declarations of love and need. In fact, ten-year-old Jill kept begging him to let her come to Hollywood; and Faulkner decided to do it. Yes, it meant bringing Estelle with her. But he missed Jill, wanted her company. Her presence on the weekends might help him get off the whiskey. He told her yes. They could come out in June. The decision lifted his spirits. He felt generous and expansive. He wrote Cho-Cho that he had found an apartment "in a quiet, convenient *not Hollywood* neighborhood." It was a small cubbyhole in a pink adobe apartment house, but maybe "Big and Little Miss" would like it. He could have a home breakfast, they could listen to some music (he was really feeling generous now), Little Missy could take riding lessons and learn fencing, which would give her poise, grace, and coordination.

He told Meta they were coming and tried to explain his position. It was mainly because of Jill. "She misses me, and Lord knows, I miss her."

Meta was furious. For the first time in their relationship, she felt cruelly put upon, her personal feelings totally ignored. She realized how much she had "the short end of the stick, the sweepings, the leavings." Estelle and Jill had everything.

"It doesn't have to make any difference—their being here," Faulkner said. "We can go on as before."

But Meta would have none of it. "Bill, I remember the way it was the last time. I'm not going through that again. Waiting for you to be able to slip away at night. Staring at the telephone as if that would make it ring and you'd be on the line."

Faulkner: "You're putting it on the basis of some kind of female morality."

Carpenter: "It's my morality—with my name engraved on it—and I'm sorry if you think I'm naive and confused."

He didn't think that, he argued. But what could he do? Tell Jill not to come?

Meta was so angry she refused to stay the night with him. He phoned her just as she entered her apartment. "I don't see how I can go back on my promise to my little girl," he said. He knew she wouldn't let him make love to her. But could he just see her? For drinks? Dinner? Anything?

"Bill," she said, "I think it will be much better if we don't see each other again—ever." He tried to protest, but she hung up. It was over then, the click of doom for him. Meta, Meta, what in the world . . . ?

ON JUNE 6, 1944, the Allies landed at Normandy, France, in the largest amphibious invasion in history. To secure their beachheads, Allied forces fought inland field by field, town by town; the fighting was savage beyond computation, with roads and hedgerows alike tangled with men and machines. Finally Allied columns broke out and pounded the Germans back in the "Battle of France." Germany was now fighting on two fronts, against Allied armies in the west and masses of Russians in the east. At the same time, U.S. forces in the Pacific were island-hopping toward the Philippines and ultimately toward Japan herself.

The war news, auspicious though it was, could only have compounded Faulkner's gloom. He still couldn't work on his fable, his contribution to the warless world to follow the current conflagration. But at least he had Jill; she was all he had, now that Meta refused to see or talk to him. Jill and Estelle arrived in late June, in the midst of the fighting in Normandy, and Faulkner moved them into the pink adobe apartment house. He set Jill up at a riding school attended by Elizabeth

Taylor, and he vowed some day to buy the horse she rode and loved there, a gentle mare named Lady Go-Lightly. Once, studying a photograph of Jill wading into the ocean, he suddenly realized that her childhood was passing. The innocent season of her life, the season he cherished so much, would be gone soon. "This is the end of it," he told Buzz Bezzerides, his fellow screenwriter. "She'll grow into a woman." It made him enormously sad.

It was a terrible summer for him—and for Estelle. Once again, he would come home furious about the idiotic movies to which Warners assigned him. He drank more, not less; he was drunk in one conference at the studio; he was drunk at home, too. Estelle, intoxicated herself, felt frightened and lost. She suspected he had taken up with Meta again, but insisted that she didn't begrudge him pleasure—she truly didn't. She had lived with the knowledge so long now. Probably she didn't know that Faulkner and Meta had broken up again. All she knew was that her marriage was hopeless. Once, in front of Buzz Bezzerides, she blurted out, "Something went wrong." She started crying. "We used to go fishing together. We loved one another."

In September, she took Jill back to Oxford for the beginning of school. Faulkner moved in with the Bezzerides family, but the furies were loose in him with a vengeance. Buzz was aghast at how much whiskey he consumed. When Buzz cut off his supply at one point, Faulkner tried to negotiate, autographing a pile of his books on Buzz's coffee table. "Now will you give me a drink?" he pleaded. On another occasion, as he sat in the living room with a bottle of Old Grand-Dad, his bourbon-soaked mind focused on his agent as the cause of all his woes. Faulkner had a Filipino knife in his hand. "I'm gonna cut Herndon up," he said. Finally Buzz had had enough. A powerful man, he picked Faulkner up bodily, forced him into the car, and drove him to a private hospital to dry out.

"God damn! Why do I do it?" Faulkner cried.

"The only one who can tell is you," Buzz said.

Faulkner moved to other lodgings—a room with a private entrance —and kept drinking. One night at Musso & Frank's, where he and Meta had spent so many evenings together, he met an actor who knew her, and the whiskey tore down his reserve: he mumbled that Meta didn't love him anymore and begged the actor to tell him how he could get her back. The actor told Meta what Faulkner said, insisting that "it was real misery and from deep down."

When she heard that, Meta's resistance crumbled. In the morning, she went to him, her mind frantically rationalizing his actions: *he had to bring Jill and Estelle out, can't you see that now? It doesn't mean he loves you any less.* When he came out of his room wearing a seersucker suit, he was startled to see her waiting for him in her car. He got in and kissed her.

"I thought it was over," he murmured. "Done with."

"So did I."

"Lord, I've missed you, m'honey."

As they drove to the studio, the morning sun blazed overhead, heating up the autumn air. Far beyond the rim of the Pacific, the United States flag now flew over Saipan, Tinian, and Guam. From makeshift airfields there, armadas of huge new American superfortresses—the B-29s—started daily round-trip missions to bomb Japan's tinderbox cities. The sun of the Japanese empire had begun to fall.

BACK IN AUGUST, Faulkner had been assigned to another Hawks film, *The Big Sleep,* loosely based on a Raymond Chandler mystery novel. It starred Humphrey Bogart as hard-boiled detective Philip Marlowe and Lauren Bacall as the millionaire's daughter Vivian Sternwood. As he struggled with bouts of alcoholism, Faulkner collaborated on the screenplay for Hawks, helping convert Marlowe and Vivian Sternwood into lovers. Faulkner himself shaped Bacall's character into a depraved woman with a large capacity for sexual evil, which suggested something of Faulkner's inner torment as far as women were concerned. But this version of the script never got beyond the censors. At that, Hawks called in another writer to patch it up, then changed it further when he started shooting in November and December. In the end, the director transformed Faulkner's Vivian into a sexy, basically good sort, with Bogey helping in the transformation as Bacall's off-camera coach.

During the early filming of *The Big Sleep,* Faulkner was in a bad way. Meta noticed that he was jumpy, morose, even peevish at times. "I have to get back to my own writing," he complained. A new novel? she asked. "I'll never get it done in this town," he said. "Sometimes I think if I do one more treatment or screenplay, I'll lose whatever power I have as a writer."

No longer needed on the set, Faulkner secured a six-month leave without pay and in mid-December headed home for Rowan Oak. On the train, he finished an assignment for the studio, then sent it off with a memorandum: "The following rewritten and additional scenes for *The Big Sleep* were done by the author in respectful joy and happy admiration after he had gone off salary and while on his way back to Mississippi. With grateful thanks to the studio for the cheerful and crowded day coach which alone saved him from wasting his time in dull and profitless rest and sleep. With love, WILLIAM FAULKNER."

IN THE FAMILIAR and secure surroundings of Rowan Oak, he tried through the winter and spring of 1945 to develop his fable into a novel. It had been ten years since he finished *Absalom, Absalom!* in a burst of triumph, ten years since he created a unitary novel with a singular vision. All his books since had been pieced together or expanded from earlier writings. He wanted more than anything to produce another great work, to prove to himself that he still had his talent, still had the courage to try for the stars—to "put all mankind's history in one sentence," as he'd told Cowley. But his fable resisted him, like a shadow eluding his reach. The voices, setting, theme—all were a universe away from his beloved Yoknapatawpha. In his imagination, he walked alien ground now, he spoke with strangers, he grappled with great ideas, striving to give them human speech and form. He tried to reincarnate Christ in the boiling smoke and mangled corpses of the First World War, to invent speeches that thundered in the heavens, only to find himself lost in a no-man's-land of empty rhetoric and have to start again. His novel did not unfold before him; he dragged it forward sentence by tentative sentence, paragraph by tenuous paragraph, trying to *will* it into being.

Meanwhile he had his usual dreams that somehow he could make enough money to live on while he finished his book. Random House did agree to advance him $2,000 or $3,000, which helped. He sent New York letters of guarded optimism, saying he thought his fable was "pretty good," unless he had "reached that time of an artist's increasing years" when he could no longer judge what he was writing. In March 1945, he told Harold Ober that it might be an "epic poem" about the crucifixion and resurrection, but confessed that he had had to throw a lot of it out, boiling 100,000 words down to about 15,000. By late May, he was rewriting "the whole thing." But at least he thought it a novel now and not just a lot of rhetoric.

Behind Faulkner's communications to New York was a suffering artist, struggling with a welter of resistant ideas, symbols, and characters. He knew what his message was going to be. But how to invent the right story to get it across? For all his incomparable skill as a novelist, he could not capture on paper the book he glimpsed in the mist. Like the great war it described, his fable went nowhere.

But the greatest war, the war that had consumed much of the planet, rushed on toward its destined end. By the spring of 1945, massive Allied armies were smashing up Nazi Germany from the west and east alike, annihilating her military forces, seizing her bombed-out towns and cities. As the Reich crumbled, her terrible death camps, at Auschwitz, Treblinka, Buchenwald, Belsec, Bergen-Belsen, stood revealed to the world with their gas chambers and unspeakable sights. Only the stark crematoriums gave hint of the millions who had vanished in smoke. With Allied columns mopping up his once mighty Reich, Hitler shot himself in a hidden bunker in Berlin, by then a smoking rubble. Berlin fell to the Russians on May 2, victory in Europe came six days later, and war-weary people everywhere surged into the streets to shout and sing in ecstasy. President Harry Truman proclaimed it "a solemn but glorious hour," as Americans danced in Times Square, on Boston Common, in the Chicago Loop, at Hollywood and Vine, in war plants and on college campuses across the land. For the moment they could forget the war in the Pacific, against an empire larger than Germany's and even more determined to fight it out to the bitter end.

In June, with Americans battling on Okinawa, Faulkner was back on the ward at Warner Bros., fighting his own anger and depression. As usual, his dream of getting enough money to finish his book had been illusory. "I ought to know now I dont sell and never will earn enough outside of pictures to stay out of debt," he said bitterly. He did collaborate on *Stallion Road,* a picture he liked, but his "wild" and "wonderful" script did not please the Warner bigwigs, who rejected it. So what else had changed? "I dont like this damn place any better than I ever did," he wrote an Oxford friend. "There is one comfort: at least I can't be any sicker tomorrow for Mississippi than I was yesterday."

He tried to work on his fable in the morning, before he left for the studio. The war news gave him an even more urgent reason to stay at it. To avoid a long and bloody campaign in the Japanese home islands, the United States unleashed a terrible new weapon that shocked the world. On August 6 and 9 respectively, American B-29s dropped an atomic bomb on Hiroshima and then another on Nagasaki, incinerating the two Japanese cities in mushrooming fireballs of destruction. The devastating power of a single atomic bomb was beyond comprehension. Four square miles of Hiroshima, once a bustling city of 344,000 people, had been vaporized. Some 75,000 to 100,000 people had been killed outright, 73,000 more had been wounded, many of them scorched and mutilated by radiation burns. Another 70,000 had perished in the port city of Nagasaki, reduced in a few moments to a pile of twisted, radioactive debris. In each city, clocks and watches had been shocked or seared to a stop at the same apocalyptic moment. Fearing annihilation, Japan surrendered unconditionally, and Americans everywhere whooped and danced in near delirium; *Time* magazine appeared with a crossed-out rising sun on its cover, and searchlights, flares, and rockets streaked the night sky over Pearl Harbor, where the Pacific conflict had begun with Japan's own air raid almost four years before.

And so the most destructive war in human history was over: 70 million people had fought in it, 49 million people had died, and trillions of dollars' worth of property had been destroyed. Cost and casualties were more than twice those of the First World War. From the Oder to the Tiber, the Seine to the Volga, Europe was a wasteland of smashed cities and scorched fields. China, Burma, Japan, and countless other Pacific islands all looked as though giant typhoons had swept across them. And no one knew what damage had been done to the human spirit. Who could measure the impact of years of hatred, emotional torment, unprecedented killing and brutality, on the moral fabric of humankind? And who knew what dangers lay ahead, in the age of the most lethal weapon ever contrived? Once the V-J celebrations had ended, somber voices said it was time to ponder the cost, time to rebuild, time to begin anew, so that it would never happen again. Perhaps from the ashes of this hellish war would yet come resurrection.

Which was the message Faulkner hoped to convey in his fable, his prophetic story of war and the Second Coming. Yet he made little headway and despaired of ever getting it written in hated "tinsel town." Two weeks after Hiroshima, he poured out his frustrations to Ober. "I think I have had about all of Hollywood I can stand. I feel bad, depressed, dreadful sense of wasting time. . . . For some time I have expected, at a certain age, to reach that period (in the early fifties) which most artists seem to reach where they admit at last that there is no solution to life and that it is not, and perhaps never was, worth living."

Yet if he left Hollywood, he had to have some means of revenue. Could Ober help him out? "My books have never sold, are out of print; the labor (the creation of my apocryphal country) of my life, even if I have a few things yet to add to it, will never make a living for me. I don't have enough sure judgment about trash to be able to write it with 50% success. Could I do some sort of editorial work, or some sort of hackwriting at home, where living won't cost me as much as now [?]"

In September, he resolved to get out of Hollywood come what may. He terminated his relationship with Herndon, refusing to pay him another dime in commissions. Herndon, of course, vowed to take him to court. But Faulkner was intractable: he had had enough of him and the crippling contract to which Herndon had shackled him. All Faulkner wanted was to go home and work on his fable, now that the time of the older men had come, the time to clean up the world's house. He tried to explain his position to the head of Warners' story department, a sympathetic fellow named Finlay McDermid, who thought it a shame to waste one of America's great novelists on "routine melodramas." Thanks to McDermid, Warners granted Faulkner another six-month leave without pay. But there were certain conditions, McDermid said. Under the terms of Faulkner's contract, he could not legally write a novel. In fact, Warners owned everything he wrote until his contract expired.

Faulkner was incredulous. This was *worse* than enslavement. Because of that despicable contract, Warners owned his very soul as an artist. He wasn't appeased when McDermid offered a compromise. McDermid had the legal department draw up a release that granted Faulkner a six-month leave to work on a novel but gave Warner Bros. first option on the movie rights. Faulkner couldn't agree to that: Bacher and Hathaway, who had conceived the idea of the fable, had the motion picture rights. He refused to sign the agreement. When the studio said he couldn't go home unless he did, Faulkner cleaned out his desk and walked off the lot and out of his contract. As far as he was concerned, the legal consequences could go to hell.

HE WOULD HAVE A SPECIAL TRAVELING COMPANION—a surprise for Jill. He had bought the horse she had loved to ride at the stable, the gentle mare named Lady Go-Lightly. He purchased a trailer for the horse and hired a driver to haul them both home to Mississippi. Lady was going to foal, though, so he had to hurry. He'd be damned, he said, if he would let a Faulkner mare foal in Hollywood.

One unhappy task remained: he had to find the courage to tell Meta. He didn't want to hurt her; he hated like hell to do that. But what choice did he have? Finally he went to her with his decision: he was finished with Hollywood, through with screenwriting. She had expected this, of course. Since they had gotten back together, she had known that he would never stay in Hollywood with her, that it could never work out between them. Yet she could not restrain her anger. Her mind raged with bitter thoughts. He wanted to console her, but what could he say? When he reached for her that night, she pushed him away.

Later he sent her a tender note, in which he called her "Honey Love" and asked to be forgiven. "If you agree that this bloke in question really means better than he does, how's for seeing your face before I leave. . . ." When she read that, she forgave him for everything. They slept together one last time, their lovemaking a benediction to all that they had shared and hoped for and lost. When he gazed down at her face, her expression was worshipful. The last thing he touched before he left the apartment was Meta's outstretched hand.

PART SIX

THE
PREREQUISITES
OF SALVATION

I T WAS OCTOBER AT ROWAN OAK, and the air was turning cool and the leaves beginning to fall. For Faulkner, it had never felt so good to be home, to putter about the place again and stroll into town for the mail. Yet he complained that he still had Hollywood in his lungs. He kept worrying about Warners and its claims on him and his writing. Finally, in mid-October, he wrote a personal appeal to Jack Warner himself, admitting that he had "made a bust at moving picture writing" and shouldn't do any more of it. He had done the best he knew how on five or six scripts, but only two of them had ever been made into movies. Even then, he felt he had received credit not for the value of his work but because of his relationship with Howard Hawks. In sum, he had spent three years trying to do work he was not equipped to do, and had therefore misspent time that, as a forty-eight-year-old novelist, he could ill afford to lose. And he did not dare misspend any more of it. Therefore, he repeated his request that the studio release him from his contract.

The studio's response came soon enough. Request denied. Not only that, the studio reasserted its claim to everything he wrote and threatened dire consequences if he tried to sell his work to an editor or anyone else. Furious and frustrated, he shelved his fable and wrote Haas that "Faulkner won't do any writing until he finds out just how much of his soul he no longer owns."

In the meantime, he immersed himself in another project, one Malcolm Cowley had proposed earlier that year. Cowley had recently published *The Portable Hemingway* and now wanted to compile a portable Faulkner, focusing on his Yoknapatawpha saga—his greatest achievement—from Indian times down to World War II. Sales would not be large, Cowley said, but the book would spotlight his work at a time of critical and popular indifference to it. What was more, it would be "a bayonet prick in the ass of Random House" to reprint his novels.

Faulkner liked the idea. By all means, let them make "a Golden Book" of his apocryphal county—he had thought of devoting his old age to doing something much like that. As for what to excerpt, he urged Cowley to include Dilsey's section of *The Sound and the Fury*, this "for the sake of the negroes." In fact, Faulkner volunteered to contribute a short synopsis of the first three sections in order to clarify hers.

In October, he set to work on the synopsis, sure that Warner Bros. couldn't block something which elucidated much earlier work. That he had no copy of *The Sound and the Fury* did not deter him, for the Compson family lived brilliantly in his mind. As he worked, his creative energies, so long frustrated in Hollywood, transformed the synopsis into a rich genealogy of the entire Compson family, with newly imagined episodes, reaching clear back to the battle of Culloden in 1746.

"Cher Maitre," he wrote Cowley. "Here it is. I should have done this when I wrote the book. Then the whole thing would have fallen into pattern like a jigsaw puzzle when the magician's wand touched it." He was happy about something else too: "that damned west coast place" had not cheapened his soul as much as he had feared.

Cowley thought the genealogy really did clarify the novel. But more than that, it was a fine addition to the portable in its own right. Cowley did fuss about factual discrepancies between the genealogy and *The Sound and the Fury*, from which he was excerpting, but Faulkner let most of them stand. For him, they simply meant that after fifteen years the book was still growing and changing.

With Faulkner offering advice from Mississippi, Cowley made his selections, and by November the book was ready for the printer. But he ran into trouble with his introduction, mainly because of contradictory information in Faulkner's public biography. *Who's Who*, for example, gave his name as "Falkner." Which was the correct spelling? Faulkner responded with a brief autobiography that sported playfully with the facts. When he first began to write, he said, maybe he was "secretly ambitious" and didn't want to ride on his grandfather's "coattails," and so he added the *u* as an easy way to strike out for himself. At least, that was what his mother and father always said. In adding the *u*, he was simply restoring what the Old Colonel, always impatient about spelling and grammar, "was said to have removed" in the first place. Then in a riotous mix of fact and fantasy, he claimed that he had easily escaped his mother's influence and more or less grown up in his father's livery stable, had dropped out of high school and Ole Miss, had acquired the rest of his education through "undirected reading" (he never mentioned Phil Stone), had painted houses, gotten fired as scout-master "for moral reasons," barnstormed airplanes, run a farm, bred and raised mules and cattle. He asserted, too, that he had worked for a New Orleans bootlegger and repeated other favorite and fanciful claims about his youthful adventures, save one. Thanks to the sobering impact of the Second World War, he did not pretend to be a wounded hero of the First: "went to RAF, returned home" was all he said.

He listed all this for Cowley's personal benefit, to clarify the entry in *Who's Who,* and hoped it would remain a private matter between the two of them. What he had written was in the public domain. What he "ate and did and when and where" was his business.

When Cowley sent him the introduction, Faulkner studied it with growing alarm. Not about Cowley's literary judgments—they were "all right, sound and correct and penetrating," Faulkner thought. Cowley was right: he probably did resemble Hawthorne in his sense of "regional peculiarity." And he did love his fictional characters "created in the image of the land." Perhaps he was guilty of certain infelicities of style, which came from working too long in solitude. But his main achieve-ment, as Cowley pointed out, was that all his books in the Yoknapataw-pha cycle were "part of the same living pattern." Each novel, each long or short story, seemed to reveal more than it stated, to deal with some-thing bigger than itself. "All the separate works are like blocks of mar-ble from the same quarry," Cowley said; "they show the veins and faults of the mother rock."

No, Faulkner had no quarrel with any of that. What he objected to was the biographical matter at the outset, the opening paragraph in particular. To develop an argument, namely that Faulkner was among the "wounded writers" of his generation, Cowley stated that Faulkner had "served at the front in the Royal Air Force, and, after his plane was damaged in combat, had crashed behind the British lines. Now he was home again and not at home, or at least not able to accept the postwar world."

Faulkner grimaced at that paragraph—"because it makes me out to be more of a hero than I was." Never mind that he had invented the myth of the gallant and wounded aviator himself, repeating it so many times that it had found its way into the public record. He didn't want it in Cowley's book, which showpieced his life's work and which he was proud of. He asked Cowley to delete the offensive paragraph and several pages of additional biographical matter.

But Cowley balked at that, insisting that the information was necessary to gain an understanding of his work. And anyway, the book was already in page proofs; he couldn't throw out the first four pages.

Faulkner warned him, "You're going to bugger up a fine dignified distinguished book with that war business," and he insisted that Cowley at least revise the beginning paragraph about his war record, saying only that he was a member of the RAF in 1918, nothing more. With Faulkner intransigent on that point, Cowley finally did as he was asked.

Immensely relieved, Faulkner wrote Cowley that he could see the need for the other opening. But to him it was false. Not to facts—he didn't care much for them. But to truth, though perhaps what he meant by that was humility and maybe what he thought was humility was really "unmitigable pride." Nevertheless, he would have preferred nothing about himself before the instant he began to write, "as though Faulkner and Typewriter were concomitant, coadjutant and without past on the moment they first faced each other at the suitable (nameless) table."

FAULKNER DID HOPE THAT COWLEY'S ANTHOLOGY would revive interest in his work in the United States. It was ironical, wasn't it? Ignored and largely forgotten in his native land, his work had an enthusiastic following abroad, especially in France. Credit Maurice Coindreau's excellent translations in part for that. For the young in France, Jean-Paul Sartre told Cowley, "Faulkner c'est un dieu." For André Gide, he was perhaps the most important American writer. For Claude Magny, he was "the only modern novelist who had lived, in all its magnitude, the literary drama of the age. . . . His work has laid down the prerequisites of Salvation."

In America, meanwhile, he won second prize—$250—for a story in the *Ellery Queen Mystery Magazine* contest. "What a commentary," he wrote Ober in January 1946. "In France I am the father of a literary movement. In Europe I am considered the best modern American and among the first of all writers. In America, I eke out a hack's motion picture wages by winning second prize in a manufactured mystery story contest."

The spring, however, brought encouraging news from Harold Ober in New York: Warner Bros. had relinquished all claims to his novel, including the option on motion picture rights, on the somewhat vague understanding that he would return to Hollywood once the fable was done, whenever that would be. Ober and Finlay McDermid had negotiated the release, and Faulkner was delighted. Maybe Ober was shy and retiring, but he looked after his authors, no doubt about that. This was not exactly Faulkner's day of jubilee: Warners had not officially liberated him from the bonds of his contract. But at least he was free until he completed his book. What was more, even his eternal money troubles seemed solved for now—Ober told him that Random House would provide $500 a month in advances to help him through his fable, which Bob Haas was anxious to publish. "I feel fine," Faulkner wrote Haas in late March, "am happy now, thanks to Harold and you."

In April came a handsome new copy of *The Portable Faulkner,* which Faulkner perused with uninhibited joy. The anthology really did illuminate his Yoknapatawpha County, from the old people—the Indians and first white settlers—down to modern times. Many of his own favorite characters paraded through its pages: a great Indian chief named Doom from an early short story; Ringo, Bayard, and Colonel John Sartoris from *The Unvanquished;* Wash Jones and Colonel Sutpen from a short story that presaged *Absalom, Absalom!;* Ike McCaslin and Sam Fathers from "The Bear"; V. K. Ratliff and the Snopeses from *The Hamlet;* Miss Emily Grierson from "A Rose for Emily"; Dilsey from *The Sound and the Fury;* the tall convict from *The Wild Palms;* Percy Grimm and Joe Christmas from the unforgettable closing scenes of *Light in August;* and the remarkable Compsons from his newly created genealogy.

"The job is splendid," Faulkner wrote Cowley. "Damn you to hell anyway. But even if I had beat you to the idea, mine wouldn't have been this good. By God, I didn't know myself what I had tried to do, and how much I had succeeded."

His life's achievement, presented in a single book for all to see, commanded for once a lot of positive critical attention—exactly what Cowley had hoped for. Caroline Gordon, Allen Tate's wife and a southern novelist herself, praised Faulkner's technical achievement and great variety of characters on the front page of *The New York Times Book Review*. But the most influential critique appeared in *The New Republic;* the author was the southern poet and novelist Robert Penn Warren, whose *All the King's Men* would come out that year and garner a Pulitzer Prize for fiction. Cowley was right, Warren said: Faulkner's was an enormous achievement, a labor of creation without equal in this time, yet it had happened "in what almost amounts to critical isolation and silence." What criticism there was tended to be "hagridden by prejudice and preconception," Warren wrote, and he cited in particular that by Maxwell Geismar, who had dismissed Faulkner's art as the "extreme hallucinations" of a "cultural psychosis." Geismar had also condemned Faulkner for his racial views, insisting that he "hated Negroes," that he portrayed them as the "tragic consequence" and "evil cause" of the collapse of the South's old order. On the contrary, Warren argued, Faulkner made it emphatically clear that slavery, not the Negro, was the South's curse. In Faulkner's world, the Negro was the black cross, the embodiment of the curse, the reminder of the guilt, the "incarnation of the problem." Yet Faulkner's legend was not simply the legend of the South; it was the legend of "our general plight and problem." What was significant in his work, Warren asserted, was the human struggle, "the capacity to make the effort to rise above the mechanical process of life, the pride to endure, for in endurance there is a kind of self-conquest."

As it turned out, *The Portable Faulkner* and Warren's widely read review did much to reverse the critical indifference to Faulkner's art. So did an essay by Jean-Paul Sartre, which ran in the *Atlantic* later that year, attesting to the influence of Faulkner and John Dos Passos on French writers like himself, Albert Camus, and Simone de Beauvoir. With a Faulkner revival well under way, Malcolm Cowley was happy both for Faulkner and for American literature. It wasn't long before he could write Faulkner that he wasn't a neglected author anymore, that they were even studying him in the colleges. At Yale, "lots of the kids think that 'The Bear' is the greatest story ever written," Cowley said, and added, "you'll have to resign yourself to bearing the expense of greatness."

IN OPPRESSIVE SUMMER HEAT, Faulkner faced the parts and pieces of his fable, which he told Cowley would be his "magnum o." He was not unaware of the irony, though: that in this strange and didactic book he had left the Yoknapatawpha world of *The Portable Faulkner,* the very world that was bringing him unprecedented attention and recognition. As the summer wore on, the fable proved as resistant as ever to all his efforts, all his stratagems. Once again, he tried to reassure himself and his publishers with grandiose assertions. "Yes, this is it," he wrote Haas. "I believe now it's not just my best but perhaps the best of my time." But it was a terrible struggle. He admitted he didn't know where the book was going. By October, he had some 250 pages completed, but they had "done no more than set the stage," he warned Haas. He hadn't even "got into the story yet." It might take him another year, maybe more, to get it right.

In truth, he was bored. "It's a dull life here," he wrote Cowley. "I need some new people, above all probably a new young woman." Yes, he needed a young woman, another Meta, someone to love him and respond to his desire. He might find a young female in New York City, if he could only get away. But alas, he couldn't afford the trip. He was stuck in Oxford.

To ease the boredom, he took morning horseback rides with Bob Farley, dean of the Ole Miss law school. As they sauntered down a country road, Faulkner would throw caution to the winds. "Let's let 'em go, Bob." And away he would go, bouncing hard in the saddle as his horse thundered down the rutted road. Farley thought this incredibly reckless for a forty-nine-year-old man. But Faulkner loved it. The galloping horse beneath him, the plunging hooves, the receding blur of the woods, the rush of the wind against his face—all made him feel young and strong and free again.

But nothing, not even whiskey, mitigated the frustrations of his novel, which progressed with depressing slowness through the long winter and into the spring of 1947. He took Easter off to hide colored eggs and jelly beans for Jill, despite the fact that she was almost fourteen years old now. Out of duty, she still went hunting for them—what else could she do? Faulkner clung to her childhood, saw in the maturing young woman only the little girl she once had been.

That spring, Faulkner consented to meet some English classes at Ole Miss, mainly to do something different and earn a little extra money. When first approached by a member of the English Department, he said no emphatically. "I have never lectured; I can't lecture; and I won't lecture." But the professor stressed how much the Ole Miss students needed to hear him, and promised, too, that none of them would take notes and no faculty would be present. Faulkner finally relented when the English Department offered him a $250 honorarium as further enticement.

In mid-April, he visited six classes, a shy, proud man with a gray mustache and thick hair flecked with white. He saw faculty members sitting with the students, but went ahead, even if the promise to him had not been kept. In response to students' questions, he talked about his writing and his characters, indicating that a "good creation" for him was "a real, three-dimensional character who stands up of his own accord and can 'cast a shadow.' " No, his characters didn't speak for him; they spoke for themselves, according to their own natures. Which were his favorite books? He read again and again, maybe once a year, the Old Testament, Shakespeare, some of Balzac, *Don Quixote, Madame Bovary, Moby Dick, Vanity Fair, The Nigger of the "Narcissus."*

When pressed to rate his contemporaries, he said he would rank Thomas Wolfe first, then Dos Passos, Hemingway, Willa Cather, and John Steinbeck. In his judgment, all had failed—that is, all had failed to match the dream, to attain the unattainable. What counted with Faulkner was the courage of the effort. "Wolfe made the grandest failure because he had a vast courage—courage in that he attempted what he knew he probably couldn't do." And so the grandest failure was to attempt the impossible, to reach for something so difficult, so pure as art, that it was doomed from the start. Which brought him to Hemingway, ranked third on his list. The trouble with Hemingway, Faulkner said, was that he had always been too careful, never attempting anything he could not do. "He had been like a poker player who plays close to his vest," Faulkner said; "he had never made mistakes of diction, style, taste, or fact; he had never used a word the meaning of which couldn't be checked in the dictionary."

A student pointed out that he hadn't ranked himself. Where would he put William Faulkner on his list?

"I'm afraid you're taxing Mr. Faulkner's modesty," a faculty member said.

At the students' insistence, Faulkner revised his list, ranking himself second to Wolfe in terms of their courage and the magnitude of their failure. He put Dos Passos third, Hemingway fourth, and Steinbeck fifth, dropping Cather from his list.

Faulkner assumed that his remarks would not go beyond the classroom, but he assumed wrong. Some students had taken notes, after all, and the Ole Miss publicity director used them to prepare a press release, which included Faulkner's ranking of the novelists. Unable to resist such wonderfully provocative copy, the New York *Herald Tribune* printed excerpts in its book section. Faulkner knew nothing about any of this until he received a registered letter from Brigadier General C. T. "Buck" Latham, a personal friend of Ernest Hemingway, who wrote to set Faulkner straight about Papa's courage. Papa had asked him to do so. In fact, Papa was angry and hurt, certain that Faulkner had called him a coward. To disabuse him of that notion, the general cited examples of Hemingway's intrepid exploits as a war correspondent in France with his 22nd Infantry Regiment.

The letter pained Faulkner to the core. Damn it all, anyway. When would he learn to keep his mouth shut? From what Latham quoted, the *Herald Tribune* excerpts seemed garbled and incomplete. Faulkner wrote Latham so and apologized for the misunderstanding. He knew about Hemingway's record in both world wars and in the Spanish Civil War, too. His comments about courage "had no reference whatever to Hemingway as a man: only to his craftsmanship as a writer." On that score, Faulkner stood by what he had said: he had measured the best of his generation by their degrees of failure, and he had placed Hemingway next to last because "he did not have the courage to get out on a limb as the others did."

Faulkner sent a copy of the letter to Hemingway, with a covering note. "I'm sorry of this damn stupid thing. I was just making $250.00. I thought informally, not for publication, or I would have insisted on looking at the stuff before it was released. I have believed for years that the human voice has caused all human ills and I thought I had broken myself of talking. Maybe this will be my valedictory lesson." He added, "I hope it wont matter a damn to you. But if or when or whe[r]ever it does, please accept another squirm from yours truly."

Back came a letter from Hemingway, dated July 23, 1947, from his villa in Cuba. It was evident that Hemingway had enjoyed more than a few daiquiris before turning to his composition. "Dear Bill: Awfully glad to hear from you and glad to have made contact. Your letter came tonight and please throw all the other stuff away, the misunderstanding, or will have to come up and we both trompel on it." As for ranking the competition, Hemingway couldn't agree with what Faulkner said about Wolfe and Dos Passos. "I never felt the link-up in Wolfe except with the N.C. stuff. Dos I always liked and respected and thought was a 2nd rate writer on acct. no ear. 2nd rate boxer has no left hand, same as ear to writer, and so gets his brains knocked out and this happened to Dos with every book. Also terrible snob (on acct. of being a bastard) (which I would welcome) and very worried about his negro blood when could have been our best negro writer if would have just been negro as hope *we* would have."

As for Hemingway's place in the rankings, he wished that Faulkner would reread *For Whom the Bell Tolls*. "Probably bore the shit out of you to re-read but as brother would like to know what you think. Anyway is as good as I can write and was takeing all chances (for a pitcher who, when has control, can throw fairly close) could take. (Probably failed.)"

As for Faulkner's place: "You are a better writer than Fielding or any of those guys and you should just know it and keep on writing. You have things written that come back to me better than any of them and I am not dopy, really. You shouldn't read the shit about living writers. You should always write your best against dead writers that we know what stature (not stature: evocative power) that they have and beat them one by one. Why do you want to fight Dostoevsky in your first fight? Beat Turgenieff—which we both did soundly. . . . Then nail yourself DeMaupassant (tough boy until he got the old rale. Still dangerous for three rounds). Then try and take Stendhal. (Take him and we're all happy.) But don't fight with the poor pathological characters of our time (we won't name). You and I can both beat Flaubert who is our most respected, honored master. . . .

"Anyway I am your Bro. if you want one that writes and I'd like us to keep in touch. . . . Excuse chickenshit letter. Have much regard for you. Would like to keep on writing [letters]." Signed: "Ernest Hemingway."

They didn't keep in touch because Faulkner didn't respond, apparently too embarrassed to do so. Unhappily for Faulkner, the episode didn't break him of talking about other writers, even about Hemingway, with whom he had another contretemps a few years later, when he made some garbled analogy about most writers being like wolves when they banded together, dogs when they ran singly, but suggested that Hemingway was a wolf without a pack. The remark enraged Papa when he read it, for he was certain that Faulkner had somehow called him "just another dog," and Papa stewed and simmered again, and contemptuously referred to Faulkner as the creator of "Anomatopoeio County." They never did meet or reconcile after that.

W HAT COUNTED FOR HIM, Faulkner said, was the courage to attempt the impossible. By that standard, how would he measure his fable? He knew he was trying for too much and so was doomed to fail. Yet if the important thing was the bravery and nobility of the effort, then he ought to feel all right about his current work. But he didn't feel all right. Unsure of himself, haunted by fears that he had lost his talent, he was still pushing his story forward line by line, then retreating to rewrite and revise, then starting tentatively forward again, as though he were an infantryman crossing a mine field. He blamed Hollywood, fretting about how much "trash and junk writing for movies" had corrupted his pen. By July 1947, he had accumulated some four hundred pages, but feared it would take a thousand to tell his story, which was only now "getting to be a tragedy of people."

By the fall, he felt tired and stale again. He worried about drawing unearned money from Random House, even though Bob Haas told him not to worry about that and just write the book. Faulkner wished he could remember that. One of the problems was the sheer size of his manuscript. "It's like standing close to an elephant," he said; "after a while you can't see the elephant anymore at all."

When *Partisan Review* rejected a long segment of the fable, which Ober had submitted, Faulkner lost confidence entirely. "Did PR give a reason for turning the piece down?" he asked Ober. "I have a notion they were disappointed in it. Did they find it dull as written?" (They found it rough as written, almost like a first draft—but Ober hadn't the heart to tell him that.) "I have an idea that this may have been PR's reason," Faulkner went on. "The world has been so beat and battered about the head during the last few years that man is in a state of spiritual cowardice: all his bottom, reserve strength has to go into physical stamina and there is nothing left to be very concerned with art. That that magazine does not exist now which would have printed sections from Ulysses as in the 1920s. And that the man crouching in a Mississippi hole trying to shape into some form of art his summation and conception of the human heart and spirit in terms of the cerebral, the simple imagination, is out of place and in the way as a man trying to make an Egyptian water wheel in the middle of the Bessemer foundry would be."

Neither Ober nor Haas had ever given him an opinion about the fable. "What is your opinion of this stuff?" he asked Ober now. "Will anybody read it in the next say 25 years? Are Random House by taking me on absolute faith as they have, wasting their money on it? My own time doesn't count; I don't believe I am wasting it or I would have stopped before now. There is nothing wrong with the book as it will be, only it may be 50 years before the world can stop to read it. It's too long, too deliberate."

He was fifty years old now. Alone in his workroom, alone in bed at night, he pondered his fate and his fable: maybe he had deceived himself, maybe the work was no good, maybe he was wasting his time. Ober now had some five hundred pages of the manuscript, and it was one of the messiest and most complicated things Faulkner had ever written. He was loath to continue; he needed a break; he heard something else anyway, voices calling from Yoknapatawpha, voices he had heard before and could no longer resist. In January 1948, he set his fable aside and started a new novel set in his apocryphal Jefferson, the idea for which he had had for some time. It was going to be a short "mystery-murder" about a black man accused of killing a white man. Faulkner was certain he could finish this one in a few weeks and finally give Random House a book. "I hope the idea will please Bob," he wrote Ober. "I've been on Random H's cuff for a long time now."

AT HOME IN YOKNAPATAWPHA COUNTY, Faulkner wrote with ease and confidence, finishing his new novel in three months. But what had started out to be "a simple quick 150 page whodunit," Faulkner told Ober, "jumped the traces" and became something longer and more significant, "a mystery story plus a little sociology and psychology." It "jumped the traces" because Faulkner found himself wanting to make a statement, which derived from his sense of moral urgency acquired during the Second World War: his belief that a new era of racial justice must follow and that older men like him must help bring it about. As the fable was to win people to the idea of peace, the new novel suggested the way to racial brotherhood. The theme, as Faulkner saw it, was that southern whites, not the North or the national government, "owe and must pay a responsibility to the Negro."

In the story itself, Faulkner stressed the relationship between Lucas Beauchamp, a mulatto farmer who refused to behave like "a nigger," and Charles "Chick" Mallison, Jr., a young white who believed in Lucas and consequently became a man almost overnight. Summoned back from a story in *Go Down, Moses,* Lucas was a grandson of Carothers McCaslin and so a blood relative of Ike McCaslin of "The Bear." Crotchety, aloof, and self-contained, Lucas had none of the violent confusions of Joe Christmas. He refused to live by the rules of either race, refused to cringe or defy. He came striding into town, dressed in a black suit and an open shirt, walking erect with a gold toothpick in his mouth, going about his business with unruffled dignity, his expression composed, detached, impersonal. Whites thought him "a damned high-nosed impudent Negro," but Lucas ignored them. When a white man screamed at him, "You goddamn biggity stiffnecked stinking burr-headed Edmonds sonofabitch," Lucas calmly replied, "I ain't a Edmonds. I don't belong to these new folks. I belongs to the old. I'm a McCaslin."

Sixteen-year-old Chick found him both fascinating and baffling. Lucas had once rescued the boy from an icy creek and given him food, but had refused to let Chick pay him back, refused even to acknowledge a relationship with him. Chick did not know what to make of Lucas or what to think. As a white in Dixie, he realized that he ought to hate Lucas for his pride and impudence, but he couldn't: he struggled with subversive feelings, with an increasing admiration and respect for the old Negro as a man.

One day the sheriff arrested Lucas, charged him with murdering a white man, and threw him in jail. But even with a lynch mob forming outside, Lucas coolly orchestrated his own deliverance: he summoned young Chick to his cell, certain that this sensitive young white boy would believe him innocent and help him prove it. Lucas was right on both counts: Chick believed him and was eager to do as Lucas said. What followed was a compelling "whodunit" in which Chick proved Lucas' innocence with the help of two loyal companions, his uncle Gavin Stevens, who served as county attorney, and the sheriff himself. In a powerful curtain scene, Lucas, free now and exonerated, appeared in Stevens' office and insisted on paying him a fee. Once again, he had his gold toothpick in his mouth. By now, Stevens himself had developed a genuine if uneasy respect for Lucas. A garrulous man in his middle years, with a thin, bony, eager face, Stevens protested that he hadn't done anything, but finally settled for $2—the price of the pen he had broken while writing down Lucas' statement. Lucas counted out $2 from his coin purse. Then he stood there, calm and intractable, while the uproar of Saturday in Jefferson rose on the bright afternoon.

"Now what?" Gavin Stevens said. "What are you waiting for now?"

"My receipt," Lucas said.

In addition to helping Lucas, Gavin Stevens played another role in the story, a didactic role. Highly educated, with a Phi Beta Kappa key from Harvard and a Ph.D. from the University of Heidelberg, Stevens represented the best and most enlightened in his generation of southern whites. In the course of the story, Faulkner let him deliver protracted speeches on freedom and southern white responsibility in the matter of race, with Chick pondering and often disputing what his uncle said.

It was the South, Stevens argued, and not the North that must free the Negro. The North had already tried that and failed, "so it will have to be us." Certainly Lucas Beauchamp deserved his freedom—he was a human being, after all. Someday he would vote as the white man did and send his children to the same school as whites and travel anywhere the white man traveled. But it would not be next Tuesday. And it could not come from legislative coercion, as northerners seemed to think, since that would drive decent southern whites into the arms of the racial fanatics and fling Lucas himself decades back into "grief and agony and violence." No, Stevens said, "man's injustice to man" could not be eradicated overnight by the police.

But Chick demurred: he thought Stevens was excusing the injustice.

"No," his uncle said. "I only say that the injustice is ours, the South's. We must expiate and abolish it ourselves, alone and without help nor even (with thanks) advice. We owe that to Lucas whether he wants it or not (and this Lucas anyway wont)."

These were Faulkner's sentiments exactly, as events were to prove. His message here was clear enough: racial change would come in the next generation of southern whites—young Chick's generation. Once they did as Chick did, once they learned to resist their racial heritage and to accept and care for the Negro as a person, they would grant him what was rightfully his and thus reform the South themselves.

Yet Faulkner did not regard his characters as merely mouthpieces for reform. He spoke of them as real people, as alive as any of the other residents of his turbulent county. He once told a friend that Gavin Stevens "was a good man, but he didn't succeed in living up to his ideal. But his nephew, the boy, I think he may grow up to be a better man than his uncle; I think he may succeed as a human being." As for Lucas Beauchamp, Faulkner seemed to feel about him as Chick and Gavin did —seemed to share the boy's "irritated awe and the man's uneasy admiration." Indeed, Faulkner showed Lucas a deference he had accorded no other character, as if to earn Lucas' own forgiveness and acceptance, and maybe even his love.

By late April 1948, Faulkner had put the finishing touches on his manuscript and mailed it off to New York, anxious to know what Haas thought. When Haas said he liked it, Faulkner was glad. He could write still, he hadn't lost his talent after all. But what to call the new book? He sought advice from Haas, from Commins and Cerf, and finally decided on a title himself: he would call it *Intruder in the Dust.*

N JULY, RANDOM HOUSE sold MGM the movie rights to *Intruder in the Dust* for $50,000. Faulkner's share, less Random House's commission, was $40,000. If Haas was "super-pleased," Faulkner was in ecstasy. His financial problems seemed over now; he could pay his taxes for this and the next three years and still have plenty of money left over. If he was careful, he wouldn't have to borrow or charge anymore, or write potboilers, or go back to Hollywood. Mark this day as his emancipation from Warner Bros. He had no intention of ever returning to the ward again, because after thirty years of indigence as a writer, he was finally on the road to financial security. He and Estelle even celebrated together, and Faulkner danced in his bare feet. "Anybody who can sell a book to the movies for $50,000 has a right to get drunk and dance in his bare feet," Faulkner told a well-wisher.

Feeling rich and happy, Faulkner even splurged on a new used car, a maroon Ford station wagon with a wooden body. Malcolm said it was a good thing: Faulkner's 1935 Ford was ready for the junkyard. The floorboards had rusted out, so that driver and passengers could see the road racing by below. Malcolm claimed that the brakes were so bad that passengers had to stick their legs through the opening and drag their feet on the pavement to stop the car.

In October, Faulkner flew to New York, to be on hand for the publication of *Intruder in the Dust*, the book that had liberated him. Also, he wanted to consult with Ober and Haas about what to do with his money—"so my friends and kinfolks dont or cant borrow and spend it," he said. He found himself quite the celebrity at Random House. The book was selling well and attracting more immediate critical attention than any of his previous novels, thanks mainly to its racial themes.

On his first night in town, Faulkner had dinner with an actress named Ruth Ford, a former Ole Miss coed who had once dated Dean Faulkner. A slim and striking woman, with bright brown eyes and black hair, she had been under contract at Warner Bros. while Faulkner had worked on the ward. He had seen her from time to time and regarded himself as her "gentleman friend." Now, in New York, he offered to be her lover. "Ruth, I've been your gentleman friend for quite a while now," he said. "Ain't it time I was promoted?" When she laughed and turned him down, his mood seemed to change. Initially cheerful, he drank more and said less now.

He did meet Malcolm Cowley at long last, at a lavish dinner party at the Haases' Fifth Avenue apartment. A year younger than Faulkner, Cowley was a brusque man with a thin mustache and thick, dark brown hair. They greeted one another like old friends, which in a way they were after their long correspondence and collaborative efforts on Cowley's *Portable*. Cowley noticed Faulkner's small, "beautifully shaped" hands and thought his face had an expression like Poe's in photographs, melancholy and a little crooked. Faulkner comported himself with an air of great dignity, Cowley observed, and spoke in a strong Mississippi accent.

It was a formal dinner in the old style, where the women withdrew afterward and the men discoursed over cigars and cognac. "There was a good deal of cognac," Cowley said. He and his wife left at two in the morning, but Faulkner and others went home with Hal Smith, Faulkner's old friend and onetime editor and publisher, for more drinking. Within a day or so, Faulkner was shut up in his hotel room and well into the cycle. At week's end, friends found him there, unconscious, and took him to a Manhattan sanitarium. But he hated it so much—"You gotta get me out of here," he kept saying—that they arranged for him to stay with Malcolm and Muriel Cowley, at their renovated farmhouse in Connecticut.

This was the true measure of friendship, and Cowley and his wife met it with unquestioning forbearance. They nursed Faulkner through the worst of the withdrawal, giving him leek and potato soup and watered-down drinks at intervals. When he was able to get up, he paced the living room with beads of cold sweat on his forehead, fighting the terrible craving until he couldn't stand it anymore. Then he would ask Muriel, politely, "Do you think I could have a beer, ma'am?"

Faulkner felt comfortable and secure with Cowley, whom he often addressed as his "dear brother." Within a couple of days, Faulkner felt well enough to confide in his friend, to open up about himself and his work. His new novel, he said, was about Christ as a corporal in the French army and about a general who was Antichrist. Cowley tried to follow Faulkner's description of the plot and theme, but it was difficult. "Symbolic and unreal," Cowley wrote in his notebook, "except for 300 wild pages about a three-legged race horse in Tennessee. Mary Magdalene and the other two Marys. There is a strange mutiny in which the soldiers on both sides simply refuse to fight. The corporal's body is chosen for that of the Unknown Soldier. Christ (or his disciple) lives again in the crowd."

Later that day, they went for a long drive into eastern New York, across the foothills of the Taconic range. It was a magnificent autumn afternoon, with falling leaves and golden skies. The maples were almost bare now, but the oaks still wore "an imperial purple," as Cowley said. Sober now, Faulkner was in a rare mood, talking away on the car trip to and from New York State and into the evening back at the Cowley farmhouse. He reminisced about his misadventures as Ole Miss postmaster, told tall tales about running rum in the bayous around New Orleans, recalled Sherwood Anderson's influence on him, and recounted how he had discovered and created Yoknapatawpha County, which borrowed scenes and features from three real Mississippi counties. He said about style: "There are some kinds of writing that you have to do very fast, like riding a bicycle on a tightrope." Cowley mentioned Hawthorne's complaint "about the devil who got into his inkpot." Faulkner said, "I listen to the voices, and when I put down what the voices say, it's right. Sometimes I don't like what they say, but I don't change it."

They also talked about *Intruder in the Dust*, which Cowley had reviewed in *The New Republic*, calling it a story about the dilemma of southern nationalism. Faulkner denied that Gavin Stevens spoke for him, which was what the artist in Faulkner would tell a critic, even one he liked. No, Faulkner said, Stevens spoke for the best type of southern liberals (which, of course, included Faulkner). "If the race problems were just left to the children," Faulkner went on, "they'd be solved soon enough. It's the grown-ups and especially the women who keep the prejudice alive." He claimed that he had once caused a mild scandal at Ole Miss when he'd asserted that blacks ought to be enrolled. He mentioned that three Negro tenant families now operated his farm and that he let them have what profits it made. He did so, he said softly, because "The negroes don't always get a square deal in Mississippi."

The next day, Faulkner felt well enough to return to New York City and thence home to Mississippi. On the way to the train station, Faulkner was "abstracted and already a little distant," Cowley thought. He wore his old, shabby English army officer's trench coat and smoked cigars, as he often did after recovering from a binge. He carried a book Cowley had lent him—Charles Jackson's harrowing story of an alcoholic, *The Lost Weekend*.

Before leaving for Mississippi, Faulkner arranged for a dozen long-stemmed roses to be sent to Muriel Cowley, as a token of his gratitude.

On NOVEMBER 24, 1948, *The New York Times* announced that Faulkner had been elected to the American Academy of Arts and Letters, the select inner body of the National Institute of Arts and Letters —further evidence of the Faulkner revival sparked by Cowley's *Portable*. Cowley now wanted to do an illustrated piece on him for *Life* magazine, but Faulkner was "convinced and determined" that this was not for him, even if Cowley was his friend. As he wrote Cowley: "It is my ambition to be, as a private individual, abolished and voided from history, leaving it markless, no refuse save the printed books; I wish I had had enough sense to see ahead thirty years ago and, like some of the Elizabethans, not signed them. It is my aim, and every effort bent, that the sum and history of my life, which in the same sentence is my obit and epitaph too, shall be them both: he made the books and he died."

Cowley was disappointed. He warned Faulkner that one day *Time, Life*, or some other magazine would send a reporter to Oxford with orders to get a story, and he would do it unscrupulously. "That's the trouble with your decision," Cowley said—"it's absolute for anyone who respects you and admires your work, but won't have any effect at all on the sons of bitches." But Faulkner refused to give in. His private life, to him, was inviolable.

"Much excitement here," he wrote New York when MGM came to town to film *Intruder in the Dust*, this in the late winter and spring of 1949. Since the Negroes in the cast couldn't lodge in public accommodations, they had to stay in the homes of local "colored leaders." Initially, white Oxonians were leery of a bunch of Hollywood people, some of them black, invading their town to make a motion picture about an averted lynching. And MGM was concerned about it, too, since a black man was actually locked up in the old city jail on a charge of raping a white woman: MGM public relations worried that the mob scene in the movie might provoke a real lynching. But nothing like that happened. The luckless Negro pleaded guilty and went off to prison, and the town and the movie group soon got along famously, in part because MGM opened a casting office and hired local people to play in bit parts and street scenes. Faulkner helped in the casting, and what he saw stirred his loins. "It's too bad," he wrote New York, "I'm no longer young enough to cope with all the local girls who are ready and eager to glide into camera focus on their backs."

Faulkner helped scout locations and made minor revisions in the shooting script, but had little to do with the actual filming. He did appear on the set one day with his aging mother; they sat in canvas chairs and watched the director and actors at work. Claude Jarman, Jr., played a creditable Chick Mallison and David Brian his voluble uncle, called John Stevens in the movie. But the real star was towering, mahogany-skinned Juano Hernandez, a former prizefighter and minstrel show singer, who was making his film debut as Lucas Beauchamp.

He *was* Lucas, with the magnificent integrity, carriage, and expression he brought to his role.

By late April, the film was done, most of the crew was gone, and Faulkner was busy with yet another book, which he'd begun in January. It was a collection of mystery stories that featured attorney Gavin Stevens. All the stories had previously appeared in magazines except the long title piece, "Knight's Gambit," which Faulkner worked on through the spring of that year. The Gavin Stevens who lived in these pages seemed a mixture of Faulkner and Phil Stone. Now "fifty plus," which was Faulkner's own age, Gavin had a shock of premature white hair, smoked a corncob pipe, and wore a suit that looked as though he had slept in it every night since he had bought it. Like Stone, he was an overeducated, "glib and talkative man who talked so much and so glibly, particularly about things which had absolutely no concern with him, that his was indeed a split personality: the one, the lawyer, the county attorney who walked and breathed and displaced air; the other, the garrulous facile voice so garrulous and facile that it seemed to have no connection with reality at all and presently hearing it was like listening not even to fiction but to literature." In amorous matters, though, Stevens resembled his creator, for in "Knight's Gambit" he set out to regain a lost love, which suggested Faulkner's own sense of loss and his corresponding need for a new young woman.

By the end of May, the typescript of *Knight's Gambit,* the title of the new collection, was on Saxe Commins' desk in New York. Faulkner had grown close to his sad-eyed, chain-smoking editor, who lovingly called him "Little Lord Fauntleroy," shared his concern about the dehumanization of the modern world, admired him enormously as a writer, and became his loyal personal friend. "I have just this minute finished with great excitement my reading of *Knight's Gambit,*" Commins reported in early June. "You must know without my telling you how deeply affected I am by its layer upon layer of implication and throbbing narrative power. My hat is off to you, Sir." That was the kind of assurance an author liked to get from his editor, even for a relatively minor work like *Knight's Gambit,* scheduled for release in the fall. Meanwhile Faulkner's fable lay in an uninviting heap on his worktable, unfinished and for all he knew unfinishable.

JILL TURNED SIXTEEN THAT JUNE, and Faulkner found it increasingly difficult to relate to her. He loved her as much as ever, yet he had no idea what he wanted her to be. He still liked the idea of "little girls in pinafores," Jill recalled, but she clearly wasn't a little girl anymore. By her own admission, she had grown into "a terrible Tom-boy" who liked to spend the day in pants on a horse, and Pappy seemed to encourage that. Jill thought he wished she were a boy. Sometimes, though, he seemed to urge her to be an independent, strong-willed female, like his mother. But at other times, he wanted her to be frail and helpless, as he saw Estelle. It was easy for him to be many people, she complained, but it was hard for her. She was so confused; she didn't know what he expected. Once, when she was downtown in shorts, Pappy walked right by her without a word. Young ladies, he lectured her later, did not dress like that in public. On another occasion, he chastised her for appearing on the square in blue jeans and Malcolm's shirt. She never wore jeans to town again.

He could be strict in other ways, too. On his orders, she could not have a radio, or a phonograph, or one of those newfangled television sets, some of which were appearing in Oxford now. Cho-Cho's second husband warned him, "Pappy, if you don't let Jill have her fun at home, she'll go outside her home for it." Finally he relented and allowed her to bring a phonograph to Rowan Oak, but she couldn't play it when he was at home.

Jill idolized her Pappy, yet feared that he didn't love and didn't want her. She was having a painful time with both parents. The hardest thing was their drinking. Sometimes when she brought friends home, they would both be inebriated, and she would feel so embarrassed and hurt. She could tell when one of Pappy's binges was coming on, and she would beg him not to start. "Think of me," she would say. "No one remembers Shakespeare's child," he once retorted. With both parents often drunk and shut up in their separate bedrooms, Jill felt isolated and lonely, an outcast, just as Faulkner had felt when he was her age. She had a recurring dream that betrayed her own turmoil: her legs were going to be amputated, and she had to figure out how she would live with her parents when she could never walk again. When they looked down at her in the dream, she got a cold feeling that they really did not care about her.

She wished she could escape from them, get out of Oxford. As Faulkner had done in his youth, Jill longed for her independence, she struggled for it. Yet her father seemed unaware of her suffering. He thought it enough that he loved her and that he stayed with Estelle mainly on her account. For him, that was the supreme sacrifice.

June drifted into July 1949. At fifty-one, Faulkner felt all used up, a "soiled and battered bloke" past his prime. He needed something to break the monotony of his life, something to convince him that it really was worthwhile, something to get him going again. In the meantime, he had a new diversion: he scraped and recaulked a sailboat he'd recently bought, put in a bottle of rum, and spent the hot July days sailing on nearby Sardis Lake, where sudden rain and thunder squalls could make things "pretty exciting" for a few minutes anyway. But deep down he still felt old, worn out. He even called his sloop *The Ring Dove*, the name of a boat in Joseph Conrad's story "The End of the Tether."

PART SEVEN

WHEN SHALL I SLEEP AGAIN?

ONE DRIZZLY AUGUST AFTERNOON IN 1949, Faulkner was standing in the pasture with his horses when a car turned into the driveway, passed the NO TRESPASSING sign he had erected at the gate, and approached the house. Who in the hell was this? Faulkner hated people who brazenly invaded his private domain. Then he recognized the driver: it was John Reed Holley, one of Malcolm's contemporaries, who used to attend Faulkner's famous Halloween parties. Holley had called him earlier that day and said something about a woman from Memphis who wanted to meet him, some would-be writer who had read his books. Faulkner had heard that line many times before; he told Holley he had other plans.

Holley got out and met Faulkner at the fence. He hoped Mr. Bill wouldn't mind, but his cousin Joan Williams, the woman he had phoned about, was in the car, and Holley would truly appreciate it if Mr. Bill would speak to her.

On the way over, Faulkner said, "Well, what does she want to see? Why does she want to meet me? Does she want to see if I have two heads?"

Holley laughed. "I don't think so. She would just like to meet you."

Faulkner assumed that Joan Williams was "a grim beldame of 40 or 50 summers, president of some limited literary circle, come out of curiosity." She turned out to be a lovely young woman, twenty or so, who sat in the back seat with a young man. When Faulkner looked inside the car and saw Joan's face, her delicate lips, green eyes, and reddish hair, he felt a tug at his heart. She would hardly look at him. In truth, she was mortified that they had intruded on him like this; it was Holley's idea. God, he was actually talking to her, the famous novelist whose books had affected her in such profound ways, standing at the car window in khakis and a T-shirt; later she was certain he wore only a pair of shorts, without a shirt. She was so embarrassed she just sat there frozen to the seat, looking away. The novelist exchanged pleasantries with Holley and his wife, who was in the front seat; then Holley got in the car and drove away.

Not long afterward, Faulkner received a letter from Joan Williams, which went like this:

Dear Mr. Faulkner:

I know you have a secretary and probably you will never see this but I have to write it anyway, as I am the girl who came here today when you told us not to, and I wanted you to know it was not for the reason you thought, to stare at you, but because I like your work so much. I am unhappy and I know you are unhappy too. I wanted to tell you you shouldn't be so unhappy and lonely when you have done so much for the world. There were so many things I had wanted to ask you because I know you have thought and felt and suffered everything I ever have and I wanted to ask you the reason for suffering. Why some people have to and others don't? In the end do you gain something from it? I knew after reading your books I could ask you everything and you would answer and I could tell you everything about myself, that my dog just got run over, and you would understand. Could I come again by myself? You don't have to worry as I know all about your drinking and that doesn't make any difference to me. My father drinks too. So don't worry or be embarrassed. I hope I have not bothered you again by writing. But I couldn't go on thinking that you thought I came there to stare when I so much did not come for that reason, at all."

For Faulkner, something charming and sweet came out of Joan's letter, like the scent of a flower in the woods, stumbled on by chance. It made him feel twenty-one again, "brave and clean and durable." He thought he might already be falling in love with her. He wrote her how much her letter meant to him, but said he wasn't sure about her coming back to Rowan Oak. He would do this, though: she could write him the questions as they occurred to her, and "sooner or later" he would answer them.

She wrote him in the fall, from Bard College in New York State, where she was a senior. She was flattered that he would even respond to her first letter; surely he could help her feel better about herself. She had had a terrible time with her parents, who had tried to push her down "every proper path," who had sent her to Miss Hutchinson's School for Girls and expected her to marry and have children, as a young lady of the 1940s was supposed to do. She had wanted to be a writer, but they had discouraged her and then crushed her attempts to rebel; when she had eloped at seventeen, they had had the marriage annulled. She hated her father and his ever-present martinis—he was a father "in name only." She felt guilty about wanting to write; her parents kept telling her she was worthless. Feeling isolated and ignorant, she clung to a childhood dream that she would someday go to a place where people would love her and she would never be hurt again.

In her letter, she asked him about the things that troubled her, about "why everything is," and he responded to the intimacy he felt in her entreaties. "These are the wrong questions," he wrote her. "A woman must ask these of a man while they are lying in bed together." But he reassured her: "dont grieve over having the problems, the questions. The kindest thing the gods can give people at twenty . . . is a capacity to ask why, a passion for something better than vegetation, even if what they get by it is grief and pain." He told her to get Housman and "read him a lot."

His sentence about lying in bed together shocked her a little. But she decided that he still just wanted to be friends. Besides, his letter consoled her. She was not the oddity to him that she was to her parents. She wrote him back, quoting Housman's *A Shropshire Lad.* "See," she said, "I always listen to you."

By October, Faulkner wanted to see Joan so badly that he almost went north. When he next wrote her, he stared at the blank page and wanted to create a love letter. During her Christmas break, they wrote back and forth, trying to set up a meeting. "Not here," he said from Oxford. "There might be . . . repercussions that would put a bad taste in the mouth." On a freezing day in early January, he rode a Southern Trailways bus to Memphis. He was not even sure he would recognize her. Belted into a trench coat, wearing a brown hat, he stepped off the bus. A slender young woman approached, with reddish hair and freckles on her face.

"Mr. Faulkner?" she asked.

"Miss Williams."

She wasn't sure where they should go. He said they had to be careful:

he couldn't be recognized. Would she drive him to the Peabody Hotel? He wanted to leave a manuscript with a typist there; it was his excuse for leaving Oxford. At that, she grew apprehensive. She had planned to meet Faulkner as Faulkner; but his need for secrecy turned it into something else: she was meeting a married man—and she only three years out of Miss Hutchinson's School for Girls!

After he dropped off his manuscript, they drove aimlessly about Memphis in freezing rain. Content with silence, he said nothing. But she was miserable: she could think of nothing to say and felt resentful that he didn't keep up a conversation, since he was so much older and more intelligent than she. Finally she stopped on a bluff overlooking the Mississippi. He spoke now. He might have guessed, he said, that she liked the river, too. Then he was silent again. The rain turned to slush on the windshield. Joan was frozen and cramped from sitting so long behind the wheel. He put a hand on her arm; she tensed, surprised, and he took his hand away. When she suggested that they have lunch, he was contrite: he forgot, he said, that at her age she had to eat in the middle of the day; at his age, he didn't.

She drove to a drive-in, and they sat in a booth inside. Since it was a weekday and past the rush hour, the place was almost empty. Good. He wouldn't be recognized here. The waitress who took their orders gazed on a demure young coed and a small, erect, middle-aged man with puffy eyes, sitting ill at ease together. On the nickelodeon, the Mills Brothers sang "You Always Hurt the One You Love."

Faulkner told Joan the song might be for her.

But why? she asked.

Because, he said, he was going to fall in love with her, or already had. Hadn't she realized what it might mean when she wrote that first letter? No, she said, apprehensive again. The colors from the nickelodeon swirled about the room in patterns of greens and lavenders.

After lunch, they set out in the car again. By the end of the day, Joan was so exhausted from the cold and the aimless driving that she took Faulkner home to meet her mother. At least her house was warm and stationary. When at last she drove him back to the bus station, Faulkner sensed how much she looked up to him. "I know," he said, "you want me to be your father." He wanted to be that and her lover, too. The idea made him flush with desire. Later, when she was back at Bard, he wrote her that thoughts of Joan Williams made him think of the painter

Bouguereau, whose *Nymphs and Satyr* showed four naked beauties dragging a virile satyr into the water of a marsh.

He resolved to help Joan become the writer she aspired to be. She had won a *Mademoiselle* short story contest, Faulkner remembered, and the story had been published. He found the issue with Joan's story and wrote her that it made him want to cry a little for "all the sad frustration of solitude, isolation, alone-ness in which every human lives, who for all the blood kinship and everything else, can't really communicate, touch." He thought the story "all right, moving and true; the force, the passion, the controlled heat," would come in time. He proposed that they write something together—the two of them collaborating "to get the good stuff out of Joan Williams." Yes, he had Shaw's Pygmalion in mind. But he didn't intend to create "a cold and beautiful statue, in order to fall in love with it." No, he hoped to take the girl he already loved and make a poet out of her. "Will you risk it?" he asked.

In February 1950, he met her in New York City and over drinks at the Biltmore outlined what he had in mind: a play they would do together called *Requiem for a Nun*. The play was to be a vehicle for his friend Ruth Ford, who'd said that she wanted most of all for him to write a play for her. Faulkner had begun *Requiem for a Nun* as a short story back in 1933, but had set it aside for *Absalom, Absalom!*

Faulkner would send notes to Joan, and she could develop them into scenes. He contended that collaborating with him would be her breakthrough as a writer. In effect, he was offering to make her his protégé. She had reservations, however, about trying to rewrite William Faulkner. Was he being serious? Then she realized that working with him would be "an excuse to offer his people and mine for our seeing one another."

She was both confused and flattered by all the attention he gave her. He took her to a party at the Haases', pointing out one guest who had magazine connections—he hoped to help her secure a magazine job after she graduated. That would get her away from her parents and out of Memphis, freeing her from the restraints of their middle-class life that stifled her as a person and an artist.

Joan struggled with her mixed feelings for Faulkner, for this courtly older man who shielded and reassured her with a warmth she had never known before. It didn't help matters when he kissed her briefly. She worried: he doesn't just want to be friends.

It's because I'm too old, isn't it, he said. *No, it isn't that,* she said, even though it was that, plus the fact that he was married. She wanted desperately not to hurt him. She needed him as a nurturing teacher and friend, somebody she could talk to, somebody who understood her. But she didn't love him that way, the way he wanted.

"If only I could have been born earlier, or you later," she said.

"No," he said. "Earlier I was too busy writing to have had time for you."

But he had time for her now. When he was with her, it was like walking in April again. For the first time in his life, he told her, he had to have somebody to write for. He had always been the cat who walked alone, but that didn't work for him anymore. "So I do need you," he wrote her later, when he was back at Rowan Oak. "Not coddling but affection, warmth. So I can believe again that work is worthwhile and do it. Sympathy. 'Fun' in a word, maybe. To talk fantasy and nonsense and good sense and truth, and to equals, to believe in the same things, believe that the same things are true and important and worth believing in. Damn it, I want somebody to give to," somebody "to say yes, yes to me and I want to say yes, yes, yes to the dear face in return."

From Rowan Oak, Faulkner sent Joan several pages of notes, reminding her that the play was hers, too. She made some effort to work on it, but she lacked the heart to do much, giving him the reason that she was too busy with her senior thesis. Don't worry, he wrote her. They could do more together this summer, when she came home. The work, he assured her, would save her from her family and "some of the lacerations and abrasions I knew." As for Joan and him, he would try to be whatever she wanted him to be, he said. But he warned her that he was "capable not only of imagining anything and everything, but even of hoping and believing."

Meanwhile Estelle was getting suspicious. An acquaintance of hers had seen Faulkner and Joan in the Memphis drive-in. Somehow Estelle knew that they had been together in New York, too. Faulkner insisted they were only collaborating on a play, but Estelle didn't believe it: why would a fifty-two-year-old novelist, with almost twenty books to his credit, want to collaborate with a neophyte college girl?

To find out for certain, Estelle arranged to meet Joan at a restaurant in the Peabody Hotel in Memphis, probably during her Easter break. Joan was amazed at how old and frail Estelle seemed: as they headed for a table, she had to hold Joan's arm for support. Seated at a table, Estelle got straight to the point. Did Joan want to marry her husband?

Astonished, Joan said no.

But Estelle persisted: why did she want to see him, then?

Because she wanted to be a writer, Joan said. Didn't Mrs. Faulkner understand? If she wanted to be a painter, wouldn't she want to know Picasso?

No, Estelle said. She thought Bill was "going through the menopause." Men had one, too, you know. Joan had no idea about that. But she did grasp Estelle's meaning: Bill needed a change. Choosing her words carefully, Joan said it was her understanding that when people had been married a long time, their feelings were not the same as they were at first. She was thinking about her parents' separate bedrooms, unaware perhaps that the Faulkners had separate bedrooms, too. Estelle misunderstood. She said she didn't consider herself too old at fifty to fall in love.

The meeting was inconclusive. Back at Rowan Oak, though, Estelle was seething, certain that Joan and Faulkner were lovers and that Joan would try to take everything away from her—her husband, her daughter, and her home. In Estelle's eyes, Joan was a worse threat than Meta had been, for pretty young Joan lived in nearby Memphis, not in California. Beset with visions of doom, Estelle wrote and then telephoned Joan's parents. When Faulkner found out, he and Estelle fought bitterly. She threatened to see Joan's parents in person, but Faulkner stopped her. At that, Estelle escaped in alcohol, often drinking in front of the servants, even in front of Jill.

In despair, Faulkner warned Joan that maybe she should end their relationship, though that was not what he wanted. She assured him she didn't want that either, despite her terrible confusions about him. She clung to his fatherly warmth; he clung to hopes and dreams that they would become lovers and fellow artists, bound together against middle-class conventions, against her domineering parents and his burdensome wife.

In late April, the American Academy of Arts and Letters awarded him the William Dean Howells Medal, given every five years for the most distinguished works in fiction during that time. Faulkner declined to attend the ceremonies in New York—"I am a farmer this time of the year," he protested. But in late spring he sent the Academy his thanks and regrets, pointing out that a writer worked for "money, women, glory; all nice to have, but glory's best, and the best of glory is from his peers." But he doubted that one's work could ever really be evaluated;

certainly none of his had ever suited him. "Then one day I was fifty and I looked back at it," he said, "and I decided that it was all pretty good —and then in the same instant I realized that that was the worst of all since that meant only that a little nearer now was the moment, instant, night: dark: sleep: when I would put it all away forever that I anguished and sweated over, and it would never trouble me anymore."

H E STRUGGLED WITH *Requiem for a Nun* that spring of 1950, only to realize that he couldn't write a play and that it was turning into "some kind of novel." By May 22, he had finished a first draft and started revisions. He told Haas that it was a story told in "seven play-scenes, inside a novel," and that it was "an interesting experiment in form. I think it's all right." His plans now called for him to do the book by himself and help Joan adapt it into a workable play script during the summer.

As he reworked his composition, Faulkner appended long historical narratives to each act, which afforded a sweeping panorama of the entire saga of Jefferson and of the state as well. He called this "the scaffolding stuff that holds my three acts in a book." In the play scenes, he called back Temple Drake and Gowan Stevens from *Sanctuary;* Stevens was the drunken young collegian who had taken Temple to the bootleggers' place, where Popeye had raped her with the corncob. Temple and Gowan were married now, a prominent couple with a baby girl. Temple had married Gowan to expunge her past—her debauchery with Popeye and Red in the Memphis bordello, her responsibility for Red's death, her perjury against Lee Goodwin. To care for her baby and share her memories, she hired a black nurse named Nancy Mannigoe, who had a sordid past too: she had been a drunkard, a cocaine addict, and a whore, but, like Temple, had apparently reformed. But for no apparent reason, Nancy murdered Temple's child in its crib one day, stood trial, and was convicted for the crime. As the play unfolded, her motive became clear; it involved Temple, of course, who hadn't changed at all, who remained as susceptible to evil as she had been in *Sanctuary.* When Red's brother had tried to blackmail her because of her past, Temple fell for the brother and told Nancy she was going to

desert her family and run away with him. At that, poor demented
Nancy killed the baby in order to save it from torment when Temple
was gone.

Temple made a final attempt to save her soul. Pressed by Gavin
Stevens, Gowan's uncle and the ubiquitous county attorney of
Faulkner's recent fiction, Temple confessed her wretched past to the
governor of Mississippi, who had already refused to stay Nancy's execu-
tion. Temple confessed so that she herself might suffer and pay a little
more for her complicity in her child's murder. When she and Gavin
visited Nancy in jail, they found that the condemned woman had given
herself to Jesus, trusting that she would be forgiven and saved.

"What about me?" cried an anguished Temple. Was there a heaven
where she might meet the child she had killed? Would she be forgiven,
too? But what if there was nobody there, nobody to forgive her?

"Believe," was all Nancy could tell her. "Believe."

Faulkner found little joy in rewriting *Requiem for a Nun,* but he
stayed at it somehow. Meanwhile Joan had graduated from Bard and
was back in Memphis for the summer, but she and Faulkner gave up
trying to meet there. They decided on Holly Springs, which was about
halfway between Memphis and Oxford. He always waited for her in the
shady courthouse square; she came down in her mother's car, or on a
Greyhound bus. Then they set off for Pott's Camp, driving along red,
dusty roads that wound through the empty countryside. He always
brought beer, and a lunch for her; he remembered that she needed to
eat in the middle of the day. Since both were laconic by nature, they
didn't talk much at the camp. They were content simply to sit and be
together in the stillness of the woods. Both perspired in the sweltering
summer heat—that he could smell of sweat made him "Bill" to her, not
William Faulkner.

She noticed little things about him, especially his manner of laughing when he remembered something humorous. He would chuckle
silently, and his hooded eyes would take on amber glints; his mustache
would wag and his thin lips would twitch. She would never forget his
soundless laughter.

Once she brought pencil and paper and said she ought to ask questions about his work and write it all down, but she didn't know what to
say. He waved his hand and said she didn't need to ask those things.
What she got from the silence and solitude was enough. They agreed
that there was not enough silence in the world, and that most would

never understand two people who enjoyed sitting all day in the woods, not caring if they talked or not. They were "soul mates," Faulkner said, and if that was sentimentality, then so be it.

"What's wrong with sentimentality?" she asked.

"People are afraid of it," Faulkner said.

One day he said he had something for her, and put in her lap the original manuscript of *The Sound and the Fury*. It was the novel closest to his heart, the one he had written only for himself, and he wanted her to have it in its purest form. In Joan he had found his real-life Caddy Compson, his own "beautiful and tragic" young woman.

He once told her that writing "was the only thing he ever found to alleviate the boredom of living." When he spoke like that or drank too much, Joan sensed how vulnerable and sensitive he was. The more she knew about him, the more Joan believed that Fate had appointed her to take care of William Faulkner "for the whole world." And she came to love the man, Bill, though she balked at becoming his lover. She couldn't overcome the strictures, drilled into her for years, against premarital intercourse, especially with a married man.

As Faulkner became more ardent, persistent, and direct about going to bed with her, Joan grew more uneasy and hesitant, which only made him unhappy. They did do a little work on the play version of *Requiem for a Nun*, but Faulkner said that it didn't matter if they never finished it; what counted was "the fun of doing it together." In the fall, she returned to Bard and went on to become assistant director of admissions there. Faulkner missed her desperately, but at least she was away from her middle-class parents, who still objected to her becoming a writer. He tried to tell her something positive about their mutual discontent. "People need trouble," he wrote in early November, "a little of frustration to sharpen the spirit on, toughen it. Artists do; I dont mean you need to live in a rathole or gutter, but they have to learn fortitude, endurance; only vegetables are happy."

ALL YEAR THERE HAD BEEN RUMORS that he would win a Nobel Prize for literature. Since no prize had been awarded for 1949, the Swedish Academy would give two this year, for 1949 and 1950, and news reports claimed that Faulkner was high on the list for one of them. He'd told Joan that he didn't want a Nobel Prize, that he would rather be in "the same pigeon hole" with Dreiser and Sherwood Anderson, who had never won, than with Sinclair Lewis and "Mrs. Chinahand Buck," who had.

On November 10, 1950, Faulkner was liming a field adjoining his house when a Swedish correspondent phoned him from New York. Faulkner hated the damn phone, but he came into the house anyway and took the call in the pantry off the kitchen. The Swedish Academy, the man said, had issued a statement that he had won the 1949 Nobel Prize for literature, "for his powerful and independent artistic contribution in America's new literature of the novel." The prize money came to $30,171. How did it feel? the correspondent asked.

Faulkner said he felt flattered, but he wouldn't go to Stockholm for the ceremonies. "It's too far away. I am a farmer down here and I can't get away."

The truth was, he was deeply moved in spite of himself. When Mac Reed, the druggist who had loyally stocked his books, came to congratulate him, Faulkner shook his hand and said, "Mac, I still can't believe it." He was guarded and reserved when reporters arrived from Memphis. But at an open house in the evening, Faulkner received friends and relatives with great courtesy, even a trace of pleasure.

The town, of course, was astounded. No one in Oxford had ever expected Count No 'Count to win the most coveted literary prize in the world. "I guess," said one Oxford man, "he's appreciated a whole lot more outside than he is around here." Phil "Moon" Mullen, editor of the Oxford *Eagle,* set out to change that: he printed the news on the front page, top and center, with reminiscences by Faulkner's friends, including Phil Stone, who wrote that "A lot of us talk about decency, about honor, about loyalty, about gratitude. Bill doesn't talk about these things: he lives them."

In New York, Faulkner's agent and editors were jubilant, too. Not only did he deserve the prize; it was certain to bring him many thousands of new readers in this country and over the world. The New York press, however, greeted the news without enthusiasm. The *Herald Tribune* preferred "the choice of a laureate more smiling in a world which is gradually getting darker." Intoned the lordly *Times:* "Incest and rape are perhaps widespread distractions in the Jefferson, Mississippi of Faulkner, but not elsewhere in the United States."

Faulkner still insisted he wouldn't go to Stockholm to get his award. "There just isn't enough gas left in the tank to go all that distance," he said. That Faulkner refused to attend the ceremonies upset American embassy officials in Sweden, who dispatched a Falkner family friend to plead with him. If he didn't go, the friend said, he would embarrass his country. But Faulkner seemed adamant until Estelle persuaded him otherwise. Take Jill with you, Estelle said. It would be the trip of her lifetime. In truth, Jill was not at all eager to go, but Pappy liked the idea. After the awards, he could show her Paris and the Luxembourg Gardens, where he once had sat and watched old men sail toy boats in the autumn of their lives. To the immense relief of everybody concerned, he capitulated. He would go to Stockholm.

By then, the hurrah and uproar at Rowan Oak were too much for him. The phone rang eternally; people seemed constantly at his door. He reached for his bottle and calculated precisely how long he had to drink before departure time, which was Wednesday, December 6. "I'll take my last drink at six o'clock Monday night," he announced. Then he shut himself up in his room and slipped away into that alcoholic void which numbed out all consciousness and all pain.

Fretful voices rose from below. The prizewinner was on a binge; what an embarrassment if the press found out. There was no telling how bad the withdrawal would be. They might have to take him to Wright's Sanitarium in Byhalia; he would miss his plane, the awards; it would be a national scandal. To forestall that, family members came up with a ruse: on Friday, December 1, they slipped into his bedroom and told him it was Monday and time to start sobering up. Faulkner grumbled, roused himself, and began spacing his drinks; then in the afternoon he called for Malcolm. Where was Malcolm? At the high school football game, someone said. Faulkner lay in bed pondering that, then raised himself with an elbow, his face glowering. "Somebody's been deceivin' me! They don't play football games on Monday." He lay back down. "I've got three more days to drink," he said.

He stopped on Monday, just as he promised, and on Wednesday was sober enough to leave, though he felt terrible, his puffy eyes blazing with truculence. Phil Stone called to wish him luck, saying, "Now, Bill, you do right." Faulkner snapped, "I'm so damn sick and tired of hearin' that. Everybody from the Swedish ambassador to my damn nigger houseboy has been tellin' me to do right!"

He and Jill flew to New York's La Guardia Airport, where a happy

Bob Haas and a bevy of aggressive reporters greeted them. "What do you consider the decadent aspect of American life today?" a female reporter demanded.

"It's what you're doing now," Faulkner shot back.

That evening, at a party thrown by the Haases, Faulkner took an antibiotic and drank Jack Daniel's and water before and after dinner. He came down with a fever the next day, but refused to stay in bed and even attended a celebration that night at Bennett and Phyllis Cerf's. Sick, mad, and sober, he had made up his mind to see this ordeal through.

By Friday, December 8, he and Jill were in snow-covered Stockholm, contending with press conferences and formal receptions. At a dinner party given by his Swedish publisher, Faulkner found himself standing alone, looking at pictures on the wall, his Swedish hosts all keeping a proper distance. He was nervous and tired; this was worse than he could ever have imagined. Presently, a tall, elegant woman approached and engaged him in conversation. She was Else Jonsson; her late husband had been an ardent Faulkner admirer and one of his first Swedish translators. Faulkner liked her at once; she had an exquisite face, with glossy red hair, blue-gray eyes, and clear, lovely skin. He felt relaxed and talkative in her company. Later, at dinner, Faulkner's Swedish publisher proposed a toast, *skål*, to Else's dead husband, and Faulkner sensed her sudden anguish: as she raised her glass, she seemed on the verge of tears. Their eyes met and something tender passed between them. Later they sat on the sofa and talked, and Else felt as though they had been friends always.

After the party, Faulkner worked on his Nobel address, begun back in Oxford and continued on the plane to Stockholm. He wanted to say something about the plight of the artist in the modern atomic age, when Russia and the United States were building nuclear arsenals and confronting one another in a cold war that threatened the very survival of humankind. The storyteller who had written so much about violence, about human depravity, failure, and doom, wrote now that man would go on nevertheless and survive any crisis, any holocaust.

On Sunday, the day of the awards, Faulkner confessed to the American ambassador that he had never given a speech before and that he was scared. At one point, he was so tense that he blurted out, "I can't stand this." But he got control of himself and showed up at the concert house dressed in a formal suit and white bow tie, but wearing his torn, oil-stained trench coat over that. He had refused to shave, and his cheeks and chin were stubbled with gray whiskers. Even so, Jill thought he looked "so very nice" and she was proud of him as they entered the great chamber, embellished with statues and tapestries, and took their respective seats. Jill was enthralled, cast in a spell by the "storybook-like atmosphere" of the entire affair.

Among the other laureates, Faulkner sat next to Lord Bertrand Russell, winner of the 1950 prize for literature, who found that talking to him was "uphill work." In a moment, two naval officers blasted a fanfare on long, flag-draped trumpets, and the award presentations began. When Faulkner's turn came, his sponsor declared him the "unrivaled master of all living British and American novelists as a deep psychologist" and the "greatest experimentalist among twentieth-century novelists." Then Faulkner stepped forward, only to stand at the edge of the platform, unsure of what to do, until King Gustaf Adolf walked to him and made his presentation.

Next came a formal banquet and acceptance speeches, held in the colonnaded town hall, which rose above the glittering waters of Lake Malar. Jill, in a fluffy blue evening gown, was mesmerized, for the room was bigger than Oxford's entire high school; the only light came from thousands of candles in silver candelabras on the tables. The dinner took place with military precision, as squads of black-coated waiters marched back and forth, bearing exotic courses. Then, with more fanfare, came the laureates' speeches. When Faulkner rose to give his, Else Jonsson thought him unforgettable, "a small elegant figure, very far away." Alas, he spoke too far from the microphone, his southern voice growing fainter as he hurried through his script. When he sat down, there was confusion in the audience. What had he said? Lord Russell complained that his voice had been completely inaudible.

After the speeches, greeting people in the gallery, Faulkner spotted Else Jonsson. "How did I look?" he asked her. "Did I behave all right?"

"Oh," she said, "you behaved beautifully."

For him, the thing had been "as long as a Mississippi funeral," and he was relieved that it was over. No goodbyes to Else, though—he intended to see her again. Back at the American embassy, where he and Jill were staying, Faulkner nursed a glass of bourbon, telling the ambassador that he would put his medal behind glass with his books. But the next day, he couldn't find the medal. An attendant assigned to him finally discovered it in a potted plant in the ambassador's residence.

Only WHEN FAULKNER'S SPEECH appeared in the newspapers did people who had been in the Nobel audience realize what he had said. It was a sensation on both sides of the Atlantic, so stunning in its eloquence that one Faulkner admirer compared it to Lincoln's Gettysburg Address. Faulkner had said, in his quick, high-pitched voice, that the award came not to him as a man but to his life's work, in which he had tried "to create out of the materials of the human spirit something which did not exist before." And so the award was his only "in trust," and he took this moment to address the young men and women who were dedicated to "the same anguish and travail," among whom was already the artist who would one day stand where he was standing.

With his mind on the nuclear age, Faulkner told his young peers, and the world beyond: "Our tragedy today is a general and universal physical fear so long sustained by now that we can even bear it. There are no longer problems of the spirit. There is only the question: When will I be blown up? Because of this, the young man or woman writing today has forgotten the problems of the human heart in conflict with itself which alone can make good writing because only that is worth writing about, worth the agony and the sweat."

The young writer must learn this again, Faulkner said, "leaving no room in his workshop for anything but the old verities and truths of the heart, the old universal truths lacking which any story is ephemeral and doomed—love and honor and pity and pride and compassion and sacrifice." Until he relearned this, he would write "as though he stood among and watched the end of man." But Faulkner refused to accept the end of man. "It is easy enough to say that man is immortal simply because he will endure: that when the last ding-dong of doom has clanged and faded from the last worthless rock hanging tideless in the last red and dying evening, that even then there will still be one more sound: that of his puny inexhaustible voice, still talking. I refuse to accept this. I believe that man will not merely endure: he will prevail. He is immortal, not because he alone among creatures has an inexhaustible voice, but because he has a soul, a spirit capable of compassion and sacrifice and endurance. The poet's, the writer's, duty is to write about these things. It is his privilege to help man endure by lifting his heart, by reminding him of the courage and honor and hope and pride and compassion and pity and sacrifice which have been the glory of his past. The poet's voice need not merely be the record of man, it can be one of the props, the pillars to help him endure and prevail."

From stockholm, father and daughter flew on to Paris and strolled together through the Luxembourg Gardens. But then Jill came down with the flu, and they had to cut their travels short, returning to New York and thence to Memphis and home. To Faulkner's surprise, Oxford gave him a hero's welcome: the high school band and seven majorettes paraded downtown, and thirty-three local businessmen took out a full-page ad in the *Eagle,* proclaiming that "Oxford and All of Us Are Very Proud of William Faulkner, One of Us, the Nobel Prize Winning Author."

"We are at home again," Faulkner wrote Haas, "lots of family, plenty of Xmas." He didn't regret going to Stockholm now, realized that it was the only thing to do. "I went, and did the best I knew to behave like a Swedish gentleman, and leave the best taste possible on the Swedish palate for Americans and Random House."

He had brought $30,171 back from Sweden, but he didn't feel right about the "damned money," because he hadn't earned it and didn't feel it was his. He used $500 of it to establish a music scholarship at Ole Miss, gave almost $3,000 to a Negro high school principal, James McGlowan, to advance his education at Hampton College and later the University of Michigan, and put $25,000 more in a trust fund.

Thanks to his rising fame, many of his books were back in print now and bringing in royalties. *The New York Times* reported that his works had sold more than 100,000 copies in Modern Library editions and almost 3 million copies in paperback. Random House had recently published *The Collected Stories of William Faulkner,* comprising forty-two of them published in magazines since 1930. It had been a Book-of-the-Month Club selection and would win a National Book Award, but for Faulkner it was no substitute for an original work.

As 1951 came on, the Nobel laureate was more unhappy than ever. Once "nothing nothing nothing else but writing" gave him peace. Now nothing at all gave him peace. He worked listlessly on revisions of

Requiem for a Nun and corresponded with Joan Williams, away in the North, as resistant as ever to his overtures. He told her she had "an emotional block," which was why her writing came hard. But he had more than her writing in mind; he was thinking of her refusal to sleep with him. "I am convinced now that is your trouble: something is frozen inside you. . . . I want it to be cured, freed; more than ever, I want to be the one to do it."

But until then, what? He thought of Else Jonsson; he thought of Meta, now remarried to Rebner—and miserable, according to her letters. They lived under the same roof, but their marriage was a wreck. When Howard Hawks asked him to come out to Hollywood and rework the script for Hawks' current motion picture, Faulkner agreed, mainly because he was bored and lonely, having trouble filling his days. He phoned Meta the news, and she met him at the Beverly-Carlton on the night of his arrival, February 1. In her forties now, she was still slender and pretty. As for Faulkner, she thought him "august, bonier, and more severe of mien, somewhat professorial." They made love that night and spent almost every night and every weekend together during his four-week stint in Hollywood. "Why did we let it happen?" he said of their broken affair. "I, more than you. This long, agonizing time away from each other. Foolish. Senseless waste. No warrant to it."

But Meta couldn't satisfy his terrible needs. From Hollywood, he wrote Joan and said he wished he could see her. At the same time, he plotted an April tryst with Else Jonsson in Paris, enlisting Bob Haas and Saxe Commins to help him set it up. Haas provided the excuse Faulkner would give his family: he needed to visit World War I battlefields to refresh his memory for his long-neglected fable.

On March 4, Meta took him to the airport, and they promised to see one another again before the year was out. Back at Rowan Oak, he wrote Commins that he was awaiting "final ratification from Europe" about his April trip. When final ratification came, Commins booked Faulkner's flight and rented two rooms for him in a Paris hotel. There, in mid-April, he and Else Jonsson slept together as man and woman, in the first of several secret rendezvous they would have. Faulkner met and liked a friend of hers, a dark, intense young writer-editor named Monique Salomon, one of the young in France who regarded Faulkner as a god. She and her husband often made a foursome with Faulkner and Else, but Monique thought Faulkner always wanted to do the same thing: order coq au vin, visit Chartres, and sip martinis. One day she swore she saw him drink twenty-three of them.

He did visit the Verdun battlefield, trying to imagine what the fighting there had been like. With pipe in mouth, he viewed the stone crosses, walked up to the forts, scanned the landscape where half a million men had died, and then headed home with military maps and a medal given him by the city of Verdun. Back in the States, he dropped by Bard College, at Annandale-on-Hudson, for a brief reunion with Joan Williams. Once he had been a solitary writer who sought refuge in a magic inner kingdom in which he gloried in creation. Now he was an aging peripatetic traveler who searched across two continents for the love that would heal him.

I N MAY OF 1951, the Nobel laureate gave the commencement address for Jill's high school graduating class. In Fulton Chapel at Ole Miss, twelve hundred graduates and parents—the largest such audience in Oxford history—heard Faulkner give a four-and-a-half-minute speech about the forces in the world trying to "use man's fear to rob him of his individuality, his soul."

Joylessly, he returned to the novel version of *Requiem for a Nun*, finally finished it in mid-June, and sent it away. He was "tired of ink and paper," he wrote Else, and looked forward to the summer's farmwork. "Don't be unhappy, damn it," he wrote Joan. "Let me be the unhappy one; sometimes I think I have enough for all, for all the world." He missed her and said he didn't like it. At fifty-three, he was too old to have to miss a young woman of twenty-two. "By now, I should have earned the right to be free of that."

To make matters worse, he had to contend with that mortal enemy of prizewinning artists: an incessant public clamor for interviews, appearances, responses, and details of his personal life. He kept insisting that his personal life belonged to him and that the only important thing about him was the work. But for those who genuinely admired him, his life was too significant, too much the wellspring of his art, to be "abolished and voided from history," as he insisted it must. For as long as the work lived, the life that created it would fascinate and inspire.

Still, that had its price. "Reporters just bring their suitcases out to his house and try to move right in," Maud said. "They walk right in the door, if it's not locked, and just look around as if the home were theirs. It's not surprising that Billy's so abrupt with them." There were the curious, too, who ignored his NO TRESPASSING sign and prowled about his property, helping themselves to whatever mementos they could find.

That fall, he and Estelle declared a brief truce and took Jill up to Wellesley, Massachusetts, where she enrolled in Pine Manor Junior College, glad to be on her own at last, away from the fighting and drinking at Rowan Oak. Faulkner stayed on in Cambridge, working with Ruth Ford and others on a stage production of *Requiem for a Nun*. Ultimately the project fell through, but Faulkner was not sorry; he didn't think it was any good anyway. Meanwhile the novel version had appeared to mixed critical notices, which Faulkner ignored. It was just as well. In assessing his most recent work, American critics announced that he had passed his zenith and was only repeating himself.

In France, though, his reputation was soaring higher than ever; from the French government came the award of the Legion of Honor, which Faulkner accepted in late October at the French consulate in New Orleans. Dressed in unshined shoes, unpressed trousers, and a hunting coat with leather elbow pads, he gave his acceptance speech in French.

Back home, he wanted and needed to work, but he felt empty, burned out. To help him write again, he added an "office" to the back of his house, complete with a fireplace and a full bathroom. He called it his office because that was the name antebellum planters gave to the room in which they transacted business. He set up his writing table by a window overlooking his paddock and stable and hung a painting over the mantel—a portrait of himself as an innocent-looking young man, done by his mother. He even moved a bed in so that he could nap and spend the night.

Away from the main traffic of the house, the office became Faulkner's special retreat from his wife, family visitors, and all other intruders. Here, in the spring of 1952, he tried to do some writing, but it had been so long since he'd "anguished over putting words together," he wrote Joan, that it seemed he had forgotten how.

Mostly he led "a dull, busy, purely physical life," tending his farm up in the hills and training a colt at Rowan Oak, on a circular riding course he had laid out there. Mounted on a horse named Sunny, he worked the colt with a lead, teaching him to trot square and steady. Faulkner was a small figure on horseback, with shoulders that sloped down now, making him appear thick, almost humped. But dressed in his jacket and riding boots, with his silver hair and mustache, he had an almost genteel look.

One day, he had the lead in his left hand, taking the horses at a good clip, when the colt suddenly whirled, reared, and snatched Faulkner clean out of the saddle. He hit the ground, hard, and lay there flat on his back in a mud puddle. But he wasn't hurt. "I learned years ago how to fall off horses," he said. On a subsequent morning, his horse shied at something and hurled him from the saddle; he landed on his back again, and this time injured his spine. The pain was excruciating. By May, he was treating it with his own remedy—downing shots of bourbon.

That same month, he flew to Paris for a cultural festival sponsored by the French government. Else Jonsson joined him there and coped with his condition the best she could. He managed a few words at the festival, in a hall packed with applauding Frenchmen. But his back was killing him, and he was drunk much of the time. His friend Monique Salomon took him to a clinic, where X-rays revealed that he had a couple of fractured vertebrae, which the doctors said required surgical fusion. Faulkner flatly refused that, but he did agree to treatment for alcoholism. Later he turned up in Oslo with Else and entered massage therapy for his back. In a week, the masseur was able to reset the injured vertebrae and the pain vanished miraculously. But now Faulkner thought something else was wrong with him. For two days in Paris, he'd suffered a spell of complete memory loss. Nothing like that had ever happened before. It was frightening.

In mid-June, he flew from Stockholm to Memphis, from Else to Joan Williams, who was back at home and trying to write despite her parents' disapproval. Sober and free of pain now, Faulkner gave her the support and encouragement she needed. At last, bursting with need for her, he broke down Joan's ambivalent defenses and succeeded in taking her to bed. Afterward, writing her from Rowan Oak, Faulkner compared himself to an aging Goethe, giddily in love with a young woman. But he felt a "terrible amount of no-peace too" and would have no peace until they went on from this beginning. "Maybe I can even do more for you then, after there is no more barrier, no more mystery, nothing to remain between us."

They saw one another when they could, either in Memphis or in the woods at Pott's Camp. In his eyes and heart, she was his honey, his shy, dear young love. At Rowan Oak, he wrote her passionate letters, often several in a row. "I love you!" he scribbled on one note. "God, how I do. . . . I mightn't say it any more—but I love you more than all the world." He would do anything for her. He read her stories, offering advice and encouragement. When she brought him one about a retarded man named Jake, he said, "This may be it." He suggested a title from Genesis, "The Morning and the Evening," and sent it to *Harper's* in her behalf, introducing her as his student. When *Harper's* turned it down, he forwarded it to Harold Ober, his agent, and asked him to try other magazines.

He wanted to make love to her again, but she couldn't do it. She was scared, unable to handle the age difference or his marriage. Her instinct was to take flight. She told him she longed to go away somewhere, to Colorado or back to New York, and be with people her age, people who had her problems. She was attracted to young men, too. She had to confess that. She didn't want to hurt him. He was so kind and sweet to her, so understanding. But she just couldn't sleep with him again.

Faulkner was crushed, guilt stricken. Had he forced her to make love against her will? What had he done? As he said once, he didn't understand women at all. Fearful of losing her, he wrote her that he would give up the physical part. He accepted her need to get away, meet people her age, even find someone else, a young man who was free as he was not. He would write New York and try to help her find a job. And if what she had told him meant goodbye, then that was all right too: "haven't I been telling you something: that between grief and nothing, I'll take grief."

But in truth he was terribly upset. He felt he had to do something. Suddenly he dug out the manuscript of his fable and set to work on it. He remembered that he had written *The Wild Palms* to stave off what he thought was heartbreak. His heart hadn't broken then. Maybe it wouldn't now, since the heart was "a very tough and durable substance."

A reply came from Joan. Yes, she said, maybe it was goodbye for them. But he refused to accept that. No, he wrote her back, "Not goodbye, not yet. I will die some day before you do, but not yet." He looked forward to seeing her again. "The big book going well, but I need something, we agreed on that: something, someone, to write, not *to* but *for.*" He needed someone to tell him, "Yes, yes. Keep on. I love you and believe in you." Please write, he said, and set a day for us to meet again.

IN MID-SUMMER, he wrote his friend and editor, Saxe Commins: "I am really sick, I think. Cant sleep too well, nervous, idle, have to make an effort not to let the farm go to pot, look forward only with boredom to the next sunrise." He had done no work in a year, did not want to do any now, and yet he had work he must do. To save his soul, to find peace and contentment, to salvage the work at least, he thought he ought to leave Estelle and his family, give them Rowan Oak and everything else, and be done with it. "Then maybe I will get to work again, and get well again. But I dont have enough time left to spend it like this." He wanted what he had always wanted: to be free. Yet "now at last I have begun to realise that perhaps I will not, I have waited, hoped too long, done nothing about it; and so now I must, or—in spirit—die."

He wrote Else much the same: "Stupid existence seeing what remains of life going to support parasites who do not even have the grace to be sycophants. Am tired, I suppose. Should either command myself to feel better, or change life itself, which I may do; if you should hear harsh things of me, dont believe all of them."

In September, Joan left for New York City to find a job, and Faulkner went to pieces. He had known he would miss her, but not like this. He drank himself into a violent state. There were ugly scenes with Estelle, and with Jill, too. Estelle claimed he "chided Jill for not having ambition like Joan" and made "several other comparisons." On September 18, he collapsed with a convulsive seizure and woke up in a psychiatric hospital in Memphis, where he spent nine days coming off alcohol and getting treatment for the broken vertebrae in his back, compounded now by a severe hypertrophic arthritis in his spine.

When he got home, Estelle confronted him about his "dreadful behavior" around Jill, who was now back at Pine Manor. He was horrified at himself. He wrote "Dear Missy" that what he'd done "was the sort of thing you can never recall, but you can express your regret and remorse for it, which I am trying to do. I love you. I believed that I would never hurt you. I wish I could recall it, which I cannot of course. But believe Pappy when he says he loves you and regrets having ever hurt at all his child, his only child, that he has always been and will always be proud of. I'm still shaky and cant write well, but well enough to say I love you and would give anything to recall that unhappy time."

Unable to bear the pain in his back or in his heart, Faulkner resorted to beer and Seconal. At one point he was so drunk that he fell down the stairs at Rowan Oak, banging himself up. Desperate, Estelle phoned Saxe Commins, and he flew down from New York to help. What he found at Rowan Oak shocked him. Faulkner lay on a couch in a stupor, his face covered with bruises and contusions, his body battered and bloated. Commins helped him to bed and began a night-long vigil. As Faulkner pleaded for a drink, tossed and mumbled deliriously, Commins alternately cajoled and threatened him. Since Faulkner couldn't control his bodily functions, Commins had virtually to carry him to the bathroom. "This is more than a case of acute alcoholism," Commins wrote his wife that morning. "It is the complete disintegration of a man."

Deeply sad, smoking one cigarette after another, Commins arranged for Faulkner to be hospitalized in Memphis again, then retreated to New York and "the amenities of publishing." The doctors sobered Faulkner up and fitted him for a steel back brace—he still would not submit to an operation. On October 21, he returned to Rowan Oak—and walked into a fusillade of drunken accusations from Estelle. "Hell's to pay here now," he wrote Commins. "While I was hors de combat, E. opened and read Joan Williams' letters to me. Now E. is drunk, and I am trying to nurse her before Malcolm sends her to a hospital, which costs like fury and does no good unless you make an effort yourself. I cant really blame her, certainly I cant criticise her, I am even sorry for her, even if people who will open and read another's private and personal letters, do deserve exactly what they get."

This was a wretched situation, Faulkner went on, "never can I remember ever being so unhappy and downhearted and despaired. I have done no work in a year, am living on my fat, will begin soon to worry about money, and I do not believe I can work here. I must get away." He wanted to go back north and finish the big book there. Yet he couldn't leave Estelle drunk at home, and anyway, if he went anywhere near New York, he feared that nothing would ever convince her it was not simply to be near Joan, "since she (E.) has never had any regard or respect for my work, has always looked on it as a hobby, like collecting stamps."

Of course, he could come up anyway, regardless of E. But he was worried about Jill. If he went east, he feared that E. would insist on some public, formal separation, and that this would hurt and humiliate Jill at school. "I will always believe that my first responsibility is to the artist, the work; it is terrible that my wife does not realise or at least accept that. But there is a responsibility too to the female child whose presence in the world I am accountable for."

Pondering Faulkner's situation at Rowan Oak, Commins was convinced that his life was in the balance. Since he refused extensive hospitalization, Commins had to get him out of Oxford, out of the unhappy conditions there that made him drink, and try to protect him from his self-destructive tendencies. Accordingly, Commins and his wife, Dorothy, offered him their place in Princeton as a retreat. But Faulkner balked at accepting, lest even that arouse Estelle's suspicions.

To compound his misery, a television crew financed by the Ford Foundation would come in a few days to make a film about him, to air over CBS. That Faulkner had consented to do the show violated everything he had ever said about keeping his private life out of the public eye. Even Estelle noticed that he seemed nervous about the filming, fretful that his voice was bad, worried about what people would think. It was all "so foreign to his nature," she wrote Commins. And Faulkner felt that, too. Nothing was right in his life; he feared his very nature was changing.

In early November 1952, the television crew invaded Faulkner's private domain, filming him at home, on his farm, on the streets of Oxford, and in Stone's law office. In the scene with Stone, Faulkner appeared stiff and distant, and well he might: over the years, he and Stone had become more estranged, in part because Stone had never repaid the $6,000 Faulkner had loaned him back in 1939. Whenever Faulkner called at his office, Stone was sure he wanted his money and would say he was too busy to talk, or slip out the back door. Stone still insisted that he was Faulkner's "closest personal friend" and basked in all the attention he received for being Faulkner's one-time mentor, yet he often impugned Faulkner as a writer ("a literary extrovert, a writer with no consistent and comprehensive theory of aesthetics") and cursed him for not taking his advice. You couldn't tell Bill anything, he complained. When you tried, he would clasp his lips shut and refuse to talk at all. It was that "damn Faulkner" in him. "Sometimes he makes me so damn tired I would like to kick the seat of his pants clean off." Frankly, he thought Faulkner was suffering from "Nobelitis" in the head.

Stone's attitude came out in the Ford Foundation show. In the scene in his law office, Stone asked Faulkner, "Did you and the King have a good time?"—a snide reference to Faulkner's trip to Stockholm. Afterward, Stone griped about how much of his time the show had taken and told Faulkner he "would be glad when he got through being famous." He wrote a literary critic that "Bill was just as gracious and patient about this [project] as possible, and I am quite alarmed about him. I want to get him to a doctor soon to be sure that he is not developing a split personality."

Faulkner still counted Stone as a friend, but was tired of his often condescending manner. "I don't see Stone as much as I used to," he told Wasson. "He's always telling me how I ought to write, whatever I'm writing." He complained to another man that "Phil never did understand what I was doing."

In mid-November, Faulkner left for Princeton. Let E. think what she might; he couldn't stay in Oxford another day. His life was on the line; he needed Commins' affection and support, couldn't go on without them. He stayed with Saxe for a few days, then moved into a comfortable room at the Princeton Inn, where Saxe and Dorothy could keep an eye on him.

At Thanksgiving, Joan came down to see him, and it relieved Faulkner immensely; it had not been goodbye, after all. They spent Thanksgiving Day at the Comminses', and walked together in the brisk outdoors, talking about writing and why he had chosen such a demanding craft. "Maybe because I wasn't as tall or as strong as I wanted to be," he said.

As it happened, the *Atlantic* had taken her story, "The Morning and the Evening," and he was glad for her. He was even happier to learn that she was writing a novel. It meant that she was an artist now, no longer a prisoner of middle-class conventions. But it would be hard for her, as it had been for him. "You must expect scorn and horror and misunderstanding from the rest of the world who are not cursed with the necessity to make things new and passionate; no artist escapes it."

He visited her later in New York, and his passion for her was more than she could resist: she went to bed with him again. For Faulkner, it was the two of them against the world, a couple of artistic vagabonds united against middle-class morality. He told her why she had returned to him. It was because she came first with him and always would. "Someday, Joan," he said, "you will know that no one will ever love you as I have."

But he still worried that he was too old for her. "Tell me if I'm too old," he kept saying. "You will tell me, won't you?"

"You are not too old," she said.

She kept telling herself: *I am taking care of him for the whole world.*

F AULKNER WAS STILL DEPRESSED and drinking heavily. Not even Joan's love, the tenderness of a young woman, could assuage his pain, his fear that he was written out, near "the bottom of the barrel." He suffered another collapse and ended up in New York's Westhill Sanitarium, where a psychiatrist prescribed electroshock therapy. During six sessions, the doctors strapped down William Faulkner, creator of *Absalom, Absalom!* and *Light in August,* inserted a hard rubber bit between his teeth, and sent electric shocks through his brain. Each time, Faulkner screamed, his whole body jumping wildly.

After the treatment was over, Faulkner was not hostile and disoriented, as were other patients who underwent electroshock. Instead, he put his arms around the psychiatrist and hugged him. Here was a man in real need of affection, the doctor thought, and he hugged Faulkner in return.

As was his custom, Faulkner wanted to spend Christmas at Rowan Oak, mainly to be with Jill. It was hard to tell Joan goodbye. She was depressed too; he could sense her distance again. She hoped he wouldn't be too unhappy at home, that he would try not to worry and to work. He gave her a little golden bell to wear over her heart, and she told him how much his letters meant to her and evidently asked him to write.

But her distance bothered him. Of course she liked his letters, he wrote from Rowan Oak. "Who wouldn't like to read the letters Faulkner wrote to the woman he loves and desires? I think some of them are pretty good literature, myself; I know what I would do if I were a woman and someone wrote them to me." He hoped she would wear her little golden bell; even if she fled from the passion in his letters, it would still sound his name for her.

Meanwhile he tried to keep "a decent daily stint" on his fable, writing mostly from sheer willpower. The day after New Year's 1953, he wrote Joan that the work wasn't going as it should, "in a fine ecstatic rush" like the orgasm they had talked about one night in New York. "But it's nice to know that I still can do that: can write anything I want to, wherever I want to, by simple will, concentration, that I can still do that. But goddamn it, I want to do it for fun again like I used to: not just to prove to bill f. that I still can."

But his momentum ran out; he had to get out of Rowan Oak if he was ever going to get it back. Estelle's response was as he feared: "Take me with you," she said. She thought Saxe and Dorothy had done wonders with him, had made him "a new man," and she wanted to go, too. But he told her no; she had severe eye trouble anyway, which necessitated operations that month to remove cataracts from both eyes. Dutifully, he stayed at home until that was over, then left for New York alone. He planned to be gone for six months—enough time, he hoped, to complete his fable at last.

HE ROOMED WITH HAL SMITH in his Manhattan apartment, saw Joan, and tried to work on his book at Random House. But Smith couldn't cope with his constant drinking and told him he had to leave. The alcohol and the aftereffects of electroshock brought on further spells of amnesia. Commins said that Jill had phoned him, but he couldn't remember talking to her. "Something is wrong with me," he wrote Else; "as you saw last spring, my nature has changed. I think now that when I fell off the horse last March, I may have struck my head too."

In March, he entered Doctors Hospital for a week of tests, but beyond his broken vertebrae and arthritis, they showed no skull injury or other organic problems, not even with his liver, which was astounding. Dr. S. Bernard Wortis, a tall, commanding psychiatrist, then subjected him to a series of nine psychological examinations. Wortis concluded that the patient was abnormally sensitive, so much so that life must have been painful for him. Alcohol, of course, was a narcotic to numb out his sensitivity. He had a powerful need for affection, too, but tended to conceal his emotions behind his mustache and a poker face. In sum, Wortis decided that Faulkner was built to suffer, to be unhappy, and to make his contributions in part from that.

Wortis speculated that Faulkner might not have had enough love from his mother. Faulkner refused to talk about it, however, and the doctor didn't press the point. But he did say that a lobe or part of Faulkner's brain was hypersensitive to alcohol. Worry, unhappiness, mental unease in any form, only lessened his tolerance. His brain was still normal, Wortis said, but it was "near the border line of abnormality." Which Faulkner knew himself: his behavior was not like him.

Before he left, Faulkner told Wortis that his next cycle of drinking would happen in May. "Well, see me or someone like me," the doctor said.

"I'll call you for an appointment myself," Faulkner said.

But he changed his mind when he received a bill for $450. Faulkner asked why it was so high, and the doctor explained that he had charged Faulkner $50 a visit for nine visits. Faulkner was incensed. All he got for that money, he complained, was a single bottle of Seconal. "Stay away from Wortis," he told Joan. "He is a psychiatrist; in my experience, psychiatrists will do anything."

Despite his hangovers and a nagging sense of doom, he kept dragging himself to Commins' small, smoke-filled office on the third floor of Random House, to type on his fable and other things too, including a long essay on Mississippi which *Holiday* had commissioned for $2,000. It amazed people at Random House that he could work in all the bedlam there, above the exhaust fumes and blaring horns of Madison Avenue.

But work he did, turning out more than ten thousand words on the Mississippi piece, a leisurely, partly fictionalized reminiscence about himself and his native state, including an affectionate portrait of Mammy Callie and a moving account of her death. He described with a bitter eloquence what he hated about Mississippi: "The intolerance and injustice: the lynching of Negroes not for the crimes they committed but because their skins were black . . . ; the inequality: the poor schools they had then when they had any, the hovels they had to live in . . . ; the bigotry which could send to Washington some of the senators and congressmen we sent there and which could erect in a town no bigger than Jefferson five separate denominations of churches but set aside not one square foot of ground where children could play and old people could sit and watch them," as they had in the Paris of his faded youth. Yet he loved Mississippi, too, remembering childhood Christmases when he had to stay in bed until dawn, the car rides to Memphis, his first sweetheart, Mammy Callie and Uncle Ned. . . . He loved "all of it even while he had to hate some of it because he knows now that you don't love because: you love despite; not for the virtues, but despite the faults."

In April, he raced back to Oxford when Estelle almost died of a hemorrhage; she required nine blood transfusions before she could leave the Oxford hospital to convalesce at Rowan Oak. Faulkner remained with Estelle for several weeks, working at his novel, too, and writing letters to Joan. Determined to will his book through to the end, he told Joan that it might be his last "major, ambitious work." But even so, looking back over his fifteen novels and various story collections, he had some perspective at last on all he had accomplished. "Now I realize for the first time what an amazing gift I had: uneducated in every formal sense, without even very literate, let alone literary, companions, yet to have made the things I have made. I dont know where it came from. I dont know why God or gods or whoever it was, selected me to be the vessel. I wonder if you have ever had that thought about the work and the country man whom you know as Bill Faulkner—what little connection there seems to be between them."

In May, Faulkner the public man gave the commencement address for Jill's graduating class at Pine Manor Junior College. In June, Faulkner the artist was back in Mississippi and off on a ten-week sprint toward the end of his fable. Estelle, recovered now, did what she could to help. "Bill has done a prodigious amount of work on his book," she wrote the Comminses, "despite interruptions of all sorts that I've been unable to prevent—But even at *that*—he is frightfully unhappy here, and Jill and I will be relieved and glad when he decides to 'take off' again." She had heard that Joan Williams had come south again; in fact, a friend of hers from Shanghai days delighted in sending Estelle "accounts that could be disturbing." But she was trying to keep "a stiff upper lip" and retain her dignity.

Later she insisted that she didn't think she had any personal animosity about all this. Certainly she didn't blame Joan, she said. "In all probability, had *I* been an aspiring young writer, and an elderly celebrity had fallen in love with me—I would have accepted him as avidly as Joan did." Estelle was indeed keeping "a stiff upper lip." Deep down, her husband's affair hurt her deeply, ravaging her self-esteem.

Faulkner did see Joan in Memphis and Holly Springs. But the awful truth was, Joan was drifting away from him again. It was because of the age thing, her need for a young man, and her own youthful and unpredictable shifts of mood. Faulkner clung to dreams. While his book was "going beautifully," he was prepared to go away with Joan—to rural New England, to Mexico, to Paris—whenever she gave the word. He even had his car overhauled and the tires recapped. But she took off for Florida instead, and it hurt. In his eyes, all he got from her was "crumbs and subterfuge."

In late August 1953, he found himself alone at Rowan Oak save for the servants. Jill had left for a semester at the University of Mexico, and Estelle had gone with her, in part to escape the gossip about Faulkner and Joan. One day he received a surprise phone call from Joan. She was at Holly Springs, on her way home from Florida. He jumped in his car, drove to Holly Springs, and convinced her to come home with him. They spent the night together at Rowan Oak.

To his despair, nothing changed. Back in Memphis, she was still remote, still in doubt. When no more meetings were forthcoming, he wrote her bitterly, "One of the nicest conveniences a woman can have is someone she can pick up when she needs or wants him; then when she doesn't, she can drop him and know that he will be right there when she does need or want him again. Only she should remember this. Sometimes when she drops him, he might break. Sometimes, when she reaches down for him, he might not be there."

Meanwhile he kept sprinting on his book somehow. He wrote Commins he was frightened that lightning might strike him dead before he could finish. He still hoped the book was the best of his time, but all that really kept him going was faith in his past talent. "Damn it, I did have genius, Saxe. It just took me 55 years to find it out."

And then suddenly, one day in early September 1953, he was done with his manuscript, or near enough to say he was done. Then, needing to show it to someone, he packed the manuscript in a briefcase and had his Negro "yard boy" drive him down to see Ben Wasson in Greenville. "I want you to be the first to read it," Faulkner said of his book. "I know it's my finest." Wasson took him to a dinner party at the country club, but Faulkner entered through the wrong door and stumbled on a teen-age dance in the ballroom. The kids all seemed to stare at the gray-haired little man, dressed in a white pongee suit, with an old-fashioned white handkerchief in his sleeve and a rosette in his buttonhole, as he made his way through them to the dining room.

After dinner, Faulkner drank liqueur with Wasson and his friends, but Faulkner couldn't stop with that. What followed was another drunken spree, the inevitable consequence of completing a book, especially one that had taken such a toll on him. Wasson and some friends finally took him home to Rowan Oak and left him with Malcolm. When Wasson returned to see about him, he found Faulkner lying in "a near comatose state" on his office floor. Gazing at his old friend and then at his mother's innocent portrait of him over the mantel, Wasson felt a pang of sadness. Bill had come a long way from those distant years when Ben had first met him at Ole Miss: he had fame and money and great honors now, but all to no avail. What secret horrors must plague him, to make him do this to himself? And his new novel was another thing: what could Wasson tell him about that? He had read it and thought some of it magnificent, but other parts were disorganized, the story often "too confused and lethargic."

Faulkner had to be hospitalized in Memphis again, but he was rest-less after only a couple of days of recuperation. To the despair of the staff, he simply walked out. In his file was a note that diagnosed him as "An acute and chronic alcoholic."

THE SQUARE IN OXFORD buzzed with the news. In his office off the square, Phil Stone felt a kind of bitter joy. The September 28 issue of *Life* magazine carried a sensational story, "The Private World of Wil-liam Faulkner," which contained family photographs and details about his personal life. The second part, "The Man Behind the Faulkner Myth," appeared in the next issue. Stone himself had assisted the au-thor, Robert Coughlan, to the extent of furnishing an eight-page cri-tique that included facts and corrections about Faulkner's personality and family background. Stone had refused to help other writers in search of personal details about his friend, but that was before Faulkner got "Nobelitis" in the head. Stone wrote Coughlan, "Your article, I think, has the town stewing. All of this I am telling you now is confidential . . . but I look for a terrific feud in the Faulkner family because they surely can't blame those family photographs on me." Stone reported that he had two friends on the street quietly gathering the gossip; sometime soon, Stone would tell Coughlan all of it "off the record."

Faulkner himself was horrified. He didn't read either issue of *Life*, but his mother did; the story upset her so much that she canceled her subscription. Faulkner could not believe this. He had not authorized the story; he had met the author once, several years ago, when he interrupted Faulkner at Rowan Oak, but had told him nothing about himself and his past, had given him no photographs. Faulkner felt betrayed. He was so mad and hurt that he drank himself back into the hospital.

When he got out, he wrote Moon Mullen, editor of the Oxford *Eagle*, what he thought about *Life*'s violation of his privacy: "I tried for years to prevent it, refused always, asked them to let me alone. It's too bad the individual in this country has no protection from journalism, I suppose they call it. But apparently he hasn't. There seems to be in this the same spirit which permits strangers to drive into my yard and pick up books or pipes I left in the chair where I had been sitting, as souvenirs.

"What a commentary. Sweden gave me the Nobel Prize. France gave me the Legion d'Honneur. All my native land did for me was to invade my privacy over my protest and my plea. No wonder people in the rest of the world dont like us, since we seem to have neither taste nor courtesy, and know and believe in nothing but money and it doesn't much matter how you get it."

In OCTOBER HE DECIDED TO RETURN to New York and put the finishing touches on his manuscript there. Joan was back in New York now, and he hoped to spend time with her when he wasn't working. His plans called for him to drive up, but he informed Joan that he was too dissipated to make the trip. Could she help him? Genuinely concerned, Joan flew to Memphis, met Faulkner at the airport, and then headed north with him in his station wagon. As it turned out, he was so weak that she had to do all the driving the first day and some of the second. Once in New York, he rented a suite in Washington Square, where she sometimes worked in the mornings, but things were still not right between them. Finally she let him know the truth: their age difference was too much for her; so was his marriage. She couldn't have the kind of relationship he wanted, or be what he desired her to be. Faulkner assumed that she had found a young man she wanted to marry. In fact, she *was* seeing a young man she was serious about; he was Ezra Bowen, the son of biographer Catherine Drinker Bowen and a writer himself, a Korean war veteran, and a sometime professional athlete.

Though Faulkner had anticipated something like this, he was devastated. Must it always be like this for him? Must it always end in rejection, in failure and pain? If only he could have been free, free of Estelle and family obligations, maybe it would have worked out for him and Joan. But even if he wasn't free, the art should have been enough to hold them. Yet it wasn't enough. She wasn't "demon-driven enough" for art; she had too much of her middle-class background telling her marriage, home, and children.

He wrote Joan that it was best that they not see one another again. Yet he wanted to preserve whatever they had shared for four years—love, sympathy, understanding, trust, belief. "You did something fine and brave and generous, and the gods will love you for it. You'll see in time. Dont regret and grieve." He assured her he would be all right. "It will just take time until I can get over it a little. It was serious with me; just because I knew all the time that the moment would come when I would have to anguish, does not make it easier."

But then he lost control, his feelings oscillating wildly between grief, denial, and rage. He lashed out with his pen: "You take too much, and are willing to give too little. . . . People have attributes like animals; you are a mixture of cat and mule and possum—the cat's secretiveness and self-centeredness, the mule's stubbornness to get what it wants no matter who or what suffers, the possum's nature of playing dead—running into sleep or its pretence—whenever it is faced with a situation which it thinks it is not going to like."

He exploded against the young people she liked and lived with in the city, warning that they would destroy her talent. They are "sophomores," he wrote her, "irresponsible parasites," who "go through the motions of art—talking about what they are going to do over drinks, even defacing paper and canvas when necessary, in order to escape the responsibility of living."

But when his fury subsided, all he felt was the pain and desolation. He remembered Housman's lines: "Look, earth and high heaven ail from the prime foundation/All thoughts to rive the heart are here, and all are vain. . . . Why did I awake? When shall I sleep again?"

"Change in people," he had written Meta that year, "the saddest thing of all, division, separation, all left is the remembering, the dream, until you almost believe that anything beautiful is nothing else but a dream."

SOMETHING DIED, but something was born too: his fable, nine long years after he'd conceived it, was finished now and on Haas' desk at Random House. Faulkner had tried to complete the final revisions himself, but the manuscript had proved too large and unwieldy for him. So he prevailed on Saxe Commins for help, notwithstanding the fact that Commins had recently suffered a heart attack and was still recuperating in Princeton. But Saxe believed so much in Faulkner, wanted so much to do his part as editor and friend, that he had Faulkner bring the manuscript down to his home. They spread pages all over the room, on a bed, a desk, and a chair, and together put them into final order. By November 4, Commins thought the script "as near perfection as we can make it." As he said later, he was "still a little bewildered by some of the rhetorical extravagances and the involuted progressions and regressions in the unfolding of a tale that is overwhelming and so simple, full of questionable coincidences and yet with a narrative substructure that holds the whole edifice from collapse."

The central character, the corporal named Stefan, was a French soldier in the First World War whose life paralleled that of Christ. He was a simple, uneducated man, this Corporal, with a "high calm composed, not wary but merely watchful, mountain face." Convinced that man could act with selfless love for all humankind, the Corporal gathered up twelve disciples and ignited a mutiny against the generals and the war, inspiring Allied and German soldiers alike to lay down their arms and stop the killing. Like Christ, the Corporal was betrayed by one of his disciples and went to prison, whereupon he found himself in a confrontation with the Supreme Commander of Allied forces, who turned out to be his father. The Supreme Commander was a condensed, bespectacled little man, "pink as an infant, ageless and serene in his aura of indomitable fidelity, invincibly hardheaded, incorrigibly opinionated and convinced, unreflectable in advice suggestion and comment and indomitably contemptuous of war and all its ramifications." In his official capacity, however, he tried to persuade his son to renounce his cause of peace and flee to safety. But the son, steadfast and laconic like his creator, rejected his father's entreaties, certain that his martyrdom would help bring tranquillity to an embattled world. In the end, the Supreme Commander had his son executed between two thieves, and Stefan's half-sisters buried him on their family farm. When the war started up again, an artillery shell blasted his body from its grave; it wound up by chance in the catacombs under Fort Valamount, whence French authorities, unaware of whose body it was, retrieved and buried it under the Arc de Triomphe as France's Unknown Soldier. Faulkner's message, if it could be fathomed in a such a confusing and complicated story, was that Christ had reappeared and sacrificed himself again in order to save humankind.

Saxe's wife, Dorothy, thought that only Faulkner could indulge in such a bewildering tale—and almost make it believeable through "sheer force of rhetorical narrative." Saxe, though he loved the book, realized how bold and provocative it was and feared that there would be "much to answer for." Bob Haas had no reservations. "I think Bill's book is simply tremendous," he told Commins. "To my mind it's one of the greatest novels that I've ever read, and I use the word 'greatest' advisedly."

Faulkner kept asserting that *A Fable* was his finest novel, maybe the best of his time, yet he didn't mean that it was necessarily a successful novel. No, when he said it was his best effort, he meant that he'd tried once again to do the impossible—to produce a perfect work of art, which was always doomed to fail. What counted for him was the daring of the effort. Certainly in this, his sixteenth novel, he had made a courageous attempt at the impossible, had reached beyond himself to the stars. God knew he had done that.

He added an acknowledgment, which credited William Bacher and Henry Hathaway of Beverly Hills, California, for the book's basic idea. Later Cerf was concerned about the acknowledgment, lest it reinforce any claim Bacher might have to the movie rights. But Faulkner insisted that he had a moral obligation to keep the acknowledgment. What it said was the truth. "I love the book, gave ten good years of my life to it," he said; "if any part of it should taste like dust on the tongue, I had better never have done it. . . . [It] must not be blemished by a squabble over rights. I would take my own name off it first and give it to anyone who would defend it from that." The acknowledgment stayed.

With *A Fable* done and in press, Faulkner plunged into an even deeper gloom. The book had been so difficult to write that he feared his life as an artist was really over now. At fifty-six, his life as a lover seemed over, too, for he was sure that he would never find another young woman, that he would never walk in April again. Ah, Joan, Joan. Not even the loss of Helen Baird had hurt so much as this.

H OWARD HAWKS HAD CALLED HIM AGAIN. He was heading for Paris and Egypt, to make *Land of the Pharaohs* for Warner Bros., and he wanted Faulkner to write the script. Faulkner complained to Saxe, "I don't want to go to Paris, I don't want to go to Egypt. I'm not well; my back bothers me." But he couldn't get out of it; he thought he owed it to Hawks. "He's done me favors in the past," Faulkner said, "and I can't let him down now."

On the night of November 30, 1953, a Random House editor and his female friend saw Faulkner off at the airport. He had expected other friends to join them, but no one else came. The editor and his companion watched Faulkner walk to the plane alone.

PART EIGHT

DARK AND DIFFICULT DAYS

It was early winter 1953, in the Suvretta House in Saint Moritz, Switzerland. In his room, Faulkner drank and wrote to Joan, unable to let her go. "I am very happy to know that you are working, and that you know that nothing basic has changed with us. It never will, no matter what course your life might take. I believe you know that until I die. I will be the best friend you ever had."

He wrote again, his pen trembling in his hand: "I think I was—am —the father which you never had—the one who never raised his hand against you, who desired, tried, to put always first your hopes and dreams and happiness." But he did not regret what had happened between them. "I know I am better for it, and I know that someday you will know that you are too."

He wrote his mother, too, promising always to let her know where he was and telling her that he loved her. Saint Moritz, he said, was in the middle of the Alps, with snow on them and moonlight. There was much skiing and bobsledding here, but too many American movie people, not to mention King Farouk of Egypt. He missed his "Moms" and "all my children"—Jill, Malcolm, and his niece Dean. He did not mention Estelle.

Faulkner had come to Saint Moritz with Hawks and his crew to work on the script for *Land of the Pharaohs.* But Faulkner was drinking so heavily that Hawks had hired a backup writer named Harry Kurnitz. None of them seemed enthusiastic about the picture. Huddled over the script, they often fell into comic repartee.

Faulkner: "I don't know how a pharaoh talks."

Hawks: "Well, I don't know. I never talked to one."

Faulkner: "Is it all right if I write him like a Kentucky colonel?"

Kurnitz: "I can't do it like a Kentucky colonel, but I'm a student of Shakespeare. I think I could do it as though it were *King Lear.*"

Hawks: "Well, you fellows go ahead, and I'll rewrite your stuff."

And so it went into the Christmas season, with Faulkner consuming each day, at lunch alone, an appetizer of two martinis and a half bottle of Montrachet. At a party on Christmas Eve, a beautiful young girl materialized before him. She was Jean Stein, the daughter of Jules Stein, the wealthy founder of the Music Corporation of America. She was studying at the Sorbonne in Paris and living with a bachelor uncle near the Arc de Triomphe; they were on holiday at Saint Moritz, staying at the Palace Hotel.

She had wanted so badly to meet William Faulkner that she asked the hostess of the party to invite him in particular. Black-haired and breathless, all of nineteen, she charmed Faulkner into a smile. He didn't care that she was almost thirty-seven years his junior. He thought her delightful. Nothing at all shy about her. Look, this was a dull, stuffy party, he said; why didn't she attend midnight mass with him? They left together, and after mass he walked her home in the cold, lamplit quiet of early morning. He liked young Jean. She was really just delightful.

He found it a queer thing, though, almost a repetition of Joan. Even her name was similar. She had come to him almost exactly as Joan had done in Oxford. She was nineteen, Joan had been twenty. An omen perhaps?

The next day he flew to Stockholm to spend time with Else. He stayed in an obscure hotel, but reporters soon found him and followed him around with cameras. Every morning, crowds of schoolchildren and old people stood in the snow outside his hotel, all wanting his autograph. "I had forgot how in Europe the artist is like the athletic champion at home," he wrote Joan.

When he returned to Saint Moritz, he assumed that Jean Stein would be gone, back in school in Paris. As it turned out, she was still in Switzerland, waiting for him. She stayed, Faulkner said, "until her momma in Venice found where she was, and ordered her back to Paris by telephone." In mid-January 1954, he met her in Paris for a few days of happiness in this otherwise melancholy time. Then he joined Hawks, Humphrey Bogart, and Lauren Bacall in Rome; Jean would meet him there later.

The script was done now, and Faulkner frequented Roman bars with Hawks, Bogart, and Bacall. It was good to see Bogey and Baby again; she was as slim and lovely as ever. She noticed how much alcohol

Faulkner consumed; sometimes she saw him drinking alone at a table in the bar at George's, but did not intrude on his privacy. One night she asked him, "Bill, why do you drink?"

He said, "When I have one martini, I feel bigger, wiser, taller. When I have a second, I feel superlative. When I have more, there's no holding me."

There was no holding him when young Jean came down from Paris. Actually, she was so uninhibited that it frightened him a little. He thought she had none of the emotional confusion that "poor Joan" had. She stayed with him until her mother found her by phone and again ordered her back to Paris.

Jean did wonders for his physical self-esteem. He felt expansive and virile. "I like this city," he wrote Joan. "It is full of the sound of water, fountains everywhere, amazing and beautiful—big things full of marble figures—gods and animals, naked girls wrestling with horses and swans with tons of water cascading over them."

In mid-February, Hawks and company went ahead to Cairo to start shooting, and Faulkner flew back to Paris for a weekend with Jean, who had just turned twenty. He hated to leave her. On his way to Cairo, he downed a bottle and a half of brandy and hurtled into a siege that sent him to the Anglo-American Hospital. Part of his anguish was the accursed script; he detested reworking the damn thing. It was a wretched picture anyway, a sort of *Red River* set in Egypt, as Faulkner described it. Hawks thought the problem was that it lacked a hero, that "everybody was a son of a bitch."

A letter came from Joan Williams, informing Faulkner that she intended to marry Ezra Bowen. Saxe Commins also wrote him about her marriage, which took place on March 6. Faulkner thanked Commins by letter, but pointed out that he had already heard about it from Joan. "I think she is too honest, even if there was nothing else, not to let me know." He hoped she would be happy. If she was, then he was "the best friend Bowen ever had."

He told Commins about his affair with Jean Stein. "I expect any day now for her to come to Cairo. She is charming, delightful, completely transparent, completely trustful. I will not hurt her for any price. She doesn't want anything of me—only to love me, be in love. You will probably meet her next fall when we are home again. The other affair would have hurt of course, except for this."

Later in March, he received a letter from Jill, who was back in

Oxford with her mother. She had momentous news to report. She had met a man she wanted to marry, a West Pointer named Paul Dilwyn Summers, Jr. He was now a first lieutenant in the army and stationed at Fort Bragg, North Carolina. She wanted her Pappy's consent to marry him; she wanted him to come home as soon as he could.

His baby wanting to marry and leave him? It troubled Faulkner that she was grown up enough to marry, that the hard march of time had made her a woman at last. It was such a long season of losses for him: Joan, his big book, and now his daughter, all irretrievably gone or going.

Put off by Faulkner's excessive drinking, Hawks released him from his contract, and Faulkner headed for Paris—saw both Jean and Else there—then left for New York and a reunion with the Comminses in Princeton. From there he raced home in his station wagon, traveling the 1,133 miles to Oxford in just thirty-six hours.

WHEN HE SAW JILL, he resigned himself to the inevitable. She was "deeply in love," as Estelle said, with "a new-found radiance" about her. In June, the three of them travelled up to Rockville, Maryland, where Paul Summers' foster parents gave him and Jill a gala announcement party. Faulkner grumbled to Commins that it was the "damndest collection of prosperous concerned stuffed-shirt republican senators and military brass hats and their beupholstered and becoiffed beldames as you ever saw. Fortunately hardly any of them ever heard of me, so I was let alone."

When they got back to Rowan Oak, Faulkner's copies of *A Fable* awaited him in the mail. "They are very fine," he wrote Commins. "I am as proud as you are; if we are right and it is my best and not the bust which I had considered it might be, I will ask nothing more." Faulkner gave Stone a copy, with the inscription: "Phil, with love/Bill." While Stone thought there was some "wonderful Faulkner writing in it," he didn't believe it was successful, because it was a book "requiring humility, which trait I have never seen in any Faulkner." Anyway, he was tired of the "whole subject" of William Faulkner. Malcolm Cowley, reviewing the book in the New York *Herald Tribune,* gave it guarded praise; but most critics, while conceding that it was a major novel by a major novelist, panned it as "murky," "difficult," and "inaccessible." No one thought it his best or the best of his time. But Faulkner claimed he didn't care. As he told Ben Wasson, "I don't write for critics. Never have."

Meanwhile Faulkner did an uncharacteristic thing: he read entire selections of his big book to Estelle and Jill. In fact, he had dedicated *A Fable* to Jill, explaining later that it was his way of saying "Good-bye to your childhood, you are grown now and you are on your way." As he read to them in a high-pitched monotone, Estelle must have had mixed feelings about the irony of this moment: he was reaching out to them in his way, holding them together with his art, and here she had been on the verge of suing him for a divorce. Last February, while he was abroad, she had written Saxe Commins that Bill had been home little in the past four years, and what time he had been there had been "a nightmare of drunkenness." She went on: "he must be very unhappy —so the only cure I know of is to help him get free legally—Heaven only knows he has been free in every other sense." She had intended to ask for divorce on the grounds of incompatibility, not adultery, even though incompatibility seemed "rather ridiculous after twenty-five years." Still, she balked at going to her lawyer. She wanted so much to do *"the right thing."* She didn't want to hurt anyone. "Please believe," she implored Saxe, "that I'm only endeavoring to make everyone concerned, a little happier—" She begged Saxe for advice. She confided details about Bill's affair with Joan, told how much it had hurt Jill. "As for me," she said, "I'm hurt, but not despairing—*Nothing* can alter my love and devotion—nor upset my faith in Bill's actual love for me— although right now, he swears he doesn't care—I'm throwing myself on your mercy and kindness, to understand—All I want is Billy's good— and to prove it, I'll do *anything* that is best—The only thing that I shudder at and might try to evade, is a divorce—and *that,* only on Jill's account." As for Billy, she thought he should be at home with a good nurse, a man he could trust, with her to tend his creature comforts. This was a shocking letter, she knew, but she just didn't know what to do. She promised Saxe this: whatever he decided, she would be brave about it and hold up her end.

Saxe evidently counseled her against divorce, because she thanked him for his "wonderfully spirit-lifting letter" and said she was "so vastly relieved" and would never be fool enough to ask for his guidance and then disregard it. But she still didn't know about Bill; he never wrote her letters, just sent notes, mostly about business. What could she think but that he was trying to drive her to a break? When she found out about Joan's marriage, she wrote Saxe that she was glad for "the child," but that it still didn't change the sad state Bill, Jill, and she were in. She felt sorry for Bill now—"He is in a mess, and I daresay is going to have a bad time of it—"

And so things stood when Bill returned for Jill's wedding: in limbo. And now, as Faulkner read from his tale about Christ's reincarnation and second crucifixion, his soft voice bound the three of them together for a fleeting moment, as if to suspend old hurts and antagonisms in the rolling cadences of his prose. . . .

At some point before the wedding, Jill came to her father, and they discussed what was best for Estelle once Jill was gone. They agreed that Pappy should open a bank account for her, so that she could be free to come and go as she wished. Jill was depending on him to do all he could to make Mama happy. In Jill's view, Mama seemed to feel that her daughter was "more or less lost to her."

With Jill and Estelle busily planning the wedding, scheduled for August 21, Faulkner attended an international writers' conference in Brazil, doing so at the invitation of the U.S. State Department. Despite a fondness for pisco, a potent brandy, Faulkner did his part "for hemispheric solidarity," reading his Nobel Prize speech at a press conference and putting in an appearance at the Writers' Congress. That he attended such a "beanfeast," as he called it, was further evidence of the changes coming over him, for he no longer felt himself an artist in interior exile, the artist he had been for a quarter of a century. Fearful that his creative work was over, he was assuming more and more the role of cultural emissary and public spokesman on a global stage.

He was back at Rowan Oak in time for Jill's wedding, an extravagant, taxing affair, with scores of friends and relatives in attendance. Ben Wasson came up from Greenville, and Faulkner gave him a copy of his fable, in which he had written: "To Ben: much love, much long time." Rowan Oak was so packed with bridesmaids and groomsmen that Faulkner had to lodge Saxe and Dorothy Commins in the Ole Miss Alumni House. At a prewedding cocktail party, they met Faulkner's mother, petite Miss Maud, as high-minded and dogmatic as ever. Dorothy was amazed at how much Faulkner resembled her: he had inherited "the cut of her face, the shape of her head, mouth, and chin."

When it was time for the ceremony, Faulkner awaited his daughter in the front hall of Rowan Oak; he got a lump in his throat when she descended in a swirl of white satin and lace. He opened a bottle of champagne, and they drank together, just the two of them. Then he escorted her outside to a limousine, which bore them away to St. Peter's Episcopal Church, where in a gust of organ music he gave away his only child.

Afterward, there was a reception at Rowan Oak, with waiters serving champagne and then white wine. Nobody seemed to mind the torrid summer heat. The Faulkners both circulated among their guests, the very picture of southern hospitality. Estelle, though, was having trouble holding back her tears; Jill was her last child to leave home. To author Shelby Foote, Faulkner seemed euphoric. "Isn't Jill the perfect virgin?" he said.

Then, all too soon, the bride and groom dashed through a shower of rice and made their getaway, heading for a honeymoon in Mexico and then a home in Charlottesville, Virginia, where Paul would attend the University of Virginia law school. Bill and Estelle stood together, with wineglasses in their hands, watching the car turn out of the cedar-lined drive and disappear.

Wasson and the Comminses stayed with them for a while. After dinner, Faulkner switched to whiskey, and Estelle was drinking heavily, too. But the next morning he was sober enough to accompany Saxe and Dorothy Commins on a car ride, with Malcolm at the wheel. Dorothy noticed that a drought had seared the countryside, drying up streams and burning corn to a withered yellow. The land seemed to lie dying in the heat. But Faulkner's imagination transported them from scorched Lafayette County into the magic kingdom of Yoknapatawpha, peopled with Sutpens, McCaslins, Sartorises, Compsons, Bundrens, Stevenses, Beauchamps, and Gibsons. As Malcolm stopped at various spots, Faulkner indicated where the different families had lived. When he pointed out the Compsons' home, Dorothy thought she could hear Dilsey speaking, with tears streaming down her face: "I've seed de first en de last, I seed de beginnin' en now I sees de endin'."

Back at Rowan Oak, Dorothy entertained everyone on the piano, her fingers dancing through Chopin, Brahms, Debussy, and a theme from Tchaikovsky's *Romeo and Juliet*, which Faulkner requested. By then, he was on the whiskey again. At dinner, the Comminses watched him down one drink after another, until Saxe had to help him to bed while Dorothy stayed with Estelle. By morning, Faulkner was unconscious and soon had to be transported to Wright's Sanitarium in Byhalia. "Poor Estelle," Dorothy said, "poor Bill, poor everybody. . . ."

Faulkner and Estelle had repeatedly said that they stayed together only because of Jill. Now they were alone at Rowan Oak, each free to make a move, see a lawyer, pack a suitcase, get out. But something held them together despite all the years of drunken combat—inertia perhaps, an inability to change after twenty-five years together. Or maybe there was more—a special bond between them, born of shared sorrows and memories. They had loved one another once; maybe a little of that remained, despite everything.

In the fall, they did reach one decision: Estelle would do some traveling of her own for five months or so, visiting the Philippines, where Cho-Cho and her husband lived, then touring across the Far and Near East to Europe. "E. leaves for Manila Friday," Faulkner wrote Commins, "still says she does not want to go, but ticket bought, trunk shipped, and apparently she is." When at last she was gone, Malcolm's wife thought Faulkner utterly amazed that "Mama" had really left him. "Perhaps a taste of being alone in that house would serve him right and do him good," she wrote Commins, a sort of family confidant by now. "I hope when he finds that no one is going to entertain him, he will return [to the North]—that would be just one more thing off our minds to worry about."

He did go north for the winter, to be with Jean Stein in New York City, where she had taken an apartment on the East River. He was still in a dark mood, depressed and disoriented without a book to do. He had enjoyed a creative burst in September, turning out a hunting story, "Race at Morning," which the *Saturday Evening Post* had bought for a record $2,500. He tried writing again, but nothing sustained his interest. Still, he was glad to have young Jean at his side: she was gorgeous and worshipful, and she helped him forget Joan, his dearest love. They spent Christmas in Princeton with the Comminses, and Faulkner told Jean what he'd said to his other mistresses: "Between grief and nothing I'll always take grief." Back in the city, he took her to the "21" Club with

Bennett and Phyllis Cerf, and they sat with novelist John O'Hara and his wife. Faulkner disliked O'Hara—"a Rutgers Scott Fitzgerald," he told Jean.

Strolling through the park on the day after New Year's 1955, he had that feeling of impending doom again. An omen of disaster about to befall him? Sometimes it was a good sign, though, so he told himself he had no reason to feel oppressed. But he couldn't help it: he felt oppressed. Despite its mixed reception, his big book had won the National Book Award for fiction, but he didn't want to attend the presentations and give a speech; he didn't even want the award, Dorothy Commins said. He had already received a National Book Award for his *Collected Stories* and thought it unfair that he should win it twice. But finally he gave in and turned up at the Hotel Commodore for the ceremonies, a short, bent, gray-haired man dressed in a blue double-breasted suit and a gray tie—a far cry from the rebellious William Faulkner who used to go about Oxford unshaven and barefoot. The ceremonies were a terrible ordeal for him. "In all my experience as a newspaperman," wrote a Memphis journalist, "I have never witnessed such a spectacle of personal discomfort." On the platform, facing seven hundred critics, publishers, and fellow writers, Faulkner spoke inaudibly about how the artist was one who "tried to create something which was not here before him"—who tried to carve "on the wall of that final oblivion beyond which he will have to pass, in the tongue of the human spirit, 'Kilroy was here.' " That, he said, "is primarily, and I think in its essence, all that we ever really tried to do. And I believe we will all agree that we failed. That what we made never quite matched and never will match the shape, the dream of perfection which we inherited and which drove us and will continue to drive us, even after each failure, until anguish frees us and the hand falls still at last."

A Fable won a Pulitzer Prize, too, but Faulkner didn't stay around for that award. By mid-March, he was back in Mississippi and embroiled in a bitter controversy that had the entire South in an uproar. Anguish had not yet freed him, had not yet stilled his hand; he had taken up his pen as public spokesman, this time in defense of the Negro in his native land.

For MORE THAN FORTY YEARS, the National Association for the Advancement of Colored People had fought racial discrimination primarily in the federal courts, marking up hard-earned victories against southern white primaries and segregated law schools in the border states. Faulkner left no record of what he thought about such victories, but he did describe himself in 1948 as "a states' rights man," who believed, as Gavin Stevens did, that "the solution to the Negro problem belongs to the South." Yet the NAACP didn't think the South would ever reform itself, and so it continued its legal battles against segregation in Dixie and the whole white supremacist philosophy that underlay it. In May 1954, the U.S. Supreme Court responded with an epochal decision that rocked the segregated South to its foundations. In *Brown* v. *Board of Education,* the court outlawed segregated public schools, thus reversing the doctrine of "separate but equal" which had prevailed in Dixie since the 1890s and handing American Negroes their most spectacular victory in the twentieth century. In one historic blow, the Supreme Court had smashed the whole legal superstructure for white supremacy, knocking down a century and a half of devious rationalizations in defense of the creed that blacks must be kept apart because they were inferior.

The decision stunned the white South, so much so that it took a while for the full impact of the decision to register. When it did, whites across the region recoiled in horror. In their frightened imaginations, integrated schools would lead inevitably to interracial dating and then interracial sex, with white girls and "nigger" boys copulating in wild abandon in bedrooms and car seats across Dixie. The whole southern "way of life" would collapse—and with it the cheap Negro labor force that had sustained the southern economy since the Civil War. With visions of catastrophe before them, southern segregationists raged at the "tyrannical" court and branded the day of the Brown decision as "black Monday." Fiery crosses burned against Texas and Florida skies, and random Klan terrorism broke out against blacks in many parts of the South. In Alabama, the state legislature "nullified" the Court decision and vowed to preserve white supremacy come what may. In Mississippi, a former football star named Tut Patterson stormed: "There won't be any integration in Mississippi. Not now, not 100 years from now, maybe not 6,000 years from now—maybe never." And he helped form the South's first White Citizens' Council to preserve the "Southern way of life" based on racial separation. In Georgia, a gubernatorial candidate stood in ninety-degree heat and expounded his "three school" plan to defeat integration: one for whites, another for colored ("the way they want it"), and a third for those insane enough to want their children in integrated schools.

When Faulkner returned to Oxford in March 1955, the southern reaction was raging at full force. He did not of course agree with his fellow white southerners. Frankly, he thought the school decision "right" and "just." If the Negro remained "patient and sensible," Faulkner believed that one day there would be "a complete equality in America." Nevertheless, he worried about the fury of his countrymen. He read the newspapers; he heard the heated talk on the courthouse square. There were many people in Mississippi who would go to any length, even resort to violence, to keep the "niggers" out of white schools. His brother John, a die-hard segregationist, vowed to use a gun if it came to that.

Faulkner was no reformer, no activist; he did not mount a soap box in the square and preach to his neighbors. But he did what he could to restrain them, with the best instrument of persuasion he had: he wrote letters to the Memphis *Commercial Appeal* that March and April, pointing out the folly of maintaining segregated schools in the poorest state in the Union. Mississippi white schools were already so bad, he said, that it was preposterous to think that they could satisfy the needs of the Negro. But it was even more absurd to appropriate public funds for separate Negro schools which at best were only equal to the poor white schools. The result was two inferior school systems. "How foolish in simple dollars and cents, let alone in wasted men and women, can we afford to be?" he asked his fellow Mississippians.

He proposed that Mississippi make the current schools the best possible in the humanities, sciences, and professions, and throw them open to the gifted students, white and Negro alike. Those eliminated could be enrolled in trade and craft schools, again without distinction of color. "I have no degrees nor diplomas from any school," he said. "I am an old veteran sixth-grader. Maybe that's why I have so much respect for education that I seem unable to sit quiet and watch it held subordinate in importance to an emotional state concerning the color of human skin."

His letters whipped up a storm of indignation in Mississippi. A state senator and a banker bawled him out in rebuttals to the *Commercial Appeal*. Anonymous callers cursed him on the phone. Abusive letters showed up in his mail. Phil Stone, an archsegregationist himself, claimed that Faulkner was simply after publicity and didn't know what he was talking about. His own brothers disputed his stand and said he deserved the outcry against him. From Oxford to Jackson, whites had a new name for Faulkner. He was "Weeping Willie, the nigger lover."

"We have much tragic trouble in Mississippi now about Negroes," Faulkner wrote Else in June. "I am afraid. I am doing what I can. I can see the possible time when I shall have to leave my native state, something as the Jew had to flee from Germany during Hitler. I hope that wont happen of course. But at times I think that nothing but a disaster, a military defeat even perhaps, will wake America up and enable us to save ourselves, or what is left. This is a depressing letter, I know. But human beings are terrible. One must believe well in man to endure him, wait out his folly and savagery and inhumanity."

In July, he left for Japan, to participate in a seminar at Nagano for fifty Japanese professors of English and American literature. He went under the auspices of the State Department, not as a literary man, he explained, but as "a simple private individual, occupation unimportant, who is interested in and believes in people, humanity, and has some concern about man's condition and his future, if he is not careful."

On the flight over, Faulkner was afraid of what lay ahead and drank heavily. What if the Japanese wanted him to be a literary man, to talk and lecture like one? He couldn't do that; he didn't know how. At flight's end, as his plane approached the Tokyo airport, he saw the shadow of the aircraft racing along the cottony hillocks below, the plane and the shadow speeding toward one another as toward headlong destruction, only to merge silently when the wheels touched the runway.

The American embassy people worried about his condition. In fact, he had drunk so much that he needed emergency medical treatment before he could meet the Japanese. "I won't let you down," he told an embassy official. "The U.S. Government commissioned me to do a job and I'll do it." And off he went, into a three-week whirlwind that would have exhausted a younger man. In addition to the seminar meetings, he spoke to the press and made other public appearances, fielding questions as best he could, trying to say something that would help the Japanese understand his country and its artists.

Art, he told them, was man's "strongest and most durable force" with which to record his ability to overcome disaster and "to postulate the validity of his hope." War and disaster—and he was mindful of what the Japanese had gone through in the last great war—reminded man that he needed a record of his endurance, his ability to survive any holocaust. In saying that, he had the American Civil War in mind, too. "I think that that is why after our own disaster there rose in my country, the South, a resurgence of good writing," he said.

The Japanese appreciated his remarks about art, but they pressed him to comment on American race problems, too. He answered forthrightly. Racial prejudice in America was "a sickness," "a cancer." But if the Negro himself had "enough sense, tolerance, wisdom" to be patient, there would be complete equality in America. His black skin would make no difference. In "a few hundred years," in fact, he would be so assimilated that he would disappear as a race, Faulkner said.

But change couldn't happen overnight, because discrimination was not basically a moral but an economic problem. If it were changed overnight, "it would mean turmoil, confusion, because it would be an upset of a working economy." There was a class of white men, he pointed out, who hated Negroes and wanted them discriminated against lest they take away white jobs. Such prejudice was peculiar to the adult population, Faulkner believed. There was no race problem among the children—they played, ate, and slept together. "I grew up with Negro children, my foster mother was a Negro woman," he said. "To me they were no different than anyone else. I noticed that with my own children." If left to the children, there would be no race problem. It was only when they grew up and inherited the southern economy, based as it was on a system of black peonage, that they accepted racial distinctions between blacks and whites.

When someone asked his opinion of Negro writers, he singled out novelist Richard Wright, who wrote one good book, Faulkner said (he had *Native Son* in mind), and then went astray because he became too concerned about racial differences and stopped being a writer and became a Negro. "It's a terrible burden that the Negro has to carry in my country," Faulkner said. "It's astonishing that any of them can disassociate themselves enough from that problem and that burden to make anything of a talent. And when one does, I think it implies a very fine talent, that it is strong enough so that he can accept the fact that he is a Negro and then stop worrying about it and be a writer. Much more difficult than the white man."

He had spoken more than he had ever thought possible. But he complained that he couldn't really communicate with his Japanese hosts: "It was like two people running at top speed on opposite sides of a plate-glass window," he said later. "You could see the mouth move, you could see the human features, the gestures, but there was no communication."

But he did like Japanese women, especially the young ones. Somehow they were much prettier than he had expected. All young females had a certain charm, he thought, but there was something about the carriage and facial structure of young Japanese women that he found especially pleasing. He would not forget the face of a geisha he had seen, her mass of blue-black lacquered hair enclosing a painted face, which crowned her slender body. "Yet behind that painted and lifeless mask," he wrote, "is something quick and alive and elfin: or more than elfin: puckish: or more than puckish even: sardonic and quizzical, a gift for comedy, and more: for burlesque and caricature: for a sly and vicious revenge on the race of men."

And there was the young woman who tended him in his room, who wore western clothes, a skirt and blouse, and seemed at first just another dumpy, nondescript young woman. She didn't speak English, yet in two days she knew his habit of rising soon after first light and always had his coffee tray awaiting him on the balcony table. When he returned from his walk, she had the room cleaned and straightened, just as he liked it, and the table set and the morning paper ready. And she asked without words for permission to sew buttons on his clothes and called him wise man and teacher when speaking of him to others. "She is proud to have me for her client and, I hope, pleased that I try to deserve that pride and match with courtesy that loyalty," Faulkner said.

And then he was on the plane again, feeling the wrench of its wheels as it rose from the runway, dragging its shadow up now and into a cloud. After a stopover in the Philippines to see Cho-Cho, he flew to Rome, where Jean Stein met him at the airport—his young Jean, with her stunning face and uninhibited ways. But the vexing race issue stalked him even in Rome. UPI called and asked for a statement about the Emmett Till murder case in Mississippi. Details were sketchy, but Till evidently had come down from Chicago that summer to visit relatives in Greenwood. He was a fourteen-year-old Negro who spoke with a stutter—the result of a childhood bout with nonparaletic polio. One night in August, two white men had kidnapped Till, shot him in the head, and flung him into the Tallahatchie River with a seventeen-pound cotton-gin fan tied to his neck with barbed wire. They murdered him because he had allegedly made a sexual remark to the wife of one of the men. Reporters from across the Union descended on Mississippi for the trial of the two killers, who ultimately went free. Why all this fuss over a dead "nigger" in the Tallahatchie? complained one Mississippi white. "That river's full of dead niggers."

In Rome, Faulkner typed a statement, which the United States Information Service released on September 6: "Perhaps the purpose of this sorry and tragic error committed in my native Mississippi by two white adults on an afflicted Negro child is to prove to us whether or not we deserve to survive. Because if we in America have reached that point in our desperate culture when we must murder children, no matter for what reason or what Color, we don't deserve to survive, and probably won't."

Mid-September found Faulkner and Jean in Paris, where she showed him off at parties in her uncle's lavish apartment. Tennessee Williams saw Faulkner there and later told Hemingway that Faulkner's "terrible, distraught eyes" had moved him to tears. But Faulkner had his humorous moments. In an interview with a pretty female reporter, he said that if his fictional world ever caught on in America as it had abroad, he could probably run one of his characters for President— maybe Flem Snopes, the scheming troglodyte of *The Hamlet.*

One late-September evening, Faulkner's French publisher, Gallimard, gave a cocktail party in his honor. The large, paneled rooms of the Gallimard house opened onto a spacious lawn with trees, one of the celebrated "secret gardens" of Paris. The family was upstairs when Faulkner arrived. Finding himself surrounded by reporters, he retreated behind "that famous wall" all Paris had been talking about, one built "of the most exquisite but the most obdurate politeness," a female journalist said. When asked a question, Faulkner would lean forward, listen, answer "yes" or "no," and then take a step backward. After forcing him to retreat step by step, the three journalists gave up and withdrew.

Then came the Gallimard family, descending on him with smiles and extended hands. The Gallimards escorted him to the reception rooms and introduced him to the arriving guests; eventually they numbered four hundred strong, and Faulkner found himself backing into the garden with only his "wall" and his bourbon to protect himself. After an hour, one of the journalists said, Faulkner had retreated as far as he could: he was standing at the end of the garden, under a tree with the heaviest foliage, his back pressed against a wrought-iron barrier. From time to time, someone would leave the reception rooms and plunge into the darkness to take Faulkner on, only to return in dismay. "It's appalling! I can't watch it; it's like something being tortured."

Finally he returned to the house and told some people, "I would like to go. I would like to say good-bye to a Gallimard." They brought him one, a fat Gallimard. "No," Faulkner said, "not that one." They fetched another, a long, thin Gallimard. "It's not that one, either," Faulkner said. "Which one do you want?" they asked. "The one who looks a little sad. The bald one," Faulkner said. "Ah, that one's gone to bed," they told him. "It doesn't matter," Faulkner said, and he went into the Paris streets, tired and a little shaky, but glad to be free.

B Y MID-OCTOBER, Faulkner was back in New York, having literally traveled round the world in three months. Then came an emergency call from Oxford: his mother, almost eighty-four now, had suffered a cerebral hemorrhage and had been rushed to the hospital. He hurried home fearing the worst, but Maud pulled through, as tough and spunky as she had ever been.

Estelle was feeling better, too, after a summer of sickness and a bout of alcoholism that had sent her to the hospital. At that, she had courageously faced the truth about herself: she had hit the bottom of her life, she was an alcoholic, and she needed help. She joined Alcoholics Anonymous, which helped her control her addiction. Soon she could talk openly about it: "I drank a lot at times," she confessed to Saxe Commins, "in fact a most unpleasant, unpredictable, alcoholic I was—Especially, when I got upset over unfortunate occurrences etc.—drink seemed to me an ideal escape." Her own mother lay sick and dying that autumn, and Estelle spent every available moment with her. Yet Estelle found the strength to withstand the temptation of alcohol.

Not so her husband, who drank and brooded about his native land, fearful that another civil war was about to break out over the race controversy. He wanted desperately to forestall that; he even went up to Memphis in November and participated in a special session on race at the annual meeting of the Southern Historical Association. A friend and fellow southern moderate, James W. Silver, chairman of the Ole Miss History Department, had persuaded him to give a paper at the session, which drew an integrated audience of seven hundred people and considerable media coverage.

A Nashville attorney named Cecil Simms spoke first. Then tall, elegant Benjamin Mays, a prominent Negro theologian and president of Atlanta's Morehouse College, gave a stem-winding oration that brought the crowd to its feet in a burst of applause. Alas, Faulkner had to follow Mays, reading a paper that was eloquent in language if not in delivery. He spoke from his heart to his fellow southerners, urging them to condemn the curse of segregation as he had. "To live anywhere in the world of A.D. 1955 and be against equality because of race or color," Faulkner said, "is like living in Alaska and being against snow." He expatiated on his theory about the economic basis of segregation, which was "our white man's shame." But when it came to integration, he was more cautious than he had been in Japan, perhaps because he was at home now and trying to proselytize. "I am not convinced that the Negro wants integration in the sense that some of us claim to fear he does," Faulkner said, with Mays and many other Negroes in his audience. "I think that what he wants is equality, and I believe that he too knows there is no such thing as equality *per se,* but only equality *to:* equal right and opportunity to make the best one can of one's life within one's capacity and capability, without fear of injustice or oppression or threat of violence. If we had given him this equal right to opportunity ninety or fifty or even ten years ago, there would have been no Supreme Court decision about how we run our schools."

In conclusion, he explained why he and other southern whites were speaking out against segregation, risking insult, ostracism, and violence. It was "because we will not sit quietly by and see our native land, the South, wreck and ruin itself twice in less than a hundred years, over the Negro question."

Faulkner's paper appeared the next day in the Memphis *Commercial Appeal* and later in a pamphlet with the other addresses; a longer, revised version would also come out in *Harper's Magazine.* In Dixie, the reaction was swift and hostile. One historian found that from Memphis to Natchez, whites talked incessantly about two things—segregation and Bill Faulkner, whom they damned for giving Mississippi "a bad press" and for being "a drunk, and a general damn fool." In Oxford,

John Faulkner was so mad at his brother that he was reportedly ready to fight. One of Faulkner's hunting comrades accused him of fanning "the flames of hate and ill will." At Rowan Oak, there were more crank phone calls in the middle of the night; one voice threatened to burn Faulkner's house down.

"Why do you continue to live here?" asked Dorothy Commins, who was down to give a piano recital at Ole Miss.

"My people live here," Faulkner said, "and this is a problem we must solve, not run away from."

To his despair, a few Negroes criticized him, too. One woman, who claimed to speak for her pastor and entire congregation, wrote in effect, "Please, Mr. Faulkner, stop talking and be quiet. You are a good man and you think you are helping us. But you are not helping us. You are doing us harm. You are playing into the hands of the NAACP so that they are using you to make trouble for our race that we dont want. Please hush, you look after your white folks' troubles and let us take care of ours."

At least the Negroes were polite and courteous. That was not the case with his white correspondents. He wrote Jean Stein, who was in the Mississippi Delta with a film crew, that he received so many threats from the Delta that he might just go over there and test them. Not long after, he met up with Jean and took her on a trip. They toured the Vicksburg battlefield, then went sightseeing in New Orleans and Pascagoula, which brought back a surge of memories for him. They stood at the site of the Stones' old beach compound, where he had written *Mosquitoes* and longed for Helen—his "amber flame"—all those years ago. As he and Jean strolled along the winter beach, a lone figure approached—a short, broad woman materializing out of Faulkner's past. It was Helen Baird Lyman. When she and Faulkner stopped to talk, Jean sensed something between them, something extraordinary. Ill and widowed now, Helen was as caustic as ever. "He had some young girl with him," she told a friend later. "But you have to expect that."

When he returned to Rowan Oak, alone, he felt creative again. Something had stirred up the Snopeses—perhaps seeing Pascagoula and New Orleans, where he had first written about them twenty-nine years before. In December 1955, he began *The Town,* the long-delayed sequel to *The Hamlet,* which had appeared in 1940. He sent some of the new work to Jean, and it lifted his spirits when she responded with enthusiasm. "Does it make you nervous to find out somebody needs you? How vain does it make you?" Faulkner asked her. "I still feel, as I did last year, that perhaps I have written myself out and all that remains now is the empty craftsmanship—no fire, force, passion anymore in the words and sentences. But as long as it pleases you, I will have to go on." He gave Saxe another reason to go on: "Miss. such an unhappy state to live in now, that I need something like a book to get lost in."

In February 1956, he went to New York to write on his book and be near Jean. But the race controversy kept intruding on his work. How could he ignore the rush of events in Dixie? In Montgomery, disciplined, hymn-singing blacks had organized an effective bus boycott, which thrust an eloquent young minister named Martin Luther King, Jr., into national prominence. In response, whites had tried to blow up King's home and threatened other violent reprisals that bitterly divided the city. In Tuscaloosa, whites rioted at the University of Alabama when a young black woman named Autherine Lucy tried to attend classes at the all-white school. For four years, the NAACP had argued her case in the federal courts; finally, under orders from the U.S. Supreme Court, a federal judge had forced the university to admit her. When Lucy appeared on campus, white mobs burned fiery crosses, chanted, "Hey, hey, ho, ho, Autherine must go," pelted her car with rocks and stones, and jumped on top of it—she thought they were going to kill her. When university trustees suspended Lucy "for her protection," NAACP lawyers filed contempt-of-court charges against them, and Lucy herself vowed to keep fighting until she received an equal education.

The rioting in Tuscaloosa upset Faulkner terribly. He was certain that "Miss Lucy" would be murdered if she ever returned to the University of Alabama campus. Then the lid would blow all over Dixie: there would be more rioting and killing, federal troops would come, another civil war would break out, the South would be vanquished again.

What appalled him was that northerners seemed unaware of the impending crisis. Damned Yankees didn't understand the South, never had. He had to do something to awaken them, to save Miss Lucy and avert the storm. He set his novel aside and penned "Letter to a Northern Editor," in which he warned that forcing integration on the South would foment massive bloodshed. The problem involved such emotional intensity that southerners would go to any extreme, against any odds, to defend their way of life. The Civil War should have taught the

North that. Now southerners appeared ready to fight again—witness events in Alabama. If they did, it would make a moderate position— Faulkner's position—utterly untenable, as all southerners would be swept up in the stampede to defend the region, their own "blood and kin." To prevent that, he would say to the NAACP and other civil rights groups: "Go slow now. Stop now for a time, a moment. . . . You have shown the Southerner what you can do and what you will do if necessary; give him a space in which to get his breath and assimilate that knowledge; to look about and see that (1) Nobody is going to force integration on him from the outside; (2) That he himself faces an obsolescence in his own land which only he can cure . . . if he, the white Southerner, is to have any peace."

Life bought Faulkner's "Letter" and agreed to publish it in late February. But that wasn't soon enough for him; the turmoil at the University of Alabama was spreading across the state. Certain that catastrophe loomed, Faulkner remembered something his brother John had told him: if "they" tried to enroll Negroes in Oxford's white schools, he would grab his gun and open fire. Faulkner asked himself: if it came to shooting and his family were involved, where would he stand? That upset him so much that he started drinking and searching frantically for a forum—a radio show, an interview, anything—in order to arouse the country before it was too late. Jean Stein tried to slow down his drinking, but Faulkner was too far gone by then. On February 21, he turned up in Saxe Commins' office for an interview with Russell Warren Howe, correspondent for the London *Sunday Times*. To Howe, who didn't know him, Faulkner appeared perfectly sober. In fact, he was so excited and drunk that he made wildly inconsistent remarks. The South, he warned, was armed for revolt. All it needed was an incident to set it off. "If that girl goes back to Tuscaloosa," Faulkner told Howe, "she will die. Then the top will blow off. The government will send its troops and we'll be back at 1860. They must stop pushing these people. The trouble is the North doesn't know that country. They don't know the South will go to war."

Yet the Negro had a right to equality, he said. That was inevitable, "an irresistible force." Still, Faulkner didn't like enforced integration any more than enforced segregation. "As long as there's a middle road, all right, I'll be on it. But"—and now his brother's remarks burst out of Faulkner's mouth—"but if it came to fighting I'd fight for Mississippi against the United States even if it meant going out into the street and shooting Negroes. After all, I'm not going to shoot Mississippians."

"You mean white Mississippians?" Howe asked.

"No," Faulkner retorted. "I said Mississippians—in Mississippi the problem isn't racial. Ninety per cent of the Negroes are on one side with the whites, against a handful like me who believe that equality is important."

He said, "We know that racial discrimination is morally bad, that it stinks, that it shouldn't exist, but it does. Should we obliterate the persecutor by acting in a way that we know will send him to his guns, or should we compromise and let it work out in time and save whatever good remains in those white people?" This seemed a loose paraphrase of King's nonviolent message from Montgomery. "The Negroes are right," Faulkner went on to say; "make sure you've got that—they're right." He had always been on their side and would go on saying that southern whites were wrong, their position unsupportable.

But if he had to make the same choice as Robert E. Lee, he would make it. Faulkner's great-grandfather had owned slaves and "must have known it was wrong," yet he fought in the Confederate Army, "not in defense of his ethical conviction but to protect his native land from being invaded."

Faulkner conceded that his middle-of-the-road position was vastly unpopular in Dixie. His fellow southerners sent him a lot of hate mail; some even phoned him at three and four in the morning and threatened to kill him.

"Do you carry a gun?" Howe asked.

"No," Faulkner said. "I don't think anyone will shoot me, it would cause too much of a stink. But the other liberals in my part of the country carry guns all the time."

When the interview appeared in the March 22 issue of *The Reporter*, it created a sensation. *Time* and *Newsweek* printed excerpts, including the remark about gunning down Negroes. Reporters hounded him for statements. Black novelist James Baldwin declared him "guilty of great emotional and intellectual dishonesty" in adhering to some chimerical middle of the road and then offering to shoot blacks in the streets. By then, Faulkner was sober and horrified. Surely he hadn't said that! He wrote *Time* that he had been misquoted. He hadn't seen the interview before it had appeared in *The Reporter*. "If I had, quotations from it which have appeared in *Time* could never have been imputed to me, since they contain opinions which I have never held, and statements which no sober man would make and, it seems to me, no sane man believe. That statement that I or anyone else in his right mind would choose any one state against the whole remaining Union of States, down to the ultimate price of shooting other human beings in the streets, is not only foolish but dangerous."

He sent *The Reporter* a similar denial. Unhappily for him, both *The Reporter* and *Time* published a rebuttal from Howe, who insisted that he'd recorded exactly what Faulkner had said. Saxe Commins, who was present during the interview, did not dispute Howe. Drunk and desperately concerned about his region and his country, Faulkner had blurted out things that would haunt him for the rest of his life. No wonder he thought that man's greatest curse was the ability to speak.

His only consolation was that Autherine Lucy elected not to return to the University of Alabama and almost certain violence at the hands of its rabid segregationists; at least the country was spared the agony of something terrible happening to her. Still, Faulkner could not shake the image of crowds rioting on the Alabama campus. He wrote a prointegration student there that segregationists seemed only to function in mobs, because they were afraid to cope with problems singly and in daylight. By then, he thought enlightened college students the best hope of his embattled homeland.

I T WAS SOMETIME after the Howe interview, and Faulkner was sitting in Jean's apartment high over Manhattan's East River, talking with her about art and writing. He had gained control of his drinking for now, and his remarks were part of an interview Jean was conducting for the prestigious *Paris Review*. At the urging of editor George Plimpton, Jean had begun the project back in Paris; she had kept a written record of Faulkner's conversations with her in Paris, New York, and elsewhere. Now her notes became the basis for Faulkner's best interview, a lucid, often profound counterpoint to his muddled and frantic session with Howe. In his talks with Jean, Faulkner was on firm ground, a master novelist sharing thoughts on his craft with an adoring disciple.

"An artist is a creature driven by demons," Faulkner said. "He don't know why they choose him and he's usually too busy to wonder why.

He is completely amoral in that he will rob, borrow, beg, or steal from anybody and everybody to get the work done." To get it done all he needed were paper, tobacco, food, and a little whiskey.

"Bourbon, you mean?" Jean asked.

"No, I ain't that particular," Faulkner said. "Between scotch and nothing, I'll take scotch."

He couldn't say how much of his fiction came from personal experience. But he did think that a writer needed three things—experience, observation, and imagination—and that his mission was "to create believable people in credible moving situations in the most moving way he can." Since words were Faulkner's talent, he preferred silence to sound, pointing out that "the image produced by words occurs in silence."

What had caused him to begin the Yoknapatawpha saga? Jean asked in closing.

"Beginning with *Sartoris,*" Faulkner said, "I discovered that my own little postage stamp of native soil was worth writing about and that I would never live long enough to exhaust it, and by sublimating the actual into the apocryphal I would have complete liberty to use whatever talent I might have to its absolute top. It opened up a gold mine of other people, so I created a cosmos of my own. I can move these people around like God, not only in space but in time too. The fact that I have moved my characters around in time successfully, at least in my own estimation, proves to me my own theory that time is a fluid condition which has no existence except in the momentary avatars of individual people. There is no such thing as *was*—only *is*. If *was* existed there would be no grief or sorrow. I like to think of the world I created as being a kind of keystone in the Universe; that, as small as that keystone is, if it were ever taken away, the universe itself would collapse. My last book will be the Doomsday Book, the Golden Book, of Yoknapatawpha County. Then I shall break the pencil and have to stop."

Faulkner worked with Jean on the final form of the interview, which appeared in the spring issue of the *Paris Review.* It was something of a coup for twenty-two-year-old Jean, who now became Feature Editor of the magazine. Grateful for her devotion, Faulkner drew sketches for her, as he had done for Meta Carpenter, and gave her an inscribed copy of *A Fable.* More than ever, he needed her to shield him from memories of Joan Williams and his own advancing years.

When he returned to Mississippi early in March, he was on a binge again. In his cups, he confessed to Estelle that he was having an affair with Jean Stein. Estelle was stoical about it, later writing Saxe Commins: "I know, as you must, that Bill feels some sort of compulsion to be attached to some young woman at all times—it's Bill—At long last I am sensible enough to concede him the right to do as he pleases, and without recrimination—it is not that I don't care—(I wish it were not so)—but all of a sudden [I] feel sorry for him—wish he could know without words between us, that it's not very important after all—"

In the ensuing days, Estelle thought they got along better than they ever had, perhaps because of her changed values and lack of anger about Miss Stein. In April, with Faulkner off bourbon and on a diet of baby food, they went to Charlottesville together to be with Jill, who was about to make them grandparents. But sobriety only made Faulkner prey to morbid anxieties, and one night he fell to talking about Dean's death. He was delighted when Jill gave birth to a fine baby boy, but depressed that he was old enough to be a grandfather. In September, he would be fifty-nine years old.

While he was in Charlottesville, the chairman of the University of Virginia English Department brought him an unexpected offer. The department wanted him to be its writer-in-residence for the spring term of 1957. Faulkner liked the idea: it was a chance to get out of Mississippi, away from racial tensions, the threatening mail and midnight phone calls, and to be near his daughter and new grandson. Besides, he liked the Charlottesville area, with its country mansions, verdant pastures, and hazy mountains. He liked the people, too. Virginians were such snobs, he said later, that they were sure to leave him alone. And so he accepted the offer, waving off the chairman's apologies about the paltry $2,000 salary. "Don't worry about money," Faulkner said. "Don't pay me anything. It would only confuse my tax situation, and besides I don't know whether I'll be any good at this or not. All I need is enough to buy a little whiskey and tobacco. Let me work at it a while and we'll see how it goes."

Back at Rowan Oak for the summer, he worked unhappily on *The Town*, contending with a bad stomach and a painful back. "Each time I begin to hope I am written out and can quit," he told Jean, "I discover I am not at all cured and the sickness will probably kill me." He couldn't tell whether the book was trash or not, but it did give him comic relief from the rotten way he felt.

In June, he took out time to write "A Letter to the Leaders in the

Negro Race," which *Ebony* had requested, urging them to follow
Gandhi's way as the blacks were doing in Montgomery. "If I were a
Negro," he said, "I would advise . . . a course of inflexible and unviolent
flexibility directed against not just the schools but against all the public
institutions from which we are interdict, as is being done against the
Montgomery, Alabama, bus lines." If he were a Negro, he would be a
member of the NAACP—a radical stance in 1956—"since nothing else
in our U.S. culture has yet held out to my race that much hope."
Echoing Martin Luther King, he counseled Negroes to be decent, quiet,
courteous, and dignified; if violence and unreason came, it must not be
from them. He added, "We must learn to deserve equality so that we
can hold and keep it after we get it. We must learn responsibility, the
responsibility of equality." In the North, white liberals and black acti-
vists scorned Faulkner as a gradualist. In Oxford, whites condemned
him as a traitor to his race and his region. When a little boy asked a
couple of them what made Faulkner different, they said he was "a
nigger lover."

In his office at Rowan Oak, Faulkner pulled a wall of silence around
him and was gone for much of the summer, off in a world that couldn't
threaten or hurt him, where he recorded the antics of the Snopeses and
the Snopes-watchers. The latter now included Gavin Stevens and Chick
Mallison, as well as V. K. Ratliff, the shrewd sewing machine salesman
and town storyteller. To Faulkner, the characters were all "quite real
and quite consistent," as *The Town* picked up the saga of Flem Snopes
where *The Hamlet* had left off. Flem came to Jefferson with his wife,
Eula, and her illegitimate daughter, Linda, and plunged into more
nefarious schemes. He was as placid and inscrutable as ever, with eyes
"like two gobs of cup grease on a hunk of raw dough." Once again, this
impotent, lowborn, froglike creature proved himself an elemental force
of invincible ambition and cunning. He outwitted the old, established
families and gained control of the powerful Sartoris bank, just as he had
seized Will Varner's little empire back in Frenchman's Bend. In his
relentless climb to power, he used people mercilessly, running rough-
shod over everybody who got in his way, from other Snopeses to his own
wife and stepdaughter.

Eula, so beautiful and doomed, fluttered helplessly in his rapacious
web. His impotence drove her to the arms of another man, the president of the Sartoris bank, whom Flem replaced and forced out of town
in disgrace. At the same time, Flem manipulated Linda ruthlessly,

turned her against Eula, and drove Eula herself to suicide, leaving his mocking signature on her tombstone: "A Virtuous Wife is a Crown to Her Husband."

He might have destroyed Linda, too, but for Gavin Stevens, the loquacious idealist with a Ph.D. from Heidelberg. This middle-aged, white-haired bachelor set out to save young Linda from being a Snopes, just as middle-aged Faulkner had tried to save Joan Williams from the middle class. Stevens was not oblivious to Linda's sensual charm: at sixteen, she was capable like her mother of arousing a man's blood, "the simple male hunger which she blazed into anguish just by being, existing, breathing." In fact, before Eula killed herself, Stevens promised her that he would marry young Linda if there was no other way to save her from Flem. But there was another way. As Faulkner had done for Joan, Stevens arranged for Linda to escape from home and resettle in Greenwich Village—"a place," he told Ratliff, "where young people of any age go to seek dreams."

Faulkner was proud of the two women characters and deeply moved by the book's ending. "It breaks my heart," he told Jean. "I wrote one scene and almost cried. I thought it was just a funny book but I was wrong." He finished it in September 1956, in Saxe Commins' office in New York City. Like *The Hamlet, The Town* was dedicated to Phil Stone, who "did half of the laughing for thirty years." Faulkner would narrate the further adventures of Flem, Linda, and Gavin in the final volume of his trilogy, to be called *The Mansion,* whose basic story he'd outlined to Bob Haas back in 1938. For now, his readers could reflect on the meaning of the water tower Flem had erected over Jefferson. At first the Snopes-watchers had thought it Flem's monument. By the close of *The Town,* they realized it was really his footprint.

In NEW YORK, Faulkner attended meetings for the People-to-People Program of the Eisenhower administration, which was designed to promote American culture behind the iron curtain. Faulkner had allowed himself to become involved because he liked the idea. What he didn't relish was the tedious work required of him as a member of the steering committee, which also included John Steinbeck and the poet Donald Hall.

He saw Jean and squired her about town. Yet something appeared to be bothering her; she seemed remote and restless. He was fifty-nine now, she was twenty-two. The age thing, then, as with Joan? He was withdrawn himself when he took her to dinner with playwright Thornton Wilder, who found her "beautiful and intelligent and charming." But "Mr. Faulkner appeared to enjoy his dinner—in silence," Wilder said. "We talked across him."

When Faulkner went home for Christmas, he found Estelle troubled, too. A man had phoned her from New York and offered to tell her something about "a Miss Stein" and her husband for $500. Estelle said she knew about Miss Stein and hung up. But he called again, and again, even after Faulkner had returned. Estelle was alarmed, Faulkner enraged. "I must know who this is and stop it," he wrote Commins. "Please go to the police, or get a private investigator if you can." Faulkner would pay for it and attend to whoever it was when he went back east after the New Year. "This is an outrage, persecution," he said, "not of me but of Estelle."

But the damage had already been done. Now Estelle was upset about him and Jean. At first she'd accepted their affair because she thought Faulkner at least had the good sense to be discreet. Now she feared that everybody in New York knew about the affair; now it was "very real" and an affront to what little dignity she had been able to salvage from his years of infidelity. She was sober and angry, and plain sick of it all.

Faulkner returned to New York in early February 1957, only to find more misery there. He was supposed to meet Jean for a date, but she phoned and broke it. Apparently she let him know that she wanted to be free now, and it plunged him into a black depression. Thrown over by another "dame"! He'd thought young Jean wanted only to love him, to be in love. But she was just like all the others. Awash in bitterness, he set himself to a protracted drunk. The women in his life, even Estelle, had all turned against him. All he had was Commins, dear Saxe, who, despite an erratic heart, stayed with him through a three-day siege at the Berkshire House hotel, until a male nurse could be found to relieve him.

By February 9, Faulkner had recovered enough to board a train for Charlottesville, where in a few days he was to begin his duties as writer-in-residence at the University of Virginia. Estelle was waiting for him there. Certain that he had reached the breaking point with her, she offered him a divorce. He kept saying he wanted to be free. Well, here was his chance. She would like to be free, too. Not from him—for once she loved, she said, it was forever—but from the false, undignified position she had occupied for the last six years. As she wrote Saxe Commins, she was tired of being "the poor deceived wife in the background," who always rationalized her reactions and saw *"his* way as a *necessity."* She had reached the point where she would welcome "a clean decisive end."

To her surprise, Faulkner turned her offer down. After the breakup with Jean, he would not even discuss a divorce. Between Estelle and nothing, Faulkner would clearly take Estelle, the mother of his only child. Perhaps he felt for her what he did for Mississippi, loving her even while hating some of her, "because he knows now that you dont love because: you love despite; not for the virtues, but despite the faults." And Estelle stayed with him, in part because she loved him the same way—despite everything. But another reason, perhaps the largest reason, was that he gave up young women, would never take up with another. He did write Joan Williams Bowen that he had never gotten over her and that she probably knew it, and he did read some manuscripts she sent him. But Estelle told Commins that this was not for her to bother about. Joan was no threat now, and neither was Jean or any other young female. Estelle was no longer "the poor deceived wife in the background." Henceforth she and Bill could try to live together as friends. Their marriage had survived. They would spend their twilight years together.

PART NINE

HOMECOMING

IT WAS A PLEASANT SPRING in Charlottesville. The Faulkners rented a two-story brick home close enough to the university for Faulkner to walk there. He met graduate and undergraduate classes in a leisurely schedule, his appearances mostly question-and-answer sessions. Leaning over a podium with his ever-present pipe, his silver hair gleaming under fluorescent lights, he treated the students with charity and good humor as they pressed him about his work. Inevitably, they wanted to know about the symbolism, the social commentary, the psychoanalytic import, intended in this or that passage. One student even asked, "Mr. Faulkner, in *As I Lay Dying*, did Jewel purchase the horse as a substitute for his mother?"

"Well, now that's something for the psychologist," Faulkner replied. "He bought that horse because he wanted that horse."

He tried to explain that he was writing about people, about the tragedy of the human heart, not about symbolism or sociology. "I don't know anything about ideas," he insisted, "don't have much confidence in them." That scarcely endeared him to the academicians, but Faulkner persisted, determined to make a point the students would not soon forget. "The writer uses environment—what he knows—and if there's a symbolism in which the lover represents the South, I don't say that's not valid and not there, but it was no intention of the writer to say: Now let's see, I'm going to write a piece in which I will use a symbolism for the North and another symbol for the South." The writer "was simply writing about people, a story which he thought was tragic and true, because it came out of the human heart, the human aspiration."

When asked about his personal goal as a writer, Faulkner repeated what he had often said: "A writer wants to make something that he knows that a hundred or two hundred or five hundred, a thousand years later will make people feel what they feel when they read Homer, or read Dickens or Balzac, Tolstoy." The writer "knows he has a short span of life, that the day will come when he must pass through the wall of oblivion, and he wants to leave a scratch on that wall."

In May, he was in New York to present John Dos Passos with the Gold Medal for Fiction from the National Institue of Arts and Letters. He made his speech mercifully brief: "Oratory can't add anything to John Dos Passos' stature, and if I know anything about writers, he may be grateful for a little less of it. So I'll say, mine is the honor to partake of his in handing this medal to him."

By now, the years of excessive drinking were taking their toll on him. His moods were unpredictable. For no apparent reason, he could be rude and insulting, even to his friends. When Lillian Hellman joined him for a drink, Faulkner asked about Dash Hammett, who had gone to jail for refusing to testify before the House Un-American Activities Committee.

"He's a very sick man," Hellman said.

"He drank too much" was all Faulkner said.

Hellman thought this so incredibly offensive that she got up and walked off.

Faulkner was just as hostile to Ben Wasson, his friend of nearly forty years. When Wasson visited him at Random House one day, Faulkner treated him as though he were an utter stranger, scarcely saying a word to him. Stung by his "inexplicable antagonism," Wasson started for the door, but Saxe Commins kept talking away, perhaps trying to make him feel better. Wasson only wanted to leave, for he realized that his long friendship with Faulkner was over. He didn't know why Faulkner had turned against him, would never know why. At the door, Wasson told Commins goodbye, then glanced back at Faulkner, who was sitting at Commins' desk.

"Good-bye, Bud," Faulkner said in a low voice.

They never saw one another again.

THE FAULKNERS SPENT THE SUMMER in sweltering Oxford, where Faulkner's longtime friend Phil Stone was ever more hostile to him. Stone rejoiced over a particularly savage review of *The Town,* which had come out in May. "I am tired of the nauseating obsequiousness that proclaims an indication of genius everything that Bill does and writes and every little remark he makes (usually borrowed from someone else)," Stone said. Without shame, he claimed that he had invented the idea of the book, as well as "a great many incidents and some of the characters." He informed one Faulkner critic that he hadn't talked to Faulkner since his return from Virginia. And it wasn't just his "Nobelitis" that infuriated Stone. It was his prointegration stand, too. "Since he has taken the position he has in turning his back on his own people and his native land," Stone said, "I don't care to ask him anything."

In September, another race crisis rocked Dixie, and Faulkner grieved again for his homeland. All month, Oxford and Memphis newspapers screamed with the news from Little Rock, Arkansas. A federal court had ordered Little Rock's Central High School to admit nine Negro students, but Governor Orval Faubus mobilized the Arkansas National Guard to keep them out. A fifteen-year-old Negro named Elizabeth Eckford, wearing bobby socks and ballet slippers, approached the school with her notebook, only to confront taunting white spectators and a line of gun-toting soldiers. She retraced her steps and stood alone at a bus stop, surrounded by jeering whites. Another attempt to enroll the students provoked such disorders that mob rule threatened Central High. Faced with the most serious challenge to federal authority since the Civil War, President Eisenhower nationalized the Arkansas National Guard and dispatched a thousand Regular Army paratroopers to maintain order in Little Rock and escort the Negro students to school. Thanks to southern white intransigence, Eisenhower became the first President since Reconstruction to send federal troops to enforce Negro rights in Dixie.

Faulkner wrote *The New York Times*—and a divided nation beyond —that "the tragedy of Little Rock" proved what everyone knew but no one wanted to admit. "This is the fact that white people and Negroes do not like and trust each other, and perhaps never can." Nevertheless, they must "federate" together or the United States was doomed. Faulkner refused to believe that in a crisis Americans could not rally their national character and show the same courage and toughness as the English had done when they stood alone against the Germans. "We, because of the good luck of our still unspent and yet unexhausted past, may have to be the rallying point for all men, no matter what color they are or what tongue they speak, willing to federate into a community dedicated to the proposition that a community of individual free men not merely must endure, but can endure."

The racial situation still troubled him when he returned to the University of Virginia for the spring term of 1958. He was convinced that Virginia, despite its segregationist governor and obstructionist school boards, must lead the South into the coming new era of race relations, and he said so in a public address at the university on the night of February 20. So as not to embarrass the university, Faulkner spoke as "a private citizen," "a citizen of Mississippi," who wished to give "A Word to Virginians," enlightened whites and segregationists alike. He began by quoting Abraham Lincoln: "This nation cannot endure half slave and half free." Or as a lesser man might put it, Faulkner went on, no nation could long endure with 10 percent of its population arbitrarily unassimilated because of physical appearance, no more so than "a town of five thousand people can get along in peace with five hundred unbridled horses."

With an eye on Virginia's segregationist leaders, he argued that the Negro perhaps was not yet ready for equality and first-class citizenship. Therefore immediate integration was unwise and dangerous, he said, for that would only provoke the emotional segment of Dixie into open violence and force the Negro himself into a role for which Faulkner thought him unprepared. Still, the problem of his second-class citizenship remained. It was up to the southern white man to solve that problem, Faulkner said, to teach the Negro "that, in order to be free and equal, he must first be worthy of it, and then forever afterward work to hold and keep and defend it." The southern white man must teach the black man rectitude and personal morality, by bringing him into white schools or giving him white teachers in his own schools. If this was not done, then the South could look forward each year to another Little Rock, another monument and milestone "to our ridicule and shame."

And the place to begin was Virginia, "the mother of all the rest of us of the South." Let Virginia show the way in preparing the Negro for his new place in society. A century ago, the hotheads of Mississippi, Georgia, and South Carolina refused to listen when Virginia tried to check their reckless course. Southerners, to their grief, ignored her then; but it would be different this time. "Show us the way and lead us in it," Faulkner said. "I believe we will follow you."

A spirited question-and-answer session followed, with several people questioning his metaphor about the wild horses. He conceded that it was unfortunate. He conceded, too, that a lot of the South's racial troubles came from violent, uneducated whites who feared that Negroes would take away the white man's economy. But Faulkner, now sixty years old, made it plain that his opinions were more conservative than they had been three years before. He agreed when a man in the audience suggested that the Negro's educational and economic standards ought to be raised while he was still segregated. "Good," Faulkner said, "that's what I'd like to do. I would like to give him such good schools that he wouldn't want to go to the white schools. I would like to give him so much equality in his own race and responsibility for it and make him have to spend so much time being responsible for his own equality that he wouldn't have time to bother with the white man's."

Did he not think race assimilation the best solution? another man asked.

"No sir," Faulkner said. "The same amount of bickering would go on. . . . I think that the only thing that will solve that problem is not integration but equality, for the Negro to know that he has just as valid rights in this country as anybody else has. That his money is just as secure, his children have a right to just as good an education as anybody else does, his vote counts as much as anybody else's." But, no, he wasn't for integration as the NAACP preached it, because he didn't think Negroes wanted to mix with white people. All the laws in the world couldn't make them do what they didn't want to do. . . .

Faulkner's arguments for equality of opportunity and freedom of choice for blacks pleased almost no one. While segregationists continued to denounce him as "small-minded Willie, the nigger-lover," integrationists of both races thought him an atavistic champion of the very doctrine of "separate but equal" the Supreme Court had nullified. Actually, he was suggesting a kind of "voluntary segregation" similar to what the great Negro leader W. E. B. Du Bois had once advocated. He wasn't defending the racist philosophy and state laws that enforced segregation in Dixie, for he hated all that as much as he ever had. He simply believed that blacks, if given a choice, would rather mix with their own race. But since most civil rights organizations in the fifties were struggling for an integrated society, his remarks struck them as offensive and reactionary. Worse still, his demeaning characterization of black people sounded unforgivably patronizing.

Later, in a visit to West Point, Faulkner made a final public pronouncement on the race issue, asserting that change was inevitable and would occur in Dixie whether southern whites liked it or not. The South would change, Faulkner suggested, because "life is motion and the only alternative to motion is stasis—death." That he equated segregation with death and change with life seemed an unequivocal indication of where his sympathies lay. Yet he remained a lonely figure in a furious crosswind, assailed by integrationists and segregationists alike. For him, the race controversy proved again that a curse was upon his homeland and that he and his entire generation were its victims.

H E WAS WORKING ON ANOTHER NOVEL that spring of 1958, the final volume of the Snopes trilogy, *The Mansion.* Always a frugal man, he typed his new work on the back of the first draft of *The Town,* banging away on his portable with two index fingers. What was he attempting in his new work? "You write a story to tell about people," he said in class that term, about "man in the ageless, eternal struggles which we inherit and we go through as though they'd never happened before, shown for a moment in a dramatic instant of the furious motion of being alive, that's all any story is." Once his "people" came alive, he told the students, they took off and he pursued them at a dead run, trying to jot down what they said and did. Certainly, Gavin Stevens and V. K. Ratliff, Linda, Flem, and Mink Snopes were up and running now, and Faulkner was doing his best to keep up with them.

He returned to Oxford for the summer and continued his composition in his office at Rowan Oak, working by the window as the dreadful heat came on. Blasted Mississippi summers; he kept swearing he would never go through another. In fact, he and Estelle were thinking seriously about buying a place in Virginia, to be near Jill and her family. Estelle had written Saxe and Dorothy Commins what a serious move this would be for her husband, but "I'm hoping and *praying* that Bill *will* see his way clear to buy a place up here—Then you can come (if you will) and stay and stay and stay—How I'd love that!"

But that would never be for Saxe, who died of a heart attack in Princeton on July 17. Faulkner was devastated. Saxe was more than an editor and a friend; he had been like a brother to Faulkner, seeing him through some of the worst ordeals of his life. Faulkner regretted that he and Estelle couldn't get to Princeton in time for the funeral; he had to settle for a personal telegram to Dorothy. Faulkner loved Saxe, as Saxe had loved him. How would he manage without such a friend? Whom would he confide in now, depend on when he drank too much or got depressed? Who would protect his memory when he had breathed his last?

Though he missed Saxe, Faulkner remained sober and at his writing table. But he grumbled to Ober that he'd had a bellyful of Oxford. "I cant keep tourists out of my front yard, rubber-necking at my house, and there is not one place in fifty miles that I have found yet where I can eat any food at all without having to listen to a juke box." By November, he couldn't wait to get back to Charlottesville. He stayed in Oxford long enough for the marriage of his niece Dean, who had grown into a delightful young woman, as effervescent and outgoing as her father had been. When Dean had died, Faulkner had vowed to be like a father to his brother's child; Faulkner had seen her through her youth, sent her to a language academy in France and then to the University of Geneva, and now he had given her away in marriage. Afterward, they placed flowers on her father's grave, and Faulkner walked home in the night, alone with his memories.

Then he was off to Charlottesville and the Blue Ridge Mountains, where in early March of 1959 he completed *The Mansion,* sending the last section off to New York. In the new work, Flem and his greedy exploits had receded into the background; Faulkner now concentrated on Mink and Linda Snopes, both of whom Flem had ruthlessly hurt, and who now became the instruments of his destruction. While Flem took over the Sartoris bank and lived in the ancestral home of a local patrician family, Mink languished in prison for murdering the farmer who had demanded a fee for pasturing his cow. Mink no longer seemed the venomous little viper he'd been in *The Town,* for Faulkner felt compassion for him now, realizing how unforgivably arrogant the farmer had appeared to Mink before Mink had blasted him to oblivion with his shotgun. In prison, Mink lived only for the day he could escape and kill Flem, who had coldly refused to save him during his trial. Finally, after spending thirty-eight years behind bars, this frantic, worn-out, obdurate little man was released, thanks to the efforts of Linda, Flem's stepdaughter, who hoped Mink would kill Flem and thus avenge the suicide of her mother.

Faulkner felt even more compassion for Linda, Flem's other victim, and drew her with great tenderness and sensitivity; it was as if she had become the new and final young woman of his heart, someone who would never reject and hurt him. In New York, where she had gone at the close of *The Town,* Linda had married a Jewish sculptor with Communist sympathies. Both had served with the loyalists in the Spanish Civil War, but he had been shot down and killed in an outmoded airplane. Linda herself had suffered punctured eardrums in an explosion and had returned to Jefferson speaking in the duck talk that deaf people used. Twenty-nine now, she was tall and slender, with fine eyes that were probably beautiful when you removed her clothes, or so Chick Mallison thought. By this time, Linda was hopelessly in love with middle-aged Gavin Stevens, who was white-haired, as Faulkner was. Linda wanted to sleep with lawyer Stevens, marry him, love him always, but Stevens, ever the idealist, could accept no gratitude from her: his role was to serve, not to receive. Well, she wanted him to marry someone then, to have that experience. Perhaps out of deference to her, he did get married—to his youthful flame, Melisandre.

Meanwhile Linda lived with Flem in his cold and silent mansion, trying to make something of her life. She worked with Negroes to improve "colored" schools, which only enraged the white folk of Jefferson, some of whom scrawled "nigger lover" and burned a cross in front of the Snopes mansion. Hating Flem, she schemed to get Mink released from prison, knowing that he would come to Jefferson and destroy the monster who had turned Linda away from her mother, Eula, and driven Eula to suicide. This was exactly what Mink did. In a climactic scene, he materialized in the mansion with a rusty pistol and a furious, single-minded determination to get his revenge; he found Flem in a downstairs room, and Flem just sat there, immobile, even detached, until Mink blasted him to eternity. In the closing scenes, Linda helped Mink escape, told Gavin goodbye in a poignant love scene, saying, "I have never loved anybody but you," and then left Jefferson and Yoknapatawpha in a new British Jaguar. Unmarried, she now belonged only to Faulkner.

But though Flem was dead, suggesting that not even a consummate devil like him could carry on with impunity, the menace of Snopesism remained. At Flem's funeral, Stevens noticed the Snopeses among the mourners, their faces suddenly springing out, identical and incontrovertible—*"like wolves,"* he thought, *"come to look at the trap where*

*another bigger wolf, the boss wolf, the head wolf, what Ratliff would
call the bull wolf, died."*

"You see?" Stevens told Ratliff. "It's hopeless. Even when you get rid
of one Snopes, there's already another one behind you even before you
can turn around."

"That's right," Ratliff said. "As soon as you look, you see right away
it aint nothing but jest another Snopes."

WITH THIS, HIS EIGHTEENTH NOVEL, Faulkner had finished his
planned labors, bringing his monumental saga of Yoknapatawpha
County down to the very edge of contemporary life. His new editor,
Albert Erskine, did worry about certain factual discrepancies between
it and the previous volumes of the trilogy, but Faulkner told him they
didn't mean a thing. "As I wrote those books, I got to know the people
better. By the time I did the third volume, I knew a lot more about
them than I did in the first volume." In the end, Random House did as
he suggested, letting *The Mansion* stand as the "definitive" volume and
correcting the earlier volumes in subsequent editions. If the discrepancies were "paradoxical and outrageous," however, Faulkner wanted
them to stand.

In June, the Faulkners bought the brick home they had been renting
in Charlottesville, with plans to spend half a year here and the other half
at Rowan Oak, which, along with the Greenville farm, they had deeded
to Jill. What they really wanted, though, was a country place in Albemarle County which they could live in permanently. Faulkner realized that a country estate would be expensive, but at age sixty-one he
no longer had to worry about money: he had $45,000 on deposit at
Random House, with royalties flowing in steadily from his books, and
movie sales of *The Sound and the Fury, Requiem for a Nun,* and *The
Hamlet*—the latter to be called *The Long Hot Summer* and to star Paul
Newman, Joanne Woodward, and Orson Welles—would bring him
about $120,000 over the next five years.

Jill was amazed at how different he seemed, how much more
relaxed. "He had in a sense finished the creative side of his life and
wanted to have something else," she recalled. "He became so much

easier for everyone to live with—not just family, but everybody." He still drank a good deal, but no longer driven by the demons of his art, and no longer in search of a young woman's acceptance and love, he did seem a little happier now.

Oh, he still had a daredevil streak in him, as he proved when he joined the fox hunts for which Albemarle County was famous. Its clubs maintained the customs of the European hunt, which had been transplanted here in the colonial era. Oscar Wilde may have characterized the fox hunt as "the uneatable pursued by the unspeakable," but Faulkner loved the sport; with its rich customs and traditions, it appealed to his patrician side. At "the meet," the gathering of the hunters and hounds, Faulkner sat stiffly on his steed, wearing the fox hunter's customary "pink" coat, top hat, pigskin gloves, and shiny top boots. At the command of the Huntsman, the hounds set off to draw a fox, and the Master, the supreme commander and strategic leader of the hunt, followed on with the field of riders. The blast of the Huntsman's horn signaled that a fox had been spotted, the baying of the hounds that they were hot on its trail. At that, the riders sallied forth in pell-mell pursuit, racing across fields, fences, and stone walls in a desperate effort to keep up with the scampering hounds. Carried away by the chase, Faulkner always rode too fast, galloping by the other horsemen with his face set, his lips grim, and taking the jumps completely out of control, with his knees out instead of tight to his horse. "One's heart was in one's mouth every time he went over a fence," said a fellow hunter, "there usually being anything from a foot to eighteen inches of sky between the seat of his trousers and the saddle."

"I love the thrill of the danger," he once said. It made him feel good; it was something he needed. But one day he paid a price for his recklessness: riding too fast on wet ground, he tried to turn his horse to face a fence, and the animal lost its footing; Faulkner leaped free as it fell, but fractured his collarbone when he slammed to the ground. Undaunted, he drank whiskey to kill the pain, and kept on riding. "It is very fine, very exciting," he wrote Joan Williams Bowen. "Even at 62, I can still go harder and further and longer than some of the others. That is, I seem to have reached the point where all I have to risk is just my bones."

By 1959, he and Joan were corresponding frequently, and he was content to leave it at that. "I'm not going to see you again, at least now," he wrote her. "It's too painful. . . . I love you but I can do it with less pain from a distance." She wrote him that she was trying to finish a novel based on her short story "The Morning and the Evening," but she was troubled. If it was published, what if people said she was imitating him?

"Have you already forgot what I always preached to you?" he replied. "Never be afraid. Never give one goddamn about what anybody says about the work, if you KNOW you have done it as honestly and bravely and truly as you could." Sure, some discerning person would see Faulkner in it. "I was in your life at an age which I think you will find was a very important experience, and of course it will show on you. But dont be afraid. There are worse people and experiences than me and ours to have influenced you. Dont be afraid. Do the work."

She did do the work and wrote him that Atheneum had accepted it. "Splendid news," Faulkner replied. "That not only justifies us but maybe absolves me of what harm and hurt I might have done you; maybe annoyance and exasperation are better words. Please keep me posted." Her novel appeared as *The Morning and the Evening* and went on to win a ten-thousand-dollar first-novel award from the Book-of-the-Month Club. Faulkner wrote Joan that he was proud of her, but urged her not to stop now. "I believe, hope you are already working on the next one."

Meanwhile his own novel had come out, with friend Cowley calling him "an epic poet in prose" in *The New York Times,* which also printed reports about his worldwide influence. But that meant little to him. What mattered were the mounting losses in his life: Harold Ober, his agent of twenty years, had died in October 1959, just before the book had appeared. "Harold will be missed," Faulkner wrote Bob Haas, "maybe by not many people, but by the sort of people I hope will miss me; there are not too many like that."

His mother was in declining health, too. When he was home, Faulkner still visited her every morning and fretted that she kept getting smaller and smaller. By the summer of 1960, she was eighty-eight years old and often in the hospital. She knew she was dying and insisted that they not give her glucose, that they just let her die. And no embalming either, she said; just put her in a plain wooden box. At her bedside, Faulkner created a fairy tale for her, describing how nice heaven would be and how much she would like it.

But Maud had reservations. "Will I have to see your father there?" she asked.

"No," Faulkner said, "not if you don't want to."

"That's good," she said. "I never did like him."

In early October, as the Faulkners were preparing to leave for Char-lottesville, Maud suffered a cerebral hemorrhage and lapsed into a coma. On the seventeenth, she was gone. Faulkner led Jack and John into her room, and one by one they kissed her forehead in death as they had in life. Her things, in orderly disarray about her room, were a testament to what she held dear: there were stacks of books and pamphlets, her easel with an unfinished oil painting on it, family paintings and photographs on the walls and tables, and near her bed Mammy Callie's small, ancient rocking chair.

As THE AUTUMN PASSED in Albemarle County, the Faulkners were often with Jill and her growing family, which included another son, born the previous December and christened William Cuthbert Faulkner Summers in honor of his grandfather. Faulkner doted on his grandsons, doing pen-and-ink drawings for them just as Maud might have done. With the little boys, he appeared a stoop-shouldered old man, with all-white hair, sagging jowls, and a drooping mustache like Mark Twain's. As baby Will learned to walk and talk, Faulkner was inordinately proud of him. When Joseph Blotner, a friend and an English professor at the university, dropped by for a drink, Faulkner said, "Listen to this." He asked Will, "What's your name, boy?" Will looked up, his hands in his pockets and his little legs planted firmly. "Will Faulkner," he said. It tickled his grandfather no end.

He and Estelle were still looking for a country place in Albemarle County, where they could spend their final years in rural serenity, sitting on a porch and gazing at the Blue Ridge Mountains. He had drawn closer to the University of Virginia, too, accepting an appointment as Balch Lecturer, which, for a modest sum, required that he give a yearly reading to the public and meet with a few classes. He said he wasn't interested in writing anymore, only in reading for pleasure the old books he'd discovered when he was eighteen. In his way, he was living like the old man he'd watched in the Luxembourg Gardens, the old man who wore a weathered derby and sailed toy boats with the children.

On July 2, 1961, a Sunday, Faulkner was visiting Jill and the boys when the news flashed over the radio that Ernest Hemingway had shot himself to death at his home in Ketchum, Idaho. "Authorities were uncertain whether Hemingway, ailing and recently released from the Mayo Clinic, shot himself deliberately or accidentally," said a UPI report. "They said it was highly unusual that the bearded novelist, an expert with guns who had survived many brushes with death, would have killed himself accidentally while cleaning his shotgun."

When Jill told him the news, Faulkner said, "It wasn't an accident. He killed himself." And Faulkner was right, as further investigation revealed. Faulkner was extremely upset. He'd said before that Hemingway boasted and protested too much, that he was trying to cover something up, and this proved it. For days, he brooded about Hemingway's suicide, thought it bad and unmanly, believed it was like saying, "death is better than living with my wife." Papa had had four wives all told. "Hemingway's mistake was that he thought he had to marry all of them," Faulkner said. A few days later he was still agitated. "I don't like a man that takes the short way home."

H E HEARD VOICES AGAIN—of characters who had first spoken to him some twenty-one years before. In the spring of 1940, he had outlined to Bob Haas a possible novel about them, but had gone on to do *Go Down, Moses* instead. Now the other story stirred in him once more, about "a sort of Huck Finn" who was really a good deal like himself as a boy. Well, Faulkner would write it and then maybe the voices would at last stop troubling him. He began the novel in Charlottesville, in the late spring of 1961, and finished it at Rowan Oak that same summer. The narrator, Lucius "Loosh" Priest, was a grandfather like Faulkner; in 1961, speaking in a kind of autumnal voice, he told his grandson about his boyhood adventures with a giant, courageous, completely unreliable child-man named Boon Hogganbeck, a shrewd, cantankerous Negro coachman named Ned McCaslin, a gentle, compassionate prostitute named Miss Corrie, and a stolen racehorse named Coppermine. In a tumultuous week with them, culminating in a dramatic racing contest in which Lucius rode Coppermine first to victory, then to defeat, the boy lost his innocence. Exposed to "debauchery and degeneracy and actual criminality," Faulkner said, Loosh would learn all the things that molded his character as a man—would learn "courage and honor and generosity and pride and pity," mostly because of "the influence of the whore." In recounting Lucius' boyhood, Faulkner utilized and forgave much of his own. In what amounted to a reconciliation with his father's memory, he even adapted Murry to the story as Maury Priest, Lucius' father and the owner of a Jefferson livery stable.

He called the new work *The Reivers*—an old Scottish term for robbers. Faulkner now had more than thirty books to his credit, including nineteen novels, five collections of stories, a collection of three short novels, two anthologies, several limited editions of his short fiction, two editions of his New Orleans sketches, and two volumes of poetry— ample testimony to the size of the mark he'd left on the wall of oblivion. He was about to turn sixty-four. Perhaps it was time to break his pencil and call it quits. When he mailed off the new manuscript at the Gathright-Reed drugstore, he told Mac Reed, "I been aimin' to quit this foolishness."

In October, he returned to Charlottesville and busied himself with horses and fox hunting. In December, he came down with a backache and a nagging respiratory infection and had to spend several days in the hospital. Two days after New Year's 1962, he was in the saddle again, riding through the wintry countryside near Charlottesville. Suddenly his horse stumbled and fell, hurling Faulkner to the ground. It knocked him senseless. He couldn't remember what had happened, but his back and head were killing him. He made it home in a daze and took whiskey and Demerol to ease the pain. By then, his left eye was badly swollen, his mouth was hurting, and he had an ugly bruise on his forehead. Two days later, he was coughing and complaining of chest pains. When a fever set in, he checked into a hospital in Richmond, where doctors said he had pleurisy or pneumonitis. Luckily for him, tests showed nothing wrong with his heart. As for his riding, Faulkner told the doctor, "I'm going to stop being a damn fool and acting like a forty-five-year-old and start living as a sixty-five-year-old and perhaps live to be an eighty-five-year-old."

Back in Oxford for a few months, he went to his doctor there and found that he'd broken three teeth as well. He had them removed and a plate inserted. "I feel now like I've got a mouse trap in my mouth," he wrote his friend Joe Blotner. "It dont hurt Jack Daniel though, thank God."

He'd resumed his habitual morning stroll down to the square, but the town no longer fascinated him as it once had. Both the town and the art it had inspired seemed behind him now. He looked forward to spending his old age in Albemarle County, even if he had seen a few Snopeses there. The longer he stayed in Virginia, the more like Mississippians the people behaved, but without some of the Mississippi vices. He still thought Virginians were snobs, he joked, but he liked that. They wanted nothing of him, gave him their hospitality, and left him alone.

At Rowan Oak, the dogwoods were in bloom; iris and daffodils had appeared in yellow and violet patches along the driveway, and the Lady Banksia rosebush that climbed into the cedars had begun to bud. As long as he could keep the tourists away, there was a peaceful serenity at Rowan Oak. He was going to miss the old place; it evoked such bittersweet memories for him. He had lived here almost thirty-two years, had written most of his great fiction here. Here his first child had died, and here his only living child had grown to maturity. The thought of giving it up tugged at his heart.

One spring day, he took a wicker chair out to some shade trees down from the house, and sat completely still as he looked out toward the cedars, where birds fluttered and cawed. Presently a young man peered around the veranda and saw Faulkner sitting in the shade, so utterly still that it seemed he had been there for weeks. The young man approached nervously and flung out his hand.

"My name is Claxton," he said. "Did you get my letter?"

"No," Faulkner said, but he shook the young man's hand and found a chair for him. His full name was Simon Claxton, and he was a British student who attended Cate School in California. He would be honored, he said, if he could ask Faulkner a few questions. Initially cool, Faulkner warmed up to the young man, perhaps because of his impeccable British manners, and told him about his writing habits and techniques. The young man was mesmerized. Throughout the interview, Faulkner rarely moved; he sat cross-legged, looking from Claxton to the trees with the same penetrating stare. His whole person was centered on the face, Claxton thought, and especially in his eyes, which were small and dark and terribly strong. "You can't escape those eyes," he wrote later. "In a way they are friendly smiling eyes, in another they are cruel. One gets a different impression every time. A withered old face . . . glittering hooded eyes."

In April, Faulkner returned to Charlottesville and then flew up to

West Point for an appearance, taking along Estelle, Jill, and her husband, Paul, a member of the class of '51. Estelle said she had a good time: "Bill and I were housed in the Presidential suite in the post hotel —and I had generals in plenty to squire me around—" Faulkner gave a reading from *The Reivers,* which would officially appear in June and would be a Book-of-the-Month Club selection. In a question-and-answer session after the reading, a cadet asked if Faulkner ever deliberately portrayed a character in an unfavorable light. Not really, Faulkner said. The first thing a writer should have was compassion for all his characters. "In his clumsy way the first thing he must do is to love all mankind, even when he hates individual ones. Some of the characters I've created I hate very much, but it's not for me to judge them, to condemn them; they are there, they are part of the scene that we all live in. We can't abolish evil by refusing to mention these people."

Back in Charlottesville, Faulkner learned that President John F. Kennedy planned to invite fifty-one American Nobel Laureates to the White House for a special dinner. "Those stuffy White House dinners," Faulkner growled, "I'm not going to go." When his invitation came, he turned it down. "I'm too old at my age to travel that far to eat with strangers," he said.

In May, he won the Gold Medal for Fiction from the National Institute of Arts and Letters, and manfully presented himself at the ceremonies in New York City. Muriel Cowley thought he had a country look, with his bronze face and white hair; "his magnificent dark eyes had the clarity that young children's often have," she told Malcolm later. During the luncheon, Faulkner spotted Lillian Hellman and went over to greet her. No doubt he wanted to make amends for offending her five years before, when he'd made the sarcastic comment about Dash Hammett's drinking. Now he recalled his good times with Hammett—"I think they were the best days of my life," he told Hellman. Somewhat mollified, she agreed that they should get together again.

To resounding applause, he mounted the stage to receive his award, presented by his fellow Mississippi writer Eudora Welty. "Mr. Faulkner, your work and our love for it have both been alive for a long time now," she said. "The most evident thing in all our minds at this moment must be that your fictional world, with its tragedy, its beauty, its hilarity, its long passion, its generations of feeling and knowing, the whole of your extraordinary world, is alive and in the room here with us now. We inhabit it; and so will they, each one for himself, the readers in days to come. . . ."

Faulkner saw Joan Williams Bowen sitting in the front row; she had won an award for *The Morning and the Evening*. After he sat down, she thought he dozed off, apparently bored stiff by the ceremonies, and did not see her when she came to the stage. After the award presentations, Malcolm Cowley found him sitting on a bench in the hallway, surrounded as always by a shield of silence. "In the bustle of members looking for their hats," Cowley said, "he seemed very much alone."

By June, he and Estelle were on the verge of a momentous decision. They had found a country place where they could live year round, a farm called Red Acres, comprising 250 of the loveliest acres to be found anywhere in the Blue Ridge Mountains. It included an impressive brick home, with a wide veranda visible from miles away, and a stable with nine box stalls, a groom's house, houses for a manager and a tenant, an implement house, a smokehouse, a silo, and two barns. The asking price was steep—$200,000—but Faulkner thought he had the resources to pay for it. He had his royalties from Random House, his home in Charlottesville, about $30,000 in the bank in Oxford, and his good name. He and Estelle wanted Red Acres. He wanted to sit in its columned splendor and bask in his material success, which with Red Acres would match the grandeur of the Old Colonel. Tired though he was, he would do anything to own Red Acres, even write other books, even lecture. By the time the Faulkners had returned to Oxford for the summer, they were prepared to gamble and make an offer.

In his last June at Rowan Oak, Faulkner worked his horses and went for rides in the country. One day he was out riding a horse named Stonewall, when suddenly the horse spooked at something and bucked, throwing Faulkner to the roadside and reinjuring his back. When the horse took off for home, Faulkner raised himself and limped after him. He was seething. That damn horse was not going to conquer him. Back at Rowan Oak, he remounted Stonewall and rode him furiously around the paddock and over the jumps. Two days later, though, his back hurt him so severely that he took to his bed. If the pain got any worse, he would treat it with his own remedy: gin and painkillers.

Then something dreadful happened. He had a premonition, saw "suddenly and close-up that wall of oblivion he had so often mentioned," said Joe Blotner. Faulkner was frightened. He told a doctor who lived nearby, "Felix, I don't want to die."

On June 26, Joan Bowen called at Rowan Oak, and Estelle politely ushered her sister off the porch where they had been sitting and left Joan and Faulkner alone. She was an attractive woman in her thirties now, but still shy. He asked if there had been any money in the envelope they had given her in New York. He hadn't been asleep after all; he had seen her come to the stage.

He walked her to her car. She thought he looked pale, but was sure he was all right and would live to be a very old man. She had to believe that. Despite all they had gone through, despite their breakup and her marriage, she still had love for him. To think of him, she thought of sun and laughter and a kind of lovely sadness. In Connecticut, where she lived, she had daydreamed of returning to Mississippi and taking care of him when he was eighty; she would put an afghan over his knees as he sat in a rocking chair, and she would listen to him again.

By July 3, he seemed distracted, complaining that his back hurt him so much he could think of little else. That night he and Estelle dined at a local restaurant called The Mansion, but Faulkner didn't enjoy his food. "I don't feel so good," he said. "Meat and bread all taste the same." That evening, he started drinking. His nephew, Jimmy, John's boy, dropped by Rowan Oak to see how he was. Faulkner was proud of Jimmy—he had been a Marine combat pilot in World War II and Korea —and very much enjoyed his company. He was a lot like Dean in his love for flying and hunting, and like him, too, in his loyalty to Faulkner. If he went on a binge, Jimmy could be counted on to help.

Faulkner went through a bad night, suffering such intense pain that he started mixing Demerol and tranquilizers with his bourbon. In his bed upstairs, he drank through Independence Day, oblivious to the anxious voices beyond his room. By July 5, his pain was all but unbearable; nothing could kill it, not even the drugs and a fifth and a half of bourbon. Miserable as he was, Faulkner did recognize Jimmy when he sat down beside him. It was time to go to Byhalia, Jimmy said, for he and Estelle hoped to end the cycle before it got any worse. Faulkner spoke earnestly to him, but Jimmy couldn't understand what he said. He seemed eager to go, though, so Jimmy and Estelle helped him out to the car and drove him up to Wright's Sanitarium, a white clapboard house situated outside Byhalia.

It was around 6 P.M. and still oppressively hot when they got Faulkner registered. By then, he was complaining of chest pains, too, but the doctor who examined him said his heart and blood pressure were normal. Once he was settled in his room, Estelle kissed him goodbye, and Jimmy said, "Brother Will. When you're ready to come home, let me know and I'll come for you."

"Yes, Jim, I will," Faulkner said.

Then he rested quietly. From a small lounge across the hall came the racket of a television set. When night closed, there was still no letup in the heat. Electric fans whirred in some of the rooms; insects buzzed at the window screens. Somewhere in the darkness a big clock sounded midnight. It was July 6 now, the Old Colonel's birthday. At about half past one in the morning, Faulkner stirred and sat up on the side of the bed, groaned, and then fell through the wall of oblivion and into the void beyond.

In the quiet of early morning, John Faulkner sat on the steps of the funeral home in Oxford, waiting for the ambulance to bring his brother there. The man who had written so powerfully about the anguish of the human heart had died of a coronary occlusion that had destroyed his own. As John sat in the gathering light, he was sure he saw his brother's people on the square. There was the the sheriff from Intruder in the Dust, *and Joe Christmas and Gail Hightower from* Light in August. *Everywhere John looked, there were Bill and his stories, Jefferson and Yoknapatawpha.*

They brought him home to Rowan Oak, home to Estelle and the gathering clan, and his kinsmen took turns sitting with him in the parlor, the same parlor where Mammy Callie had lain when he had given her eulogy. On July 7 of his sixty-fifth year, a hearse bore William Faulkner on his last ride through the little lost town he had immortalized, round the square now, past the courthouse and the Confederate monument that had captivated him from boyhood, past the closed stores and staring people. In the funeral procession, novelist William Styron found himself deep in memory, as Dilsey and Benjy and all the Compsons, Hightower and Byron Bunch and Flem Snopes and the gentle Lena Grove, all these people and scores of others came swarming back in Styron's mind with a sense of utter reality, along with the tumultuous landscape, the fierce and gentle weather, and the whole "maddened, miraculous vision of life" that had created them.

Under a blazing sky, they buried Faulkner in St. Peter's Cemetery, not in the old section where his grandfather, Maud, Dean, and Mammy

Callie were buried, for that was full now; but in a new section, a hot dry field overlooking a housing project. Then the crowd was gone, and Faulkner lay alone between two oaks, on a gentle slope where the earth that held him fast would draw him breath again. "He has stepped into an eternal tomorrow that has left him forever in Yoknapatawpha County," John said. "He can never leave us again."

ACKNOWLEDGMENTS

I could not have written this volume without the generosity of others. Chancellor Joseph D. Duffey, Provost Richard D. O'Brien, Dean Murray M. Schwartz of the College of Humanities and Fine Arts, and Chairman Robert W. Griffith of the History Department helped secure a named chair for me at the University of Massachusetts, Amherst, which provided a research assistant and travel funds that facilitated my work immensely. The university not only awarded me an additional faculty research grant, but provided a timely sabbatical that allowed me to write full time. I appreciate the university's strong support of my biographical efforts, and am proud to be associated with it.

The following archivists and librarians offered indispensable assistance in the research stage of my work, and I am in their debt: Edmund Berkeley, Jr., Curator of Manuscripts and University Archivist, Michael Plunkett, Associate Curator of Manuscripts, Joan St. C. Crane, Curator of Literature Collections, Gregory A. Johnson, Senior Public Services Assistant, and the Faulkner Access Committee, the Alderman Library of the University of Virginia, Charlottesville; Decherd Turner, Director, and Cathy Henderson, Research Librarian and Faulkner collection specialist, the Harry Ransom Humanities Research Center at the University of Texas, Austin; Wilbur E. Meneray, Head of Rare Books and Manuscripts, the Howard-Tilton Memorial Library, Tulane University; the staff of the Rare Books and Manuscripts Division, New York Public Library; Thomas Verich, University Archivist and Curator of Special Collections, University of Mississippi Library; and the entire reference departments in the library of the University of Massachusetts, Amherst, and the libraries of Amherst College and Smith College.

In Oxford, Jack and Wylene Dunbar, Dean Faulkner Wells, and the staff of the Center for the Study of Southern Culture at the University of Mississippi, especially Director William Ferris and Frank Childree, aided me in my research, and I am obliged to them for their courtesies. I owe a particular debt to my assistants, Eva Langlois and especially Karen Smith, who tracked down obscure facts, probed collateral issues, criticized drafts, read proof, and performed sundry other tasks with enthusiastic and unflagging professionalism. Members of the Amherst Creative Biography Group, including Dorothy Clark, Debra Craig, Peter Eddy, Sandra Katz, William Kimbrel, Elizabeth Lloyd-Kimbrel, Ann Meeropol, Will Ryan, Harriet Sigerman, and Leslie Stainton, heard parts of the manuscript during our monthly readings, and I thank them for their spirited and constructive criticism of the book as biography. Professor Barry O'Connell, chairman of the English Department at Amherst College, took time from his busy schedule to give the manuscript a thorough reading and to make trenchant annotations that helped me enormously. At Harper & Row, Daniel Bial, Frances Lindley, and M. S. "Buz" Wyeth, Jr., my longtime friend and editor, also furnished a vigorous critique, and Marjorie Horvitz did a superior job of copyediting the manuscript; I am grateful to all of them and to production editor Daril Bentley for making this a better book than it otherwise would have been. My additional thanks to Daniel Bial for alerting me to the fact that Faulkner's lines to Estelle, after she decided to marry Cornell Franklin, came originally from a poem by François Coppée. My gratitude, too, to Joan Williams, L. D. Brodsky, Professor Arthur F. Kinney of the University of Massachusetts, and Professor Doreen Fowler and Professor Evans Harrington of the University of Mississippi for their help and encouragement.

I am also grateful to Gerard McCauley, my longtime agent, for his unstinting support; to Rachel Clifton for her friendship and keen appreciation of the art of evoking personality; to the members of my biography seminar, from 1972 to 1987, for teaching me as I taught them; and to Betty L. Mitchell, Frederick Turner, and T. H. Watkins, my friends and fellow biographers, for sharing their experience and insights. To Carol Kendall, her lovely daughters, Callie and Gillian, and her son-in-law, Rob, I offer a special thanks.

NOTES

The sources listed below are abbreviated in the references according to the key on the left. All other sources are identified in the notes. For bibliographies of Faulkner's works, see Linton R. Massey (comp.), *"Man Working," 1919–1962: William Faulkner, A Catalogue of the William Faulkner Collections at the University of Virginia* (Charlottesville, 1968), part one, and Leland H. Cox, *William Faulkner: Biographical and Reference Guide* (Detroit, 1982). Space does not permit me to cite all the critical works and articles I consulted and profited from. For bibliographies of the secondary literature, see Beatrice Ricks, *William Faulkner: A Bibliography of Secondary Works* (Metuchen, N.J., and London, 1981), John Earl Bassett, *Faulkner: An Annotated Checklist of Recent Criticism* (Kent, Ohio, 1983), and the Modern Language Association's annual international bibliographies.

ALOP   Abadie, Ann, ed. *William Faulkner: A Life on Paper.* Jackson, Miss., 1980.

SAM   *Sherwood Anderson Memoirs: A Critical Edition.* Ed. Ray Lewis White. Chapel Hill, N.C., 1969.

NYPL   Berg, Dr. Albert A., Collection. New York Public Library.

FAB   Blotner, Joseph. *Faulkner: A Biography.* 2 vols. New York, 1974.

FAB(1)   Blotner, Joseph. *Faulkner: A Biography.* One-volume ed. New York, 1984.

BCB   Brodsky, Louis Daniel, and Hamblin, Robert W., eds. *Faulkner: A Comprehensive Guide to the Brodsky Collection.* Vol. I: The Bibliography. Jackson, Miss., 1982.

BCL   Brodsky, Louis Daniel, and Hamblin, Robert W., eds. *Faulkner: A Comprehensive Guide to the Brodsky Collection.* Vol. II: The Letters. Jackson, Miss., 1984.

IMC   Broughton, Panthea Reid. "An Interview with Meta Carpenter Wilde," *Southern Review* (Oct. 1982), 776–801.

SCW   Commins, Dorothy. *What Is an Editor? Saxe Commins at Work.* Chicago, 1978.

PWWF   Coughlan, Robert. *The Private World of William Faulkner.* New York, 1954.

FCF   Cowley, Malcolm. *The Faulkner-Cowley File: Letters and Memories, 1944–1962*. New York, 1966.

AFR   Dahl, James. "A Faulkner Reminiscence: Conversations with Mrs. Maud Faulkner," *Journal of Modern Literature* (April 1974), 1026–30.

FOM   Falkner, Murry C. *The Falkners of Mississippi: A Memoir*. Baton Rouge, 1967.

FWP   Fant, Joseph L., III, and Ashley, Robert, eds. *Faulkner at West Point*. Paperback reprint 1964 ed. New York, 1969.

MBB   Faulkner, John. *My Brother Bill: An Affectionate Reminiscence*. New York, 1963.

HRHRC   Faulkner, William. Collection. Harry Ransom Humanities Research Center, University of Texas, Austin.

UVA   Faulkner, William. Collections. Alderman Library, University of Virginia.

EPP   Faulkner, William. *Early Prose and Poetry*. Ed. Carvel Collins. Boston, 1962.

ESPL   Faulkner, William. *Essays, Speeches, & Public Letters*. Ed. James B. Meriwether. New York, 1965.

HAC   Faulkner, William. *Helen: A Courtship* and *Mississippi Poems*. Introductory essays by Carvel Collins and Joseph Blotner. New Orleans and Oxford, 1981.

FLT   Faulkner, William. Letters. Howard-Tilton Memorial Library, Tulane University.

SL   Faulkner, William. *Selected Letters*. Ed. Joseph Blotner. New York, 1977.

MD   Faulkner, William. *Mayday*. Introduction by Carvel Collins. Notre Dame, 1976.

NOS   Faulkner, William. *New Orleans Sketches*. Ed. Carvel Collins. New York, 1958.

FYY   Fowler, Doreen, and Abadie, Ann J., eds. *Fifty Years of Yoknapatawpha: Faulkner and Yoknapatawpha, 1979*. Jackson, Miss., 1980.

BLWF   Franklin, Malcolm. *Bitterweeds: Life with William Faulkner at Rowan Oak*. Irving, Tex., 1977.

FR   Gardner, Paul. "Faulkner Remembered," *A Faulkner Perspective* (Franklin Center, Pa., 1976), 1–29.

AFC   Gresset, Michel. *A Faulkner Chronology*. Jackson, Miss., 1985.

FIU   Gwynn, Frederick L., and Blotner, Joseph, eds. *Faulkner in the University: Class Conferences at the University of Virginia, 1957–1958*. Charlottesville, Va., 1959.

FAF   Kawin, Bruce F. *Faulkner and Film*. New York, 1977.

AFM   Meriwether, James B., ed. *A Faulkner Miscellany*. Jackson, Miss., 1974.

ISF   Meriwether, James B., ed. "An Introduction for *The Sound and the Fury*," *Southern Review* (Oct. 1972), 705–10. Reprinted as "Faulkner, Lost and Found" in *The New York Times* (Nov. 5, 1972), 6–7.

LIG Meriwether, James B., and Millgate, Michael, eds. *Lion in the Garden: Interviews with William Faulkner, 1926–1962.* Reprint of 1968 ed. Lincoln, Neb., 1980.

OFA Sensibar, Judith L. *The Origins of Faulkner's Art.* Austin, Tex., 1984.

PSY Snell, Susan. *Phil Stone of Yoknapatawpha.* Ann Arbor, 1978.

COF Spratling, William. "Chronicle of a Friendship: William Faulkner in New Orleans," *Texas Quarterly* (Spring 1966), 34–40.

CNC Wasson, Ben. *Count No 'Count: Flashbacks to Faulkner.* Jackson, Miss., 1983.

WFO Webb, James W., and Green, A. Wigfall (ed.). *William Faulkner of Oxford.* Baton Rouge, 1965.

DSF Wells, Dean Faulkner. "Dean Swift Faulkner: A Biographical Study." Unpublished M.A. thesis, University of Mississippi, 1975.

ALG Wilde, Meta Carpenter, and Borsten, Orin. *A Loving Gentleman: The Love Story of William Faulkner and Meta Carpenter.* New York, 1976.

TNCA Williams, Joan. "Twenty Will Not Come Again," *Atlantic Monthly* (May 1980), 58–65.

page   PREFACE

xi **"pure" biography:** Paul Murray Kendall, *The Art of Biography,* 2nd ed. (New York, 1985), ix, 13–14, 28.

xi **"is an artist upon oath":** Quoted in ibid., 15.

xii **"spark of creation":** See Frank E. Vandiver's essay in Stephen B. Oates, ed., *Biography as High Adventure: Life-Writers Speak on Their Art* (Amherst, Mass., 1986), 50–65.

xii **"not only each book":** *LIG,* 255.

PART ONE: FUMBLING IN WINDY DARKNESS

3 **train ride and Oxford:** *FOM,* 3–4; *WFO,* 10.

4 **Murry and the Young Colonel:** *FAB,* 51–70; *DSF,* 1–2.

4 **Murry:** *FOM,* 9–10; *FAB(1),* 17–18.

5 **"How can I be older":** *FAB,* 87. See also *PWWF,* 42.

5 **Mammy Callie:** *ESPL,* 16–17, 40; *FOM,* 12–15; *WFO,* 11; *MBB,* 49; *AFR,* 1028.

6 **parental troubles:** *FOM,* 11–12, 25; *FAB,* 79, 90; *FAB(1),* 18; *DSF,* 2–4, 35, 116–17. See also *OFA,* 48, 52.

6 **"DON'T COMPLAIN—DON'T EXPLAIN":** *FOM,* 9–10. See also *MBB,* 122.

7 **WF in his grandfather's library:** *ESPL,* 179.

7 **"light of my life":** *FAB,* 1516.

7 **little white house:** DSF, 5–6.

7 **fruit trains:** *FOM,* 78–80; *WFO,* 17–18.

8 **"William Falkner":** *FAB,* 94.

8 **Sallie Murry:** ibid., 105, 107; *MBB,* 47.

page

9   **Dean:** DSF, 7–8, 31, 35; *MBB*, 47; *FAB*, 108.

9   **WF and his grandfather:** *MBB*, 73; *FOM*, 6–7, 68–69.

9   **"proudest boy":** *FAB*, 125.

9–11 **Old Colonel:** Ibid., 9–50; *PWWF*, 27–38; also Donald Philip Duclos, *Son of Sorrow: The Life, Works and Influences of Colonel William C. Falkner, 1825–1829* (Ann Arbor, 1962); Phil Stone, "William Faulkner, the Man and His Work," *Mississippi Quarterly* (Summer 1964), 153–56; Robert Cantwell's essay in Frederick J. Hoffman and Olga W. Vickery, eds., *William Faulkner: Three Decades of Criticism* (paperback reprint of 1960 ed., New York, 1963), 55–56, 63–66; Cantwell's foreword in William Faulkner, *Sartoris* (paperback reprint of 1929 ed., New York, 1957), ix–xvi; Thomas L. McHaney, "The Falkners and the Origin of Yoknapatawpha County: Some Corrections," *Mississippi Quarterly* (Summer 1972), 249–64; and Walter Taylor, *Faulkner's Search for a South* (Urbana, 1983), 6–9.

11 **"I want to be a writer":** *PWWF*, 43; *FOM*, 6; also Faulkner's remarks in *FWP*, 108–9.

11 **"Even at my age":** *MBB*, 85.

11 **"Nolia, see that little boy":** *FAB*, 85.

11 **"Snake-Lips":** ibid., 187; *OFA*, 50, 236.

11 **"the cure":** *FAB*, 45–48. Cf. David Minter, *William Faulkner: His Life and Work* (Baltimore and London, 1980), 15, with *FAB*, 98–100.

12 **"given to solitary walks":** *WFO*, 218; also 29.

12 **"He would do anything":** *FAB*, 123.

12 **"If he couldn't turn her off":** *MBB*, 220.

12 **"shrill cricket voice":** William Faulkner, "And Now What's to Do," in *AFM*, 145–46. This unfinished piece is clearly autobiographical, as James B. Meriwether notes.

12 **"one of the best books":** *FAB*, 146. See also *ESPL*, 197–98.

13 **Faulkner and the Civil War:** Faulkner's remarks *FIU*, 249; *ESPL*, 15–16.

13 **"It got so":** *PWWF*, 43.

13 **submitted a drawing:** *MD*, 10.

14 **"Thank you, *sir*":** FAB, 178–89. See also H. Edward Richardson, *William Faulkner: The Journey to Self-Discovery* (Columbia, Mo., 1969), 34.

14 **WF's longing to be tall:** Author interview with Dean Faulkner Wells; *OFA*, 177; *FYY*, 259.

14 **WF's burning eyes:** *WFO*, 96.

14 **"looked after the same girls":** *AFM*, 146. Judith Bryant Wittenberg, *Faulkner: The Transfiguration of Biography* (Lincoln, Neb., 1979), 28, makes a similar point.

14 **WF and off-color stories:** *WFO*, 66, 172, 184.

14–15 **WF and Estelle:** *FAB*, 152, 155, 157, 159, and *FAB(1)*, 41; *MBB*, 122.

15 **"He was generally":** *FAB*, 154.

page

15–17   **WF and Stone:** *PSY,* 33–34, 37–51, 180–99; *PWWF,* 47–49; *MBB,* 130.

17   **"springing from some tortured undergrowth":** *EPP,* 114–16; *NOS,* xiv–xv. See also Cleanth Brooks, *William Faulkner: Toward Yoknapatawpha and Beyond* (New Haven and London, 1978), 2–3, 19, and Gary Lee Stonum, *Faulkner's Career* (Ithaca and London, 1979), 44, 70.

17   **born out of his time and place:** Brooks, *Toward Yoknapatawpha,* 19.

17–18   **WF and Estelle:** *FAB,* 174–76; *MBB,* 122.

19   **"Learned the medicinal value":** Marshall J. Smith, "Faulkner of Mississippi," *The Bookman* (Dec. 1931), 416.

19   **"Hell, he ain't ever":** *ALOP,* 33. See also *FAB,* 179; *PWWF,* 43, 58.

19   **WF's drawings:** *EPP,* 36, 37.

19   **"sure is a nut":** *CNC,* 25–26.

20   **Estelle's marriage:** *FAB,* 193–96; *PSY,* 257; *HAC,* 26; William Faulkner, *Light in August* (Modern Library ed., New York), 158; *MBB,* 133.

20–21   **song lyrics:** Blotner quotes Faulkner's use of the lyrics in *FAB,* 195, but fails to note that Faulkner copied them from H. de Fontenailles's song "Obstination: A Resolve," whose lyrics de Fontenailles had taken from Coppée's poem "Obstination." The song, with English translation done before 1903, was available in sheet music for voice and piano. See *56 Songs You Like to Sing* (New York, 1937), 148–50. The poem is in François Coppée's *Poésies* (Paris, n.d.), 227–28.

21   **"Humanity . . . must be mad":** *The American Heritage History of World War I* (New York, 1964), 185.

22   **WF's dreams of aviators:** *ESPL,* 180.

22   **"It's too late":** *FAB,* 204.

22–23   **the cadet:** *FAB(1),* 60–67.

23   **"disgusted sorrow":** William Faulkner, *Soldiers' Pay* (New York, 1926), 7.

23   **"Hush, Buddy" and WF homecoming:** *MBB,* 137–39.

23–24   **WF's posturing:** *FAB,* 224–25; *OFA,* 3, 6–7; *DSF,* 39–40; also *WFO,* 96–98, and *BCL,* 21–24. For a discussion of Faulkner's various personae, see Louis Daniel Brodsky, "Faulkner's Life Masks," *Southern Review* (Autumn 1986), 738–65.

25   **"world owed no man":** *WFO,* 7–8, 226; *PSY,* 342, 445, 486.

25   **"like curs on a cold trail":** *EPP,* 117.

25   **"reason for being born":** Ibid.

25   **"ripening thighs":** *WFM,* 146–47.

25   **WF's pastoral poems:** *OFA,* 8–11, 24–30; Brooks, *Toward Yoknapatawpha,* 4–6, 17–18.

26   **"He gave the impression":** *FAB,* 232.

26   **WF inscription:** *OFA,* 24.

page

26 "lascivious dreaming knees": *EPP,* 39; Stonum, *Faulkner's Career,* 55.

26 "Bill and I felt": *BCL,* 261.

26 "I am sending you a drawing": *FAB,* 247.

27 Murry: DSF, 42–43.

27 "beauutiful man" and "Count No 'Count": *CNC,* 19–20, 25; *FAB,* 264, 269.

28 "young Galahad" and "Listen to those horns": *CNC,* 26, 34–36.

28 The Lilacs: *OFA,* 61–71; *MD,* 9.

28 "You'll have to admit": *CNC,* 52–53.

28–29 The Marionettes: William Faulkner, *The Marionettes* (Charlottesville, Va., 1977), 20; *OFA,* 21–25.

29 "a shadowy fumbling": Faulkner, *The Marionettes,* 82.

29 "yelping pack," etc.: *EPP,* 74; *OFA,* 105–6, 122; *CNC,* 32–33.

30 Vision in Spring: William Faulkner, *Vision in Spring* (Austin, 1984), passim; *OFA,* 107–205. See also Brooks, *Toward Yoknapatawpha,* 11–15.

31 "I have given": *FAB(1),* 55.

31 "That damn Billy": *PSY,* 329.

31 "Mr. Murry": *FAB(1),* 102.

32 Memphis brothel with Stone: *PSY,* 217, 291, 314–15. Said Edith Brown Douds in *WFO,* 53: "Phil wore a hat all the time, indoors and out."

32 "the perfect milieu": *LIG,* 239.

32 "I know whores": *ALG,* 52. See also *HAC,* 64, and *FAB(1),* 101.

32 Gertrude Stegbauer: *PSY,* 306–9; *MBB,* 146; *HAC,* 28; *MD,* 17–18.

33 One Oxonian remembered: *WFO,* 92. See also DSF, 58–59.

33–34 WF's grandfather: *AFM,* 145; *FOM,* 111.

34 "anyone who wrote fiction": *PSY,* 346.

34 "old Walt Whitman": *CNC,* 33. See also *PWWF,* 48.

34–35 Balzac and Wright: *PSY,* 348, 350–53; *WFO,* 228; *FAB,* 300–1, 320–21; Martin Kreiswirth, *William Faulkner: The Making of a Novelist* (Athens, Ga., 1983), 5–6, 18–36. For the influences of the "novelists of consciousness," see Arthur F. Kinney, *Faulkner's Narrative Poetics* (Amherst, Mass., 1978), 41–67.

35 doomed to write: *ESPL,* 180; also *LIG,* 220–21, and *FYY,* 10.

35 "shy, almost singing voice": *FAB(1),* 116.

36 suit-box lid: *PSY,* 368, 517.

36 "It's beautiful": *FAB,* 350.

36 "get some recognition": *PSY,* 368–69.

36 WF's emotional crisis: Faulkner to Wasson, undated, HRHRC; *CNC,* 66.

36 Stone and *Marble Faun: PSY,* 368ff.; Stone's correspondence in *BCL,* 9, 21, 184; Stone to Yale Alumni Weekly, Oct. 15, 1924, and to Dear Friend, undated, HRHRC. See also Stone to *Atlan-*

page

tic Monthly, Nov. 13, 1924, and correspondence with Four Seas, ibid.

37 "imperceptive" and "I believe my book": *CNC,* 65–67.

37 WF's autobiographical sketch: *SL,* 7.

38 "Thank God": *FAB,* 365; also *FR,* 4.

38 "able to walk in the sunlight": Faulkner to Wasson, undated, HRHRC.

38 "these blue hills": *HAC,* 156.

38 WF and Wasson: *CNC,* 72.

38 "By God, that's a man": Ibid., 71.

39 "cut from black paper": William Faulkner, *Mosquitoes* (New York, 1927), 14–15.

39 "I didn't think": *FIU,* 230. See also Elizabeth Anderson and Gerald R. Kelly, *Miss Elizabeth: A Memoir* (Boston, 1969), 40.

39–40 Anderson profile: Draws from Irving Howe, *Sherwood Anderson* (reprint of 1951 ed., Stanford, Cal., 1968), 44ff.; *SAM,* passim, and Anderson and Kelly, *Miss Elizabeth,* 47–94.

40 "after a few drinks": *FAB,* 371.

40 "a little Southern man" and "write like Shelley": Irving Howe, *William Faulkner: A Critical Study* (3d ed., rev., Chicago, 1975), 16.

PART TWO: A COSMOS OF MY OWN

45 "colonial mansions": *FAB,* 329.

45 "a skinny little guy": *COF,* 34.

45 "drank enough whiskey": Don Lee Keith, "Faulkner in New Orleans," *The Delta Review* (May 1969), 47.

46 WF's sketches: *NOS,* xii–xxxiv and passim; *HAC,* 82.

46 "WHAT'S THE MATTER": *FAB,* 397.

46 "shaped to a brush": *NOS,* xxiii.

46 "abundant liquor": *COF,* 35.

47 "ignorant, unschooled fellows" and "that little patch": *EPP,* 8–9.

47 "warm, generous, merry" and "figures and symbols": *ESPL,* 9.

48 "You've got too much talent": Ibid., 7. See Howe, *Anderson,* 145–46, for Anderson's insecurities.

48–49 race argument: *SAM,* 462; Howe, *Anderson,* 145; Schevill, *Anderson,* 195–96. Elizabeth Anderson gave a somewhat different version in *Miss Elizabeth,* 100–1.

49 "those decayed families" and "lot of the same old bunk": *SAM,* 474.

49 "Good God!" and "damn manuscript": *FIU,* 22; *FAB,* 430; also Anderson and Kelly, *Miss Elizabeth,* 96, and *SAM,* 462, 465. Faulkner himself gave various other versions of Anderson's response. See for example *LIG,* 118, 218, 249, and Faulkner, *ESPL,* 9–10; also *PWWF,* 60.

49–50 first novel: Textual quotations from *Soldiers' Pay.* See also Witten-

page

berg, *Faulkner,* 46–47; *HAC,* 16–17, 80; Kreiswirth, *Faulkner,* 37–69.

50–51   **Helen Baird meeting:** Faulkner to Helen Baird, undated, FLT; *FAB,* 419–20; Brooks, *Toward Yoknapatawpha,* 52; *HAC,* 22–23, 93.

51   **"single stubborn leaf":** *HAC,* 126. WF composed a version of this in March or so, 1925.

51   **"the moon looks like":** *FAB(1),* 151–53; *HAC,* 10, 17–18, 28; *CNC,* 14.

51–52   **WF's poems and sonnets:** *HAC,* 112, 111, 116, 117, 122.

52   **Helen's mother and Helen's indifference:** *HAC,* 23–24; *FAB,* 439, and *FAB(1),* 151, 153.

52   *Let there be no farewell: HAC,* 123.

52–53   **"damn fine book"** and **"didn't seem to care":** *PSY,* 431, and *WFO,* 51.

53   **dreamed of Helen:** *HAC,* 121–22.

53   **"only two basic compulsions":** *COF,* 38.

53   **"frozen music," "covered with gargoyles," "Full of Americans," "all stones and cobbles," "people eat and sleep":** *SL,* 9, 10.

54   **"I have just written":** Ibid., 17.

54   **"When I am old enough," "Makes me look sort of," "could see right through it," "It looked as if a cyclone":** Ibid., 19–20, 18, 25; *FAB,* 469.

54–55   **"greasy," "tramping again," "most restful country":** *SL,* 29, 30.

55   **"on the strength":** *FAB(1),* 172. See also *SAM,* 462, 465.

55   **"Enclosed at your usual rate":** *BCL,* 5.

55–56   **WF and Helen:** *HAC,* 19.

56   **"to thee":** *MD,* 45.

56   **BB gun:** *COF,* 36; William Spratling, *File on Spratling: An Autobiography* (Boston, 1967), 28.

56   **"most noteworthy":** *FAB,* 505.

56–57   **WF and Anderson:** Sherwood Anderson, *Letters* (ed. Howard Mumford Jones and Walter B. Rideout, Boston, 1953), 152, 153; *SL,* 293; Anderson and Kelly, *Miss Elizabeth,* 100–1; *ESPL,* 132–39; Schevill, *Anderson,* 225–26.

58   textual quotations from *Mosquitoes* (New York, 1927).

58   **"amber flame":** *HAC,* 92; Faulkner to Helen Baird, undated, FLT.

59   **"Helen, your name":** Faulkner to Helen Baird, UVA.

59   **"proud and self-sufficient beast":** *FAB,* 1437; *BCL,* 94.

59   **"You don't commit suicide"** and **"So I can't write poetry":** Faulkner, *Mosquitoes,* 228, 249. Faulkner wrote Liveright, June 4, 1926, HRHRC, that *Mosquitoes* was a better novel than *Soldiers' Pay* and that he needed an advance to continue it, but the language is Phil Stone's, as Snell, *PSY,* 453–54, points out. Later Faulkner conceded that *Mosquitoes* was "not an important book on my list" (*FIU,* 257). For a discussion, see Michael Millgate, *The Achievement of William Faulkner* (New York, 1966), 68–75.

60   **"primer-like style"** and **"We have one priceless":** *ESPL,* 6, 174–75.

page

60   "warm and delicate": *COF*, 36.

60–61   Anderson: *SAM*, 462–65. 466; Howe, *Anderson*, 202.

61   WF on Anderson: *ESPL*, 4–6, 10; also *WFO*, 135, and *LIG*, 118–19.

61   "on the verge": Faulkner, "Trial Preface to *Sartoris*" in Max Putzel, "Faulkner's Trial Preface to *Sartoris:* An Eclectic Text," *Papers of the Bibliographical Society of America* (Oct. and Dec. 1980), 374–75.

62   "bolt of lightning": *FIU*, 90. For Stone's influence here, see Kreiswirth, *Faulkner*, 101–4, and *PSY*, 473–76.

62   "little postage stamp of native soil": *LIG*, 255, plus Faulkner's "Trial Preface" cited above. See also *FAB*, 532–34.

62   "While Cornell": *FAB(1)*, 189; also 197–98 and *FR*, 12. In *The Wishing Tree*, Faulkner's gift book for Cho-Cho, the mother resembles Estelle "with her grave unhappy eyes" and "slender hands."

63   "Her name is Helen Baird": *CNC*, 75.

63   "the whole face": *ESPL*, 28.

63   "Be still, my heart": *HAC*, 88.

64   "Helen Helen Helen": FLT. Other Faulkner letters to Helen are also located here.

64   "heights or depths": Courtesy Ralph Newman.

64   "little, lost town": Faulkner's subsequent description. See *FAB(1)*, 253.

64–66   kingdom and characters: From *Flags in the Dust*, which went through at least five drafts; also Faulkner, "Trial Preface," 374–76. As he worked, he was "staking out his territorial claim" (Millgate in *FYY*, 26–27). See also Cleanth Brooks, *William Faulkner: The Yoknapatawpha Country* (New Haven, 1972), 107, and *Toward Yoknapatawpha*, 165–77; Kinney, *Faulkner's Narrative Poetics*, 1–4, 123–39; Kreiswirth, *Faulkner*, 112–27.

66   Stone recognized himself: *BCL*, 21.

66   "the stuff": *SL*, 37. Stone, too, thought *Flags in the Dust* outclassed Faulkner's previous novels (Stone to H. V. Kincannon, Oct. 29, 1927, HRHRC).

66   "Phil Stone lent me": *FAB(1)*, 204. See also *PSY*, 500, and Minter, *Faulkner*, 92.

67   "I have written THE book": Faulkner to Liveright [Oct. 16, 1927], UVA. The published version in *SL*, 38, omits the lines about the "lady friend."

67   Liveright's letter and WF's reaction: *FAB*, 559–60; *SL*, 39.

67   "Every day or so": *SL*, 40–41.

68   fifth draft: Merle Wallace Keiser in *FYY*, 48.

68   "Will you please": *FAB*, 563; *CNC*, 84–86.

68   morbid lyrics and death: *WFO*, 94; Minter, *Faulkner*, 92.

68   "utter charm" and "lovely vase": *BCL*, 8.

68   "difficulties of an intimate kind": *FAB*, 571.

73–75   writing *The Sound and the Fury:* Faulkner gave consistent state-
        ments about how he wrote this, the novel he most loved. My para-
        graphs draw from Maurice Coindreau, "Preface to 'The Sound and
        the Fury,' " *Mississippi Quarterly* (Summer 1966), 108–9; James B.
        Meriwether, ed., "An Introduction to *The Sound and the Fury,*"
        Mississippi Quarterly (Summer 1973), 412–15; *ISF,* 708–10; *ESPL,*
        176–77; *FIU,* 1, 6, 31–32, 64, 77, 84; *LIG,* 46, 245; *WFO,* 130; *FWP,*
        109, 111; *FAB(1),* 209–21.

75   "the hackneyed accidents": Faulkner, *Mosquitoes,* 339; Minter,
        Faulkner, 102.

75   "there is actually something": *ISF,* 709.

75–77   reading to Stone: *PSY,* 494–95; *BCL,* 154, 278. Wittenberg, *Faulkner,*
        76–77, 80–85, also points out Faulkner's and Quentin's similarities.
        For discussions of *The Sound and the Fury,* see Cleanth Brooks,
        William Faulkner: First Encounters (New Haven, 1983), 43–77, and
        Millgate, *Achievement,* 86–103.

77   "a fine woman" and "good human being": *WFO,* 131; *FIU,* 85.

77   "tale told by an idiot": *BCL,* 154.

77   "dark story": Coindreau "Preface," *Mississippi Quarterly,* 109.

78   Liveright ought to be a stockbroker: *COF,* 38.

78   "Well, I'm going to be published": *SL,* 41.

79   "The trouble is" and "shady but ingenious shapes": *FAB,* 584.

79   "You've done a good job": *CNC,* 89. For Wasson's editorial work, see
        ibid., 86–89, and Keiser's discussion in *FYY,* 49–51. I agree with
        Kinney, *Faulkner's Narrative Poetics,* 1, that *Sartoris* was a "much
        diminished thing." *Flags in the Dust* was finally published in 1973.

79   "Read this one": *CNC,* 89.

80–81   genesis of *Sanctuary:* FAB, 429–31, 604–17.

81   "again as a printed object": *ESPL,* 177.

81   "That is all right": *SL,* 43.

81   "You're the only damn fool": *FAB(1),* 241.

81–82   Stone's advice to WF: *FAB,* 612. Stone gave other versions. See *BCL,*
        278, 312, and *Oxford Eagle,* Nov. 14, 1950.

82   "anything without pictures": *SL,* 43.

82   "Major Oldham's yard boy": *FAB(1),* 239.

82   "about a girl," "how all this evil," "women are completely impervi-
        ous": *FAB,* 613. See also *WFO,* 131, and Wittenberg, *Faulkner,*
        90–91, 102.

83   "It's horrible": *FAB,* 617. See also Noel Polk, *Sanctuary: The Origi-
        nal Text* (New York, 1981).

83   You're damned: *ESPL,* 177.

83–84   Faulkner and Estelle: *FAB,* 618–19. Estelle's self-doubts are clear
        from her letters in *BCL.*

84   "Hal, I want $500.00": NYPL.

page
85　"Mr. Lem": *FAB,* 619–20.
85　"a regular Chesterfield": Ibid., 626; also *BLWF.*
86　"Read it again": *AFC,* 29.
86　"he could say things": *FAB(1),* 246.
86　"Don't make any more additions": *SL,* 44–45.
86–87　Estelle's attempted suicide: *FAB,* 629–30.
88　"flighty": *OFA,* 209. Maud and her sons' loyalty from author's interview with Dean Faulkner Wells; DSF, 55–56; *FAB,* 631.
88　Cornell and Dallas visit: *FAB(1),* 245.
89　"water flowing slow": So Faulkner said in *LIG,* 133–34.
89　"I found out": *LIG,* 255.
89　"deliberate": *ISF,* 709; *FAB,* 634; *FCF,* 25.
89　"the finest sound": NYPL.
90–91　textual quotations from *As I Lay Dying* (New York, 1930). See also Howe, *Faulkner,* 175–91, and Brooks, *First Encounters,* 78–95.
91　he would stand or fall: *ESPL,* 178.
92–94　Rowan Oak: *FAB,* 138–39, 652–61; Jill Faulkner quoted in *FAB(1),* 261; *BLWF,* 27, 28; *FR,* 9–10. Faulkner spelled it Rowanoak and Rowan Oak. I've used the latter for consistency.
94　Mammy Callie's storytelling: *BLWF,* 109.
94　Uncle Ned: *ESPL,* 39; *MBB,* 183; *BLWF,* 115; *FAB,* 52, 658–60, 998.
95　"that back, that stride": *ESPL,* 39.
95　"generally like an angel": Gordon Price-Stephens, "The British Reception of William Faulkner, 1929–1962," *Mississippi Quarterly* (Summer 1965), 122–23.
96　WF's breakfasts: *LIG,* 27; *BLWF,* 89.
96　"No one can get in": *LIG,* 26.
96　"forbidden items": *BLWF,* 33.
96　"natural and sustained aversion": *FOM,* 197.
96–97　WF's writing habits: *LIG,* 23, 71–72; *FCF,* 112; *FIU,* 49, 193–94, 273–74; *FWP,* 99; *FYY,* 262, 267; *FR,* 14–15. I benefited from perusing the collection of manuscripts called "The Rowan Oak Papers," which are located in the University of Mississippi Library. They give one a good sense of the way Faulkner wrote and the way his fiction developed.
97　bitterweeds: *BLWF,* 81, 84.
97　sneered and laughed: *BCL,* 171; *PSY,* 507–8.
97–98　WF's noon, afternoon, and evening: *FR,* 14–15; *BLWF,* 84; *FIU,* 285.
98　Judith Shegog's ghost: Dean Faulkner Wells, *The Ghosts of Rowan Oak: William Faulkner's Ghost Stories for Children* (Oxford, Miss., 1980), 13–35; *BLWF,* 86–87; *WFO,* 26, 86–87; *FAB,* 669–70.
99　"That has to be Judith": *BLWF,* 88.
99　Armistice Day: Ibid., 46.
99–100　"You can't print it," "might sell," "pay for the privilege": *LIG,* 123; *ESPL,* 178.

page

100–2   textual quotations from *Sanctuary* (New York, 1931). For discussions of Faulkner's revisions, see Millgate, *Achievement,* 113–23, and Polk, *Sanctuary: The Original Text,* 293–306. Wittenberg, *Faulkner,* 102, found more of a physical resemblance between Estelle and Temple than I did. I benefited from the point about Popeye in Howe, *Faulkner,* 152, and from Kinney's discussion, *Faulkner's Narrative Poetics,* 177–94.

102   **WF on Temple and Popeye:** *CNC,* 115–16; *FWP,* 83; *FIU,* 74.

102   **"at a time" and "passing coal":** *FAB,* 676; *FIU,* 91.

103–4   **Alabama's death:** *CNC,* 106–8; *MBB,* 222; *FAB,* 682–83.

104   **"putrid":** *FAB,* 684–86.

105   **Oxford reaction:** *PWWF,* 77, 78, 125; *MBB,* 171; DSF, 121–23; *FAB,* 687, 751.

105   **Stone quotations:** *PSY,* 530–31; *BCL,* 124.

106   **Stone on WF:** Stone to Tulsa Bookshop, July 18, 1931, HRHRC; *WFO,* 4, 8, 228; James B. Meriwether, ed., "Early Notices of Faulkner by Phil Stone and Louis Cochran," *Mississippi Quarterly* (Summer 1964), 148–64.

107   **"I may be up":** *SL,* 51.

107   **Inception of *Light in August:*** FAB, 701–4; *FIU,* 74, 199.

108   **"I was deliberately choosing":** *ISF,* 709.

108   **"I don't think":** UVA. Quoted by permission of Jill Faulkner Summers. *SL,* 38, omits this portion of the letter.

108–9   **WF at UVA conference:** Emily Clark, "A Week-end at Mr. Jefferson's University," *New York Herald Tribune Books* (Nov. 8, 1931), 1; Anderson, *Letters,* 252–53; *FAB,* 710–16, 719–20.

109   **"my one friend":** *FAB,* 726.

109   **"It's just like I was":** *SL,* 53.

109   **"I have created":** Ibid.

110   **WF and Dorothy Parker:** *CNC,* 105, 108–11, 114; *FAB,* 731.

110   **Hammett and Lillian Hellman Kober:** Diane Johnson, *Dashiell Hammett: A Life* (New York, 1983), 94–103; Jackson R. Bryer, ed., *Conversations with Lillian Hellman* (Jackson, Miss., 1986), 64, 222; *CNC,* 110. Lillian was then estranged from her husband, Arthur Kober; they would soon divorce.

111   **Knopf party:** *FAB,* 742–43.

111   **Estelle to New York:** Ibid., 745–46; *LIG,* 25–27. *CNC* gives a different version, 125–26.

111–12   **Estelle in New York:** *ALOP,* 68; *FR,* 17; *FAB(1),* 295–96; James B. Meriwether, *The Making of William Faulkner's Books, 1929–1937: An Interview with Evelyn Harter Glick* (Columbia, S.C., 1979), 21–22.

112   **"so tired of literary people":** *WFO,* 217.

113   **"There is the first stage":** *LIG,* 32.

113–17   textual quotations from *Light in August* (New York, 1932). Faulkner

page

quotations ("tragic, central idea" and "didn't know whether") from *FIU,* 72, 118, and *FWP,* 83. See also Brooks, *First Encounters,* 160–91, and Howe, *Faulkner,* 66, 152.

117 "captain of her soul" and "one of the calmest": *LIG,* 253.

117 Estelle and *Light in August:* FAB, 765.

117 WF's finances and MGM contract: *SL,* 61, 62; *FAC,* 36; *FAB,* 767–68.

117 Murry Falkner: DSF, 133; *FAB,* 781–82.

118 WF's fears: *New York Times,* Dec. 25, 1932.

PART FOUR: SOJOURNS DOWN RIVER

121 WF in Hollywood: *FAB,* 771–77; *FAB(1),* 305; *SL,* 66, 110; *FAF,* 69–75. See also Estelle Faulkner to Robert Haas, [Fall 1932?], UVA.

121 "most talented writers": *FAF,* 2.

121–22 WF and Howard Hawks: Joseph McBride, *Hawks on Hawks* (Berkeley, 1982), 10–14, 57; Gerald Mast, *Howard Hawks, Storyteller* (New York, 1982), 3–16; *FR,* 19; *FAF,* 12, 76–78, 125. See also Tom Dardis, *Some Time in the Sun* (New York, 1976), 80–86.

122 "I like working for Hawks": *FAB,* 780.

123 "It was a natural role": *FOM,* 200–1.

123 "Then it is me": *SL,* 65.

123 "O.K. damn it": *FAB,* 784.

123 "stand as it is": *SL,* 66.

123 "Things are going pretty well": NYPL.

123 "thank God" and "justifiably pleased": *SL,* 66; *WFO,* 104.

124 "didn't even want to see": *ISF,* 710.

124 "He was simply protecting himself": *MBB,* 172.

124 dispiriting December: *SL,* 69, 70.

125 "sojourn down river": See ibid., 72. Faulkner often referred to Hollywood in terms of slavery.

125 WF and flying: *FAB,* 795–97; *FOM,* 126; DSF, 143–44; *WFO,* 21.

125 "peace in the sky": *FAC,* 39–40.

125–26 Jill's birth: *BLWF,* 46–47; *FAB(1),* 318; *SL,* 71. For WF's loss of resolve about drinking, see WF to Bennett Cerf, Dec. 12, 1933, UVA.

126 "spasmodically": *SL,* 71.

126 WF and Dean: DSF, 115–51, 165.

126 "a nigger woman" and WF to Smith: *SL,* 75, 78.

127 "more or less violent breakup": Ibid., 78–79. The short stories that led to the new novel were "Evangeline" and "Wash." The latter appeared in *Harper's,* Feb. 1934. Faulkner's initial title for the novel was *Dark House;* his outline and précis and trial drafts are in the Rowan Oak Papers, University of Mississippi.

127 "something frenetic": *FIU,* 36. See also *FAB(1),* 327–30.

128 "trash": *SL,* 84.

128 "fingernail chewing stage": Ibid., 82–83. See also Faulkner to "My

page

dear Jill Baby," July 7, 1934, and to Estelle, July 12 and 21, 1934, UVA.

128   "hot as hell here" and "I still do not know": *SL,* 83–84.

129   Dean's marriage: DSF, 149–65.

130   "ephemera and phenomena" and "as ephemeral": *FIU,* 36.

130   "Lo!": see *SL,* 87. For Faulkner's Indians, see Lewis M. Dabney, *The Indians of Yoknapatawpha: A Study in Literature and History* (Baton Rouge, 1974).

130–31   troubled marriage and rival views: My portrait draws from author's interview with Dean Faulkner Wells; *ALOP,* 105; Estelle's parody about her husband in HRHRC; *ALG,* 51–52, 103; IMC, 789; *FAB(1),* 358–60; *FAB,* 940, 943. Cf. Minter, *Faulkner,* 160–61.

131   "to beat hell" and "I cannot and will not": *SL,* 87, 90–91.

132   aborted binge: *FAB,* 887.

132   "inchoate fragments": *FIU,* 76.

132   "pinch of necessity": *SL,* 91, also 92.

132   "good and ready" and "I have settled": *SL,* 92–93. See also *FAB,* 901–2, 904.

133–34   Dean's death and funeral and WF's guilt: DSF, 172–84; *FOM,* 130–32. See also *FAB(1),* 354–57, and *FAB,* 1603.

135   "I am working like hell": *SL,* 93.

135   "tour of duty": *AFC,* 45.

135   don't get drunk: FAF, 89.

135–37   Meta Carpenter: *ALG,* 14–57; *IMC,* 777, 788–89, 796.

138   "I think it's the best novel": *ALOP,* 83.

138   "temporarily due to illness": *FAB,* 928.

139–43   textual quotations from *Absalom, Absalom!* (New York, 1936). Faulkner quotation (held "the thing to something of reality") is from *FIU,* 75. The critical literature is prodigious. For discussions of the characters, plot, and structure, see Brooks, *First Encounters,* 192–224, and Kinney, *Faulkner's Narrative Poetics,* 194–215, among many other fine studies.

143   WF's love-hate for the South: *ESPL,* 36–43.

144   "because one has got to belong" and "he violated": *FIU,* 80–81, 35.

144   "greatest possible adornment": *FAB,* 929. See also Bennett Cerf, *At Random* (New York, 1977), 129.

144–45   WF reads to Stone: *WFO,* 98; *BCL,* 29, also 55. As for Stone's advice about Meta and Estelle, Meta suggested that this occurred while Faulkner was in Oxford in June and July, 1936 (*ALG,* 132). But the logic of events argues that it actually happened while Faulkner was home in February of that year.

145–48   WF and Meta: *ALG,* 24, 62–79, 126–27, 137–38, 140, 222, 248; *IMC,* 777, 783–800; *HAC,* 49, 59–61, 71, 97.

148   "That is the girl": *CNC,* 143.

148   "I wish I was at home": *SL,* 34–35. Meta saw WF's counterpull (*IMC,* 788).

page

148 "You're spying on me": *CNC,* 134–35.

149 "They're going to get me": *ALG,* 142–44. *IMC,* 777, suggests that this incident might have happened in the fall of 1936.

149 "Damn this being an orphan": UVA. Quoted by permission of Jill Faulkner Summers.

149 goodbye to Meta: *ALG,* 88–90, 96. Panthea Broughton, the interviewer in *IMC,* dated the leavetaking scene as occurring in January 1936. But the logic of events convinces me that it happened when Faulkner departed in May, as Meta implied in *ALG.* It isn't clear, however, that he went home by train, as she remembered.

149 WF wrote Meta: *ALG,* 97, 100.

150 "blind, staggering" and "for things like": Ibid., 127, 103.

150 "I will not be responsible": Memphis *Commercial Appeal,* June 22, 1936, and Oxford *Eagle,* June 25, 1936. See *FAB,* 938–39.

150 "famed novelist" and "It's just a matter": *Time,* July 6, 1936.

151–52 "keystone in the Universe" and "about honor, truth, pity": *LIG,* 255, and *SL,* 142; also *WFO,* 132, *FCF,* 14–15, and *FIU,* 87, 197. See also Elizabeth M. Kerr, *Yoknapatawpha: Faulkner's 'Little Postage Stamp of Native Soil'* (2nd rev. ed., New York, 1976).

152–53 WF and Meta: *ALG,* 164–67, 127–29.

153 marital tensions: *FAB,* 944–45.

153–57 WF and Meta: *ALG,* 167–95; *IMC,* 777, 789, 794, 789–90, 801; *CNC,* 145–49.

157 drunk at Wasson's: *CNC,* 149–52.

157 "I do not have to tell you": *FAB,* 952.

158 fight with Estelle, goodbye to Meta: *ALG,* 194–95; *IMC,* 777, 790.

158 WF's binge: *FAB,* 956; Spratling, *File on Spratling,* 30–31. See also Stephen Longstreet, "My Friend, William Faulkner," *Cavalier* (April 1965), 60.

158 "skin and bones": *ALG,* 195.

159 "Take care of my little baby": UVA. Quoted by permission of Jill Faulkner Summers.

159–60 textual quotations from *The Unvanquished* (New York, 1938). See also *FYY,* 71–89. Wittenberg, *Faulkner,* 166, argues that *The Unvanquished* "is Faulkner's final expression of his recurrent attempt to come to terms with his personal family history."

160 "worn out from them": *SL,* 101.

160 trip home with Wasson: *CNC,* 154–58.

161 "did not understand": *Current Biography 1941* (New York, 1941), 146.

161–62 WF and Anderson: *SAM,* 466; *ESPL,* 10.

162–63 WF's binge and burn: *FAB,* 975; *ALG,* 223–25; Cerf, *At Random,* 129–30.

163 "Carpenter? Are you happy?": *ALG,* 229–30.

167 "in order to stave off": *SL*, 338.

167 "it needed emphasis": *LIG*, 247–48, also 132.

168 "He kept me alive": *FAB*, 979.

168 "to hell with it" and "if the pen still wrote": *SL*, 105, 106.

168–70 textual quotations from *The Wild Palms* (New York, 1939). See also *FIU*, 173, Carvel Collins's introductory essay in *HAC*, 86–97, and his introduction in *MD*, 13–15, and Thomas L. McHaney, *William Faulkner's* The Wild Palms: *A Study* (Jackson, Miss., 1975).

170 "I am in fair shape": *SL*, 104.

170 "I'm not a literary man": *PWWF*, 96.

171 "I think Bill" and "My brother is the most": Sidney Alexander, "The Nobel Prize Comes to Mississippi," *Commentary* (Aug. 1951), 177, and *FAB*, 1062; also *MBB*, 176–90, 205–11, and Jim Faulkner, *Across the Creek: Faulkner Family Stories* (Jackson, Miss., 1986), 4.

171 "horribly shy": *SL*, 342.

171–72 WF's description of the projected trilogy: *SL*, 107–9.

172 "going to be pretty damned sound": Received Feb. 17, 1939, UVA.

172 "a social historian" and "the most talented": *Time* (Jan. 23, 1939), 45.

173 "a jungle of rank creepers": Frederick J. Hoffman and Olga W. Vickery, eds., *William Faulkner: Three Decades of Criticism* (paperback reprint 1960 ed., New York, 1963), 135.

173–74 Meta again: *ALG*, 241–44.

174 "I have known him": *SL*, 111, 112–13. See also *PSY*, 526–29.

174 "Maybe what I need" and "I am the best": *SL*, 114, 113.

174–76 Textual quotations from *The Hamlet* (New York, 1940). See also Howe, *Faulkner*, 84–88, 249, and especially Brooks, *First Encounters*, 96–128.

177–78 Mammy Callie's death: *ESPL*, 40–42, 117–18; *FOM*, 146–48; *FCF*, 107; *SL*, 118–19; *FAB*, 1034–35.

179 "that impenetrable wall": Faulkner, "The Old People," written probably in the late spring or summer of 1939 and included in *Go Down, Moses* (New York, 1942).

179–80 textual quotations from ibid.

180 Faulkner and segregation: See my pages 282–97 and 305–8 for a full account.

180 Collier's rejection of "Pantaloon": *FAB*, 1039.

180–81 WF's dire financial troubles: *SL*, 119, 120–24; Haas to WF, May 1, 1940, UVA; *AFC*, 54.

181 "What a hell of a time": *SL*, 125.

181 "It's probably vanity" and "a more or less": Ibid., 128–32, also 125; *AFC*, 56–57; *LIG*, 49.

181–82 Viking and Random House negotiations: *FAB*, 1048–56; *SL*, 132–35.

182 "I am doing no writing": *SL*, 136.

182 "fret and stew": Ibid., 138, also 137 and *PSY*, xi.

183 **fall hunt:** *SL,* 138. See John B. Cullen, *Old Times in the Faulkner Country* (Baton Rouge, 1961) for an account of Faulkner on the hunting expeditions; also *FAB,* 1063–64, and Faulkner's story "Tall Men," which, as Blotner points out, contains some of Faulkner's strongest convictions.

183 **"drunk bed":** *BLWF,* 18–19.

184 **"relationship between":** *SL,* 139.

184 **WF and Jill:** WF to Mrs. B. I. Wiley, June 23, 1942, FLT; *LIG,* 45; *FAB(1),* 397–98, 446; *FYY,* 266; *FR,* 15.

185–87 **textual quotations** from *Go Down, Moses;* see also Francis Lee Utley, Lynn Z. Bloom, and Arthur F. Kinney, eds., *Bear, Man, and God: Seven Approaches to William Faulkner's "The Bear"* (New York, 1964); Brooks, *First Encounters,* 129–59; and Howe, *Faulkner,* 88–98.

187 **"I think it's good stuff":** *SL,* 147.

187 **"the earth a little":** WF to Mrs. B. I. Wiley, June 23, 1942, FLT. WF's efforts to enlist from *FAB,* 1103–4.

188 **"Harrassed to hell," "I know where the trouble lies," "I have been trying":** *SL,* 151, 153.

188 **Meta:** *ALG,* 275–76; *IMC,* 791.

188–89 **Herndon imbroglio:** *SL,* 156–60; *FAB,* 1106–13.

189–90 **reunion with Meta:** *ALG,* 273, 276–79.

190 **"You authorized me" and "for getting things bitched up":** *SL,* 196, 162.

190 **"You're all schmucks":** *FAB,* 1196–97, also 1121–36.

190 **"inexplicable, confounding, passionate fascination":** *ALOP,* 7; also *FAF,* 95, 108.

190–92 **with Meta:** *IMC,* 796; *ALG,* 284–88. See also *FAB(1),* 446, and WF to Jill, undated but probably 1942, UVA, used by permission of Jill Faulkner Summers.

192 **lord of his manor:** *ALG,* 293.

192 **"worst bloody rotten bad cold":** *SL,* 169.

192 **"a cold-blooded man":** WF to "Dear Moms," April 25 (?), 1943, UVA.

192 **"pittance of a salary" and "about to bust":** *SL,* 177.

193 **condolences to Haas:** *SL,* 175; also to Malcolm, 175–76.

193 **"A change will come":** *SL,* 175–76. For Faulkner and *Battle Cry,* see *FAF,* 108, and William Faulkner, *Battle Cry: A Screenplay* (vol. V of *Faulkner, A Comprehensive Guide to the Brodsky Collection,* ed. Louis Daniel Brodsky and Robert W. Hamblin, Jackson, Miss., 1985).

194 **"We are fighting" and "When you and Jim":** *BLWF,* appendix. See also Minter, *Faulkner,* 198–99, and Brodsky, "Faulkner's Life Masks," *Southern Review* (Autumn 1986), 747–48.

194–95 **projected Hawks partnership:** *SL,* 177; *FAB(1),* 452.

195 **"a fable, an indictment of war":** *SL,* 178. See also Stephen Longstreet, "My Friend, William Faulkner" *Cavalier* (May 1965), 51.

page
195　"We are repeating": *SL,* 180; also 178–79.

196　"That goddamned piece of junk": *FAF,* 109–11; *FR,* 22.

196　"just smelled something": *Life* (June 12, 1944), 55.

197　"I'm supposed to say all that?": *FAB,* 1157. For WF's role in *To Have and Have Not,* see *FAF,* 109–11, and Bruce F. Kawin, ed., *To Have and Have Not* (Madison, Wis., 1980), 53.

197　Bogart: *Life* (June 12, 1944), 55–60; Kirtley Baskette, "Hollywood's Trigger Man," *The American Magazine* (June 1943), 43, 63–64.

198　"Bogie's got a new girl friend": *FAB,* 1156.

198　"sublimation and glorification": *SL,* 181.

198　Cowley to WF: *FCF,* 5, 8–9.

198　"I think (at 46)": *SL,* 182.

199　"all mankind's history": Ibid., 185–86; also *FCF,* 12–15.

199　WF to Cho-Cho: *SL,* 181.

199–200　breakup with Meta: *ALG,* 300–3.

201　"This is the end of it" and "Something went wrong": *FAB,* 1169, and *FAB(1),* 459.

201　WF's drinking: *FAB,* 1173–74; *ALG,* 306–7.

202　"I thought it was over": *ALG,* 307–8.

202　The Big Sleep: *FAF,* 113–20.

202　"I have to get back": *ALG,* 309.

203　"rewritten and additional scenes": *FAB,* 1176.

203–4　working on *A Fable:* SL, 188, 191, 192; *LIG,* 132; *FIU,* 27.

204　"I ought to know": *SL,* 191.

204　"wild" and "wonderful" script: Longstreet, "My Friend, William Faulkner," *Cavalier* (May 1965), 50.

204　"I dont like this damn place": *SL,* 198.

205–6　"I think I have had about all" and "My books have never sold": Ibid., 199.

206　Herndon and Warners: *SL,* 193, 195; *BCL,* 33–34, 39.

207　Faulkner mare foal: Longstreet, "My Friend, William Faulkner," *Cavalier* (May 1965), 86.

207　goodbye to Meta: *ALG,* 311–12.

PART SIX: THE PREREQUISITES OF SALVATION

211　"made a bust": *SL,* 204–5. *FAF,* 137, speculates that the five or six film scripts WF referred to were *To Have and Have Not, The Big Sleep, Battle Cry, Country Lawyer, Stallion Road,* and possibly *Fog Over London* or *The DeGaulle Story.*

211　"Faulkner won't do any writing": *SL,* 210.

211–14　Cowley and *The Portable Faulkner:* from *FCF,* 23–91, and *SL,* 197–98, 203–9, 211–17, 219–20, 222–23; Cowley, ed., *The Portable Faulkner* (rev. and expanded ed., 1967), vii–xxxiii.

214　"Faulkner c'est un dieu": *FCF,* 24.

page
214 "the only modern novelist": *PWWF,* 128.
214 "What a commentary": *SL,* 217–18.
215 Warners negotiations: *BCL,* 35, 38–39, 41, 43; *SL,* 223–26; *FAB,* 1203–12.
215 "I feel fine" and "The job is splendid": *SL,* 232, 233.
216 Warren's review: Hoffman and Vickery, eds., *Faulkner,* 109–24.
216 "lots of the kids": *FCF,* 100. See also Young, ed., *Conversations with Malcolm Cowley,* 13, 109, 194–95.
217 "magnum o": *SL,* 233.
217 "Yes, this is it" and "done no more": Ibid., 237, 244, 247.
217 "It's a dull life here": *SL,* 245. Faulkner's "sexual key," said Meta, "was the image of a young woman, fresh and fragrant of skin beneath her summer cotton dress, tremblingly responsive to his desire" (*ALG,* 127). Said Dean Faulkner Wells: "Oh, I think Pappy loved pretty girls. . . . Of course these young women are not a threat to him and they adore him and that's very attractive to an aging man." Author's interview.
217 "Let's let 'em go": *FAB,* 1222.
217 Easter eggs: *FAB,* 1228–29.
218–19 WF at Ole Miss: *WFO,* 127–39.
219–20 Hemingway episode: *SL,* 250–52; Carlos Baker, ed., *Ernest Hemingway: Selected Letters, 1917–1961* (New York, 1981), 623–25.
220–21 second contretemps with Hemingway: *SL,* 333–34. See also *FAB,* 1427–28.
221 "trash and junk writing," "getting to be a tragedy," "It's like standing," "Did PR give a reason": *SL,* 248, 258, 261–62.
222 "mystery-murder" and "I hope the idea": Ibid., 262.
222–23 "a simple quick 150 page" and "owe and must pay": Ibid., 266, 262; also *FIU,* 141–42.
223–24 textual quotations from *Intruder in the Dust* (New York, 1948); also Howe, *Faulkner,* 99–101, 129, and Millgate, *Achievement,* 215–20. I do not suggest, of course, that Faulkner shared all of Gavin Stevens's moral, ethical, and social views, particularly those in other novels and stories in which Stevens appeared. Sometimes, as Cleanth Brooks points out, Faulkner treated Gavin "as a figure of fun" (Brooks, *The Yoknapatawpha Country,* 194.)
225 "was a good man": *Time* (July 17, 1964), 45.
225 WF and Lucas Beauchamp: Howe, *Faulkner,* 130.
225 "super-pleased" and WF's reaction: Haas to Faulkner, July 12, 1948, UVA; *SL,* 270.
225–26 "Anybody who can sell a book": *FAB,* 1257.
226 WF's cars: *MBB,* 252–53.
226 "so my friends and kinfolks": *SL,* 270.
226 Ruth Ford: *FAB,* 1265; *FAB(1),* 497; *FR,* 25.
226 Cowley meeting: *FCF,* 103–4.

page
227 "You gotta get me out of here": *FAB*, 1267.
227–28 with Cowley: *FCF*, 104–14.
228–29 "It is my ambition": *SL*, 285.
229 "That's the trouble": *FCF*, 127.
229 "Much excitement here" and "It's too bad": *SL*, 286. See also James W. Silver, *Running Scared: Silver in Mississippi* (Jackson, 1984), 39, 48.
229 WF's part in the filming: *FAB*, 1277–84.
230 WF's similarity to Gavin Stevens: *SL*, 280; *FAB(1)*, 504.
230 WF and Commins: *SCW*, 202; Commins to Faulkner, Oct. 16, 1950, UVA; *BCL*, xvii.
230 "I have just this minute": Commins to Faulkner, June 2, 1949, UVA.
231–32 WF and Jill: *OFA*, 209–10; *ALOP*, 31–32, 67, 91, 92; *FR*, 13–15; *FAB*, 1291; *LIG*, 162. See also WF to Missy (circa 1952), UVA, telling her she has always been "sensible and dependable." Quoted by permission of Jill Faulkner Summers.
232 "soiled and battered bloke": *TNCA*, 61.
232 "pretty exciting": *SL*, 292.

PART SEVEN: WHEN SHALL I SLEEP AGAIN?

235–36 Joan Williams: *TNCA*, 60–61; *WFO*, 87–88; *FAB*, 1292. The Faulkner–Joan Williams correspondence, housed in the Alderman Library of the University of Virginia, is currently closed to researchers, which is a great pity for Faulkner biography. A sanitized version of some of Faulkner's letters to Joan did appear in *SL*—with all the intimate details carefully deleted. With the publication of Meta Carpenter's *ALG*, Joan Williams's own *TNCA*, and the Brodsky Collection letters, we now know about Faulkner's involvement with Meta, Joan Williams, Else Jonsson, and later Jean Stein. As a consequence, there seems no reason to keep the Faulkner-Williams correspondence locked up. I expect that those letters will reveal in greater detail what we already know: namely, that Faulkner was very much in love with Joan and that he was a passionate and suffering older lover.

As Faulkner's official biographer, Joseph Blotner saw the Faulkner-Williams correspondence and used some of it in preparing *FAB*, published first in 1974, and we are all indebted to him for quoting what material he does from that file. Actually, the most candid and complete account of Faulkner's relationship with Joan can be found in her novel about it, *The Wintering* (New York, 1971). While it is fiction and "a lot of it is made up," as Joan told me, the characters —Amy Howard and Jeff Almoner—are nevertheless close replicas of Joan Williams and William Faulkner. Moreover, the story follows the general facts of their lives and involvement, and it contains excerpts from actual letters and apparently actual conversations as well.

Which brings me to Joan's letter, quoted in my text. This is the version in *The Wintering*, 57–58, but it is so close to Joan's paraphrase of the actual document in *TNCA*, 60, and Blotner's brief paraphrase of it in *FAB*, 1293, that I'm convinced it is almost word-for-word the genuine article. I could not, of course, quote from the actual document, for that is apparently in the restricted Faulkner-Williams correspondence. Since I wanted to show why Faulkner reacted to the letter as passionately as he did, I had no recourse but to use the version in *The Wintering*—the only such liberty I've taken.

236–38 **correspondence with Joan and Memphis meeting:** *TNCA*, 58, 59, 61–63 (cf. *The Wintering*, 78–90); *OFA*, note 19, chap. 9; author's interview with Joan Williams; also *FAB*, 1299, and *FAB(1)*, 511.

238 **Joan reminded him of Bouguereau:** *FAB(1)*, 508.

239 **"all the sad frustration,"** and **"to get the good stuff":** *SL*, 297, and *FAB*, 1302–3, *FAB(1)*, 512.

239–40 **NYC and collaboration with Joan:** Author's interview with Joan Williams; *TNCA*, 63–64. Cf. *The Wintering*, 108–22. See also *SL*, 298, and *FAB*, 1306.

240 **"So I do need you":** *ALOP*, 104; also *SL*, 307.

240 **"some of the lacerations"** and **"capable not only of imagining":** *FAB*, 1319, and *FAB(1)*, 516; also *SL*, 300.

240–41 **Estelle and Joan:** *TNCA*, 62 (cf. *The Wintering*, 158); *BCL*, 135; author's interview with Joan Williams; *FAB*, 1327.

241 **"I am a farmer"** and **"money, women, glory":** *SL*, 302, and *ESPL*, 206.

242 **"some kind of novel"** and **"seven play-scenes":** *SL*, 304, 305.

242 **"scaffolding stuff":** *FAB(1)*, 520.

242–43 textual quotations from *Requiem for a Nun* (New York, 1951). See also Noel Polk, *Faulkner's* Requieum for a Nun: *A Critical Study* (Bloomington, Ind., 1981).

243–44 **Pott's Camp meetings:** *TNCA*, 59, 60, 63–64; author's interview with Joan Williams. Cf. *The Wintering*, 133–44.

244 **"the fun of doing it together"** and **"People need trouble":** *FAB*, 1327–28, and *SL*, 308.

245 **"the same pigeon hole":** *SL*, 299.

245 **"for his powerful and independent"** and **"It's too far away":** *FAB*, 1338; also *PWWF*, 131.

245 **"Mac, I still can't believe it"** and **"I guess he's appreciated":** *WFO*, 186, and *PWWF*, 132, also 131.

245 **"A lot of us talk":** Oxford *Eagle* (Nov. 14, 1950).

245 **New York press:** *AFC*, 81.

246 **"There just isn't enough gas":** *MBB*, 242.

246 **WF's binge:** *FAB*, 1349–52.

246 **"Now, Bill, you do right":** *PWWF*, 185. Stone thought that the saga

page

of getting Faulkner off to Sweden resembled "one of his Snopes tales." *BCL,* 64.

247   "What do you consider": *FAB,* 1353.

247   Else Jonsson: Ibid., 1360–61.

247   "I can't stand this": Ibid., 1362.

248   "so very nice" and "storybook-like atmosphere": *BCL,* 59, and Memphis *Commercial Appeal,* Jan. 7, 1951.

248   award presentation and banquet: Ibid.; Oxford *Eagle,* Jan. 4, 1951, and July 12, 1962; *FAB,* 1362–69.

249   comparison to Gettysburg Address: *BCL,* 67.

249–50   WF's Nobel Prize address: *ESPL,* 119–20.

250   "Oxford and All of Us": *FAB,* 1371.

250   "We are at home again": *SL,* 310–11.

250   "damned money": *FAB,* 1370; also *SL,* 444, and *BCL,* 62n.

250   "nothing nothing nothing else": *SL,* 312.

251   "emotional block" and "I am convinced": *FAB,* 1373.

251   with Meta: *ALG,* 319–20.

251   WF to Joan: *SL,* 312.

251   tryst with Else: *BCL,* xiii, 62–66; also Monique Salomon references in *FAB,* 1380–83.

252   "use man's fear": *ESPL,* 122–24; *FAB,* 1385–86.

252   "tired of ink and paper" and "Don't be unhappy": *SL,* 315, and *FAB,* 1395.

252   "abolished and voided from history": *SL,* 285.

253   "Reporters just bring their suitcases": *AFR,* 1027.

253   WF at French consulate: *FOM,* 192.

253   "anguished over putting words together" and "dull, busy": *SL,* 331; also Faulkner to Commins, April 12 (?), 1952, UVA.

254   "I learned years ago": *SL,* 328; also Faulkner to "Dear Missy," postmarked March 5, 1952, UVA.

254   Paris and Oslo with Else: *BCL,* 73, 75, 77, 101; *SL,* 346; *FAB(1),* 534–35.

254   Joan's lover: *FAB,* 1426–27, 1431. Cf. *The Wintering,* 240–44.

255   "I love you!": Undated, unsigned, UVA. Quoted by permission of Jill Faulkner Summers. This is filed in the Faulkner family letters, but is clearly written to Joan. According to Blotner, *FAB(1),* 559, Faulkner wrote her four letters in one twenty-four-hour period, plus two more in a few days.

255   "This may be it": *TNCA,* 64. Yet he did suggest changes in the story. See *BCL,* 80–81, and *SL,* 338–39, also 337.

255–56   strain with Joan: *FAB(1),* 559 (cf. *The Wintering,* 172–73, 236); *SL,* 336–37, 338; *TNCA,* 63.

256   "I am really sick" and "Stupid existence": *BCL,* 80, and *SL,* 339. See also *BCL,* 81, 82.

256   "chided Jill": *BCL,* 135.

page

256   "dreadful behavior" and "Dear Missy": Sept. (29?), 1952, UVA. Quoted by permission of Jill Faulkner Summers.

257   "This is more than a case": *BCL*, 89–91. See also *SL*, 342.

257   "Hell's to pay": *BCL*, 94, also 95–97, 134–36. See Faulkner's letter to Joan quoted in *FAB*, 1437. Joan's novel, *The Wintering*, 264–65, suggests the kind of letters that Estelle found and read. In the novel, Amy (Joan) wrote Almoner (Faulkner): "Please keep writing me. Your letters are so beautiful. I hope knowing that just your writing me gives me a certain faith in things, makes you happy. Aside from unhappiness about me, are you happy? Try not to worry and to work. That's the important thing. Despite its all being so hard, this is a wonderful wonderful time in my life because of knowing you. I hope all this adoration isn't irritating. I read once, and I don't know where, adoration is a universal sentiment; it differs in degrees in different natures. I can't help being emotional about knowing you. Others feel as strongly as I, but happen not to write you. I'm afraid you don't understand that nothing in your life has been worthless. You must be proud knowing your writing can inspire me so much that I write you the way, at eleven, I wrote to movie stars. And now I feel silly!" Such letters convinced Estelle that "Billy is completely enamoured, and Joan professes her love in no uncertain terms." See *BCL*, 135.

258   Commins's offer: *BCL*, xviii. See also Commins to Faulkner, Oct. 2, 1952, UVA.

258   "so foreign to his nature": *BCL*, 96. See also *SL*, 347.

258–59 Stone's attitude toward WF: *PSY*, xii, 529; *BCL*, xix, 47, 53, 56, 29, 68, 84; *CNC*, 166.

259   "would be glad" and "Bill was just as gracious": *BCL*, 106, 99.

259   "I don't see Stone" and "Phil never did understand": *CNC*, 166–67, and *PSY*, xiv.

259   "Maybe because I wasn't as tall": *FAB*, 1442; also *BCL*, 101.

259   "You must expect": *SL*, 343.

260   "Someday, Joan": *TNCA*, 65. Cf. Almoner's remark to Amy in *The Wintering*, 304: "Someday you'll know, Amy, no one will ever love you as I have."

260   "Tell me if I'm too old" and I am taking care of him: *TNCA*, 65.

260   electroshock therapy: *FAB*, 1442. See also Faulkner to Jill, Nov. 20, 1952, UVA.

260   goodbye to Joan and "Who wouldn't like to read": *FAB*, 1444–45; *HAC*, 33.

261   "decent daily stint," "fine ecstatic rush," "Take me with you": *BCL*, 104, 107; and *SL*, 344. See also *BCL*, 105, 107–8.

261   "Something is wrong with me": *SL*, 347, also 346. See, too, WF to Jill, postmarked Feb. 16, 1953, UVA.

261   psychological examinations: *FAB*, 1453–54; *SL*, 347.

262   at Random House: *LIG*, 74–76; *SCW*, 199–200.

page

262–63   Mississippi: *ESPL*, 11–43.

263   "major, ambitious work" and "Now I realize": *SL*, 348. For Estelle's hemorrhage, see *BCL*, 111–12.

263–64   "Bill has done a prodigious amount of work" and "In all probability": *BCL*, 116–17, 136.

264   WF and Joan: *FAB*(1), 571, 572–73; author's interview with Joan Williams; *SL*, 350.

264   "Damn it, I did have genius": *SL*, 352.

265   binge at Wasson's: *CNC*, 177–89; *FAB*, 1465.

265   "An acute and chronic alcoholic": *FAB(1)*, 574.

266   "Your article, I think": *BCL*, 120, also 83–89, 92–93, 121.

266   "I tried for years": *SL*, 354.

267–68   breakup with Joan: Author's interview with Joan Williams; *BCL*, 126, 138; *SL*, 357; *FAB*, 1469–70, 1474–77.

268   "Change in people": *HAC*, 97.

268   "as near perfection" and "still a little bewildered": *BCL*, 126, and *SCW*, 202.

268–69   textual quotations from *A Fable* (New York, 1954). *A Fable* also includes a long story, originally published in a limited edition as *Notes on a Horsethief* (1951), about a lame race horse, an English groom named Mr. Harry, and his faithful black friend. The two men wound up in France, where both died in an artillery barrage. Faulkner himself, in *FIU*, 27, described the novel as a tour de force. He had begun with the idea that it was Christ "under that fine big cenotaph with the eternal flame burning on it," he said, but "then it became *tour de force*, because I had to invent enough stuff to carry this notion." Howe, *Faulkner*, 269, called *A Fable* "another of those 'distinguished' bad books that flourish in America." For a sympathetic discussion, see Millgate, *Achievement*, 227–34. As far as its message was concerned, Millgate concluded that *A Fable* was "a kind of extended gloss upon" Faulkner's Nobel Prize speech.

269   "sheer force of rhetorical narrative," "much to answer for," "I think Bill's book": *SCW*, 202, and *BCL*, 122.

270   "I love the book": *SL*, 361–62.

270   "I don't want to go to Paris" and "He's done me favors": *SCW*, 206; *FAB(1)*, 578; also *SL*, 356.

270   airport: This is Blotner's version (*FAB*, 1478). Dorothy Commins, Saxe's wife, claimed that Saxe alone put Faulkner on the plane. See *SCW*, 206.

PART EIGHT: DARK AND DIFFICULT DAYS

273   WF to Joan: *FAB*, 1484.

273   "all my children": *SL*, 358.

273   comic repartee: McBride, *Hawks*, 60.

page

274   Jean Stein meeting: *BCL,* 138; *FAB,* 1484–85; author's conversation with Jean Stein.

274   "I had forgot": *SL,* 358.

274   "until her momma in Venice": *BCL,* 138.

275   "Bill, why do you drink?" *FAB,* 1487.

275   "poor Joan" and "It is full of the sound": *BCL,* 138, and *SL,* 360.

275   "everybody was a son of a bitch": McBride, *Hawks,* 60; also *SL,* 362, and Memphis *Press-Scimitar* (June 14, 1955), quoted in *FAB(1),* 599.

275   "I think she is too honest" and "expect any day now": *BCL,* 138.

276   "deeply in love" and "new-found radiance": Ibid., 144.

276   "damndest collection" and "They are very fine": *SL,* 365.

276   "Phil, with love," "wonderful Faulkner writing," "requiring humility": *BCL,* 217, 130, 142–43, 221.

277   "I don't write for critics": *CNC,* 191. See Lawrence Thompson's devastating critique of *A Fable* in *BCL,* 149–51, and Perry Miller's defense of it in *SCW,* 211–12.

277   "Good-bye to your childhood": *LIG,* 162.

277–78 Estelle to Commins: *BCL,* 134–38.

278   "more or less lost to her": Ibid., 161.

278   "for hemispheric solidarity": *SL,* 368; *BCL,* 158–60.

278   "To Ben: much love" and "the cut of her face": *CNC,* 190, and *SCW,* 212–13.

278–80 Jill's wedding and WF's binge: *CNC,* 190–93; *SCW,* 213–15; *FAB,* 1507–10.

280   "E. leaves for Manila" and "Perhaps a taste": *BCL,* 169, 170.

280–81 "Between grief and nothing" and "Rutgers Scott Fitzgerald": *FAB,* 1520, 1522.

281   "In all my experience": Memphis *Commercial Appeal* (Jan. 30, 1955); *SCW,* 219.

281   WF's speech: *ESPL,* 143.

282   "a states' rights man": *LIG,* 60. For a discussion of Faulkner's views on race up to 1954, see Charles D. Peavy, *Go Slow Now: Faulkner and the Race Question* (Eugene, Oreg., 1971), 11–58.

283   "right" and "just," "patient and sensible," "complete equality": *LIG,* 90, 89.

283–84 WF's letters to Memphis *Commercial Appeal:* ESPL, 215–16, 221–22, 93; Memphis *Commercial Appeal,* March 27, April 10, 1955; *BCL,* 179–80; *MBB,* 268.

284   "We have much tragic trouble": *SL,* 381.

284   "simple private individual": Ibid., 384.

284   flight to Japan: *LIG,* 188; *ESPL,* 76.

284   "I won't let you down": *FAB,* 1546.

284–85 WF's remarks in Japan: From *LIG,* 84–188.

286   "It was like two people": *FIU,* 89.

286   WF on young Japanese women: *LIG,* 100–1; *ESPL,* 78–81.

page

287   "That river's full": Dan Wakefield, *Revolt in the South* (New York, 1960), 32–33.

287   WF's statement: *ESPL,* 222–23.

287   "terrible, distraught eyes": Kenneth Tynan, "Papa and the Playwright," *Esquire* (May 1963), 140; *FAB(1),* 611.

287–88 WF at Gallimards': *LIG,* 228–31.

288   "I drank a lot at times": *BCL,* 199–200.

289   WF's speech at the Southern Historical Association: *ESPL,* 146–51; *BCL,* 185–86, 242–43, 290; Silver, *Running Scared,* 59–62.

289–90 "a drunk, and a general damn fool," "the flames of hate," "Why do you continue to live here?": *SCW,* 222; Cullen, *Old Times in the Faulkner Country,* 56.

290   "Please, Mr. Faulkner": *ESPL,* 89–90.

290   WF with Jean Stein: *SL,* 388; *HAC,* 97–98; *FAB,* 1585–86; author's conversation with Jean Stein.

290–91 "Does it make you nervous" and "Miss. such an unhappy state": *FAB,* 1587; *SL,* 391, 390. See also *BCL,* 189–90.

291   "Hey, hey, ho, ho": *Time* (Feb. 20, 1956), 40.

291–92 "Letter to a Northern Editor": Published as "A Letter to the North," *Life* (March 5, 1956), in *ESPL,* 86–91.

292   WF upset and drunk over Lucy crisis: *SL,* 408–9; Peavy, *Go Slow Now,* 73–75; *FAB(1),* 617–18.

292–93 Howe interview: from the *Reporter* version in *LIG,* 258–64; Howe's remarks in Peavy, *Go Slow Now,* 73–74. See also the cogent analysis in Louis Daniel Brodsky's "Sorting Faulkner's Mail: March–April 1956," in *Faulkner and Race: Faulkner and Yoknapatawpha 1986.*

293   "guilty of great emotional and intellectual dishonesty": James Baldwin, *Nobody Knows My Name* (New York, 1961), 121.

293–94 WF's letters to *Time* and *The Reporter:* ESPL, 226, 225. See also Howe's rebuttal in *LIG,* 265–66.

294   WF to prointegrationist student: *SL,* 396.

294–95 Stein interview: *LIG,* 237–55; *FAB,* 1594–95; author's conversation with Jean Stein.

296   "I know, as you must": *BCL,* 200.

296   "Don't worry about money": *FAB,* 1605.

296   "Each time I begin to hope": *SL,* 402; also 399 and 400.

296–97 "A Letter to the Leaders in the Negro Race": Published as "If I Were a Negro," *Ebony* (Sept. 1956), in *ESPL,* 107–12.

297   "quite real and quite consistent": *FIU,* 78.

297–98 textual quotations from *The Town* (New York, 1957). Warren Beck described Gavin Stevens as a "protagonist of a humanistic ethic," one who tended to ascribe loftier motives to people than they actually had. In Faulkner's treatment, said Beck, this was "the humane man's most dangerous vulnerability; yet its alternative, a complete defensive cynicism, must be worse." See Beck, *Man in Motion: Faulkner's Trilogy* (Madison, 1961), 11, 52.

page
298 "It breaks my heart": *SL,* 402; also *BCL,* 193.

299 "beautiful and intelligent and charming": *FAB,* 1626.

299 crank phone calls: *BCL,* 205–6.

299 thrown over by another "dame": See *FAB,* 1629.

299 three-day siege: *BCB,* 263.

299–300 Estelle and divorce: *BCL,* 206.

300 WF to Joan Williams: Ibid., 213; also 214.

300 reconciliation: See *BCL,* xvi, and Silver, *Running Scared,* 41; also author's interview with Dean Faulkner Wells.

PART NINE: HOMECOMING

303–4 WF in class: *FIU,* 109, 9–10, 58, 61; also 19, 26, 47, 147.

304 "Oratory can't add anything": *FCF,* 146–47.

304 Lillian Hellman: *FAB,* 1666–67.

304 Wasson: *CNC,* 198–99, 6.

304–5 strain with Stone: *BCL,* 215, 217, 220, also 191–92, 208, 219, 285, xxi–xxiv.

305–6 WF's letter to *NYT:* ESPL, 230–31; also in *BCL,* 219–20.

306–7 WF's UVA speech (Feb. 20, 1958): *FIU,* 209–27.

307 "small-minded Willie": *Time* (July 17, 1964), 48.

308 "life is motion": *FWP,* 98. For contemporary assessments of Faulkner's racial views, see Silver, *Running Scared,* 93; Evans Harrington in *BCL,* 320; Moon Mullen in *WFO,* 164; and Baldwin, *Nobody Knows My Name,* 117–26. For subsequent assessments, see, for example, Howe, *Faulkner,* 116–37; Peavy, *Go Slow Now;* Margaret Walker Alexander, "Faulkner & Race," in Evans Harrington and Ann J. Abadie, eds., *The Maker and the Myth: Faulkner and Yoknapatawpha, 1977* (Jackson, 1978), 105–22; Walter Taylor, *Faulkner's Search for a South* (Urbana, Ill., 1983); and Erskine Peters, *William Faulkner: The Yoknapatawpha World and Black Being* (Darby, Pa., 1983).

308 "You write a story": *FIU,* 239, 120.

308 "I'm hoping and *praying*": *BCL,* 484; also *SL,* 455, for Faulkner and Mississippi summers.

308–9 Commins's death and "I cant keep tourists out": *SL,* 415.

309 Dean's wedding: Author's interview with Dean Faulkner Wells; *FAB,* 1702–3.

310–11 textual quotations from *The Mansion* (New York, 1959). Back in May 1957, Faulkner had told a UVA class that Linda was "one of the most interesting people I've written about yet, I think. Her story will be in the next book." For an analysis of the Snopes trilogy, see Beck, *Man in Motion.*

311 "As I wrote those books": Cerf, *At Random,* 133; also *SL,* 426, 429–31, 433; *FAC,* 103–4.

311 WF's income: *FAB,* 1717.

page

311   "He had in a sense finished the creative side": *FAB(1),* 671.

312   "One's heart was in one's mouth" and "I love the thrill": *FAB,* 1748, and *FAB(1),* 658.

312   "It is very fine": *SL,* 439, also 429.

312–13 "I'm not going to see you," "Have you already forgot," "Splendid news": *FAB(1),* 675; *FAB,* 1730–31, 1761; also *BCL,* 269.

313   "I believe, hope": *BCL,* 287; also 285 and *TNCA,* 65.

313   "Harold will be missed": *SL,* 438.

313–14 Maud's death: *FOM,* 188–89; *FAB,* 1761–62, 1764–65.

314   "Listen to this": *FAB,* 1767–68.

315   Hemingway's death: UPI report July 2, 1961, as printed in Amarillo *News,* July 3, 1961; *FAB,* 1790, and *FAB(1),* 690.

315–16 "a sort of Huck Finn" and "debauchery and degeneracy": *SL,* 123–24. See also Minter, *Faulkner,* 246.

316   WF's books: As Faulkner did, I'm counting *The Unvanquished* and *Go Down, Moses,* as novels. The fifth story collection was *Big Woods,* published by Random House in 1955; it consisted of four hunting stories that had previously appeared. The first anthology was Cowley's *Portable Faulkner;* the second was *The Faulkner Reader,* published by Random House in 1954; it included all of *The Sound and the Fury,* several short stories from the *Collected Stories,* and three previously published novellas or long stories: "The Bear" (from *Go Down, Moses*), "Old Man" (from *Wild Palms*), and "Spotted Horses," which Faulkner had incorporated into *The Hamlet.* In 1958, Random House published the novellas again under the title *Three Famous Short Novels.* The limited or special editions of Faulkner's short fiction comprise *Idyll in the Desert* (1931), *Miss Zilphia Gant* (1932), *Salmagundi* (1932), *A Rose for Emily and Other Stories* (1945), and *Notes on a Horsethief* (1951). A limited edition of Faulkner's New Orleans sketches, *Mirrors of Chartres Street,* appeared in 1953. Five years later Random House brought out a trade edition, *New Orleans Sketches,* edited by Carvel Collins. A number of other Faulkner titles would appear posthumously. See *AFC,* 109–13, and Massey (comp.), *"Man Working," 1919–1962: A Catalogue of the William Faulkner Collections at the University of Virginia.*

316   "I been aimin' to quit": *WFO,* 187; also Oxford *Eagle,* July 12, 1962.

316   "I'm going to stop being a damn fool" and "I feel now": *FAB,* 1810, and *SL,* 459.

317   WF and Virginians: *FIU,* 12, 282.

317   Claxton interview: *LIG,* 273–74.

318   "Bill and I were housed": *BCL,* 301.

318   "In his clumsy way": *FWP,* 82.

318   "Those stuffy White House dinners" and "I'm too old": *FAB,* 1817, and *Newsweek* (May 14, 1962), 27. The *New York Times* (May 19, 1962), and Estelle in *BCL,* 301, give slightly different versions.

page

318 "his magnificent dark eyes" and "I think they were the best days": *FCF*, 148; *FAB*, 1823; Bryer, *Conversations with Lillian Hellman*, 64.

318 "Mr. Faulkner, your work": *Proceedings of the American Academy of Arts and Letters and the National Institute of Arts and Letters* (2nd ser., no. 13, New York, 1963), 225–26.

319 "In the bustle of members": *FCF*, 150; also *TNCA*, 65.

319 Red Acres: *SL*, 461–62. See also Faulkner to "Dear Missy," Sunday [1962], UVA.

319 "suddenly and close-up" and "Felix, I don't want": *FAB*, 1830, 1829.

319–20 Joan Williams Bowen: *TNCA*, 65; author's interview with Joan Williams. See also *The Wintering*, 324.

320 "Meat and bread all taste the same": Memphis *Commercial Appeal*, July 7, 1962.

320–21 WF's death: *FAB*, 1835–39; author's interview with Dr. Chester McLarty.

321 John Faulkner: *WFO*, 213; *WFO*, x.

321 "maddened, miraculous vision": William Styron, *This Quiet Dust and Other Writings* (New York, 1982), 262.

322 "He has stepped into an eternal tomorrow": *WFO*, 213.

INDEX

About the Author

Stephen B. Oates is a professional biographer with an international reputation. He is especially acclaimed for his Civil War Quartet, comprising biographies of four central figures of the Civil War era and its century-old legacies: *To Purge This Land with Blood: A Biography of John Brown* (1970, 1984), *The Fires of Jubilee: Nat Turner's Fierce Rebellion* (1975), *With Malice Toward None: The Life of Abraham Lincoln* (1977), and *Let the Trumpet Sound: The Life of Martin Luther King, Jr.* (1982). *With Malice Toward None,* hailed as the best one-volume life of Lincoln, won a Christopher Award for "affirming the highest values of the human spirit, artistic and technical proficiency, and significant degree of public acceptance," and the Barondess/Lincoln Award of the New York Civil War Round Table. *Let the Trumpet Sound* won a Christopher Award too, plus the Robert F. Kennedy Memorial Book Award. The two volumes have also appeared in several languages. Mr. Oates' other biographical works include *Rip Ford's Texas* (1963, 1987), *Portrait of America* (2 volumes, 1973, 1986), *Our Fiery Trial: Abraham Lincoln, John Brown, and the Civil War Era* (1979), *Abraham Lincoln: The Man Behind the Myths* (1984), and *Biography as High Adventure* (1986), a collection of essays by Mr. Oates and others who have practiced biography as a literary art. An elected member of the Society of American Historians, Mr. Oates has been a Fellow of the John Simon Guggenheim Foundation and a Senior Summer Fellow of the National Endowment for the Humanities. He is currently Paul Murray Kendall Professor of Biography, Professor of History, and Adjunct Professor of English at the University of Massachusetts, Amherst, where he teaches a nationally recognized seminar in the art and technique of biography.

There's an epidemic with 27 million victims. And no visible symptoms.

It's an epidemic of people who can't read.

Believe it or not, 27 million Americans are functionally illiterate, about one adult in five.

The solution to this problem is you... when you join the fight against illiteracy. So call the Coalition for Literacy at toll-free **1-800-228-8813** and volunteer.

Volunteer Against Illiteracy. The only degree you need is a degree of caring.